The Case for Case Studies

This book seeks to narrow two gaps: first, between the widespread use of case studies and their frequently "loose" methodological moorings; and second, between the scholarly community advancing methodological frontiers in case study research and the users of case studies in development policy and practice. It draws on the contributors' collective experience at this nexus, but the underlying issues are more broadly relevant to case study researchers and practitioners in all fields. How does one prepare a rigorous case study? When can causal inferences reasonably be drawn from a single case? When and how can policy-makers reasonably presume that a demonstrably successful intervention in one context might generate similarly impressive outcomes elsewhere, or if massively "scaled up"? No matter their different starting points – disciplinary base, epistemological orientation, sectoral specialization, or practical concerns – readers will find issues of significance for their own field, and others across the social sciences. This title is also available Open Access.

Jennifer Widner is Professor of Politics and International Affairs at Princeton University and Director of Innovations for Successful Societies. Her research focuses on government performance, democratization, and constitutional design. Much of her work uses qualitative process-tracing case studies focused on institutional change, implementation, and service delivery.

Michael Woolcock is Lead Social Scientist with the World Bank's Development Research Group, and an Adjunct Lecturer in Public Policy at Harvard Kennedy School. He is the coauthor of *Contesting Development: Participatory Projects and Local Conflict Dynamics in Indonesia* (2011) and *Building State Capability: Evidence, Analysis, Action* (2017).

Daniel Ortega Nieto is a Senior Public Sector Specialist at The World Bank. He assisted the Global Delivery Initiative and led a team developing DeCODE, an evidence-based system that helps anticipate delivery challenges. He was an advisor to the Mexican Government and holds degrees from the LSE and Georgetown University.

Strategies for Social Inquiry

Editors
Colin Elman, *Maxwell School of Syracuse University*
John Gerring, *Boston University*
James Mahoney, *Northwestern University*

Editorial Board
Bear Braumoeller, David Collier, Francesco Guala, Peter Hedström, Theodore Hopf, Uskali Maki, Rose McDermott, Charles Ragin, Theda Skocpol, Peter Spiegler, David Waldner, Lisa Wedeen, Christopher Winship

This book series presents texts on a wide range of issues bearing upon the practice of social inquiry. Strategies are construed broadly to embrace the full spectrum of approaches to analysis, as well as relevant issues in philosophy of social science.

Published Titles
Colin Elman, John Gerring and James Mahoney, *The Production of Knowledge: Enhancing Progress in Social Science*
John Boswell, Jack Corbett and R. A. W. Rhodes, *The Art and Craft of Comparison*
John Gerring, *Social Science Methodology: A Unified Framework, 2nd edition*
Michael Coppedge, *Democratization and Research Methods*
Thad Dunning, *Natural Experiments in the Social Sciences: A Design-Based Approach*
Carsten Q. Schneider and Claudius Wagemann, *Set-Theoretic Methods for the Social Sciences: A Guide to Qualitative Comparative Analysis*
Nicholas Weller and Jeb Barnes, *Finding Pathways: Mixed-Method Research for Studying Causal Mechanisms*
Andrew Bennett and Jeffrey T. Checkel, *Process Tracing: From Metaphor to Analytic Tool*
Diana Kapiszewski, Lauren M. MacLean and Benjamin L. Read, *Field Research in Political Science: Practices and Principles*
Peter Spiegler, *Behind the Model: A Constructive Critique of Economic Modeling*
James Mahoney and Kathleen Thelen, *Advances in Comparative-Historical Analysis*
Jason Seawright, *Multi-Method Social Science: Combining Qualitative and Quantitative Tools*
John Gerring, *Case Study Research: Principles and Practices, 2nd edition*

The Case for Case Studies

Methods and Applications in International Development

Edited by

Jennifer Widner
Department of Politics, Princeton University

Michael Woolcock
Development Research Group, World Bank

Daniel Ortega Nieto
Governance Global Practice, World Bank

CAMBRIDGE
UNIVERSITY PRESS

CAMBRIDGE
UNIVERSITY PRESS

University Printing House, Cambridge CB2 8BS, United Kingdom

One Liberty Plaza, 20th Floor, New York, NY 10006, USA

477 Williamstown Road, Port Melbourne, VIC 3207, Australia

314–321, 3rd Floor, Plot 3, Splendor Forum, Jasola District Centre,
New Delhi – 110025, India

103 Penang Road, #05–06/07, Visioncrest Commercial, Singapore 238467

Cambridge University Press is part of the University of Cambridge.

It furthers the University's mission by disseminating knowledge in the pursuit of
education, learning, and research at the highest international levels of excellence.

www.cambridge.org
Information on this title: www.cambridge.org/9781108427272
DOI: 10.1017/9781108688253

First published 2022

A catalogue record for this publication is available from the British Library.

Library of Congress Cataloging-in-Publication Data
Names: Widner, Jennifer A., editor.
Title: The case for case studies : methods and applications in international development / edited by
Jennifer Widner, Michael Woolcock, Daniel Ortega Nieto.
Description: New York, NY : Cambridge University Press, 2022. | Series: Strategies for social inquiry
| Includes bibliographical references and index.
Identifiers: LCCN 2021049586 (print) | LCCN 2021049587 (ebook) | ISBN 9781108427272
(hardback) | ISBN 9781108688253 (ebook)
Subjects: LCSH: Social sciences – Methodology. | Social sciences – Case studies.
Classification: LCC H61 .C273 2022 (print) | LCC H61 (ebook) | DDC 300.72–dc23/eng/20220105
LC record available at https://lccn.loc.gov/2021049586
LC ebook record available at https://lccn.loc.gov/2021049587

ISBN 978-1-108-42727-2 Hardback
ISBN 978-1-108-44798-0 Paperback

Contents

Figures

Tables

Boxes

Contributors

Christopher Achen is Roger Williams Straus Professor of Social Sciences, and Professor of Politics, in the Department of Politics at Princeton University.

Andrew Bennett is Professor of International Relations in the Department of Government in the College and the School of Foreign Service at Georgetown University.

Melani Cammett is Clarence Dillon Professor of International Affairs in the Department of Government and chair of the Harvard Academy of International and Area Studies at Harvard University.

Nancy Cartwright is Professor of Philosophy at the University of California at San Diego and the University of Durham.

Sarah Glavey is Research Manager at Trinity College, Dublin, Ireland.

Maria Gonzalez de Asis is Practice Manager for the Social Development Global Practice in the Latin America and Caribbean region of the World Bank.

Oliver Haas is Senior Partner, Kessel & Kessel Consultants, Germany; he was formerly the Head of the Global Division on "Health, Education, Social Inclusion" in Deutsche Gesellschaft für Internationale Zusammenarbeit (GIZ).

Margaret Levi is the Sara Miller McCune Director of the Center for Advanced Study in the Behavioral Sciences (CASBS) at Stanford University, Professor of Political Science at Stanford, and Jere L. Bacharach Professor Emerita of International Studies in the Department of Political Science at the University of Washington.

Andrew Moravcsik is Professor of Politics and Director of the European Union Program at Princeton University.

Daniel Ortega Nieto is Senior Public Sector Specialist in the Governance Global Practice at the World Bank.

Tommaso Pavone is Assistant Professor of Law and Politics in the School of Government and Public Policy at the University of Arizona.

Claudio Santibanez is Senior Advisor, Public Sector Partnerships, at UNICEF, based in New York.

Barry R. Weingast is the Ward C. Krebs Family Professor in the Department of Political Science at Stanford University, and a Senior Fellow at the Hoover Institution.

Jennifer Widner is Professor of Politics and International Affairs in the Department of Politics at Princeton University, and Director of Innovations for Successful Societies, a Woodrow Wilson School research program on improving government performance.

Michael Woolcock is Lead Social Scientist in the Development Research Group at the World Bank. For many years he has also taught part-time at Harvard Kennedy School.

Preface and Acknowledgments

This volume was conceived, as we suspect are many such ventures, during an informal conversation – in this instance, in Berlin in December 2014, at the launch of the Global Delivery Initiative.[1] All three of us were engaged with different aspects of international development, and were producing or using case studies with some frequency, but we found ourselves noting that while case studies remained widely deployed across the social sciences, and that expressions such as "the case of" were ubiquitous even in everyday speech, case studies per se remained in something of a residual methodological space: they were popularly conceived as "qualitative," for example, yet one could find many instances in which the constituent elements of a given "case" in economics were exclusively quantitative (or in medicine, for example, physiological; or in law, jurisprudential). If a singular case was indeed primarily qualitative, the key question asked by Christian Lund – "Of what is this a case?"[2] – still remained to be answered, which logically meant that the case had to be connected in some way (empirically, theoretically) to broader instances or manifestations of a phenomenon. Was this a "typical" case? A randomly selected case? An outlier? How does one know?

Moreover, if a common critique of case studies was either that their underlying methodological quality was highly variable (selection bias! selecting on the dependent variable!), or that generalizing from them was at best problematic, then there surely needed to be a serious scholarly response to such concerns. Can causal inferences reasonably be drawn from a single case? If so, under what conditions? In development practice, when and how can

---

[1] Details on the history, structure, and function of the Global Delivery Initiative (GDI) are discussed in several of the chapters in this volume. The GDI's secretariat was based at the World Bank from 2015 to 2021, but the GDI itself was essentially a membership-based entity coordinating the contributions of 50 development organizations from around the world, with case studies being one of the 3 primary means by which policy implementation lessons were shared between them. More than 165 such case studies were prepared during this period; they are now hosted by the Global Partnership for Effective Development Cooperation, and can be accessed (by selecting "Case Studies" in the "Resource Type" category) at: www .effectivecooperation.org/search/resources.

[2] Christian Lund (2014) "Of what is this a case? Analytical movements in qualitative social science research," *Human Organization*, 73(3), 224–234.

policy-makers reasonably presume that a demonstrably successful intervention in one context might generate similarly impressive outcomes elsewhere, or if massively "scaled up"? For their part, social science methodologists have in fact made impressive advances on these fronts in recent years, yet much of this analysis remains disconnected from development practice and/or grounded in comparative "cases" of large meta-categories of country characteristics – "democracy," "revolutions," "constitutions," "rule of law" – that are not the units of analysis at which the vast majority of practitioners think and act about development problems and solutions (which is: how to design and implement particular policies/projects that will achieve particular development objectives for particular groups in particular places despite numerous constraints and likely some form of political opposition). In short, we discerned two serious mismatches: first, between the ubiquity of case studies and their rather "loose" methodological moorings; and second, between the epicenter of serious scholarly activity advancing the methodological frontier of case study research ("producers") and the place where most users ("consumers") of case studies – at least in development policy and practice – actually resided.

Narrowing these twin gaps, then, became the mission of this book. While it draws on our collective experience at the nexus of development research and practice, we like to think that the underlying issues are more broadly relevant. As such, we hope readers engaging with case studies from many different starting points – disciplinary base, epistemological orientation, sectoral specialization, or practical concerns – will find issues of significance for them discussed in this volume. More generally, we hope the ideas, strategies, and challenges outlined herein prompt further advances from both researchers and practitioners, on the basis of more fruitful and informed dialogue between them – if only because the kinds of questions in play here, as elsewhere, are unlikely ever to be solved by a lone genius.

Transforming this volume from an idea to a reality took the combined efforts of many people across two rather different organizations – Princeton University and the World Bank – and we are eternally grateful to them, especially those who do a lot of the support work behind the scenes but rarely receive adequate recognition or reward. An author's conference hosted at Princeton by the Initiative for Successful Societies program greatly helped to refine the content and quality of each individual chapter while also enabling us to discern a more coherent structure for the volume as a whole. In addition to the chapter authors, other invited participants (especially Dan Honig and Mark Moran) at the author's conference, and subsequent comments from anonymous reviewers, have helped to sharpen the volume's focus and utility, since edited books work to the extent the whole is indeed greater than the sum of its parts. We particularly thank Princeton University and the World Bank's Research Support Budget, funding from which has made this entire venture possible.

1   Using Case Studies to Enhance the Quality of Explanation and Implementation

Integrating Scholarship and Development Practice

Jennifer Widner, Michael Woolcock, and Daniel Ortega Nieto

1.1   Introduction

In recent years the development policy community has turned to case studies as an analytical and diagnostic tool. Practitioners are using case studies to discern the mechanisms underpinning variations in the quality of service delivery and institutional reform, to identify how specific challenges are addressed during implementation, and to explore the conditions under which given instances of programmatic success might be replicated or scaled up.[1] These issues are of prime concern to organizations such as Princeton University's Innovations for Successful Societies (ISS)[2] program and the Global Delivery Initiative (GDI),[3] housed in the World Bank Group (from 2015–2021), both of which explicitly prepare case studies exploring the dynamics underpinning effective implementation in fields ranging from water, energy, sanitation, and health to cabinet office performance and national development strategies.

In this sense, the use of case studies by development researchers and practitioners mirrors their deployment in other professional fields. Case studies have long enjoyed high status as a pedagogical tool and research

---

The views expressed in this chapter are those of the authors alone, and should not be attributed to the organizations with which they are affiliated.

[1] For example, see Barma, Huybens, and Viñuela (2014); Brixi, Lust, and Woolcock (2015); and Woolcock (2013).

[2] See https://successfulsocieties.princeton.edu/.

[3] GDI's case studies are available (by clicking on "Case studies" under the search category "Resource type") at www.effectivecooperation.org/search/resources.

method in business, law, medicine, and public policy, and indeed across the full span of human knowledge. According to Google Scholar data reported by Van Noorden, Maher, and Nuzzo (2014), Robert Yin's *Case Study Research* (1984) is, remarkably, the sixth most cited article or book *in any field, of all time.*[4] Even so, skepticism lingers in certain quarters regarding the veracity of the case study method – for example, how confident can one be about claims drawn from single cases selected on a nonrandom or nonrepresentative basis? – and many legitimate questions remain (Morgan 2012). In order for insights from case studies to be valid and reliable, development professionals need to think carefully about how to ensure that data used in preparing the case study is accurate, that causal inferences drawn from it are made on a defensible basis (Mahoney 2000; Rohlfing 2012), and that broader generalizations are carefully delimited (Ruzzene 2012; Woolcock 2013).[5]

How best to ensure this happens? Given the recent rise in prominence and influence of the case study method within the development community and elsewhere, scholars have a vital quality control and knowledge dissemination role to play in ensuring that the use of case studies both accurately reflects and contributes to leading research. To provide a forum for this purpose, the World Bank's Development Research Group and its leading operational unit deploying case studies (the GDI) partnered with the leading academic institution that develops policy-focused case studies of development (Princeton's ISS) and asked scholars and practitioners to engage with several key questions regarding the foundations, strategies, and applications of case studies as they pertain to development processes and outcomes:[6]

- What are the distinctive virtues and limits of case studies, in their own right and vis-à-vis other research methods? How can their respective strengths be harnessed and their weaknesses overcome (or complemented by other approaches) in policy deliberations?

---

[4] Van Noorden et al. (2014) also provide a direct link to the dataset on which this empirical claim rests. As of this writing, according to Google Scholar, Yin's book (across all six editions) has been cited over 220,000 times; see also Robert Stake's *The Art of Case Study Research* (1995), which has been cited more than 51,000 times.

[5] In addition to those already listed, other key texts on the theory and practice of case studies include Feagin, Orum and Sjoberg (1991), Ragin and Becker (1992), Bates et al. (1998), Byrne and Ragin (2009), and Gerring (2017). See also Flyvbjerg (2006).

[6] As such, this volume continues earlier dialogues between scholars and development practitioners in the fields of history (Bayly et al. 2011), law (Tamanaha et al. 2012), and multilateralism (Singh and Woolcock, forthcoming).

- Are there criteria for case study selection, research design, and analysis that can help ensure accuracy and comparability in data collection, reliability in causal inference within a single case, integrity in statements about uncertainty or scope, and something akin to the replicability standard in quantitative methods?
- Under what conditions can we generalize from a small number of cases? When can comparable cases be generalized or not (across time, contexts, units of analysis, scales of operation, implementing agents)?
- How can case studies most effectively complement the insights drawn from household surveys and other quantitative assessment tools in development research, policy, and practice?
- How can lessons from case studies be used for pedagogical, diagnostic, and policy-advising purposes as improvements in the quality of implementation of a given intervention are sought?
- How can the proliferation of case studies currently being prepared on development processes and outcomes be used to inform the scholarship on the theory and practice of case studies?

The remainder of this chapter provides an overview of the distinctive features (and limits) of case study research, drawing on "classic" and recent contributions in the scholarly literature. It provides a broad outline of the key claims and issues in the field, as well as a summary of the book's chapters.

1.2   The Case for Case Studies: A Brief Overview

We can all point to great social science books and articles that derive from qualitative case study research. Herbert Kaufman's (1960) classic, *The Forest Ranger*, profiles the principal–agent problems that arise in management of the US Forest Service as well as the design and implementation of several solutions. Robert Ellickson's (1991) *Order Without Law* portrays how ranchers settle disputes among themselves without recourse to police or courts. Judith Tendler's (1997) *Good Government in the Tropics* uses four case studies of Ceara, Brazil's poorest state, to identify instances of positive deviance in public sector reform. Daniel Carpenter's (2001) *The Forging of Bureaucratic Autonomy*, based on three historical cases, seeks to explain why reformers in some US federal agencies were able to carve out space free from partisan legislative interference while others were unable to do so. In "The Market for Public Office," Robert Wade (1985) elicits the strategic structure of a particular kind of spoiler problem from a case study conducted in India. In economics, a longitudinal study of poverty dynamics in a single village in India (Palanpur)[7] has usefully informed understandings of these processes across the subcontinent (and beyond).

What makes these contributions stand out compared to the vast numbers of case studies that few find insightful? What standards should govern the choice and design of case studies, generally? And what specific insights do case studies yield that other research methods might be less well placed to provide?

The broad ambition of the social sciences is to forge general insights that help us quickly understand the world around us and make informed policy decisions. While each social science discipline has its own distinctive approach, there is broad agreement upon a methodological division of labor in the work we do. This conventional wisdom holds that quantitative analysis of large numbers of discrete cases is usually more effective for testing the veracity of causal propositions, for estimating the strength of the association between readily measurable causes and outcomes, and for evaluating the sensitivity of correlations to changes in the underlying model specifying the relationship between causal variables (and their measurement). By contrast, qualitative methods generally, and case studies in particular, fulfill other distinct epistemological functions and are the predominant method for:

1. Developing a theory and/or identifying causal mechanisms (e.g., working inductively from evidence to propositions and exploring the contents of the "black box" processes connecting causes and effects)
2. Eliciting strategic structure (e.g., documenting *how* interaction effects of one kind or another influence options, processes, and outcomes)
3. Showing how antecedent conditions elicit a prevailing structure which thereby shapes/constrains the decisions of actors within that structure
4. Testing a theory in novel circumstances
5. Understanding outliers or deviant cases

The conventional wisdom also holds that in an ideal world we would have the ability to use both quantitative and qualitative analysis and employ "nested" research designs (Bamberger, Rao, and Woolcock 2010; Goertz and Mahoney

---

[7] The initial study in what has become a sequence is Bliss and Stern (1982); for subsequent rounds, see Lanjouw and Stern (1998) and Lanjouw, Murgai, and Stern (2013). This study remains ongoing, and is now in its seventh decade.

2012; Lieberman 2015). However, the appropriate choice of method depends on the character of the subject matter, the kinds of data available, and the array of constraints (resources, politics, time) under which the study is being conducted. The central task is to deploy those combinations of research methods that yield the most fruitful insights in response to a specific problem, given the prevailing constraints (Rueschemeyer 2009). We now consider each of these five domains in greater detail.

1.3   Developing a Theory and/or Identifying Causal Mechanisms

Identifying a causal mechanism and inferring an explanation or theory are important parts of the research process, especially in the early stages of knowledge development. The causal mechanism links an independent variable to an outcome, and over time may become more precise: to cite an oft-used example, an initial awareness that citrus fruits reduced scurvy became more refined when the underlying causal mechanism was discovered to be vitamin C. For policy purposes, mechanisms provide the basis for a compelling storyline, which can greatly influence the tone and terms of debate – or the space of what is "thinkable," "say-able," and "do-able" – which in turn can affect the design, implementation, and support for interventions. This can be particularly relevant for development practitioners if the storyline – and the mechanisms it highlights – provides important insights into how and where implementation processes unravel, and what factors enabled a particular intervention to succeed or fail during the delivery process.

In this way, qualitative research can provide clarity on the factors that influence critical processes and help us identify the mechanisms that affect particular outcomes. For example, there is a fairly robust association, globally, between higher incomes and smaller family sizes. But what is it about income that would lead families to have fewer children – or does income mask other changes that influence child-bearing decisions? To figure out the mechanism, one could conduct interviews and focus groups with a few families to understand decision-making about family planning. Hypotheses based on these family case studies could then inform the design of survey-based quantitative research to test alternative mechanisms and the extent to which one or another predominates in different settings. Population researchers have done just that (see Knodel 1997).

Case studies carried out for the purpose of inductive generalization or identifying causal mechanisms are rarely pure "soak and poke" exercises uninformed by any preconceptions. Indeed, approaching a case with a provisional set of hypotheses is vitally important. The fact that we want to use a case to infer a general statement about cause and effect does not obviate the need for this vital intellectual tool; it just means we need to listen hard for alternative explanations we did not initially perceive and be highly attentive to actions, events, attitudes, etc., that are at odds with the reasoned intuition brought to the project.

An example where having an initial set of hypotheses was important comes from a GDI case on scaling-up rural sanitation. In this case, the authors wanted to further understand how the government of Indonesia had been able to substantially diminish open defecation, which is the main cause of several diseases in thousands of villages across the country.[8] The key policy change was a dramatic move from years of subsidizing latrines that ended up not being used to trying to change people's behavior toward open defecation, a socially accepted norm. The authors had a set of hypotheses with respect to what triggered this important policy shift: a change in cabinet members, the presence of international organizations, adjustments in budgets, etc. However, the precise mechanism that triggered the change only became clear after interviewing several actors involved in the process. It turns out that a study tour taken by several Indonesian officials to Bangladesh was decisive since, for the first time, they could see the results of a different policy "with their own eyes" instead of just reading about it.[9]

There are some situations, however, in which we may know so little that hypothesis development must essentially begin from scratch. For example, consider an ISS case study series on cabinet office performance. A key question was why so many heads of government allow administrative decisions to swamp cabinet meetings, causing the meetings to last a long time and reducing the chance that the government will reach actual policy decisions or priorities. One might have a variety of hypotheses to explain this predicament, but without direct access to the meetings themselves it is hard to know which of these hypotheses is most likely to be true (March, Sproul, and Tamuz 1991). In the initial phases, ISS researchers deliberately left a lot of space for the people interviewed to offer their own explanations. They anticipated that not all heads of state might want their cabinets to work as forums for decision-making and coordination, because ministers who had a lot of political and military clout might capture the stage or threaten vital interests of weaker members – or because the head of state benefited from the

---

[8] Glavey and Haas (2015).   [9] Glavey and Haas (2015).

dysfunction. But as the first couple of cases unfolded, the research team realized that part of the problem arose from severe under-staffing, simple lack of know-how, inadequate capacity at the ministry level, or rapid turn-over in personnel. In such situations, as March, Sproul, and Tamuz (1991: 8) aptly put it,

[t]he pursuit of rich experience ... requires a method for absorbing detail without molding it. Great organizational histories, like great novels, are written, not by first constructing interpretations of events and then filling in the details, but by first identifying the details and allowing the interpretations to emerge from them. As a result, openness to a variety of (possibly irrelevant) dimensions of experience and preference is often more valuable than a clear prior model and unambiguous objectives.

In another ISS case study on the factors shaping the implementation and sustainability of "rapid results" management practices (e.g., setting 100-day goals, coupled with coaching on project management), a subquestion was when and why setting a 100-day goal improved service delivery. In interviews, qualitative insight into causal mechanisms surfaced: some managers said they thought employees understood expectations more clearly and therefore performed better as a result of setting a 100-day goal, while in other instances a competitive spirit or "game sense" increased motivation or cooperation with other employees, making work more enjoyable. Still others expected that an audit might follow, so a sense of heightened scrutiny also made a difference. The project in question did not try to arbitrate among these causal mechanisms or theories, but using the insight from the qualitative research, a researcher might well have proceeded to decipher which of these explanations carried most weight.

In many instances it is possible and preferable to approach the task of inductive generalization with more intellectual structure up front, however. As researchers we always have a few "priors" – hunches or hypotheses – that guide investigation. The extent to which we want these to structure initial inquiry may depend on the purpose of our research, but also on the likely causal complexity of the outcome we want to study, the rapidity of change in contexts, and the stock of information already available.

1.4 Eliciting Strategic Structure

A second important feature of the case study method, one that is intimately related to developing a theory or identifying causal mechanisms, is its ability to elicit the strategic structure of an event – that is, to capture the interactions that produce an important outcome. Some kinds of outcomes are "conditioned": they vary with underlying contextual features like income levels or geography. Others are "crafted" or choice-based: the outcome is the product of bargaining, negotiating, deal-cutting, brinkmanship, and other types of interaction among a set of specified actors. Policy choice and implementation fall into this second category. Context may shape the feasible set of outcomes or the types of bargaining challenges, but the only way to explain outcomes is to trace the process or steps and choices as they unfold in the interaction (see Bennett and Checkel 2015).

In process tracing we want to identify the key actors, their preferences, and the alternatives or options they faced; evaluate the information available to these people and the expectations they formed; assess the resources available to each to persuade others or to alter the incentives others face and the expectations they form (especially with regard to the strategies they deploy); and indicate the formal and informal rules that govern the negotiation, as well as the personal aptitudes that influence effectiveness and constrain choice. The researcher often approaches the case with a specific type of strategic structure in mind – a bargaining story that plausibly accounts for the outcome – along with a sense of other frames that might explain the same set of facts.

In the 1980s and 1990s, the extensive literature on the politics of structural adjustment yielded many case studies designed to give us a better understanding of the kinds of difficulties ministers of finance faced in winning agreement to devalue a currency, sell assets, or liberalize trade or commodity markets, as well as the challenges they encountered in making these changes happen (e.g., Haggard 1992). Although the case studies yielded insights that could be used to create models testable with large-N data, in any individual case the specific parameters – context or circumstance – remained important for explaining particular outcomes. Sensitivity to the kinds of strategic challenges that emerged in other settings helped decision-makers assess the ways their situations might be similar or different, identify workarounds or coalitions essential for winning support, and increase the probability that their own efforts would succeed. It is important to know what empirical relationships seem to hold across a wide (ideally full) array of cases, but the most useful policy advice is that which is given in response to specific people in a specific place responding to a specific problem under specific constraints; as such, deep knowledge of contextual contingencies characterizing each case is vital.[10]

---

[10] For example, if it can be shown empirically that, in general, countries that exit from bilateral trade agreements show a subsequent improvement in their "rule of law" scores, does this provide warrant for

For example, consider the challenge of improving rural livelihoods during an economic crisis in Indonesia. In "Services for the People, By the People," ISS researchers profiled how Indonesian policy-makers tried to address the problem of "capture" in a rural development program. Officials and local leaders often diverted resources designed to benefit the poor. The question was how to make compliance incentive compatible. That is, what did program leaders do to alter the cost–benefit calculus of the potential spoiler? How did they make their commitment to bargains, deals, pacts, or other devices credible? In most cases, the interaction is "dynamic" and equilibria (basis for compliance) are not stable. Learning inevitably takes place, and reform leaders often have to take new steps as circumstances change. Over time, what steps did a reformer take to preserve the fragile equilibrium first created or to forge a new equilibrium? Which tactics proved most effective, given the context?

In this instance, leaders used a combination of tactics to address the potential spoiler problem. They vested responsibility for defining priorities in communities, not in the capital or the district. They required that at least two of three proposals the communities could submit came from women's groups. They set up subdistrict competitions to choose the best proposals, with elected members of each community involved in selection. They transferred money to community bank accounts that could only be tapped when the people villagers elected to monitor the projects all countersigned. They created teams of facilitators to provide support and monitor results. When funds disappeared, communities lost the ability to compete. Careful case analysis helped reveal not only the incentive design, but also the interaction between design and context – and the ways in which the system occasionally failed, although the program was quite successful overall.

A related series of ISS cases focused on how leaders overcame the opposition of people or groups who benefited from dysfunction and whose institutional positions enabled them to block changes that would improve service delivery. The ambition in these cases was to tease out the strategies reform leaders could use to reach an agreement on a new set of rules or practices; if they were able to do so, case studies focused on institutions where spoiler traps often appear: anticorruption initiatives, port reform (ports, like banks, being "where the money is"), and infrastructure. The strategies or tactics at the focus in these studies included use of external agencies of restraint (e.g., the Governance and Economic Management Assistance Program [GEMAP] in Liberia); "coalitions

advising (say) Senegal that if it wants to improve its "rule of law" then it should exit from all its bilateral trade agreements? We think not.

with the public" to make interference more costly in social or political terms; persuading opponents to surrender rents in one activity for rewards in another; pitting strong spoilers against each other; and altering the cost calculus by exposing the spoiler to new risks. The cases allowed researchers both to identify the strategies used and to weigh the sensitivity of these to variations in context or shifts in the rules of the game or the actors involved. The hope was that the analysis the cases embodied would help practitioners avoid the adoption of strategies that are doomed to fail in the specific contexts they face. It also enabled policy-makers to see how they might alter rules or practices in ways that make a reformer's job (at least to a degree) easier.

A couple of GDI cases provide further illustration of how to elicit strategic structure. In a case on how to shape an enabling environment for water service delivery in Nigeria,[11] the authors were able to identify the political incentives that undermine long-term commitments and overhaul short-run returns, and which generate a low-level equilibrium trap. This has led to improvements in investments in rehabilitation and even an expansion of water services, yet it has not allowed the institutional reforms needed to ensure sustainability to move forward. In the case of Mexico, where the government had been struggling to improve service delivery to Indigenous communities, a World Bank loan provided a window of opportunity to change things. A number of reformers within the government believed that catering services to these populations in their own languages would help decrease the number of dropouts from its flagship social program, Oportunidades.[12] However, previous efforts had not moved forward. A World Bank loan to the Mexican government triggered a safeguards policy on Indigenous populations and it became fundamental for officials to be able to develop a program to certify bilingual personnel that could service these communities. Interviews with key officials and stakeholders showed how the safeguards policy kick-started a set of meetings and decisions within the government that eventually led to this program, changing the strategic structures within government.

1.5 Showing How an Antecedent Condition Limits Decision-Makers' Options

Some types of phenomena require case study analysis to disentangle complex causal relationships. We generally assume the cause of an outcome is

---

[11] Hima and Santibanez (2015).   [12] Estabridis and Nieto (2015).

exogenous, but sometimes there are feedback effects and an outcome inten-
sifies one of its causes or limits the range of values the outcome can later
assume. In such situations, case studies can be helpful in parsing the structure
of these causal relationships and identifying which conditions are prior.
Some of the case studies that inform *Why States Fail* (Acemoglu and
Robinson 2012), for example, perform this function. More detailed case
studies of this type appear in political science and sociological writing in
the "historical institutionalism" tradition (see Thelen and Mahoney 2009;
Mahoney and Thelen 2015).

Case studies are also useful in other instances when both the design of
a policy intervention and the way in which it is implemented affect the
outcome. They help identify ways to distinguish the effects of policy from
the effects of process, two things that most quantitative studies conflate. To
illustrate, take another ISS case study series on rapid turnarounds observed in
some types of public sector agencies: the quick development of pockets of
effectiveness. The agencies at the focus of this project provided business
licenses or identity documents – actions that required relatively little exercise
of judgment on the part of the person dispensing the service and where the
number of distribution points is fairly limited. Businesses and citizens felt the
effects of delay and corruption in these services keenly, but not all governments put reformers at the helm and not all reformers improved performance. The ISS team was partly interested in the interventions that produced
turnarounds in this type of activity: was there a secret recipe – a practice that
produced altered incentives or outlooks and generated positive results? The
literature on principal–agent problems offered hypotheses about ways to
better align the interests of leaders and the people on the front-line who
deliver a service, but many of these were inapplicable in low-resource
environments or where removing personnel and modifying terms of service
was hard to do. But ISS was also interested in how the mode of implementation affected outcomes, because solving the principal–agent problem often
created clear losers who could block the new policies. How did the successful
reformers win support?

The team refined and expanded its initial set of hypotheses through
a detailed case study of South Africa's Ministry of Home Affairs, and traced
both the influence of the incentive design and the process used to put the new
practices into effect. Without the second part, the case study team might have
reasoned that the results stemmed purely from changed practices and tried to
copy the same approach somewhere else, but in this instance, as in many
cases, the mode of implementation was critical to success. The project leader

could not easily draw from the standard toolkit for solving principal–agent problems because he could not easily remove poorly performing employees. He had to find ways to win union acceptance of the new policies and get people excited about the effort. This case study was an example of using qualitative methods to identify a causal mechanism and to develop explanations we can evaluate more broadly by conducting other case studies.

An example from the GDI is a case on addressing maternal and child mortality in Argentina in the early 2000s.[13] As a result of the 2001 economic crisis, thousands of people lost their jobs and hence were unable to pay for private healthcare; consequently, the public health system suddenly received a vast and unexpected influx of patients. Given that the Argentine public health system had been decentralized over the preceding decades and therefore the central government's role in the provinces was minor, policy-makers had to work around a set of conditions and do it fast, given the context. The case disentangled how the central government was able to design one of the first results-based finance programs in the health sector and how this design was critical in explaining the maternal and child mortality outcomes. Policy-makers had to react immediately to the pressure on the health system and were able to make use of a provincial coordination mechanism that had become mostly irrelevant. By reviving this mechanism and having access to international funds, the central government was able to reinstate its role in provincial health care and engage key local decision-makers. Through the case study, the authors were able to assess the relevance of the policy-making process and how it defined the stakeholders' choices, as well as the effect of the process in the Argentine healthcare system.

1.6   Testing a Theory in Novel Circumstances

Case study analysis is a relatively weak method for testing explanations derived from large sample sizes but it is often the only method available if the event is relatively uncommon or if sample sizes are small. Testing a theory against a small number of instrumentally chosen cases carries some peril. If we have only a few cases to study, the number of causal variables that potentially influence the outcome could overwhelm the number of observations, making it impossible to infer anything about the relationship between two variables, except through intensive tracing of processes.

---

[13] Ortega Nieto and Parida (2015).

Usually theory testing with case studies begins with a "truth table" or matrix, with the key independent variable(s) arrayed on one axis and the outcome variable arrayed on the other. The researcher collects data on the same variables in each case. The names of the cases in the cells of the table are then arranged and comparisons made of expected patterns with the actual pattern. The proportion of cases in each cell will track expectations if there is support for the theory.

An example of this kind of use of case studies appears in Alejandro Portes's collaborative project on institutional development in Latin America (Portes and Smith 2008). In each country, the project studied the same five agencies. The research team listed several organizational characteristics that prior theories suggested might be important. In the truth table, the characteristic on which the successful agencies clustered was having a merit system for making personnel decisions. Having a merit system distinguished the successful agencies from the unsuccessful agencies in each of the five country settings in which the research took place. (A slightly different design would have allowed the researchers to determine whether an antecedent condition shaped the adoption of merit systems in the successful cases and also exercised an independent effect on the outcome.)

In the ISS project about single-agency turnarounds, the aim was to make some tentative general statements about the robustness of a set of practices to differences in context. Specifically, the claim was that delays would diminish and productivity would rise by introducing a fairly standard set of management practices designed to streamline a process, increase transparency, and invite friendly group competition. In this kind of observational study, the authors had a before-and-after or longitudinal design in each individual case, which was married with a cross-sectional design.[14] The elements of the intervention were arrayed in a truth table and examined to see which of them were present or absent in parallel interventions in a number of other cases. The team added cases with nearly identical interventions but different underlying country contexts. ISS then explored each case in greater detail to see whether implementation strategy or something else having to do with context explained which reforms were successful and which were not.

---

[14] In the best of all possible worlds, we would want to draw the cases systematically from a known universe or population, but the absence of such a dataset meant we had to satisfice and match organizations on function while varying context means. Conclusions reached thus need to be qualified by the recognition that there could be more cases "out there," which, if included in the analysis, might alter the initial results.

Small-scale observational studies (the only type of study possible in many subject areas) suffer from a variety of threats, including inability to control for large numbers of differences in setting. However, the interview data and close process tracing helped increase confidence in two respects. First, they helped reveal the connection between the outcomes observed and the practices under study. For example, it was relevant that people in work groups could describe their reactions when a poster showing how many identity documents they had issued had increased or decreased compared to the month before. Second, the information the interviews delivered about obstacles encountered and workarounds developed fueled hypotheses about robustness to changes in setting. In short, the deep dive that the case study permitted helped alleviate some of the inferential challenges that inevitably arise when there are only small numbers of observations and a randomized controlled trial is not feasible.

Rare events pose special problems for theory testing. Organizations must often learn from single cases – for example, from the outcome of a rare event (such as a natural disaster, or a major restructuring). In this circumstance it may be possible to evaluate impact across several units within the organization or influences across policy areas. However, where this approach is impossible few organizations decline to learn from experience; instead, they look closely at the history of the event to assess the sequence of steps by which prevailing outcomes obtained and how these might have been different had alternative courses of action been pursued.

1.7   Understanding Outliers or Deviant Cases

A common and important use of case studies is to explore the case that does not conform to expectations. An analysis comparing a large number of cases on a few variables may find that most units (countries, agencies, etc.) cluster closely around a regression line whose slope shows the relationship between the causal variables and the outcome. However, one or two cases may lie far from the line. We usually want to know what's different about those cases, and especially how and why they differ. For example, there is generally a quite robust relationship between a country's level of spending on education and the quality of outcomes that country's education system generates. Why is Vietnam in the bottom third globally in terms of its spending on education, yet in the upper third globally in terms of outcomes (as measured by student performance on standardized examinations)? Conversely, why is Malaysia in the upper third on spending and bottom third on outcomes?

In the study of development, outliers such as these hold particular fascination. For example, several scholars whose contributions are ordinarily associated with use of quantitative methods have employed schematic case studies to ponder why Botswana seems to have stronger institutions than most other African countries (Acemoglu, Johnson, and Robinson 2003). Costa Rica and Singapore attract attention for the same reason.[15] This same approach can be used to explore and explain subnational variation as a basis for deriving policy lessons. Brixi, Lust, and Woolcock (2015), for example, deploy data collected from household surveys to map the wide range of outcomes in public service delivery across countries in the Middle East and North Africa – countries which otherwise have highly centralized line ministries, which means roughly the same policies regarding (say) health and education apply across any given country. The wide variation in outcomes is thus largely a matter of factors shaping policy *implementation*, which are often highly contextual and thus much harder to assess via standard quantitative instruments. On the basis of the subnational variation maps, however, granular case studies were able to be prepared on those particular locations where unusually high (and low) outcomes were being obtained; the lessons from these cases, in turn, became inputs for a conversation with domestic policy-makers about where and how improvements might be sought. Here, the goal was not to seek policy reform by importing what researchers deemed "best practices" (as verified by "rigorous evidence") from abroad but rather to use *both* household surveys and case studies to endogenize research tools into the ways in which local practitioners make difficult decisions about strategy, trade-offs, and feedback, doing so in ways regarded as legitimate and useful by providers and users of public services.

---

[15] The ISS program began with a similar aim. The questions at the heart of the program were "What makes the countries that pull off institutional transformation different from others? What have they done that others could do to increase government capacity? What can be learned from the positive deviants, in particular?" For a variety of reasons having to do with the nature of the subject matter, the program disaggregated the subject and focused on responses to particular kinds of strategic challenges within countries and why some had negotiated these successfully in some periods and places but not in others.

1.8 Ensuring Rigor in Case Studies: Foundations, Strategies, and Applications

There is general agreement on some of the standards that should govern qualitative case studies. Such studies should:[16]

- respond to a clear question that links to an important intellectual debate or policy problem
- specify and define core concepts, terms, and metrics associated with the explanations
- identify plausible explanations, articulating a main hypothesis and logical alternatives
- offer data that allow us to evaluate the main ideas or discriminate between different possible causal mechanisms, including any that emerge as important in the course of the research
- be selected according to clear and transparent criteria appropriate to the research objective
- be amenable to replication – that is, other researchers ought to be able to check the results

Together, this book's three parts – on Internal and External Validity Issues, Ensuring High-Quality Case Studies, and Applications to Development Practice – explore how the content and realization of these standards can be applied by those conducting case studies in development research and practice, and how, in turn, the fruits of their endeavors can contribute to a refinement and expansion of the "ecologies of evidence" on which inherently complex decisions in development are made.

We proceed as follows. Part I focuses on the relative strengths and weaknesses of qualitative cases versus frequentist observational studies (surveys, aggregate data analysis) and randomized controlled trials (RCTs). Its constituent chapters explore the logic of causal inference and the logic of generalization, often framed as problems of internal and external validity.

In Chapter 2, philosopher of science Nancy Cartwright walks us through the logic behind RCTs on the one hand, and qualitative case studies on the other. RCTs have gained considerable prominence as a 'gold standard' for

---

[16] These general standards, importantly, are consistent with a recent interdisciplinary effort to define rigor in case study research, which took place under the auspices of the US National Science Foundation. See Report on the Workshop on Interdisciplinary Standards for Systematic Qualitative Research. Available at: https://oconnell.fas.harvard.edu/files/lamont/files/issqr_workshop_rpt.pdf.

establishing whether a given policy intervention has a causal effect, but what do these experiments actually tell us and how useful is this information for policy-makers? Cartwright draws attention to two problems. First, an RCT only establishes a claim about average effects for the population enrolled in an experiment; it tells us little about what lies behind the average. The policy intervention studied might have changed nothing in some instances, while in others it triggered large shifts in behavior or health or whatever is under study. But, second, an RCT also tells us nothing about when we might expect to see the same effect size in a different population. To assess how a different population might respond requires other information of the sort that qualitative case studies often uncover. RCTs may help identify a cause, but identifying a cause is not the same as identifying something that is generally true, Cartwright notes. She then considers what information a policy-maker would need to predict whether a causal relationship will hold in a particular instance, which is often what we really want to know.

The singular qualitative case study has a role to play in addressing this need. Cartwright begins by asking what are the support factors that enable the intervention to work, and are they present in a particular situation? She suggests we should use various types of evidence, both indirect and direct. In the "direct" category are many of the elements that case studies can (and should) document: 1) Does O occur at the time, in the manner, and of the size to be expected that T caused it? 2) Are there symptoms of cause – by-products of the causal relationship? 3) Were requisite support factors present? (i.e., was everything in place that needed to be in order for T to produce O?), and 4) Were the expected intermediate steps (mediator variables) in place? Often these are the key elements we need to know in order to decide whether the effects observed in an experiment will scale.

Political scientist Christopher Achen also weighs the value of RCTs versus qualitative case studies with the aim of correcting what he perceives as an imbalance in favor of the former within contemporary social science. In Chapter 3 he shows that "the argument for experiments depends critically on emphasizing the central challenge of observational work – accounting for unobserved confounders – while ignoring entirely the central challenge of experimentation – achieving external validity." Using the mathematics behind randomized controlled trials to make his point, he shows that once this imbalance is corrected, we are closer to Cartwright's view than to the current belief that RCTs constitute the gold standard for good policy research.

As a pivot, Achen takes a 2014 essay, a classic statement about the failure of observational studies to generate learning and about the strengths of RCTs. The authors of that essay argued that

[t]he external validity of an experiment hinges on four factors: 1) whether the subjects in the study are as strongly influenced by the treatment as the population to which a generalization is made, 2) whether the treatment in the experiment corresponds to the treatment in the population of interest, 3) whether the response measure used in the experiment corresponds to the variable of interest in the population, and 4) how the effect estimates were derived statistically. (Gerber et al. 2014, 21)

But Achen finds this list a little too short: "The difficulty is that those assumptions combine jaundiced cynicism about observational studies with gullible innocence about experiments," he writes. "What is missing from this list are the two critical factors emphasized in the work of recent critics of RCTs: heterogeneity of treatment effects and the importance of context." For example, in an experiment conducted with Michigan voters, there were no Louisianans, no Democrats, and no general election voters; "[h]ence, no within-sample statistical adjustments are available to accomplish the inferential leap" required for generalizing the result.

Achen concludes: "Causal inference of any kind is just plain hard. If the evidence is observational, patient consideration of plausible counterarguments, followed by the assembling of relevant evidence, can be, and often is, a painstaking process." Well-structured qualitative case studies are one important tool; experiments, another.

In Chapter 4, Andrew Bennett help us think about what steps are necessary to use case studies to identify causal relationships and draw contingent generalizations. He suggests that case study research employs Bayesian logic rather than frequentist logic: "Bayesian logic treats probabilities as degrees of belief in alternative explanations, and it updates initial degrees of belief (called 'priors') by using assessments of the probative value of new evidence vis-à-vis alternative explanations (the updated degree of belief is known as the 'posterior')."

Bennett's chapter sketches four approaches: generalization from 'typical' cases, generalization from most- or least-likely cases, mechanism-based generalization, and typological theorizing, with special attention to the last two. Improved understanding of causal mechanisms permits generalizing to individuals, cases, or contexts outside the initial sample studied. In this regard, the study of deviant, or outlier, cases and cases that have high values on the independent variable of interest (theory of change) may prove helpful, Bennett suggests, aiding the identification of scope conditions, new explanations, and omitted variables.

In "Will it Work Here?" (Chapter 5), Michael Woolcock focuses on the utility of qualitative case studies for addressing the decision-maker's perennial external validity concern: What works there may not work here. He asks how to generate the facts that are important in determining whether an intervention can be scaled and replicated in a given setting. He focuses our attention on three categories. The first he terms causal density, or whether 1) there are numerous causal pathways and feedback loops that affect inputs, actions, and outcomes, and 2) there is greater or lesser openness to exogenous influence. Experiments are often helpful when causal density is low – deworming, use of malaria nets, classroom size – but they fail when causal density is high, as in parenting. To assess causal density, Woolcock suggests we pay special attention to how many person-to-person transactions are required; how much discretion is required of front-line implementing agents; how much pressure implementing agents face to do something other than respond constructively to the problem; and the extent to which implementing agents are required to deploy solutions from a known menu or to innovate in situ.

Woolcock's two other categories of relevant fact include implementation capability and reasoned expectations about what can be achieved by when. With respect to the first, he urges us not to assume that implementation capacity is equally available in each setting. Who has the authority to act? Is there adequate management capacity? Are there adequately trained front-line personnel? Is there a clear point of delivery? A functional supply chain? His third category, reasoned expectations, focuses on having a grounded theory about what can be achieved by when. Should we anticipate that the elements of an intervention all show results at the same time, as we usually assume, or will some kinds of results materialize before others? Will some increase over time, while others dissipate? Deliberation about these matters on the basis of analytic case studies, Woolcock argues, are the main method available for assessing the generalizability of any given intervention. Woolcock supplements his discussion with examples and a series of useful summary charts.

Part II of the book builds upon these methodological concerns to examine practical strategies by which case studies in international development (and elsewhere) can be prepared to the highest standards. Although not exhaustive, these strategies, presented by three political scientists, can help elevate the quality and utility of case studies by focusing on useful analytical tools that can enhance the rigor of their methodological foundations.

In Chapter 6, Jennifer Widner, who directs Princeton University's Innovations for Successful Societies program, reflects on what she and others have learned about gathering reliable information from interviews. Case study researchers usually draw on many types of evidence, some qualitative and some quantitative. For understanding motivation/interest, anticipated challenges, strategic choices, steps taken, unexpected obstacles encountered, and other elements of implementation, interviews with people who were "in the room where it happens" are usually essential. There may be diary entries or meeting minutes to help verify personal recall, but often the documentary evidence is limited or screened from view by thirty-year rules. Subject matter, proximity to elections or other sensitive events, interviewer self-presentation, question sequence, probes, and ethics safeguards are among the factors that shape the reliability of information offered in an interview. Widner sketches ways to improve the accuracy of recall and the level of detail, and to guard against "spin," drawing on her program's experience as well as the work of survey researchers and anthropologists.

Political scientist Tommaso Pavone analyzes how our evolving under-standing of case-based causal inference via process tracing should alter how we select cases for comparative inquiry (Chapter 7). The chapter explicates perhaps the most influential and widely used means to conduct qualitative research involving two or more cases: Mill's methods of agreement and difference. It then argues that the traditional use of Millian methods of case selection can lead us to treat cases as static units to be synchronically compared rather than as social processes unfolding over time. As a result, Millian methods risk prematurely rejecting and otherwise overlooking (1) ordered causal processes, (2) paced causal processes, and (3) equifinality, or the presence of multiple pathways that produce the same outcome. To address these issues, the chapter develops a set of recommendations to ensure the alignment of Millian methods of case selection with within-case sequential analysis. First, it outlines how the use of processualist theories can help reformulate Millian case selection designs to accommodate ordered and paced processes (but not equifinal processes). Second, it proposes a new, alternative approach to comparative case study research: the method of inductive case selection. By selecting cases for comparison after a causal process has been identified within a particular case, the method of inductive case selection enables researchers to assess (1) the generalizability of the causal sequences, (2) the logics of scope conditions on the causal argument, and (3) the presence of equifinal pathways to the same outcome. A number of concrete examples from development practice illustrate how the method of inductive case selection can be used by both scholars and policy practitioners alike.

One of the common criticisms of qualitative research is that a case is hard to replicate. Whereas quantitative researchers often share their research designs and their data and encourage one another to rerun their analyses, qualitative researchers cannot as easily do so. However, they can enhance reliability in other ways. In Chapter 8, Andrew Moravcsik introduces new practices designed to enhance three dimensions of research transparency: *data transparency*, which stipulates that researchers should publicize the data and evidence on which their research rests; *analytic transparency*, which stipulates that researchers should publicize how they interpret and analyze evidence in order to generate descriptive and causal inferences; and *production transparency*, which stipulates that social scientists should publicize the broader set of design choices that underlie the research. To respond to these needs, Moravcsik couples technology with the practice of discursive footnotes common in law journals. He discusses the rationale for creating a digitally enabled appendix with annotated source materials, called Active Citation or the Annotation for Transparency Initiative.

Part III – this volume's concluding section – explores the ways in which case studies are being used today to learn from and enhance effectiveness in different development agencies.

In Chapter 9, Andrew Bennett explores how process tracing can be used in program evaluation. "Process tracing and program evaluation, or contribution analysis, have much in common, as they both involve causal inference on alternative explanations for the outcome of a single case," Bennett says:

Evaluators are often interested in whether one particular explanation – the implicit or explicit theory of change behind a program – accounts for the outcome. Yet they still need to consider whether exogenous nonprogram factors … account for the outcome, whether the program generated the outcome through some process other than the theory of change, and whether the program had additional or unintended consequences, either good or bad.

Bennett discusses how to develop a process-tracing case study to meet these demands and walks the reader through several key elements of this enterprise, including types of confounding explanations and the basics of Bayesian analysis.

In Chapter 10, with a focus on social services in the Middle East, political scientist Melani Cammett takes up the use of positive deviant cases – examples of sustained high performance in a context in which good results are uncommon – to identify and disentangle causal complexity and understand the role of context. Although the consensus view on the role of deviant cases is that they are most useful for exploratory purposes or discovery and theory building, Cammett suggests they can also generate insights into the identification and operation of causal mechanisms. She writes that "analyses of positive deviant cases among a field of otherwise similar cases that operate in the same context . . . can be a valuable way to identify potential explanatory variables for exceptional performance." The hypothesized explanatory variables can then be incorporated in subsequent quantitative or qualitative studies in order to evaluate their effects across a broader range of observations. The chapter discusses how to approach selection of positive deviant cases systematically and then works through a real example.

In Chapter 11, on "Analytical Narratives and Case Studies," Margaret Levi and Barry Weingast focus on a particular type of case in which the focus is on an outcome that results from strategic interaction, when one person's decision depends on what another does. "A weakness of case studies per se is that there typically exist multiple ways to interpret a given case," they begin. "How are we to know which interpretation makes most sense? What gives us confidence in the particular interpretation offered?" An analytic narrative first elucidates the principal players, their preferences, key decision points and possible choices, and the rules of the game. It then builds a model of the sequence of interaction including predicted outcomes and evaluates the model through comparative statics and the testable implications the mode generates. An analytic narrative also models situations as an extensive-form game. "The advantage of the game is that it reveals the logic of why, in equilibrium, it is in the interest of the players to fulfill their threats or promises against those who leave the equilibrium path," the authors explain. Although game theory is useful, there is no hard rule that requires us to formalize. The particular findings do not generalize to other contexts, but an analytic narrative points to the characteristics of situations to which a similar strategic logic applies.

The book's final chapters focus on the use of case studies for refining development policy and practice – in short, for learning. In Chapter 12, Sarah Glavery and her coauthors draw a distinction between explicit knowledge, which is easily identified and shared through databases and reports, and tacit knowledge – the less easily shared "know how" that comes with having carried out a task. The chapter explores ways to use case study preparation, as well as a case itself, as a vehicle for sharing "know how," specifically with respect to program implementation. It considers the experiences of four different types of organizations that have used case studies as part of their decision-making as it pertains to development issues: a multilateral agency (the World Bank), a major bilateral agency (Germany's GIZ), a leading think tank (Brookings), and a ministry of a large country (China's Ministry of Finance), which are all linked through their involvement in the GDI.

Finally, in Chapter 13, Maria Gonzalez and Jennifer Widner reflect more broadly on the intellectual history of a science of delivery and adaptive management, two interlinked approaches to improving public services, and the use of case studies to move these endeavors forward. They emphasize the ways in which case studies have become salient tools for front-line staff whose everyday work is trying to solve complex development challenges, especially those pertaining to the implementation of policies and projects, and how, in turn, case studies are informing a broader turn to explaining outcome variation and identifying strategies for responding to complex challenges and ultimately seeking to enhance development effectiveness. The chapter discusses seven qualities that make a case useful to practitioners, and then offers reflections on how to use cases in a group context to elucidate core ideas and spark innovation.

1.9 Conclusion

In both development research and practice, case studies provide unique insights into implementation successes and failures, and help to identify why and how a particular outcome occurred. The data collected through case studies is often richer and of greater depth than would normally be obtained by other research designs, which allows for (potentially) richer discussions regarding their generalizability beyond the defined context of the case being studied. The case study method facilitates the identification of patterns and provides practical insights on how to navigate complex delivery challenges. Case studies can also capture the contextual conditions surrounding the delivery case, trace the detailed dynamics of the implementation process, provide key lessons learned, and inform broader approaches to service delivery (e.g., by focusing attention on citizen outcomes, generating multidimensional responses, providing usable evidence to enhance real-time implementation, and supporting leadership for change).

The core idea behind recent initiatives seeking to expand, formalize, and catalogue case studies of development practice is that capturing implementation processes and building a cumulative body of operational knowledge and know-how can play a key role in helping development practitioners deliver better results. Systematically investigating delivery in its own right offers an opportunity to distill common delivery challenges, and to engage constructively with the nontechnical problems that often hinder development interventions and prevent countries and practitioners from translating technical solutions into results on the ground.

Doing this well, however, requires drawing on the full array of established and leading approaches to conducting case study research. As this volume seeks to show, the last twenty years have led to considerable refinements and extensions of prevailing practice, and renewed confidence among scholars of case study methods that they have not merely addressed (or at least identified defensible responses to) long-standing concerns regarding the veracity of case studies but actively advanced those domains of inquiry in which case studies enjoy a distinctive epistemological 'comparative advantage'. In turn, the veritable explosion of case studies of development processes now being prepared by academic groups, domestic governments, and international agencies around the world offers unprecedented opportunities for researchers to refine still further the underlying techniques, methodological principles, and theory on which the case study itself ultimately rests. As such, the time is ripe for a mutually beneficial dialogue between scholars and practitioners of development – a dialogue we hope this volume can inspire.

References

Acemoglu, D., Johnson, S., and Robinson, A. (2003) "Botswana: An African success story" in Rodrik, D. (ed.) *In search of prosperity: Analytic narratives on economic growth*. Princeton, NJ: Princeton University Press, pp. 80–119.

Acemoglu, D. and Robinson, J. A. (2012) *Why nations fail: The origins of power, prosperity and poverty*. New York: Crown Business.

Bamberger, M., Rao, V., and Woolcock, M. (2010) "Using mixed methods in monitoring and evaluation: Experiences from international development" in Tashakkori, A. and Teddlie, C. (eds.) *Handbook of mixed methods in social and behavioral research* (2nd revised edition). Thousand Oaks, CA: Sage Publications, pp. 613–641.

Barma, N., Huybens, E., and Viñuela, L. (2014) *Institutions taking root: Building state capacity in challenging contexts*. Washington, DC: World Bank.

Bates, R. H., Avner Greif, M. L., Rosethal, J. L., and Weingast, B. (eds.) (1998) *Analytic narratives*. Princeton, NJ: Princeton University Press.

Bayly, C. A., Rao, V., Szreter, S., and Woolcock, M. (eds.) (2011) *History, historians and development policy: A necessary dialogue*. Manchester: Manchester University Press.

Bennett, A. and Checkel, J. T. (eds.) (2015) *Process tracing: From metaphor to analytic tool*. New York: Cambridge University Press.

Bliss, C. and Stern, N. (1982) *Palanpur: The economy of an Indian village*. Oxford: Oxford University Press.

Brixi, H., Lust, E., and Woolcock, M. (2015) *Trust, voice and incentives: Learning from local success stories in service delivery in the Middle East and North Africa*. Washington, DC: World Bank.

Byrne, D. and Ragin, C. C. (eds.) (2009) *The Sage handbook of case-based methods*. Los Angeles: Sage Publications.

Carpenter, D. (2001) *The forging of bureaucratic autonomy: Reputations, networks and policy innovation in executive agencies, 1862–1928*. Princeton, NJ: Princeton University Press.

Ellickson, R. (1991) *Order without law: How neighbors settle disputes*. Cambridge, MA: Harvard University Press.

Estabridis, C. A. and Nieto, D. O. (2015) *How to overcome communications and cultural barriers to improve service provision to indigenous populations*. Washington, DC: World Bank, Global Delivery Initiative Case Study.

Feagin, J. R., Orum, A. M., and Sjoberg, G. (eds.) (1991) *A case for the case study*. Chapel Hill: University of North Carolina Press.

Flyvbjerg, B. (2006) "Five misunderstandings about case-study research," *Qualitative Inquiry*, 12(2), 219–245.

George, A. and Bennett, A. (2005) *Case studies and theory development in the social sciences*. Cambridge, MA: MIT Press.

Gerring, J. (2017) *Case study research: Principles and practices, 2nd ed*. New York: Cambridge University Press.

Glavey, S. and Haas, O. (2015) *How to scale up rural sanitation service delivery in Indonesia*. Washington, DC: World Bank.

Goertz, G. and Mahoney, J. (2012) *A tale of two cultures: Qualitative and quantitative research in the social sciences*. Princeton, NJ: Princeton University Press.

Haggard, S. (1992) *The politics of economic adjustment: International constraints, distributive conflicts, and the state*. Princeton, NJ: Princeton University Press.

Hima, H. and Santibanez, C. (2015) *Against the current: How to shape an enabling environment for sustainable water service delivery in Nigeria*. Washington, DC: World Bank.

Kaufman, H. (1960) *The forest ranger: A study in administrative behavior*. Washington, DC: Resources for the Future.

Knodel, J. (1997) "A case for nonanthropological qualitative methods for demographers," *Population and Development Review*, 23(4), 847–853.

Lanjouw, P., Murgai, R., and Stern, N. (2013) "Nonfarm diversification, poverty, economic mobility, and income inequality: A case study in Village India," *Agricultural Economics*, 44 (4–5), 461–473.

Lanjouw, P. and Stern, N. (1998) *Economic development in Palanpur over five decades*. Oxford: Oxford University Press.

Lieberman, E. S. (2015) "Nested analysis: Toward the integration of comparative-historical analysis and other social science methods" in Mahoney, J. and Thelen, K. (eds.). *Advances in comparative-historical analysis.* New York: Cambridge University Press, pp. 240–263.

Mahoney, J. (2000) "Strategies of causal inference in small-n analysis," *Sociological Methods & Research*, 28(4), 387–424.

Mahoney, J. and Thelen, K. (eds.) (2015) *Advances in comparative-historical analysis.* New York: Cambridge University Press.

March, J. G., Sproull, L. S., and Tamuz, M. (1991) "Learning from samples of one or fewer," *Organization Science*, 2(1), 1–13.

Morgan, M. (2012) "Case studies: One observation or many? Justification or discovery?" *Philosophy of Science*, 79(5), 667–677.

Ortega Nieto, D. and Parida, I. (2015) *How to ensure quality healthcare and coverage to uninsured populations: Argentina's Plan Nacer/Programa Sumar.* Washington, DC: World Bank.

Portes, A. and Smith, L. D. (2008) "Institutions and development in Latin America: A comparative analysis," *Studies in Comparative International Development*, 43(2), 101–128.

Ragin, C. and Becker, H. (1992) *What is a case? Exploring the foundations of social inquiry.* New York: Cambridge University Press.

Rohlfing, I. (2012) *Case studies and causal inference: An integrative framework.* Basingstoke: Palgrave Macmillan.

Rueschemeyer, D. (2009) *Useable theory: Analytic tools for social and political research.* Princeton, NJ: Princeton University Press.

Ruzzene, A. (2012) "Drawing lessons from case studies by enhancing comparability," *Philosophy of the Social Sciences*, 42(1), 99–120.

Singh, J. P. and Woolcock, M. (eds.) (forthcoming) Special issue of *Global Perspectives* on the future of multilateralism and global development.

Stake, R. E. (1995) *The art of case study research.* Thousand Oaks, CA: Sage Publications.

Tamanaha, B., Sage, C., and Woolcock, M. (eds.) (2012) *Legal pluralism and development policy: Scholars and practitioners in dialogue.* New York: Cambridge University Press.

Tendler, J. (1997) *Good government in the tropics.* Washington, DC: Johns Hopkins University Press.

Thelen, K. and Mahoney, J. (eds.) (2009) *Explaining institutional change: Ambiguity, agency and power.* New York: Cambridge University Press.

Van Noorden, R., Maher, B. and Nuzzo, R. (2014) "The top 100 papers: Nature explores the most cited research of all time," *Nature*, October 29. Available at www.nature.com/news/the-top-100-papers-1.16224 (accessed January 19, 2020).

Wade, R. (1985) "The market for public office: Why the Indian state is not better at development," *World Development*, 13(4), 467–497.

Woolcock, M. (2013) "Using case studies to explore the external validity of 'complex' development interventions," *Evaluation*, 19(3), 229–248.

Yin, R. K. (1984) *Case study research: Design and methods.* Beverly Hills, CA: Sage Publications. [Now in its sixth edition, 2017.]

Part I

Internal and External Validity Issues in Case Study Research

How to Learn about Causes in the Single Case

Nancy Cartwright

2.1 Introduction

The case study is a broad church. Case studies come in a great variety of forms, for a great variety of purposes, using a great variety of methods – including both methods typically labelled 'qualitative' and ones typically labelled 'quantitative'.[1] My focus here is on case studies that aim to establish causal conclusions about the very case studied. Much of the discussion about the advantages and disadvantages of case study methods for drawing causal conclusions supposes that the aim is to draw causal conclusions that can be expected to hold more widely than in the case at hand. This is not my focus. My focus is the reverse. I am concerned with using knowledge that applies more widely, in consort with local knowledge, to construct a case study that will help predict what will happen in the single case – *this* case, involving *this* policy intervention, *here* and *now*. These involve what philosophers call a 'singular causal claim' – a claim about a causal connection in a specific single individual case, whether the individual is a particular person, a class, a school, a village or an entire country, viewed as a whole. It is often argued that causal conclusions require a comparative methodology. On this view the *counterfactual* is generally supposed to be the essence of singular causality: In situations where treatment T and outcome O both occur, 'T caused O' means[2] 'If T had

---

[1] For a nice discussion of case study types see Morgan (2014); see Byrne and Ragin (2009) for a good text surveying case-based methods.

[2] Or at least it is supposed that the causal claim is true if and only if the counterfactual is. This has led to endless discussion in philosophy of how to treat putative counterexamples, for example cases of overdetermination and preemption. For further discussion, see Menzies (2014).

not occurred, then O would not have'.[3] And it is additionally supposed that the only way to establish that kind of counterfactual is by contrasting cases where T occurs with those where T does not occur in circumstances that are the same as the first with respect to all other factors affecting O other than the occurrence of T and its downstream effects.

My discussion aims to show that neither of these suppositions is correct.[4] Nor do we take them to be correct, at least if the dictum 'actions speak louder than words' is to be believed. We all regularly, in daily life and in professional practice, bet on causal claims about single individuals and guide our actions by these bets without the aid of comparison. Juries decide whether the defendant committed the crime generally without consulting a case just like this one except for the defendant's actions; I confidently infer that it was my second daughter (not the first, not my granddaughter, not Santa) who slipped *Northanger Abbey* into my Christmas stocking; and the NASA investigating team decided that the failure of an O-ring seal in the right solid rocket booster caused the Challenger disaster in which all seven crew were killed.

It might be objected that these causal judgments are made without the rigor demanded in science and wished for in policy. That would be surprising if it were generally true since we treat a good many of these as if we can be reasonably certain of them. Some 975 days after the Challenger disaster, Space Shuttle Discovery – with redesigned solid rocket boosters – was launched with five crew members aboard (and it returned safely four days later). Though not much of practical importance depends on it, I am sure who gave me *Northanger Abbey*. By contrast, people's lives are seriously affected by the verdicts of judges, juries, and magistrates. Though we know that mistakes here are not uncommon, nobody suggests that our abilities to draw singular causal conclusions in this domain are so bad that we might as well flip a coin to decide on guilt or innocence.

I take it to be clear that singular causal claims like these can be true or false, and that the reasoning and evidence that backs them up can be better or worse. The question I address in Section 2.3, with a 'potted' example in Section 2.4, is: What kinds of information make good evidence for singular causal claims about the results of policy interventions, both post-hoc evaluations – 'Did this intervention achieve the targeted outcome when it was implemented here in this individual case?' – and ex ante predictions – 'Is this intervention likely to produce the targeted outcome if implemented here

---

[3] Cf. Menzies (2014).   [4] For a more detailed discussion, see Cartwright (2017a).

in this individual case?' I believe that the catalogue of evidence types I outline wears its plausibility on its face. But I do not think that is enough. Plausible is, ceteris paribus, better than implausible, but it is better still when the proposals are grounded in theory – credible, well argued, well-warranted theory. To do this job I turn to a familiar theory that is commonly used to defend other conventional scientific methods for causal inference, from randomized controlled trials (RCTs) to qualitative comparative analysis, causal Bayes nets (Bayesian networks) methods, econometric instrumental variables, and others. In Section 2.5, I outline this theory and explain how it can be used to show that the kinds of facts described in the evidence catalogue *are* evidence for causation in the single case.

So, what kinds of facts should we look for in a case study to provide evidence about a singular casual claim there – for instance, a claim of the kind we need for program evaluation: Did this program/treatment (T) as it was implemented in this situation (S) produce an outcome (O) of interest here? Did T cause O in S?

I call the kinds of evidence one gets from case studies for singular causal claims *individualized* evidence. This is by contrast with RCTs, which provide what I call *anonymous* evidence for singular causal claims. I shall explain this difference before proceeding to my catalogue because it helps elucidate the relative advantages and disadvantages of RCTs versus case studies for establishing causal claims.

2.2   What We Can Learn from an RCT

Individualized evidence speaks to causal claims about a particular identified individual; *anonymous* evidence speaks about one or more unidentified individuals. RCTs and group-comparison observational studies provide anonymous evidence about individual cases. This may seem surprising since a standard way of talking makes it sound as if RCTs establish general causal claims – 'It works' – and not claims about individuals at all. But RCTs by themselves establish a claim only about averages, and about averages only in the population enrolled in the experiment. What kind of claim is that? To understand the answer a little formalism is required. [See Appendix 2.1 for more complete development.]

A genuinely positive effect size in an RCT where the overall effects of other 'confounding' variables are genuinely balanced between treatment and control groups – let's call this an 'ideal' RCT – would establish that at least some individuals in the study population were caused by the treatment to have the targeted outcome. This is apparent in the informal argument that positive results imply causal claims: 'If there are more cases of the outcome in the treatment than in the control group, something must have caused this. If the only difference between the two groups is the treatment and its downstream effects, then the positive outcomes of at least some of the individuals in the treatment group must have been caused by the treatment.'

This is established more formally via the rigorous account of RCT results in common use that traces back to Rubin (1974) and Holland (1986), which calls on the kind of theory appealed to in Section 2.5. We assume that whether one factor causes another in an individual is not arbitrary but that there is something systematic about it. There is a fact of the matter about what factors at what levels in what combinations produce what levels for the outcome in question for each individual. Without serious loss of generality, we can represent all the causal possibilities that are open for an individual i in a simple linear equation, called a *potential outcomes equation*:

$$POE(1): \quad O(i)c= \alpha(i)T(i) + W(i)$$

In this equation the variable O on the left represents the targeted outcome; $c=$ signifies that the two sides of the equation are equal and that the factors on the right are causes of those on the left. $T(i)$, which represents the policy intervention under investigation, may or may not genuinely appear there; that is, $\alpha(i)$ may be zero. The equation represents the possible values the outcome can take given various combinations of values a complete set of causes for it takes. $W(i)$ represents in one fell swoop all the causes that might affect the level of the outcome for this individual that do not interact with the treatment.[5] α represents the overall effect of factors that *interact* with the treatment. 'Interact' means that the amount the treatment contributes to the outcome level for individual i depends on the value of $\alpha(i)$. Economists and statisticians call these 'interactive' variables; psychologists tend to call them 'moderator' variables; and philosophers term them 'support' variables. For those not familiar with support factors, consider the standard philosopher's example of striking a match to produce a flame. This only works if there is oxygen present; oxygen is a support factor without which the striking will not produce a flame.

---

[5] $W(i)$ can include a variable that represents a pure individual effect not shared with others in the population.

Interactive/support variables really matter to understanding the connection between the statistical results of an RCT and the causal conclusions inferred from them. The statistical result that is normally recorded in an RCT is the effect size. 'Effect size' can mean a variety of things. But all standard definitions make it a function of this: the difference in outcome means between treatment and control groups. What can this difference in the average value of the outcome in the two groups teach us about the causal effects of the treatment on individuals enrolled in the experiment? What can readily be shown is that in an ideal RCT this difference in means between treatment and control is the mean value of $\alpha(i)$, which represents the support factors – the mean averaged across all the individuals enrolled in the experiment. So the effect size is a function of the mean of the support/interactive variables – those variables that determine whether, and to what extent, the treatment can produce the outcome for the individual. If the average of $\alpha(i)$ is not zero, then there must be at least some individuals in that population for which $\alpha(i)$ was not zero. That means that for some individuals – though we know not which – T genuinely did contribute to the outcome. Thus, we can conclude from a positive mean difference between treatment and control in an ideal RCT that 'T caused O in some members of the population enrolled in the experiment.'[6]

You should also note one other feature of $\alpha(i)$. Suppose that we represent the value of the policy variable in the control group from which it is withheld by 0. This is another idealization, especially for social experiments and even for many medical ones, where members of the control groups may manage to get the treatment despite being assigned to control. But let's suppose it. Then $\alpha(i)T(i) - \alpha(i)C(i) = \alpha(i)T(i) - 0 = \alpha(i)T(i)$, letting C represent the value of the treatment when that treatment is not experienced. So $\alpha(i)$ represents also the 'boost' to O that i gets from receiving the policy treatment. This is often called 'the individual treatment effect'.

When could we expect the same positive average effect size in an RCT on a new population? In the abstract that is easy to say. First, T must be *capable* of producing O in the new population. There must be possible support factors that can get it to work. If there aren't, no amount of T will affect O for anyone. Again, philosophers have a potted example: No amount of the fertility drug Clomiphene citrate will make any man get pregnant. In

---

[6] It may be useful to be reminded that the reverse is not true. The mean in treatment and control groups can be the same not only because the treatment is ineffective but also if it is helpful to some and harmful to others and the effects averaged over the treatment group balance out.

development studies we might use Angus Deaton's (2010) fanciful example of a possible World Bank proposal to reduce poverty in China by building railway stations, a proposal that is doomed to failure when looked at in more detail because the plan is to build them in deserts where nobody lives. Then the two experiments will result in the same effect size just in case the mean of T's support factors is the same in the two. And how would we know this? That takes a great deal of both theoretical and local knowledge about the two populations in question – knowledge that the RCTs themselves go no way toward providing.[7]

Much common talk makes it sound as if RCTs can do more, in particular that they can establish what holds generally or what can be expected in a new case. Perhaps the idea is that if you can establish a causal conclusion then somehow, because it is causal, it is general. That's not true, neither for the causal results established for some identified individuals in an RCT nor for a causal result for a single individual subject that might be established in a case study. Much causality is extremely local: local to toasters of a particular design, to businesses with a certain structure, to fee-paying schools in university towns in the south of England, to families with a certain ethnic and religious background and immigration history ... The tendency to generalize seems especially strong if 'the same' results are seen in a few cases – which they seldom are, as can be noted from a survey of meta-analyses and systematic reviews. But that is induction by simple enumeration, which is a notoriously bad way to reason (swan 1 is white, swan 2 is white ... so all the swans in Sydney Harbour are white).

A study – no matter whether it is a case study or it uses the methodology of the RCT, Bayes nets methods for causal inference, instrumental variables, or whatever – by itself can only show results about the population on which the data is collected. To go beyond that, we need to know what kinds of results travel, and to where. And to do that takes a tangle of different kinds of studies, theories, conceptual developments, and trial and error. This is underlined by work in science studies[8] and by recent philosophical work on evidence and induction. See, for instance, John Norton's (2021) material theory of induction: Norton argues that inductive inferences are justified by facts, where facts include anything from measurement results to general

---

[7] For further discussion, see Cartwright and Hardie (2012). For a wonderful technical treatment of conditions under which different results travel from one population to another, see Bareinboim and Pearl (2013).

[8] Cf. Hasok Chang's (2007) *Inventing Temperature* or Peter Howlett and Mary Morgan's (2010) *How Well Do Facts Travel?*

principles. Parallel lessons follow from the theory of evidence I endorse (Cartwright 2013), the *argument theory*, in which a fact becomes evidence for a conclusion in the context of a good argument for that conclusion, an argument that inevitably requires other premises.

What I want to underline here with respect to RCTs is that, without the aid of lots of other premises, their results are confined to the population enrolled in the study; and what a positive result in an ideal RCT shows is that the treatment produced the outcome in some individuals in that population. For all we know these may be the only individuals in the world that the treatment would affect that way. The same is true if we use a case study to establish that T caused O in a specific identified individual. Perhaps this is extremely unlikely. But the study does nothing to show that; to argue it – either way – requires premises from elsewhere.

I also want to underline a number of other facts that I fear are often underplayed.

- The RCT provides *anonymous* evidence. We may be assured that T caused O in some individuals in the study population, but we know not which. I call this 'Where's Wally?' evidence. We know he's there somewhere, but the study does not reveal him.
- The study establishes an average; it does not tell us how the average is made up. Perhaps the policy is harmful as well as beneficial – it harms a number of individuals, though on average the effect is positive.
- We'd like to know about the variance, but that is not so easy to ascertain. Is almost everyone near the average or do the results for individuals vary widely? The mean of the individual effect sizes can be estimated directly from the difference in means between the treatment and the control groups. But the variance cannot be estimated without substantial statistical assumptions about the distribution. Yet one of the advantages of RCTs is supposed to be that we can get results without substantial background assumptions.
- I have been talking about an ideal RCT in a very special sense of 'ideal': one in which the net effect of confounding factors is genuinely balanced between treatment and control. But that is not what random allocation guarantees for confounders even at baseline. What randomization buys is balance 'in the long run'. That means that if we did the experiment indefinitely often on exactly the same population, the observed difference in means between treatment and control groups would converge on the true difference.

- That's one reason we want experiments to have a large number of partici-pants: it makes it more likely that what we observe in a single run is not far off the true average, though we know it still should be expected to be off a bit, and sometimes off a lot. Yet many social experiments, including many development RCTs, are done on small experimental populations.
- Randomization only affects the baseline distribution of confounders. What happens after that? Blinding is supposed to help control differences, but there are two problems. First, a great many social experiments are poorly blinded: often everybody knows who is in treatment versus control – from the study subjects themselves to those who administer the policy to those who measure the outcomes to those who do the statistical analyses – and all of these can make significant differences. Second, without reasonable local background knowledge about the lives of the study participants (be they individuals or villages), it is hard to see how we have reason to suppose that no systematic differences affect the two groups post randomization.
- Sometimes people say they want RCTs because RCTs measure average effect sizes and we need these for cost–benefit analyses. They do, and we do. But the RCT measures the average effect size in the population enrolled in the experiment. Generally, we need to do cost–benefit analysis for a different population, so we need the average effect size there. The RCT does not give us that.

I do not rehearse these facts to attack RCTs. RCTs are a very useful tool for causal inference – for inferring anonymous singular causal claims. I only list these cautions so that they will be kept in mind in deciding which tool – an RCT or a case study or some other method or some combination – will give the most reliable inference to singular causal claims in any particular case.

I turn now to the case study and how it can warrant singular causal claims – in this case, individualized ones.

2.3   A Category Scheme for Types of Evidence for Singular Causation That a Case Study Can Provide

Suppose a program T has been introduced into a particular setting S in hopes of producing outcome O there. We have good reason to think O occurred. Now we want to know whether T, as it was in fact implemented in S, was (at least partly) responsible.[9] What kinds of information should we try to collect

---

[9] Material in this section and the next draws on Cartwright (2017a, 2017b).

in our case study to provide evidence about this? In this section I offer a catalogue of types of evidence that can help. I start by drawing some distinctions. However, it is important to make a simple point at the start. I aim to lay out a catalogue of kinds of evidence that, if true, can speak for or against singular causal claims. How compelling that evidence is will depend on:

- how strong the link, if any, is between the evidence and the conclusion,
- how sure we can be about the strength of this link, and
- how warranted we are in taking the evidence claim to be true.

All three of these are hostages to ignorance, which is always the case when we try to draw conclusions from our evidence. In any particular case we may not be all that sure about the other factors that need to be in place to forge a strong link between our evidence claim and our conclusion, we may worry whether what we see as a link really is one, and we may not be all that sure about the evidence claim itself. The elimination of alternatives is a special case where the link is known to be strong: If we have eliminated alternatives then the conclusion follows without the need for any further assumptions. But, as always, we still face the problem of how sure we can be of the evidence claim. Have we really succeeded in eliminating all alternatives? No matter what kind of evidence claim we are dealing with, it is a rare case when we are sure our evidence claims are true and we are sure how strong our links are, or even if they are links at all. That's why, when it comes to evidence, the more the better.

The first distinction that can help provide a useful categorization for types of evidence for singular causal claims is that between direct and indirect evidence:

- *Direct:* Evidence that looks at aspects of the putative causal relationship itself to see if it holds.
- *Indirect:* Evidence that looks at features outside the putative causal relationship that bear on the existence of this relationship.

Indirect. The prominent kind of indirect evidence is evidence that helps eliminate alternatives. If O occurred in S, and anything other than T has been ruled out as a cause of O in S's case, then T must have done it. This is what Alexander Bird (2010, 345) calls 'Holmesian inference' because of the famous Holmes remark that when all the other possibilities have been eliminated, what remains must be responsible even if improbable. RCTs provide indirect evidence, eliminating alternative explanations by (in the ideal) distributing all the other possible causes of *O* equally between treatment and control groups. But we don't need a comparison group to do this. We can do this in the case study as well, if we know enough about what the other causes might be like, and/or about the history of the situation *S*. We do this in physics experiments regularly. But we don't need physics to do it. It is, for instance, how I know it was my cat that stole the pork chop from the frying pan while I wasn't looking.

Direct. I have identified at least four different kinds of direct evidence possible for the individualized singular causal claim that *T* caused *O* in *S*:

1. The character of the effect: Does *O* occur at the time, in the manner, and of the size to be expected had *T* caused it? (For those who are familiar with his famous paper on symptoms of causality, Bradford Hill (1965) endorses this type of evidence.)
2. Symptoms of causation: Not symptoms that *T* occurred but symptoms that *T* caused the outcome, side effects that could be expected had *T* operated to produce *O*. This kind of inference is becoming increasingly familiar as people become more and more skilled at drawing inferences from 'big data'. As Suzy Moat puts it, "People leave this large amount of data behind as a by-product of simply carrying on with their lives." Clever users of big data can reconstruct a great deal about our individual lives from the patterns they find there.[10]
3. Presence of requisite support factors (moderator/interactive variables): Was everything in place that needed to be in order for *T* to produce *O*?
4. Presence of expectable intermediate steps (mediator variables): Were the right kinds of intermediate stages present?

Which of these types of evidence will be possible to obtain in a given case will vary from case to case. Any of them that we can gather will be equally relevant for post-hoc evaluation and for ex ante prediction, though we certainly won't ever be able to get evidence of type 2 before the fact. I am currently engaged in an NSF-funded research project, *Policy Prediction: Making the Most of the Evidence*, that aims to use the situation-specific causal equations model (SCEM) framework sketched in Section 2.5 to expand this catalogue of evidence types and to explore more ways to use it for policy prediction.

---

[10] At a *Spaces of Evidence* conference, Goldsmiths, University of London, Sept. 26, 2014. See Moat et al. (2014).

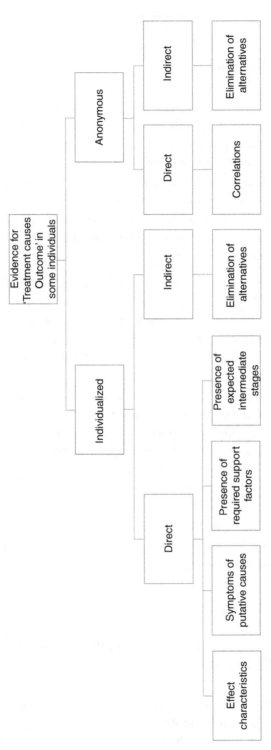

Figure 2.1 Categories of evidence

2.4 A Diagrammatic Example

Let me illustrate with one of those diagrammatic examples we philosophers like, this one constructed from my simple-minded account of how an emetic works. It may be a parody of a real case study, but it provides a clear illustration of each of these types of evidence.

Imagine that yesterday I inadvertently consumed a very harmful poison. Luckily, I realized I had done so and thereafter swallowed a strong emetic. I vomited violently and have subsequently not suffered any serious symptoms of poisoning. I praise the emetic: It saved me! What evidence could your case study collect for that?

- Elimination of alternatives: There are very low survival rates with this poison. So it is not likely my survival was spontaneous. And there's nothing special about me that would otherwise explain my survival having consumed the poison. I don't have an exceptional body mass, I hadn't been getting slowly acclimatised to this poison by earlier smaller doses, I did not take an antidote, etc.
- Presence of required support factors (other factors without which the cause could not be expected to produce this effect): The emetic was swallowed before too much poison was absorbed from the stomach.
- Presence of necessary intermediate step: I vomited.
- Presence of symptoms of the putative causes acting to produce the effect: There was much poison in the vomit, which is a clear side effect of the emetic's being responsible for my survival.
- Characteristics of the effect: The amount of poison in the vomit was measured and compared with the amount I had consumed. I suffered just the effects of remaining amount of poison; and the timing of the effect and size were just right.

2.5 Showing This Kind of Information Does Indeed Provide Evidence about Singular Causation

I developed the scheme in Section 2.3 for warranting singular causal claims bottom-up by surveying case studies in engineering, applied science, policy evaluation, and fault diagnoses, inter alia. But a more rigorous grounding is possible: these types all provide information relevant for filling in features of a *situation-specific causal equations model* (SCEM). Once you see what a SCEM is, this is apparent by inspection, so I will not belabor that point. Instead, I will spend time defending the SCEM framework itself.

A SCEM is a set of equations that express (one version of) what is sometimes called the 'logic model' of the policy intervention: a model of how the policy treatment T is supposed to bring about the targeted outcome O, step by step. Each of the equations is itself what in Section 2.2 was called a 'potential outcomes equation'. (In situations where the kind of quantitative precision suggested by these equations seems impossible or inappropriate, there is an analogous Boolean form for yes–no variables, familiar in philosophy from Mackie (1965) and in social science from qualitative comparative analysis [e.g., Rihoux and Ragin 2008].)

To build a SCEM, start with the outcome O of interest. Just what should the policy have led to at the previous stage that will produce O at the final stage? Let's call that 'O_{-1}'. Recalling that a single cause is seldom enough to produce an effect on its own, what are the support factors necessary for O_{-1} to produce O? Represent the net effect of all the support factors by 'α_{-1}'. Establishing that these support factors were/will be in place or not provides important evidence about whether O can be brought about by O_{-1}. If not, then certainly T cannot produce O (at least not in the way you expect). Consider as well what other factors will be in place at the penultimate stage that will affect O. These affect the size or level of O. You want to know about those because they provide alternative explanations for the level of O that occurs; they are also relevant for judging the size T's contribution would have to be if T were to contribute to the outcome. Represent the net effect of all these together by 'W_{-1}'. How O depends on all these factors can then be represented in a potential outcomes equation like this:

$$POE\ (2):\ \ O(i)\ c= \alpha_{-1}(i)O_{-1}(i) + W_{-1}(i).$$

Work backwards, step by step, constructing a potential outcomes equation for each stage until the start, where T is introduced. The resulting set of equations is the core of the SCEM for this case.

But there is more. Think about the support factors (represented by the αs) that need to be in place at each stage. These are themselves effects; they have a causal history that can be expressed in a set of potential outcomes equations that can be added to the core SCEM. This is important information too: Knowing about the causes of the causes of an effect is a clue to whether the causes will occur and thus to whether the effect can be expected. The factors that do not interact with O_{-1} (represented by W_{-1}) but that also affect O have causal histories as well that can be represented in a series of potential outcomes equations and added to the SCEM. So too with all the Ws in the chain. For purposes of evaluation, we may also want to include equations in which O figures as a cause since seeing that the effects of O obtain gives good evidence that O itself occurred. We can include as much or as little of the causal histories of various variables in the SCEM as we find useful.

I am not suggesting that we can construct SCEMs that are very complete, but I do suggest that this is what Nature does. Even in the single case, what causes what is not arbitrary – at least not if there is to be any hope that we can make reasonable predictions, explanations, and evaluations. There is a system to how Nature operates, and we have learned that generally this is what the system is like: Some factors *can* affect O in this individual and some *cannot*. All those that can affect an outcome appear in Nature's own potential outcomes equation for that outcome. Single factors seldom contribute on their own so the separate terms in Nature's equations will generally consist of combinations of mutually interacting factors. So Nature's equations look much like ours. Or, rather, when we do it well, ours look much like Nature's since hers are what we aim to replicate.

So: A successful SCEM for a specific individual provides a concise representation of what causal sequences are possible for that individual given the facts about that individual and its situation – what values the quantities represented can take in relation to values of their causes and effects. Some of the features represented in the SCEM will be ones we can influence, and some of these are ones we would influence in implementing the policy; others will take the values that naturally evolve from their causal past. The interpretation of these equations will become clearer as I defend their use.

I offer three different arguments to support my claim that SCEMs are good for treating singular causation: 1) their use for this purpose is well developed in the philosophy literature; 2) singular causation thus treated satisfies a number of common assumptions; 3) the potential outcomes equations that make up a SCEM are central to the formal defense I described in Section 2.2 that RCTs can establish causal conclusions.[11]

1) The SCEM framework is an adaptation for variables with more than two values of J. L. Mackie's (1965) famous account in which causes are INUS conditions for their effects. In the adaptation, causes are INUS conditions

---

[11] As mentioned in Section 2.2, they are similarly central to the defense of a variety of other methods for causal inference, though I do not show that here.

for *contributions* to the effect,[12] where an INUS condition for a contribution to $O(i)$ is an **I**nsufficient but **N**ecessary part of an **U**nnecessary but **S**ufficient condition for a contribution to it. Each of the additive terms ($\alpha(i)T(i)$ and $W(i)$) on the right of the equation $O(i) \; c= \alpha(i)T(i) + W(i)$ represents a set of conditions that together are *sufficient* for a contribution to $O(i)$ but they are *unnecessary* since many things can contribute to O; and each component of an additive term (e.g., $\alpha(i)$ and $T(i)$) is an *insufficient* but *necessary* part of it – both are needed and neither is enough alone. This kind of situation-specific causal equations model for treating singular causation is also familiar in the contemporary philosophy of science literature, especially because of the widely respected work of Christopher Hitchcock.[13]

2) The SCEM implies a number of characteristics for singular causal relations that they are widely assumed to have:
   - the causal relation is irreflexive (nothing causes itself)
   - the causal relation is asymmetric (if T causes O, O does not cause T)
   - causes occur temporally before their effects
   - there are causes to fix every effect
   - causes of causes of an effect are themselves causes of that effect (since substituting earlier causes of the causes in an equation yields a POE valid for a different coarse-graining of the time)[14]
   - causal relations give rise to noncausal correlations.[15]

3) Each equation in a SCEM is a potential outcomes equation of the kind that is used in the Rubin/Holland argument I laid out in Section 2.2 to show that RCTs can produce causal conclusions: A SCEM is simply a reiteration of the POE used to represent singular causation in the treatment of RCTs, expanded to include causes of causes of the targeted outcome and, sometimes, further effects as well. So, if we buy the Rubin/ Holland argument about why a positive difference in means between treatment and control groups provides evidence that the treatment has caused the outcome in at least some members of the treatment group, it seems we are committed to taking POEs, and thus SCEMs, as a good

---

[12] Note: stating that all causes are INUS conditions does not imply that all INUS conditions are causes.

[13] Cf. Hitchcock (2007).

[14] Philosophers sometimes reject this assumption, but it is important for predicting effects separated by longish time periods from the policy initiation.

[15] For example, consider a cause c with two effects, e_1 and e_2, with no other causes. Supposing determinism, e_1 obtains if and only if e_2 obtains. That is not among the causal equations. But it obtains on account of them.

representation of the causal possibilities open to individuals in the study population.

Warning: Equations like these are sometimes treated as if they represent 'general causal principles'. That is a mistake. To see why, it is useful to think in terms of a threefold distinction among equations we use in science and policy, and similarly for more qualitative principles:

- Equations and principles that represent the context-relative causal possibilities that obtain for a specific single individual, as in the SCEMs discussed here.
- Equations and principles that represent the context-relative causal possibilities for a specific population. These often look just like a SCEM so it appears as if the causal possibilities are the same for every member of the population. This can be misleading for two reasons. First, for some individuals in the population some of the $\alpha(i)$s may be fixed at 0 so that the associated cause can never contribute to the outcome for them. Second, the $W(i)$s can contain a variable that applies only to the single individual i (as noted in footnote 5). So there can be unique causal possibilities for each member of the population despite the fact that the equation makes it look as if they are all the same.
- Equations and principles that hold widely. I suggest reserving the term 'general principles' for these, which are relatively context free, like the law of the lever or perhaps 'People act so as to maximize their expected utility.' These are the kinds of principles that we suppose ground the single-case causal possibilities represented in SCEMs and the context-relative principles that describe the causal possibilities for specific populations. These general principles tend to employ very abstract concepts, by contrast with the far more concrete, operationalizable ones that describe study results on individuals or populations – abstract concepts such as 'utility', 'force', 'democracy'. They are also generally different in form from SCEMs. Think, for instance, about the form of Maxwell's equations, which ground the causal possibilities for any electromagnetic device: these are not SCEM-like in form at all. It is in an instantiation of these in a real concrete arrangement located in space and time that genuine causal possibilities, of the kind represented in SCEMs, arise.

I note the differences between equations representing general principles and those representing causal possibilities for a single case or for a specific population to underline that knowing general principles is not enough to tell us what we need to know to predict policy outcomes for specific individuals, whether these are individual students or classes or villages, considered as a whole, or specific populations in specific places. Knowing Maxwell's principles will not tell you how to repair your Christmas-tree lights. For that you need context-specific local knowledge about what the local arrangements are that call different general principles into play, both together and in sequence. That's what will enable you to build a good SCEM that you can use for predicting and explaining outcomes. The same unfortunately is true for the use of general principles to predict the results of development and other social policies. Good general principles should be very reliable, but it takes a lot of thinking and a lot of local knowledge to figure out how to deploy them to model concrete situations. This is one of the principal reasons why we need case studies.

Thinking about how local arrangements call different general principles into play or not is key to how to make good use of our general knowledge to build local SCEMs. Consider a potted version of the case of the failure of the class-size reduction program that California implemented in 1996/97 based on the successes of Tennessee's STAR project (which was attested by a good RCT) and Wisconsin's SAGE program. Let us suppose for purposes of illustration that these three general principles obtain widely:

- Smaller classes are conducive to better learning outcomes.
- Poor teaching inhibits learning.
- Poor classroom facilities inhibit learning.

Imagine that in Tennessee there were good teacher-training schools with good routes into local teaching positions and a number of new schools with surplus well-equipped classrooms that had resulted from a vigorous, well-funded school-building program. In California there was a great deal of political pressure and financial incentivization to introduce the program all at once (it was rolled out in most districts within three months of the legislation being passed); there were few well-trained unemployed teachers and no vigorous program for quick recruitment; and classrooms, we can suppose, were already overcrowded. These arrangements in California called all three principles into play at once; thus – so this story goes – the good effects promised by the operation of the first principle were outweighed by the harmful effects of the other two. Learning outcomes did not improve across the state, and in some places they got worse.[16] The arrangements in

---

[16] For a serious account of what happened, see Stecher and Bohrnstedt (2002).

Tennessee called into play only the first principle, which accounts for the improved outcomes there.

How would you know whether to expect the results in California to match those of Tennessee and Wisconsin? Not by looking for superficial 'similarities' between the two. I recommend a case study, one that builds a SCEM for California, modelling the sequential steps by which the policy is supposed to achieve the targeted outcomes and then modelling what factors are needed in order for each step to lead to the next and what further causes are supposed to ensure that these factors are in place. We can't do this completely, but reviewing the California case, it seems there was ample evidence – evidence of the kinds laid out in the catalogue of Section 2.3 – to fill in enough of the SCEM to see that a happy outcome was not to be expected.

2.6 Conclusion

How much evidence of the kinds in my catalogue and in what combinations must a case study deliver, and how secure must it be, in order to provide a reasonable degree of certainty about a causal claim about the case? There's no definitive answer. That's a shame. But this is not peculiar to case studies; it is true for all methods for causal inference.

Consider the RCT. If we suppose the treatment does satisfy the independence assumptions noted in Appendix 2.1, we can calculate how likely a given positive difference in means is if the treatment had no effect and the difference was due entirely to chance. But for most social policy RCTs there are good reasons to suppose the treatment does not satisfy the independence assumptions. The allocation mechanism often is not by a random-outcome device; there is not even single blinding let alone the quadruple we would hope for (of the subjects, the program administrators and overseers, those who measure outcomes, and those who do the statistical analysis); numbers enrolled in the experiment are often small; dropouts, noncompliance, and control group members accessing the treatment outside the experiment are not carefully monitored; sources of systematic differences between treatment and control groups after randomization are not well thought through and controlled; etc. – the list is long and well known. Often this is the best we can do, and often it is better than nothing. The point is that there are no formulae for how to weigh all this up to calculate what level of certainty the experiment provides that the treatment caused the outcome in some individuals in the experimental population. Similarly with all other methods of causal inference. Some things can be calculated – subject to assumptions. But there is seldom a method for calculating how the evidence that the assumptions are satisfied stacks up, and we often have little general idea about what that evidence should even look like. Judgment – judgment without rules to fall back on – is required in all these cases. I see no good arguments that the judgments are systematically more problematic in case studies than anywhere else.

The same holds when it comes to expecting the same results elsewhere. Maybe if you have a big effect size in an RCT with lots of subjects enrolled and good reason to think that the independence assumptions were satisfied, you have reason to think that in a good number of individuals the treatment produced the outcome. For a single case study, you can have at best good reason to think that the treatment caused the outcome in one individual. Perhaps knowing it worked for a number of individuals gives better grounds for expecting it to work in the next. Perhaps not. Consider economist Angus Deaton's (2015) suggestions about St. Mary's school, which is thinking about adopting a new training program because a perfect RCT elsewhere has shown it improves test scores by X. But St. Joseph's down the road adopted the program and got Z. What should St. Mary's do? It is not obvious, or clear, that St. Joseph's is not a better guide than the RCT, or indeed an anecdote about another school. After all, St. Mary's is not the mean, and may be a long way from it. Which is a better guide – or any guide at all – depends on how similar, in just the right ways, the individual/individuals in the study are to the new one we want predictions about. And how do we know what the right ways are? Well, a good case study at St. Joseph's can at least show us what mattered for it to work there, which can be some indication of what it might take to work at St. Mary's since they share much underlying structure.[17] In this case it looks like the advantage for exporting the study result may lie with the case study and not with the higher numbers.

Group-comparison studies do have the advantage that they can estimate an effect size – for the study population. That may be just what we need – for instance, in a post-hoc evaluation where the program contractors are to be paid by size of result. But we should beware of the assumption that this number is useful elsewhere. We have seen that it depends on the mean value

---

[17] Here's yet another source of uncertainty in both cases. The – often unknown or ill-understood – underlying structure matters to what can help a cause to operate. What enables a cause to work in one given underlying structure need not enable it to work where other structures obtain. Putting gas in my Volvo enables the car to go when I turn the ignition on, but not in a diesel Audi 3; and reducing class sizes in Tennessee and Wisconsin improved learning outcomes, but not in California.

of the net contribution of the interactive/support factors in the study population. It takes a lot of knowledge to warrant the assumption that the support factors at work in a new situation will have the same mean.

What can we conclude in general, then, about how secure causal conclusions from case studies are or how well they can be exported? Nothing. But other methods fare no better.

There is one positive lesson we can draw. We often hear the claim that case studies may be good for suggesting causal hypotheses but it takes other methods to test them. That is false. Case studies can test causal conclusions. And a well-done case study can establish causal results more securely than other methods if they are not well carried out or we if have little reason to accept the assumptions it takes to justify causal inference from their results.

Appendix 2.1

The Rubin/Holland analysis, which is also widely adopted by economists discussing RCTs, begins with a singular counterfactual difference: that between the value that the outcome (say $x_k(i)$) would have in the individual case i were i subject to the treatment ($x_k^T(i)$) and the value it would have in i were i subject to the control ($x_k^C(i)$). It is assumed that the possible values x_k can take for i are determined[18] by a complete set of possible causes of x_k that might act on i during the relevant time period given the actual situation of i, including possibly the treatment T (which in this simple case gets value 1 in the treatment group and 0 in the control). This gets represented in the potential outcomes equation:

POE: $x_k(i) \ c= \alpha_T(i)T(i) + \Sigma\alpha_j(i)x_j(i)$

In this equation the variables on the left represent the targeted outcome; $c=$ signifies that the two sides of the equation are equal and that the factors on the right are causes of those on the left. $T(i)$ may or may not genuinely appear there (i.e., $\alpha_T(i)$ may be zero). The equation represents the possible value the outcome can take given various combinations of values a complete set of causes for it take. Besides the treatment there are J possible additive causes as well as those that make up the interactive factor $\alpha_T(i)$ (which may turn out to be 0), most unknown or unobservable.

---

[18] The scheme can be adapted to deal with merely probabilistic causation, but I won't do that here to keep notation simple.

Now consider treatment (T = 1) and control (T = 0) groups and calculate averages. Imagine that random assignment and blinding have succeeded as hoped in ensuring that T is orthogonal in the mean to the net effect of other causal factors ($\alpha_T(i)$ and $\Sigma\alpha_j(i)x_j(i)$), in which case, using *Exp* for 'expectation'

$$Exp\left(x_k^T(i) - x_k^C(i)\right) = Exp\, x_k^T(i) - Exp\, x_k^C(i) = Exp\alpha_T(i) \tag{1}$$

So the middle term (the difference in means between the treatment and control groups, which is observable) is an unbiased estimator of *Exp* $\alpha_T(i)$. Given the causal interpretation proposed of the potential outcomes equation, a genuinely positive effect size shows that $\alpha_T(i) \neq 0$ for some *i*: that is, that (in the long run of experiment repetitions) the treatment will have caused the outcome in at least some individuals in the treatment group. Note that the observed effect size is the estimated mean of the *individual* treatment effects, which in turn is the estimated mean of $\alpha_T(i)$. By inspection $\alpha_T(i)$ represents the net effect of the interactive/support factors that fix whether, and to what degree, *T* can contribute to x_k in individual case *i*.

Appendix 2.2

A SCEM is a set of equations in block triangular form:[19]

$$x_1(i)\, c = \mu \tag{1}$$
$$x_2(i)\, c = a_{21}(i)\, x_1(i)$$

$$x_n c = \sum a_{nj}(i) x_j(i)$$

SCEMs provide a concise representation of what causal sequences are possible in a specific case given the facts about that case – that is, what values the quantities represented can take in relation to values of their causes and effects. Each equation is itself a potential outcomes equation (POE). The variables are time ordered so that for $x_{j<k}$, x_j occurs simultaneous with, or earlier than, x_k. As with a single POE, variables on the left represent effects, one of which will be the targeted outcome; $c=$ signifies that the two sides of the equation are equal and that the factors on the right are causes of those on the left.

---

[19] *Block* triangularity allows for multiple simultaneous effects with the same causes.

Warning. In addition to the warning in Section 2.5, I offer some further, more technical cautions here. The linear simultaneous equations forms that appear in a SCEM are also familiar within social science, for example from the work of Herbert Simon (1957) on causality, in path analysis, in econometrics, as the basis for Judea Pearl's causal Bayesian networks,[20] etc. I say 'warning' because I see two related problems cropping up. First, the equations show relations between quantities but they do not express which populations of individual cases these relations hold for, and often this is not made clear in social science uses. I use these equations for *identified* individual cases. Second, generally some of the variables are labelled 'exogenous' (determined outside the system of equations, indicated by the μ in the first equation) and a joint probability is supposed for them. This supposes some population of individual cases to which this probability applies, but again, which population that is – or why we should suppose there is a probability to be had for those variables in that population – is usually not specified.

References

Bareinboim, E. and Pearl, J. (2013) "A general algorithm for deciding transportability of experimental results," *Journal of Causal Inference*, 1(1), 107–134.

Bird, A. (2010) "Eliminative abduction: Examples from medicine," *Studies in History and Philosophy of Science*, 41(4), 345–352.

Bradford Hill, A. (1965) "The environment and disease: Association or causation?" *Proceedings of the Royal Society of Medicine*, 58(5), 295–300.

Byrne, D. and Ragin, C. (2009) *The SAGE handbook of case-based methods*. Thousand Oaks, CA: Sage.

Cartwright, N. (2013) "Evidence, argument and prediction" in Karakostas, V. and Dieks, D. (eds.) *EPSA11 Perspectives and Foundational Problems in Philosophy of Science, The European Philosophy of Science Association Proceedings 2*, pp. 3–18. Also in *Evidence: For Policy and Wheresoever Rigor is a Must*. Order Project Discussion Paper Series. London: London School of Economics. Available at https://nyudri.wordpress.com/initiatives/deaton-v-banerjee/ (accessed December 20, 2021).

Cartwright, N. (2017a) "Single case causes: What is evidence and why" in Chao, H., Chen, S., and Reiss, J. (eds.) *Philosophy of science in practice*. Dordrecht: Springer, pp. 11–24.

Cartwright, N. (2017b) "How to learn about causes in the single case." Durham University: CHESS Working Paper No. 2017-04.

Cartwright, N. and Hardie, J. (2012) *Evidence based policy: A practical guide to doing it better*. New York: Oxford University Press.

---

[20] Cf. Pearl (2000).

Chang, H. (2007) *Inventing temperature: Measurement and scientific progress.* Oxford: Oxford University Press.

Deaton, A. (2010) "Instruments, randomization and learning about development," *Journal of Economic Literature*, 48(2), 424–455.

Deaton, A. (2015) "Deaton v Banerjee." NYU Development Research Institute. Available at https://nyudri.wordpress.com/initiatives/deaton-v-banerjee/ (accessed January 20, 2020).

Hitchcock, C. (2007) "Prevention, preemption, and the principle of sufficient reason," *Philosophical Review*, 116(4), 495–532.

Holland, P. (1986) "Statistics and causal inference," *Journal of the American Statistical Association*, 81(396), 945–960.

Howlett, P. and Morgan, M. (eds.) (2010) *How well do facts travel?* Cambridge: Cambridge University Press.

Mackie, J. L. (1965) "Causes and conditions," *American Philosophical Quarterly*, 2(4), 245–264.

Moat, H. S., Preis, T., Olivola, C.Y., Liu, C., and Chater, N. (2014) "Using big data to predict collective behavior in the real world," *Behavioral and Brain Sciences*, 37(1), 92–93.

Morgan, M. (2014) "Case studies" in Cartwright, N. and Montuschi, E. (eds.), *Philosophy of social science: A new introduction.* New York: Oxford University Press, pp. 288–307.

Menzies, P. (2014) "Counterfactual theories of causation" in Zalta, E. N. (ed.), *The Stanford encyclopedia of philosophy* (Spring 2014 Edition). Available at: http://plato.stanford.edu/archives/spr2014/entries/causation-counterfactual/ (accessed January 20, 2020).

Norton, J. (2021) *The material theory of induction.* Calgary: University of Calgary Press.

Pearl, J. (2000) *Causality: Models, reasoning, and inference.* Cambridge: Cambridge University Press.

Rihoux, B. and Ragin, C. (eds.) (2008) *Configurational comparative methods: Qualitative comparative analysis (QCA) and related techniques.* Los Angeles: Sage Publications.

Rubin, D. (1974) "Estimating causal effects of treatments in randomized and nonrandomized studies," *Journal of Educational Psychology*, 66(5), 688–701.

Simon, H. (1957) *Models of man: Social and rational.* New York: John Wiley and Sons.

Stecher, B. and Bohrnstedt, G. (2002) "Class size reduction in California: Findings from 1999–00 and 2001–02" [online]. Available at: https://citeseerx.ist.psu.edu/viewdoc/download?doi=10.1.1.694.7009&rep=rep1&type=pdf (accessed January 20, 2020).

3 RCTs versus Observational Research

Assessing the Trade-Offs

Christopher H. Achen

3.1 Introduction

Experiments of all kinds have once again become popular in the social sciences (Druckman et al. 2011). Of course, psychology has long used them. But in my own field of political science, and in adjacent areas such as economics, far more experiments are conducted now than in the twentieth century (Jamison 2019). Lab experiments, survey experiments, field experiments – all have become popular (for example, Karpowitz and Mendelberg 2014; Mutz 2011; and Gerber and Green 2012, respectively; Achen 2018 gives an historical overview).

In political science, much attention, both academic and popular, has been focused on field experiments, especially those studying how to get citizens to the polls on election days. Candidates and political parties care passionately about increasing the turnout of their voters, but it was not until the early twenty-first century that political campaigns became more focused on testing what works. In recent years, scholars have mounted many field experiments on turnout, often with support from the campaigns themselves. The experiments have been aimed particularly at learning the impact on registration or turnout of various kinds of notifications to voters

I thank participants at the authors' workshop (at which drafts of chapters now comprising this volume were presented) for helpful advice. Sue Stokes and Larry Bartels provided timely suggestions. The responsibility for remaining errors and misjudgments remains with me.

that an election was at hand. (Green, McGrath, and Aronow 2013 reviews the extensive literature.)

Researchers doing randomized experiments of all kinds have not been slow to tout the scientific rigor of their approach. They have produced formal statistical models showing that an RCT is typically vastly superior to an observational (nonrandomized) study. In statistical textbooks, of course, experimental randomization has long been treated as the gold standard for inference, and that view has become commonplace in the social sciences. More recently, however, critics have begun to question this received wisdom. Cartwright (2007a, 2017, Chapter 2 this volume) and her collaborators (Cartwright and Hardie 2012) have argued that RCTs have important limitations as an inferential tool. Along with Heckman and Smith (1995), Deaton (2010) and others, she has made it clear what experiments can and cannot hope to do.

So where did previous arguments for RCTs go wrong? In this short chapter, I take up a prominent formal argument for the superiority of experiments in political science (Gerber et al. 2014). Then, building on the work of Stokes (2014), I show that the argument for experiments depends critically on emphasizing the central challenge of observational work – accounting for unobserved confounders – while ignoring entirely the central challenge of experimentation – achieving external validity. Once that imbalance is corrected, the mathematics of the model leads to a conclusion much closer to the position of Cartwright and others in her camp.

3.2   The Gerber–Green–Kaplan Model

Gerber, Green, and Kaplan (2014) make a case for the generic superiority of experiments, particularly field experiments, over observational research. To support their argument, they construct a straightforward model of Bayesian inference in the simplest case: learning the mean of a normal (Gaussian) distribution. This mean might be interpreted as an average treatment effect across the population of interest if everyone were treated, with heterogeneous treatment effects distributed normally. Thus, denoting the treatment-effects random variable by X_t and the population variance of the treatment effects by σ_t^2, we have the first assumption:

$$X_t \sim N(\mu, \sigma_t^2) \tag{1}$$

Gerber et al. implicitly take σ_t^2 to be known; we follow them here.[2]

In Gerber et al. (2014)'s setup, there are two ways to learn about μ. The first is via an RCT, such as a field experiment. They take the view that estimation of population parameters by means of random sampling is analogous to the estimation of treatment effects by means of randomized experimentation (Gerber et al. 2014, 32 at fn. 8). That is, correctly conducted experiments are always unbiased estimates of the population parameter.

Following Gerber et al.'s mathematics but making the experimental details a bit more concrete, suppose that the experiment has a treatment and a control group, each of size n, with individual outcomes distributed normally and independently: $N(\mu, \sigma_e^2/2)$ in the experimental group and $N(0, \sigma_e^2/2)$ in the control group. That is, the mathematical expectation of outcomes in the treatment group is the treatment effect μ, while the expected effect in the control group is 0. We assume that the sampling variance is the same in each group and that this variance is known. Let the sample means of the experimental and control groups be $\bar{x}_e$ and $\bar{x}_c$ respectively, and let their difference be $\hat{\mu}_e = \bar{x}_e - \bar{x}_c$.

Then, by the textbook logic of pure experiments plus familiar results in elementary statistics, the difference $\hat{\mu}_e$ is distributed as:

$$\hat{\mu}_e \sim N(\mu, \sigma_e^2/n) \tag{2}$$

which is unbiased for the treatment effect μ. Thus, we may define a first estimate of the treatment effect by $\hat{\mu}_e = \bar{x}_e - \bar{x}_c$: It is the estimate of the treatment effect coming from the experiment. This is the same result as in Gerber et al. (2014, 12), except that we have spelled out here the dependence of the variance on the sample size.

Next, Gerber et al. assume that there is a second source of knowledge about μ, this time from an observational study with m independent observations, also independent of the experimental observations. Via regression or other statistical methods, this study generates a normally distributed estimate of the treatment effect μ, with known sampling variance σ_o^2/m. However, because the methodology is not experimental, Gerber et al. (2014, 12–13) assume that the effect is estimated with confounding, so that its expected value is distorted by a bias term β. Hence, the estimate from the observational study $\hat{\mu}_o$ is distributed as:

$$\widehat{\mu}_o \sim N(\mu + \beta, \sigma_o^2/m) \tag{3}$$

We now have two estimates, $\widehat{\mu}_e$ and $\widehat{\mu}_o$, and we want to know how to combine them. One can proceed by constructing a minimum-mean-squared error estimate in a classical framework, or one can use Bayesian methods. Since both approaches give the same result in our setup and since the Bayesian logic is more familiar, we follow Gerber et al. in adopting it. In that case, we need prior distributions for each of the unknowns.

With all the variances assumed known, there are just two unknown parameters, μ and β. An informative prior on μ is not ordinarily adopted in empirical research. At the extreme, as Gerber et al. (2014, 15) note, a fully informative prior for μ would mean that we already knew the correct answer for certain and we would not care about either empirical study, and certainly not about comparing them. Since our interest is in precisely that comparison, we want the data to speak for themselves. Hence, we set the prior variance on μ to be wholly uninformative; in the usual Bayesian way we approximate its variance by infinity.[1]

The parameter β also needs a prior. Sometimes we know the likely size and direction of bias in an observational study, and in that case we would correct the observational estimate by subtracting the expected size of the bias, as Gerber et al. (2014, 14) do. For simplicity here, and because it makes no difference to the argument, we will assume that the direction of the bias is unknown and has prior mean zero, so that subtracting its mean has no effect. Then the prior distribution is:

$$\beta \sim N(0, \sigma_\beta^2) \tag{4}$$

Here σ_β^2 represents our uncertainty about the size of the observational bias. Larger values indicate more uncertainty. Standard Bayesian logic then shows that our posterior distribution for the observational study on its own is $\widehat{\mu}_{op} = N(\mu, \sigma_o^2/m + \sigma_\beta^2)$.

Now, under these assumptions, Bayes' Theorem tells us how to combine the observational and experimental evidence, as Gerber et al. (2014, 14) point out. In accordance with their argument, the resulting

---

[1] Without this assumption, the Bayesian treatment estimate would differ from the minimum mean squared error estimate.

combined or aggregated estimate $\widehat{\mu}_a$ is a weighted average of the two estimates $\widehat{\mu}_{op}$ and $\widehat{\mu}_e$:

$$\widehat{\mu}_a = p\widehat{\mu}_{op} + (1-p)\widehat{\mu}_e \qquad (5)$$

where p is the fraction of the weight given to the observational evidence, and

$$p = \frac{\sigma_e^2/n}{\sigma_e^2/n + \sigma_o^2/m + \sigma_\beta^2} \qquad (6)$$

This result is the same as Gerber et al.'s, except that here we had no prior information about μ, which simplifies the interpretation without altering the implication that they wish to emphasize.

That implication is this: Since σ_e^2, σ_o^2, n, and m are just features of the observed data, the key aspect of p is our uncertainty about the bias term β, which is captured by the prior variance σ_β^2. Importantly, Gerber et al. (2014, 15) argue that we often know relatively little about the size of likely biases in observational research. In the limit, they say, we become quite uncertain, and $\sigma_\beta^2 \to \infty$. In that case, obviously, $p \to 0$ in Equation (6), and the observational evidence gets no weight at all in Equation (5), not even if its sample size is very large.

This limiting result is Gerber et al.'s (2014, 15) Illusion of Observational Learning Theorem. It formalizes the spirit of much recent commentary in the social sciences, in which observational studies are thought to be subject to biases of unknown, possibly very large size, whereas experiments follow textbook strictures and therefore reach unbiased estimates. Moreover, in an experiment, as the sample size goes to infinity, the correct average treatment effect is essentially learned with certainty.[2] Thus, only experiments tell us the truth. The mathematics here is unimpeachable, and the conclusion and its implications seem to be very powerful. Gerber et al. (2014, 19–21) go on to demonstrate that under conditions like these, little or no resources should be allocated to observational research. We cannot learn anything from it. The money should go to field experiments such as those they have conducted, or to other experiments.

---

[2] That is, the posterior distribution collapses around the true treatment effect μ, or in classical terms, $\text{plim}\,\widehat{\mu}_e = \mu$.

3.3   A Learning Theorem with No Thumb on the Scale

Gerber et al.'s Illusion of Observational Learning Theorem follows rigorously from their assumptions. The difficulty is that those assumptions combine jaundiced cynicism about observational studies with gullible innocence about experiments. As they make clear in the text, the authors themselves are neither unrelievedly cynical nor wholly innocent about either kind of research. But the logic of their mathematical conclusion turns out to depend entirely on their becoming sneering Mr. Hydes as they deal with observational research, and then transforming to kindly, indulgent Dr. Jekylls when they move to RCTs.

To see this, consider the standard challenge of experimental research: external validity, discussed in virtually every undergraduate methodology text (for example, Kellstedt and Whitten 2009, 75–76). Gerber et al. (2014, 22–23) mention this problem briefly, but they see it as a problem primarily for laboratory experiments because the inferential leap to the population is larger than for field experiments. The challenges that they identify for field experiments consist primarily in administering them properly. Even then, they suggest that statistical adjustments can often correct the biases induced (Gerber et al. 2014, 23–24). The flavor of their remarks may be seen in the following sentence:

The external validity of an experiment hinges on four factors: whether the subjects in the study are as strongly influenced by the treatment as the population to which a generalization is made, whether the treatment in the experiment corresponds to the treatment in the population of interest, whether the response measure used in the experiment corresponds to the variable of interest in the population, and how the effect estimates were derived statistically. (Gerber et al. 2014, 21)

What is missing from this list are the two critical factors emphasized in the work of recent critics of RCTs: heterogeneity of treatment effects and the importance of context. A study of inducing voter turnout in a Michigan Republican primary cannot be generalized to what would happen to Democrats in a general election in Louisiana, where the treatment effects are likely to be very different. There are no Louisianans in the Michigan sample, no Democrats, and no general election voters. Hence, no within-sample statistical adjustments are available to accomplish the inferential leap. Biases of unknown magnitude remain, and these are multiplied when one aims to generalize to a national population as a whole. As Cartwright (2007a;

Chapter 2 this volume), Cartwright and Hardie 2012, Deaton (2010), and Stokes (2014) have spelled out, disastrous inferential blunders occur commonly when a practitioner of field experiments imagines that they work the way Gerber et al. (2014) assume that they work in their Bayesian model assumptions. Gerber et al. (2014, 32 at fn. 6) concede in a footnote: "Whether bias creeps into an extrapolation to some other population depends on whether the effects vary across individuals in different contexts." But that crucial insight plays no role in their mathematical model.

What happens in the Gerber et al. model when we take a more evenhanded approach? If we assume, for example, that experiments have a possible bias γ stemming from failures of external validity, then in parallel to the assumption about bias in observational research, we might specify our prior beliefs about external invalidity bias as normally and independently distributed:

$$\gamma = N(0, \sigma_\gamma^2) \tag{7}$$

Then the posterior distribution of the treatment estimate from the experimental research would be $\widehat{\mu}_{ep} = N(\mu, \sigma_e^2/n + \sigma_\gamma^2)$, and the estimate combining both observational and experimental evidence would become:

$$\widehat{\mu}_{ab} = q\widehat{\mu}_{op} + (1 - q)\widehat{\mu}_{ep} \tag{8}$$

where q is the new fraction of the weight given to the observational evidence, and

$$q = \frac{\sigma_e^2/n + \sigma_\gamma^2}{\sigma_e^2/n + \sigma_\gamma^2 + \sigma_o^2/m + \sigma_\beta^2} \tag{9}$$

A close look at this expression (or taking partial derivatives) shows that the weight given to observational and experimental evidence is an intuitively plausible mix of considerations.

For example, an increase in m (the sample size of the observational study) reduces the denominator and thus raises q; this means that, all else equal, we should have more faith in observational studies with more observations. Conversely, increases in n, the sample size of an experiment, raise the weight we put on the experiment. In addition, the harder that authors have worked to eliminate confounders in observational research (small σ_β^2), the more we believe them. And the fewer the issues with external validity in an experiment (small σ_γ^2), the more weight we put on the experiment. That is what follows from Gerber et al.'s line of analysis when all the potential biases are put on the table, not just half of them. But, of course, all these implications have been familiar for at least half a century. Carried out evenhandedly, the Bayesian mathematics does no real work and brings us no real news.

Gerber et al. arrived at their Illusion of Observational Learning Theorem only by assuming away the problems of external validity in experiments. No surprise that experiments look wonderful in that case. But one could put a thumb on the other side of the scale: Suppose we assume that observational studies, when carefully conducted, have no biases due to omitted confounders, while experiments continue to have arbitrarily large problems with external validity. In that case, $\sigma_\beta^2 = 0$ and $\sigma_\gamma^2 \to \infty$. A look at Equations (8) and (9) then establishes that in that case, we get an Illusion of Experimental Learning Theorem: Experiments can teach us nothing, and no one should waste time and money on them. But of course, this inference is just as misleading as Gerber et al.'s original theorem.

Gerber et al. (2014, 11–12, 15, 26–30) concede that observational research sometimes works very well. When observational biases are known to be small, they see a role for that kind of research. But they never discuss a similar condition for valid experimental studies. Even in their verbal discussions, which are more balanced than their mathematics, they continue to write as if experiments had no biases: "experiments produce unbiased estimates regardless of whether the confounders are known or unknown" (Gerber et al. 2014, 25). But that sentence is true only if external validity is never a problem. Their theorem about the unique value of experimental work depends critically on that assumption. Alas, the last decade or two have taught us forcefully, if we did not know it before, that their assumption is very far from being true. Just as instrumental variable estimators looked theoretically attractive when they were developed in the 1950s and 1960s but often failed in practice (Bartels 1991), so too the practical limitations of RCTs have now come forcefully into view.

Experiments have an important role in political science and in the social sciences generally. So do observational studies. But the judgment as to which of them is more valuable in a particular research problem depends on a complex mixture of prior experience, theoretical judgment, and the details of particular research designs. That is the conclusion that follows from an evenhanded set of assumptions applied to the model Gerber et al. (2014) set out.

3.4 Conclusion

Causal inference of any kind is just plain hard. If the evidence is observational, patient consideration of plausible counterarguments, followed by the assembling of relevant evidence, can be, and often is, a painstaking process.[3] Faced with those challenges, researchers in the current intellectual climate may be tempted to substitute something that looks quicker and easier – an experiment.

The central argument for experiments (RCTs) is that the randomization produces identification of the key parameter. That is a powerful and seductive idea, and it works very well in textbooks. Alas, this modus operandi does not work nearly so well in practice. Without an empirical or theoretical understanding of how to get from experimental results to the relevant population of interest, stand-alone RCTs teach us just as little as casual observational studies. In either case, there is no royal road to secure inferences, as Nancy Cartwright has emphasized. Hard work and provisional findings are all we can expect. As Cartwright (2007b) has pungently remarked, experiments are not the gold standard, because there is no gold standard.

References

Achen, C. H. (2018) *Cycles in academic fashions: The case of experiments*. Mimeo, Department of Politics, Princeton University.

Achen, C. H. and Bartels, L. M. (2018) "Statistics as if politics mattered," *Journal of Politics*, 80 (4), 1438–1453.

Bartels, L. M. (1991) "Instrumental and quasi-instrumental variables," *American Journal of Political Science*, 35(3), 777–800.

Bross, I. D. J. (1960). "Statistical criticism," *Cancer*, 13(2), 394–400.

Cartwright, N. (2007a) *Hunting causes and using them*. New York: Cambridge University Press.

Cartwright, N. (2007b) "Are RCTs the gold standard?" *BioSocieties*, 2(1), 11–20.

Cartwright, N. (2017) "Single case causes: What is evidence and why" in Chao, H. and Reiss, J. (eds.) *Philosophy of science in practice: Nancy Cartwright and the nature of scientific reasoning*. New York: Springer International Publishing, pp. 11–24.

---

[3] Plausible counterarguments, but not just any speculative counterargument, a point not always understood by critics of observational evidence: see Bross (1960); Achen and Bartels (2018).

Cartwright, N. and Hardie, J. (2012). *Evidence-based policy: A practical guide to doing it better.* Oxford: Oxford University Press.

Deaton, A. (2010) "Instruments, randomization, and learning about development," *Journal of Economic Literature,* 48(2), 424–455.

Druckman, J. N., Green, D. P., Kuklinski, J. H., and Lupia, A. (2011) *Cambridge handbook of experimental political science.* New York: Cambridge University Press.

Gerber, A. S. and Green, D. (2012). *Field experiments.* New York: Norton.

Gerber, A. S., Green, D. and Kaplan, E. H. (2014) "The illusion of learning from observational research" in Teele, D. L. (ed.) *Field experiments and their critics.* New Haven, CT: Yale University Press, pp. 9–32.

Green, D. P., McGrath, M. C., and Aronow, P. M. (2013) "Field experiments and the study of voter turnout," *Journal of Elections, Public Opinion and Parties,* 23(1), 27–48.

Heckman, J. J. and Smith, J. A. (1995) "Assessing the case for social experiments," *Journal of Economic Perspectives,* 9(2), 85–110.

Jamison, J. C. (2019) "The entry of randomized assignment into the social sciences," *Journal of Causal Inference,* 7(1). http://dx.doi.org/10.1515/jci-2017-0025 (accessed January 21, 2020).

Karpowitz, C. F. and Mendelberg, T. (2014) *The silent sex: Gender, deliberation and institutions.* Princeton, NJ: Princeton University Press.

Kellstedt, P. M. and Whitten, G. D. (2009) *The fundamentals of political science research.* New York: Cambridge University Press.

Mutz, D. C. (2011) *Population-based survey experiments.* New York: Oxford University Press.

Stokes, S. C. (2014) "A defense of observational research," in Teele, D. L. (ed.) *Field experiments and their critics.* New Haven, CT: Yale University Press, pp. 33–57.

Teele, D. L., ed. (2014) *Field experiments and their critics.* New Haven, CT: Yale University Press.

4 Drawing Contingent Generalizations from Case Studies

Andrew Bennett

4.1 Introduction

What lessons can be learned from the international community's slow and piecemeal response to the Ebola epidemic in Guinea, Sierra Leone, and Liberia in 2014? Are the histories and outcomes of microfinance programs in one country or by one lender relevant beyond each country or lender? How can we judge whether the early results of a medical or other experiment are so powerfully indicative of either success or failure that the experiment should be stopped even before all cases are treated or all the evidence is in?

Case studies are one approach to addressing such questions. Yet one of the most common critiques of case study methods is that the results of individual case studies cannot be readily generalized. Oxford professor Bent Flyvbjerg notes that when he first became interested in in-depth case study research in the 1990s, his teachers and colleagues tried to dissuade him from using case studies, arguing "you cannot generalize from a single case." Flyvbjerg concluded that this view constitutes a conventional wisdom that "if not directly wrong, is so oversimplified as to be grossly misleading" (Flyvbjerg, 2006: 219). Similarly, the present chapter notes that the conventional wisdom is not fully wrong, as techniques for generalizing from individual case studies are complex and potentially fallible. The chapter concurs with Flyvbjerg, however, in concluding that we have means of assessing which findings will and will not generalize. For some case studies and some findings, generalization beyond the individual case is not warranted. In other contexts, we can make contingent generalizations from one or more case studies, or generalizations to a subset of a population that shares a well-defined set of features. In still other instances, sweeping generalizations to large and diverse populations are possible even from a single case study. The answer to whether case studies generalize is "It depends." It depends on our prior causal knowledge, our prior knowledge of populations of cases and of the frequency of contextual variables that enable or disable causal mechanisms, the evidence that emerges from process tracing on case studies (see Chapter 7), and how that evidence updates our prior knowledge of causal mechanisms and the contexts in which they do and do not operate.

A second, and related, critique of case studies is that their findings do not cumulate into successive improvements in theories. The present chapter, in contrast, argues that case studies can contribute to developing two different kinds of progressively better theories. First, case studies can lead to improved theories about individual causal mechanisms and the scope conditions under which they operate. Claims about causal mechanisms are one of the most common kinds of theory in both the social and physical sciences. Second, case studies can contribute to improved "typological theories," or theories about how combinations of causal mechanisms interact in specified issue areas and distributions of resources, stakeholder interests, legitimacy, and institutions. Later case studies can build upon, test, qualify, and extend typological theories developed in earlier ones.

This chapter first clarifies different conceptions of "generalization" in statistical and case study research. It then discusses four kinds of generalization from case studies: generalization from the selection and study of "typical" cases, generalization from most- and least-likely cases, mechanism-based generalization, and generalization via typological theories. The chapter uses studies of the 2014 Ebola epidemic as a running example to illustrate many of these kinds of generalization, and it draws on studies of microfinance programs and medical experiments to illustrate particular kinds of generalization.

4.2 Statistical Versus Case Study Views on "Generalization"

While the accurate explanation of individual historical cases is important and useful, the ability to generalize beyond individual cases is rightly considered a key component of both theoretical progress and policy relevance. Theories are abstractions that simplify the task of perceiving and operating in the world, and without some degree and kind of generalization little simplification is possible. But "generalization" can take on several meanings, and scholars and policy-makers vary in their views on what kinds of generalizations are either possible or pragmatically useful, partly depending on whether their methodological training was mostly in quantitative or qualitative approaches. Thus, it is important to clarify the different meanings that scholars in different methodological traditions typically give to the term "generalization."

Among researchers whose main methods are statistical analysis of observational data, "generalization" is commonly treated as a question of the "average effect" observed between a specified independent variable and the dependent variable of interest in a population. This average effect is represented by the coefficients on the statistically significant independent variables in a regression equation.[1] Similarly, for researchers who use experimental methods, generalization takes the form of the estimated "average treatment effect," measured as the average difference in outcomes between the treated and untreated groups from a large number of randomly selected units.[2]

Generalization from statistical analysis of observational data depends on several assumptions, most notably: 1) that the treatment of one unit does not affect the outcome of another unit (the Stable Unit Treatment Value Assumption, or SUTVA); and, 2) that independent variables have "constant effects" across the units (or, related, the "unit homogeneity" assumption that two units will have the same value on the dependent variable when they have the same value on the explanatory variable).[3] These are very demanding assumptions, and they do not hold up when there are interaction effects among independent variables, or when there are learning or selection effects through which the outcome (or expected outcome) in one individual or group affects the behavior, treatment, or outcome of another individual or group.

For statistical methods, the possibility that there may in fact be interaction effects, selection effects, and learning can create what is known as the "ecological inference problem." Specifically, even if a statistical correlation holds up for a population, and even if the correlation is causal, it is a potential fallacy to infer that any one case in the population is causally explained by the

---

[1] King, Keohane, and Verba (1994). The present discussion for the most part sets aside the issue of whether this average "effect" is treated as a descriptive finding or a potentially causal relationship.

[2] In experiments, there is a stronger presumption that any difference in average outcomes between treated and untreated units is causal, and experimenters can also analyze differences in the standard deviation of outcomes between treated and untreated groups.

[3] King, Keohane, and Verba (1994: 91).

correlation that is observed at the population level. When interaction effects exist, a variable that raises the average outcome for a population may have a greater or smaller effect, or zero effect or even a negative effect, on the outcome for an individual case.

For example, in the 1960s, on the basis of statistical and other evidence, it became generally (and rightly) accepted as true that smoking increases the general prevalence of lung cancer for large groups of people. This generalization is an adequate basis for the policy recommendation that governments should discourage smoking. Yet the generalization that smoking on average increases the incidence of lung cancer does not tell us whether any one individual contracted lung cancer due to smoking.[4] Some people who smoke develop lung cancer but others do not, and some people who do not smoke develop lung cancer.[5] Scientists using statistical methods to assess epidemiological and experimental data have more recently begun to understand some of the genetic, environmental, and behavioral factors (in addition to the decision on whether to smoke) that affect the probability that a specific individual will develop lung cancer. This supports more targeted policy recommendations on whether an individual with particular genes is at especially high risk if they choose to smoke. For example, recent studies indicate that individuals with a mutation in a region on chromosome 15 will have a greatly increased risk of contracting lung cancer if they smoke (Pray 2008: 17). Even in this subgroup, however, it cannot be said with certainty that any one individual developed lung cancer because of smoking, as not every individual with this mutation gets lung cancer even if they smoke.[6]

Statistical researchers are well aware that strong assumptions are required to extend inferences from populations to individual cases, and they are

---

[4] This is related to the "fundamental problem of causal inference" (Holland 1986), which is that we cannot run a perfect experiment in which we rerun history, changing only one intervention or treatment, to compare an individual case that is treated in one world and untreated in the other. Here, we cannot compare the world in which an individual smokes cigarettes to the counterfactual world in which the same individual did not smoke.

[5] With other kinds of treatments or interventions, the effects on individual cases are even more uncertain. Smoking probably does not *decrease* the likelihood of lung cancer for anyone, but some medicines can cause life-saving effects in some cases, fatal allergies in others, and little or no effects in still other individuals. The language of "average effects" can be very misleading if it does not include discussion of the variance of effects: we would rightly ban a medicine that has a very small positive effect on average (say, increasing life span by a few hours) but terrible effects in a small number of cases (such as death by allergic reaction).

[6] The mechanism linking mutations on chromosome 15 to lung cancer is still under debate: the mutation could either create an indirect effect by increasing susceptibility to nicotine addiction, or a direct effect by creating molecular paths to cancer, or both (Pray 2008).

typically careful to make clear that their models do not necessarily explain individual cases (although the results of statistical studies are often oversimplified in media reports and applied to individual cases). Case study researchers in the social sciences tend to be particularly skeptical about strong assumptions regarding constant effects, unit homogeneity, and independence of cases. These researchers often think that high-order interaction effects, interdependencies among cases across space or time, and other forms of complexity are common in social life. Consequently, qualitative researchers in the social sciences typically doubt whether there are many nontrivial single-variable generalizations that apply in consistent ways across large populations of cases in society.

Case study researchers thus face the obverse of the ecological inference problem: often it is neither possible nor desirable to "generalize" from one or a few case studies to a population in the sense of developing estimates of average causal effects. Yet, at the same time, case study researchers do aspire to derive conclusions from case studies that are useful beyond the specific cases studied. Instead of seeking estimates of average effects for a population, case study researchers attempt to identify narrower "contingent generalizations" that apply to subsets of a population that share combinations of independent variables. Case study researchers thus develop "typological" or "middle range" theories about how similar combinations of variables lead to similar outcomes through similar processes or pathways. These researchers often focus on hypothesized causal mechanisms and their scope conditions, posing research questions in the following form: "Under what conditions does this mechanism have a positive effect on the outcome, under what conditions does it have zero effect, and under what conditions does it have a negative effect?"

Contingent generalizations are similar in form to the generalizations sought by statistical researchers: they apply to defined populations, they may have anomalous cases whose outcomes do not fit the generalization, and they are potentially fallible as even cases that have the expected outcome may have arrived at that outcome through mechanisms different from those associated with the theory behind the generalization. The difference is that case studies arrive at generalizations through methods that are for the most part associated with Bayesian rather than frequentist logic (see Chapter 7). Bayesian logic treats probabilities as degrees of belief in alternative explanations, and it updates initial degrees of belief (called "priors") by using assessments of the probative value of new evidence vis-à-vis alternative explanations (the updated degree of belief is known as the "posterior").

With ample cases and strong or numerous independent pieces of evidence, Bayesian and frequentist methods converge on similar conclusions, but unlike frequentism, Bayesian analysis does not need a minimum number of cases to get off the ground. Bayesianism is thus better suited to contexts in which cases are few or diverse, as is often true in the study of complex phenomena such as development.[7]

These different logics translate into differences in practice on what constitutes an acceptable generalization. Case study researchers are often happy with a generalization that holds up well for, say, five or six cases that share similar values on a half-dozen independent variables, and they are also usually curious about or troubled by individual cases that do not fit such a generalization. This is because case study researchers base their arguments on the probative value of evidence within a Bayesian framework. Within this framework, a single piece of powerful evidence can sharply discriminate between one explanation and many alternative explanations, while many pieces of weak evidence cannot support any updating unless all or most of them point in the same direction. In a frequentist framework, which treats probabilities as constituting the likelihood that a sample drawn from a population is or is not representative of the population, nothing can be said about five or six cases with seven or eight independent variables because of the "degrees of freedom" problem. Frequentists also often have little curiosity about individual cases that do not fit a correlation established through a large sample, as they expect that such outliers will occasionally happen, whether by quantum randomness or by the fact that numerous weak variables left out of a model can sometimes line up in ways that create outliers.

The different logics also lead to different ways of establishing generalizations. The above-described frequentist approach starts and ends with populations: the population is studied at the population level through the study of the full population (or the random selection of cases from the population) to make population-level claims on average effects. Case studies, in contrast, begin from within-case analysis of individual cases, or process tracing, of cases not selected at random. Process tracing uses Bayesian logic to make inferences from the evidence within a single case about alternative explanations of the outcome of that case (see Chapter 7). Depending on the results

---

[7] This is particularly true for rare events. Researchers sometimes closely study rare but high-consequence events such as nuclear accidents and airplane crashes, and "close calls" of events that have never happened, such as accidental use of nuclear weapons, to derive lessons for preventing rare but costly outcomes; see March, Sproull, and Tamuz (1991).

of the within-case analysis and the principle used in selecting the cases studied, case study researchers decide whether to generalize contingently (to populations that share several specified features), widely (to populations that share fewer features), or not at all. The decision on whether and how to generalize depends on the understanding that emerges from the case study regarding the mechanisms that generated the outcome of the case, and also on new and prior knowledge about the nature and prevalence of the contexts that enable those mechanisms to operate. Put another way, the study of an individual case can lead to a new understanding of causal mechanisms and the scope conditions in which they do and do not operate, and the researcher may have prior knowledge on the frequency with which the necessary scope conditions exist (and hence of the population to which the case findings are relevant).

This overall description of generalizing from case studies includes four approaches to developing generalizations: generalization from "typical" cases, generalization from most- or least-likely cases, mechanism-based generalization, and typological theorizing.[8] The sections that follow address each in turn.

4.3 Generalization from a "Typical" Case

A first approach to generalization from cases is to select a case that is thought to be "typical" or representative of a population (Gerring and Seawright 2008: 299–301). In the medical literature, for example, case studies are often presented as being typical of a particular disease or condition. If indeed a case is representative of a population – a key assumption – then process tracing on the case can identify or verify relationships that generalize to the population. If an existing theory predicts a population-level correlation, and statistical analysis of the relevant population exhibits the expected correlation, close study of a typical case can strengthen the inference that the correlation is causal if process tracing on the case shows the hypothesized mechanisms were indeed in operation. A typical case can also undermine causal claims if it shows that no plausible mechanisms connect the hypothesized independent variable to the outcome, or if it demonstrates that the

---

[8] The present discussion sets aside fuzzy-set Qualitative Comparative Analysis (fsQCA), an approach that uses fuzzy-set measures of variables, case comparisons, and Boolean algebra to find patterns on which combinations of variables relate to different outcomes; see Ragin (2006).

mechanisms that generated the outcome were different from those initially theorized (Gerring and Seawright 2008: 299).

These inferences all depend on whether the case studied is in fact representative of the population. One way to choose a case that may be typical is to construct a statistical model and then identify a case with a small error term vis-à-vis the model, or to choose randomly from among several cases with small error terms (Gerring and Seawright 2008: 299). Added criteria for typicality could include choosing a case that is near the mean or median values on most or all variables. One problem with these criteria is that if the statistical model is mis-specified – for example, if it omits relevant variables – a case may appear to be representative when it is in fact atypical (Gerring and Seawright 2008: 300). For example, the case may include two omitted variables that occur only rarely, one of which pushes the case toward the outcome of interest and one of which inhibits or lessens the outcome, so these variables may have cancelled out each other's effects and resulted in a low error term. The case would have therefore had a low error term for reasons that would not apply to the majority of cases in the population that do not have the rare variables. One way to reduce the likelihood of this problem is to do process tracing on several cases thought to be typical.

When the population of cases is small and the hypothesized relationship involves interaction effects or different paths to the outcome that have little in common, it may be difficult or impossible to specify or identify a case that is "typical." When these conditions hold, as they often do in the study of social phenomenon, the more theory-based forms of generalization discussed herein may prove more useful than attempts to generalize from a "typical" case.

4.4   Generalization from Most- or Least-Likely Case Studies

The most-likely and least-likely cases approach uses extant theories and preliminary knowledge about the values of the variables in particular cases to estimate case-specific priors on how likely it is that alternative theories will prove to be good explanations of a case. A case is most-likely for a theory, or an easy test case, if we expect the theory to be a strong explanation for the case's outcome. The case is least-likely for a theory, or a tough test case, if we have reason to believe the theory should not account very well for the outcome of the case. The degree to which we can generalize from a case then depends on whether the theory passes or fails tough or easy test cases. A theory that succeeds in a least-likely case might be given broader scope conditions. For example, if a study shows that anarchist groups are hierarchically organized even though we should have expected them to be the least-likely kind of social organization to be hierarchical, we might conclude that hierarchy is a common feature in a wide range of social groups. Conversely, a theory that fails in a most-likely case should be assigned narrower scope conditions.[9] A theory's successful explanation of most-likely cases, or its failure to explain least-likely cases, has little impact on our estimates of its scope conditions.

Determining whether a case is most- or least-likely for a theory depends on whether the variables in the theory point strongly to an outcome, whether the variables in alternative theories point strongly to an outcome, and whether the main theory of interest and the collective alternative explanations point to the same outcome or to different outcomes. The strongest possible basis for generalizing from a case is when a theory modestly pushes toward one outcome, countervailing alternative explanations point strongly to the opposite outcome, and the first theory proves correct regarding the outcome. The strongest basis for narrowing the scope conditions of a theory exists when the theory and all the alternative explanations point strongly to the same outcome, and yet they are all wrong. Other combinations lead to different degrees of updating of scope conditions (Rapport, 2015).

An analysis of the international response to the 2014 West Africa Outbreak illustrates these issues.[10] In this outbreak the US government mobilized considerable resources – albeit later than it should have – and the UK government stepped in to assist in Sierra Leone, while France was slower to play a role and the UN system lagged.[11] There are several possible alternative explanations for the variation in these responses.[12] One possible

---

[9] Similarly, claims of necessity or sufficiency can be cast into doubt, in Bayesian fashion, by one or a few contrary cases.

[10] Thanks to Jennifer Widener and Michael Woolcock for providing an analysis of this example and the case codings for the USA, the WHO, and the UK (on the capacity and cohesion variables) in Table 4.1; the remaining codings and question marks are the author's. For more on this subject, see the multi-author case study series published in 2016–2017 by Princeton University's Innovations for Successful Societies research program, available at https://successfulsocieties.princeton.edu/publications/all-hands-deck-us-response-west-africa%E2%80%99s-ebola-crisis-2014-2015.

[11] Notably, each country focused on the Ebola outbreak in the African country with which it had the strongest historical ties: the USA on Liberia, the UK on Sierra Leone, and France on Guinea.

[12] We can substantially discount a fifth possible explanation – differing awareness of the problem – as it is not consistent with the variation in outcomes. The USA and the UN both had public health officials on the ground shortly after the initial cases appeared through April 2014. Although both were mistaken in thinking the epidemic had ended in April, each had kept the situation on the radar and all four governments were aware when new infections began to appear, thanks to Medicins sans frontieres (MSF).

Table 4.1 Mobilization during 2014 Ebola outbreak: World Health Organization, United States, United Kingdom, and France

Country or International Organization	Finance	Capacity	Authority	Cohesion	Expected Outcome (E) and Observed Outcome (O)
WHO	N	N	N	N	E: Little Mobilization O: Little Mobilization
United States	Y	Y	Y	Y	E: Mobilization O: Mobilization
United Kingdom	Mixed	Y	Mixed	Y	E: Slow Mobilization O: Slow Mobilization
France	N	?	?	?	E: Little Mobilization O: Little mobilization

explanation for the pattern of assistance that emerged is "Finance": the ability to summon substantial financial resources quickly. A second is "Capacity": ability to mobilize organizational resources, transportation, and medical materials rapidly. A third is "Authority": Whether there is an interagency process that allows institutions responsible for medical emergencies to work with institutions responsible for disaster response, without having to create a whole new organization for that purpose. A fourth is "Cohesion": Whether the decision to act lies within the power of one person or a few people, or whether there are many veto points.

With respect to "Finance," the USA had disaster response discretionary funds it could use to put people on the ground quickly, while the UK and France could mobilize money less easily and the UN system would have to pass the hat for contributions from member states. With respect to "Capacity," the WHO's emergency response capacity had eroded, while the USA had an Office of Foreign Disaster Assistance with a rapid response capability in place. With respect to "Authority," there was no quick way within the UN system to merge a public health or medical response (a World Health Organization matter) with a disaster response (based at the UN Office for the Coordination of Humanitarian Affairs). Finally, with respect to "Cohesion," in the USA a single decision-maker, the president, could authorize action, while the UN agencies required the assent of member-state representatives.

In this instance, there are no strong or generalizable surprises from the most- and least-likely cases: the USA was the most-likely case for early and strong mobilization, the WHO was the least likely, and both had the expected outcomes. Had the USA failed to mobilize, or the WHO succeeded in doing so, these cases might challenge the four-factor theory of mobilization and its scope conditions.

The most interesting and strongest generalization to emerge from the international response to the 2014 Ebola outbreak is that the main bottleneck internationally was not finances or capacity, which would require financial investments to fix, but authority and cohesion, which require political attention to fix. The UK, France, and especially the USA had unused capacity in their militaries and national health systems for addressing Ebola, and the USA in particular mobilized substantial resources. However, many of these resources translated into operations only after the number of new infections per week had started to diminish. The USA deployed 3,000 troops to build 11 Ebola treatment centers in Africa, but only 28 Ebola patients received treatment at these centers, and 9 of the 11 centers never treated a single Ebola patient (Onishi 2015). In the UK, Public Health England (PHE) and the Department for International Development (DFID) coordinated in responding to Ebola, but only after initial delays that a parliamentary report attributed to over-reliance on WHO medical warning systems and DFID's inflexibility in dispersing small amounts of money early in the outbreak (House of Commons, 2016: 3). In addition, some UK health care personnel willing to volunteer for the fight against Ebola in Africa had to first negotiate leaves of absence from their respective organizations (Reece et al. 2017). A stronger and more coordinated early response would have been less costly and more effective than the slow and piecemeal responses that emerged.

4.5 Mechanism-Based Generalization from Cases

Typical, most-likely, and least-likely cases can provide a basis for a general claim that scope conditions should be broadened or narrowed, but they do not provide much detail on exactly how, or to what subpopulations, they might be extended, or from what subpopulations they might be withdrawn. The third, mechanism-based approach to generalizing from case studies provides some clues to this process, often by building on new theories about causal mechanisms derived from the study of individual cases.

To understand the logic of this kind of generalization, consider two polar opposite examples, the first of which leads to very limited generalizability and the second of which leads to sweeping generalizations. In the first example, imagine that a researcher studying voter behavior finds evidence that a voter, according to the variables identified by every standard theory of voter choice (party affiliation, ideology, etc.) should have voted for candidate A, but in fact it is known that the voter chose candidate B. Imagine further that the researcher is able to ask the voter "Why did you vote for B?" and the voter replies "B is my sister-in-law." This new variable, which we might call "immediate kinship relations," provides a convincing explanation, but the mechanisms involved in the explanation suggest that it will generalize only to a very small number of cases in any election involving a large electorate.[13]

Now consider an opposite example: Charles Darwin undertook an observational study of several bird species and came up with the theory of evolutionary selection. In view of the mechanisms that this theory posits, the theory should apply to an extremely large group: all living things. Here again, the hypothesized mechanisms involved in the theory – genetic mutation, procreation, and environmental selection – provide clues on the expected scope conditions of the theory. In part, these expectations are built, in Bayesian fashion, on prior knowledge of the base rates of the enabling conditions of the theory: immediate relatives of a candidate are rare among big populations of voters, whereas living things are common.

The lessons experts drew from the early mishandling of the 2014 Ebola outbreak[14] provide a real example of generalization from an improved understanding of causal mechanisms. Here, findings on the relevant causal mechanisms are not only those concerning the medical details of the Ebola virus itself, but the interaction of the virus with local health systems, international organizations, social media, and local customs. An early opportunity to suppress the 2014 outbreak was missed because international experts did not realize that reported numbers of cases had dropped not because the outbreak had been contained, but because fearful communities had chased away health workers and sick patients were avoiding health clinics, which

---

[13] One could change the variable "immediate kinship relations" to a more general category of social relations (neighbors, coworkers, ethnic groups, etc.) that might apply to more cases. In cases where "ethnic voting" is common, for example, last names that are viewed as signals of ethnicity can affect voting behavior.

[14] The first cases in Guinea appeared at the very end of 2013, but for present purposes almost all the salient events unfolded in 2014 and into 2015.

they associated with high rates of death (Sack, Fink, Belluck, and Nossiter, 2014). In addition, the virus spread in part because of cultural commitments to hands-on washing of the dead, which points to the need for "culturally appropriate outreach and education" to prevent the spread of future outbreaks (Frieden et al., 2014). These findings, and not just differences in the availability of health care and quarantine technologies, help explain why Ebola spread rapidly in West Africa but not in Europe or the United States despite the arrival of infected patients in the latter regions.

Generalizations based on improved theories about causal mechanisms have two very important properties. First, they can be highly relevant for making policy decisions. For many policy decisions, we are less interested in questions such as "what is the average causal effect of X on Y in a population" than in questions such as "what will be the effect of increasing X in this particular case." Improved knowledge of how causal mechanisms work, and of the contexts in which they have positive and negative effects on the outcome of interest, is directly relevant to estimating case-specific effects.

Second, an improved understanding of causal mechanisms can allow generalizing to individual cases, and kinds of cases or contexts, that are different from or outside of the sample of the cases studied. This is a very important property of theoretical understandings derived from the close observation of causal mechanisms in individual cases, as both statistical studies and artificial intelligence algorithms are often weak at "out of sample" predictions. A powerful example here is the development of an effective "cocktail" of drugs to treat HIV-AIDS. This medical advance was greatly fostered by the close study of individual patients who responded far better to treatments than other patients. Researchers concluded upon close examination of such patients that administration of a combination of drugs earlier in the progression of the disease than previous experimental treatments could keep it in check (Schoofs, 1998). This illustrates that when a researcher comes up with a new theory or explanation from the study of a case, their new understanding of the hypothesized mechanisms through which the theory operates can itself give insights into the expected scope conditions of the theory, as in the above-mentioned "sister-in-law" and Darwin examples.

While researchers might derive new understandings of causal mechanisms from many types of case studies, two kinds of case selection are particularly oriented toward developing new understandings of mechanisms and their scope conditions: studies of "deviant" (or outlier) cases, and studies of cases that have high values on an independent variable of interest.[15] Deviant cases, or cases with an unexpected outcome or a high error term relative to extant theories, are good candidates for the purpose of looking inductively for new explanations or omitted variables. In these cases, new insights and theories may arise from the inductive use of process tracing to connect "clues" – pieces of evidence that do not on first examination fit into extant theories – in a new explanation.[16]

An interesting and important dilemma here concerns decisions on whether to stop trial experiments on medical or other treatments sooner than planned when the early subjects undergoing the treatment show signs of either catastrophic failures or remarkable successes. Continuing a trial after a treatment has shown signs of being powerfully effective can be unethical as it delays treatment of other individuals or communities who might benefit. Even worse, continuing a trial treatment after catastrophic outcomes arise in early cases can cost lives. Much of the discussion of this issue in the medical literature warns against premature termination of medical experiments, regardless of unexpectedly good or bad early results, due to the frequentist argument that small samples can be unrepresentative and do not allow powerful conclusions. There is indeed a risk that trials stopped early for benefit might catch the observed treatment effect at a "random high," which later can yield to a "regression to the truth effect" in subsequent trials or clinical use (Montori et al., 2005). Yet qualitative evidence from individual cases can provide additional analytical leverage over decisions on whether to continue experiments after strong early results, particularly when that evidence, combined with existing expert knowledge, strongly illuminates the causal mechanisms at work. Experts on clinical trials have thus noted that "formal statistical methods should be used as tools to guide decision-making rather than as hard rules" (Sydes et al., 2004: 60) and that "predefined statistical stopping boundaries for benefit provide a useful objective guide-line, but the reality of making wise judgements on when to stop involves an evaluation of the totality of evidence available" (Pocock, 2006: 516).

Bayesian logic and process tracing provide a useful perspective on this issue. As noted, whereas frequentism treats probabilities as representing the likelihood that a sample is representative of a population, Bayesians view probability as representing degrees of belief in different explanations.

---

[15] Recent research on case selection has placed renewed emphasis on the value of deviant and "high on the independent variable" cases as sources of insights on causal mechanisms (Seawright, 2016).

[16] A large error term can also arise from the combined effects of many different weak variables, or from measurement error, rather than from one or a few strong omitted variables.

Consequently, when evidence is uniquely consistent with one explanation, Bayesians can update their confidence in alternative explanations even with small numbers of cases. In medical applications, this involves looking at process-tracing evidence on *why* a treatment succeeded or failed, not just whether it succeeded or failed. While much of the thinking behind clinical trials still reflects a frequentist outlook, a more Bayesian and process-tracing approach has been influential in epidemiology and experimental medicine as well. Early on in the debates on the relationship between smoking and cancer, the English epidemiologist Sir Austin Bradford Hill developed nine criteria for assessing evidence on a potential causal relationship between a presumed cause and an observed effect. These include process-tracing types of criteria, such as the specificity of the observed relationship, the temporal precedence of the cause over the effect, and the existence of a plausible theorized mechanism linking the cause and the effect. As a later study of Hill's criteria concluded: "Whereas a trial is often open to the objection that it is an anomaly or not generalizable, if we supplement the evidence from the trial with strong mechanistic and parallel evidence, it becomes increasingly diffi-cult to question the results of the study and its applicability to a wider target population" (Howick, Glasziou, and Aronson, 2009: 193).

An example here concerns the early application of chimeric antigen receptor T-cell (CAR-T) therapy. In CAR-T therapy, physicians alter a patient's T-cells (a type of white blood cell critical to the immune system) so that these T-cells can better target and destroy cancer cells. The physicians then introduce the altered T-cells back into the patient's body. Of the first patients with ordinarily fatal cancers given this experimental treatment, three had complete remissions, four improved without a full remission, one improved and then relapsed, and two showed no effect. While these early results included too few cases for any strong conclusion using frequentist statistics, they looked promising given the extremely low remission rates of untreated patients with the kinds of cancers included in the initial study, and research on CAR-T therapy continued.

The most revealing case arose when doctors chose to administer CAR-T therapy in 2012 to Emily Whitehead, a young patient with a likely terminal case of Acute Lymphoblastic Leukemia. Like some previous CAR-T patients, within a few days Emily developed life-threatening immune response symp-toms, including a fever of 105 degrees, and appeared to be hours away from death. Fortunately, her doctors quickly found that the cause was an elevation of cytokines, inflammatory factors secreted by T-cells and their target cells. Emily had one cytokine in particular, IL-6, that was 1,000 times higher than normal. In a sense, given her doctors' already well-developed understanding of their therapeutic approach, this showed that the CAR-T process was working: the chimeric T-cells were targeting and destroying cancer cells at an astonishing rate. Yet the associated side effect of inflammation might have killed Emily, as it had a previous patient named Jesse Gelsinger. Luckily, one of Emily's doctors knew of a recently approved drug that blocks IL-6, and Emily experienced a remarkably quick and full recovery once she received this drug. Seven years later, she remained cancer-free (Mukherjee, 2019).

This example demonstrates that the efficacy and generalizability of an intervention should rely not only on the number of successes or failures and frequentist statistical assumptions about sampling, but also on Bayesian inference, prior theoretical knowledge, and process-tracing evidence. Here, despite the small number of prior cases, the results were striking: deadly in some cases, remarkably curative for some who survived the inflammatory response. Emily's case provided the key process-tracing clue regarding the "cytokine storm" that was threatening patients. Fortunately, a drug was at hand to treat her particular IL-6 cytokine spike, and doctors used their prior causal knowledge to decide to administer this drug. Emily's recovery spurred further CAR-T research, and while not every patient has benefited in trials and several challenges remain, the therapy continues to show promise. Yet given the frequentist tilt of extant practices in medical research, the future of CAR-T therapy hinged on Emily's personal outcome to a far larger degree than it should have. As one physician later commented (Rosenbaum, 2017: 1314):

anecdote can easily break a field rather than make it: the death of Jesse Gelsinger in a trial at Penn had set the field of gene therapy back at least a decade. And as both June and Stephan Grupp, the Children's Hospital oncologist and principal investigator of the CART-19 trial in children, emphasized, had Emily died, the CAR-T field would probably have died with her.

In addition to studying cases with remarkable outcomes on the dependent variable, the study of cases with high values on an independent variable of interest can contribute to better and generalizable understandings of causal mechanisms. This is often the intuition behind selecting cases that have high value on both an independent variable and the dependent variable. An example here is a study of "hybrid" microfinance organizations, or commercial organizations that combine elements of profit-making lending and development-oriented lending, by Julie Battilana and Silvia Dorado. These authors chose two such organizations in Bolivia that they knew to be "pioneering" and high-performing in order to carry out a "comparative inductive study" (Battilana and Dorado, 2010:1435) of the factors behind their success. They concluded from close study of these two organizations that their innovative hiring and socialization processes accounted for their high portfolio growth. The authors suggest that this finding is relevant to hybrid organizations more generally, although they also note "limits to the influence of hiring and socialization policies in mitigating tensions between institutional logics within organizations" (Battilana and Dorado, 2010: 1420).

Of course, researchers can make mistakes in either over-generalizing or under-generalizing the expected scope conditions that emerge from their understanding of a new theory. For this reason, while researchers may have warrant for making claims on the scope conditions of new theories derived from cases, these claims must remain provisional pending testing in other cases. Researchers should be particularly careful of selecting "best practices" cases on the basis of performance or outcomes, or selecting on the dependent variable, and then making inferences on the practices in these cases as the causes of high performance. If a population is large, some units may perform well even over long periods of time just by chance. Researchers have often claimed to have found the best practices that underlie unusually good perform-ance in companies' stock market strategies and management practices, for example, only to find later that the same companies later experienced average or even below average performance, exhibiting regression toward the mean.[17]

4.6 Typological Theorizing and Generalization

The fourth approach to generalization from case studies, typological theor-izing, systematically combines process tracing and small-N comparisons. The goal is to develop a theory on different combinations of independent variables, or types, so that contingent generalizations can be made about the processes and outcomes of cases within each type.[18] To develop and test these

---

[17] A well-known example here is the popular management book *In Search of Excellence* (Peters and Waterman, 1982), which studied high-performing businesses and claimed to have found the common principles that led to their above-average returns. Within a few years of the book's publication, most of the businesses that were the basis of the study experienced average or poor returns.

[18] Qualitative Comparative Analysis (QCA) is similar to typological theorizing in that it focuses on cases as combinations of variables, but as traditionally practiced QCA relies on cross-case comparisons rather than within-case analysis. More recently, some QCA methodologists have advocated using QCA for the purpose of selecting cases for process tracing, which is more similar to typological theorizing (Schneider and Rohlfing 2013).

contingent generalizations, researchers first build a typological theory, starting deductively and then iterating between their initial theoretical understanding of the phenomenon they are studying and their initial knowledge of the measures of the variables in the cases in the relevant population. Once they have built a typological theory using this initial knowledge, the researchers can use it to choose which cases they will study, and then they can use process tracing (see Chapter 7) to study those cases.

While a full discussion of typological theorizing is beyond the scope of this chapter,[19] the paragraphs that follow outline a process for developing typological theories. As an illustrative example, the discussion considers the puzzle of why, in response to epidemics such as Ebola or flu, governments sometimes resort to isolation strategies while at other times they employ quarantines. Isolation involves treating and limiting the movement of symptomatic patients suspected of having a contagious disease, while quarantines seek to limit the movement into and out of designated areas (including neighborhoods or whole cities) of individuals who may have been exposed to an illness but are not themselves symptomatic. Isolation is uncontroversial, while quarantines raise more difficult issues regarding civil liberties. Quarantines can also create unintended consequences by inhibiting patients who might be sick from seeking care, or motivating individuals to flee from high-infection quarantined areas to low-infection areas, possibly spreading the epidemic in the process. For present purposes of illustrating a typological theory, however, I focus not on the policy question of when quarantines might be efficacious, or the ethical question of when they might be justified, but the political question of when they are attempted.

To build a typological theory, the researcher first defines or conceptualizes the outcome of interest (the dependent variable) and decides how to measure this outcome. Often in typological theories the dependent variable is categorized by nominal measures (such as "democracy" and "non-democracy"), but it can also be categorized by ordinal measures (such as high, medium, and low levels of growth in the percentage of children attending school), or by conceptual typologies (such as combinations of variables that constitute three types of "welfare capitalism" (Esping-Andersen, 1990)). In our example of isolation

One advantage of QCA is that it allows the derivation of two different measures relating to generalization. The first measure, "consistency," assesses the degree to which cases that share a condition or a combination of variables have the same outcome. The second measure, "coverage," estimates the degree to which any variable or combination covers the total of instances of the outcome of interest. This is a measure of the importance of the variable or combination (Ragin, 2006).

[19] See George and Bennett (2005) and Bennett (2013).

versus quarantine, there are gradations of both (How many symptoms qualify a patient for isolation? How geographically broad or narrow is a quarantine and does it allow many or few exceptions for work or family reasons?), but the overall conceptual difference between isolation and quarantine is clear. For present purposes, the discussion therefore uses a simple dichotomized dependent variable of isolation versus quarantine, but subsequent research could consider gradations and kinds of isolations and quarantines.

Second, the researcher draws on existing theories to identify the key independent variables from individual theories, or constituent theories that relate to the outcome of interest. By convention, these independent variables constitute the columns in a table laying out the typological theory, while the individual cases (or clusters of cases with the same combination of independent variables, or "types") constitute the rows in the typological table. In our example I offer three independent variables that may affect choices between isolation strategies and quarantines. First, airborne epidemics, which typically spread quickly, are more likely to be subject to quarantine than those transmitted only by direct bodily contact. This may even be a nearly sufficient condition for quarantines. Second, isolation is more likely when a country has a high-capacity health care system that can treat a large number of individuals. Third, quarantines are a more tempting option when individuals in the quarantined area have few transportation or other options for escaping the quarantine area. Additional variables may matter as well, such as levels of social media, levels of trust or distrust in the government and the health system, and state capacity for coercion, but for illustrative purposes the present example includes only three independent variables and treats each as dichotomous.

Third, the researcher builds a table – a "typological space" (sometimes called a "possibility space" or a "property space" in the philosophy of logic) of all the possible combinations of the independent variables of the constituent theories.[20] Because a typological space becomes combinatorially more complex with additional variables and finer levels of measurement of these variables, for the purpose of presenting and thinking through the typological table, researchers typically include six or fewer independent variables and use nominal, dichotomous, or trichotomous measures of these variables. Researchers can relax the simplifications on the number and measurement

---

[20] For discussion and a compilation of examples of theoretical typologies, see Collier, Laporte, and Seawright (2012).

Table 4.2 A typological theory on government choices of isolation versus quarantine strategies in epidemics

Case	Air or Direct Transmission	High or Low Health Care Capacity	High or Low Ability to Escape Quarantine	Outcome: Expected (E) and Observed (O)
SARS 2003 in Taiwan, Canada,	Air	H	H	Unclear Prediction; Quarantine (O)
SARS 2003 in Hong Kong, Singapore	Air	H	L	Quarantine (E) Quarantine (O)
SARS 2003 in Vietnam	Air	L	H	Quarantine (E) Quarantine (O)
SARS 2003 in China	Air	L	L	Quarantine (E) Quarantine (O)
Ebola 2013–2015 in the United States, EU countries	Direct	H	H	Isolation (E) Isolation (O)
No cases	Direct	H	L	Isolation (E)
Ebola 2013–2015 in Guinea, Liberia, Sierra Leone	Direct	L	H	Unclear Prediction; Liberia attempted quarantine, others did not
No cases	Direct	L	L	Unclear Prediction

of variables as they move from the simplified typological theory to the within-case analysis of individual cases. In our example, with three dichotomous variables, we have two to the power of three or eight possible combinations. These are outlined in Table 4.2.

Fourth, the researcher deductively thinks through how each combination of variables might interact and what the expected outcome should be for each row. This is the step at which the researcher integrates the constituent theories that created the typological space into a single typological theory that provides the expected outcome for every combination of variables. In practice, a typological theory is rarely fully specified, as the researcher may lack a strong theoretical prior for every possible combination of the independent variables. Still, it is useful to think through possible interactions and specify expected outcomes deductively to the extent possible. Table 4.2 identifies the expected outcome for combinations that lead to clear and strong predictions on outcomes, such as combinations where all three independent variables point to the same expected outcome and interaction effects are unlikely. Table 4.2 codes a question mark for combinations in which the independent variables push toward different outcomes.

Fifth, after this deductive construction of the first draft of the typological theory, the researcher can use their preliminary empirical knowledge of extant historical cases to classify these cases into their respective types or rows. This stage allows for some iteration between the researcher's preliminary theoretical expectations and their initial knowledge of the empirical cases. Quick initial comparisons of the cases might lead to revisions to the theoretical typology and/or to the remeasurement and reclassification of cases. For example, if cases are in the same row – that is, they have fully similar combinations of the values of the independent variables – but they have different outcomes, they pose anomalies for the emerging theory. A quick examination of these cases might lead to revisions in the typology or the measurement of the variables in the cases in question, or deeper process tracing may be necessary to analyze why the cases have different outcomes. The example in Table 4.2 includes countries that had a significant number of SARS cases in 2003 or Ebola cases in 2013–2015, and it also includes some countries that had a few Ebola cases but public debates over a possible quarantine. The codings are based on very limited and preliminary knowledge of the values of the variables in each case, particularly the measurement of the ability of individuals to escape quarantined areas.

After iterating between the typological theory and the classification of extant cases to resolve all the discrepancies that can be addressed quickly and easily with the benefit of secondary sources, the researcher can undertake the sixth step: using the refined typological theory to select cases for deeper research that uses process tracing. The refined typological theory makes it easy to assess which cases fit various comparative research designs and inferential purposes: most-similar cases (cases that differ on one independent variable and on the outcome), least-similar cases (cases with the same outcome and only one independent variable in common), deviant cases (cases without the predicted outcome), cases with a high value on one independent variable, and typologically similar cases (cases in the same type or row and with the same outcome). In this example, interesting cases worth studying are those of Liberia, Sierra Leone, and Guinea. The theory does not make a strong prediction for the combination of variables evident in the cases of Sierra Leone, Guinea, and Liberia in 2013–2015 because the high ability of individuals to escape quarantine and the low capacity to isolate and treat patients push in opposite directions. Comparisons among these cases could prove fruitful in understanding why only Liberia attempted a quarantine.

Vietnam is also an interesting case worthy of study, as it was fairly successful in containing SARS despite limited health resources (Rothstein et al., 2003: 107). This makes it a least-likely case that succeeded. Canada and Taiwan are worthy of study as well, as the theory does not give a strong prediction on how countries with high health care capacity (and here, strong democratic cultures) would respond to airborne epidemics, and both countries resorted to quarantines.

This is a "building block" approach in several senses: it builds on theories about individual variables or mechanisms, theorizes about different combinations of these variables, uses individual case studies to validate the theorization on each combination of variables or "type" of case, and cumulatively charts out different types or paths to the outcome of interest. If there are limited interaction effects, individual variables, or even combinations of variables, will behave similarly across types, but typological theorizing does not presume or require such constant or simple interaction effects. Its strongest generalizations focus on the cases within each type. This prioritizes theoretical intension – making strong statements about well-defined subtypes that cover relatively few cases – while it sacrifices some degree of parsimony, as each combination or path can have its own explanation. Typological theorizing does not necessarily aspire to single-variable generalizations that apply to the whole population, but if such generalizations exist, it can still uncover them. In our example, both the theory and the extant cases suggest that quarantines are far more likely for airborne epidemics.

4.7 Generalizing – Carefully and Contingently – from Cases

Researchers in both the qualitative and quantitative traditions are rightly cautious about generalizing from individual case studies to broad populations. Case studies are not optimal for generalizing in the sense of estimating average effects for a population, as statistical studies aim to do. In addition, when process tracing reveals that the outcome in a case was due to mechanisms whose enabling conditions are rare or unique, little or no generalization beyond the case is possible. Even when findings do generalize from individual cases, it can be difficult to identify exactly the scope conditions in which they apply.

Yet case studies contribute to forms of generalization that are different from average population-level effects and that are pragmatically useful for policy-makers. Cases that are typical, most-likely, least-likely, deviant, and high on the value of a particular independent variable can all contribute to various forms of generalization even if they do not always provide clear guidelines on the scope conditions for generalizations. And sometimes cases do allow inferences about scope conditions – the clearer understanding of causal mechanisms that often emerges from process tracing can provide information on the conditions under which these mechanisms operate, and prior knowledge can indicate how common those conditions are. Just as a case study can uncover causal mechanisms that are relatively unique, it can also identify mechanisms that prove generalizable to large populations. In addition, typological theorizing can develop contingent generalizations about cases that share combinations of variables. Researchers can also develop cumulatively better knowledge of a phenomenon as they build upon and revise typological theories through the study of additional or subsequent cases.

These forms of generalization from case studies are Bayesian in the sense that they depend on prior theoretical knowledge and knowledge about the prevalence of the scope conditions thought to enable causal mechanisms to operate. Prior knowledge on both how causal mechanisms operate and where/under what conditions they operate can be updated through the study of individual cases. As prior knowledge is usually incomplete, however, generalization from cases is potentially fallible. Researchers can make the mistake of either over-generalizing or under-generalizing from cases. Process-tracing research on additional cases, as well as statistical studies of newly modeled mechanisms, can further test whether generalizations about causal mechanisms hold, and whether they need to be modified. Careful generalizations from case studies can thus contribute to cumulating policy-relevant knowledge about causal processes and the conditions under which they operate.

References

Battilana, J. and Dorado, S. (2010) "Building sustainable hybrid organizations: The case of commercial microfinance organizations," *Academy of Management Journal*, 53(6), 1419–1440.

Bennett, A. (2013) "Causal mechanisms and typological theories in the study of civil conflict" in Checkel, J. (ed.) *Transnational dynamics of civil war*. New York: Cambridge University Press, pp. 205–230.

Collier, D., Laporte, J., and Seawright, J. (2012) "Putting typologies to work: Concept formation, measurement, and analytic rigor," *Political Research Quarterly*, 65(1), 217–232.

Esping-Andersen, G. (1990) *The three worlds of welfare capitalism*. Hoboken, NJ: John Wiley and Sons.

Flyvbjerg, B. (2006) "Five misunderstandings about case-study research," *Qualitative Inquiry*, 12(2), 219–245.

Frieden, T., Damon, I., Bell, B., Kenyon, T., and Nichol, S. (2014) "Ebola 2014 – New challenges, new global response and responsibility," *New England Journal of Medicine*, 371(13), 177–1180.

George, A. L. and Bennett, A. (2005) *Case studies and theory development in the social sciences*. Cambridge, MA: MIT University Press.

Gerring, J. and Seawright, J. (2008) "Case selection techniques in case study research: A menu of qualitative and quantitative options," *Political Research Quarterly*, 61(2), 294–308.

Holland, P. W. (1986) "Statistics and causal inference," *Journal of the American Statistical Association*, 81(396), 945–960.

House of Commons International Development Committee. (2016) "Ebola: Responses to a public health emergency," Second Report of Session 2015–2016.

Howick, J., Glasziou, P., and Aronson, K. (2009) "The evolution of evidence hierarchies: What can Bradford Hill's 'guidelines for causation' contribute?" *Journal of the Royal Society of Medicine*, 102(5), 186–194.

King, G., Keohane, R., and Verba, S. (1994) *Designing social inquiry*. Princeton, NJ: Princeton University Press.

March, J., Sproull, L., and Tamuz, M. (1991) "Learning from samples of one or fewer," *Organization Science*, 2(1), 1–13.

Montori, V. M., Devereaux, P. J., Adhikari, N. K., et al. (2005) "Randomized trials stopped early for benefit: A systematic review," *JAMA*, 294(17), 2203–2209.

Mukherjee, S. (2019) "The promise and price of cellular therapies," *The New Yorker*, July 15.

Onishi, N. (2015) "Empty Ebola clinics in Liberia are seen as misstep in US relief effort," *The New York Times*, April 11.

Peters, T. and Waterman, R. (1982) *In search of excellence: Lessons from America's best-run companies*. New York: Harper and Row.

Pocock, S. J. (2006) "Current controversies in data monitoring for clinical trials," *Clinical Trials*, 3(6), 513–521.

Pray, L. (2008) "Genes, smoking, and lung cancer," *Nature Education*, 1(1), 73.

Ragin, C. (2006) "Set relations in social research: Evaluating their consistency and coverage," *Political Analysis*, 14(3), 291–310.

Ragin, C. (2008) *Redesigning social inquiry: Fuzzy sets and beyond*. Chicago, IL: University of Chicago Press.

Rapport, A. (2015) "Hard thinking about hard and easy cases in security studies," *Security Studies*, 24(3), 431–465.

Reece, S., Brown, C. S., Dunning, J., Chand, M. A., Zambon, M. C., and Jacobs. M. (2017) "The UK's multidisciplinary response to an Ebola epidemic," *Clinical Medicine*, 17(4), 332–337.

Rosenbaum, L. (2017) "Tragedy, perseverance, and chance – The story of CAR-T therapy," *The New England Journal of Medicine*, 377(14), 1313–1315.

Rothstein, M. A., Alcalde, M. G., Elster, N. R., et al. (2003) *Quarantine and isolation: Lessons learned from SARS*. A Report to the Centers for Disease Control and Prevention.

Sack, K., Fink, S., Belluck, P., and Nossiter, A. (2014) "How Ebola roared back," *The New York Times Magazine*, December 29.

Schneider, C. and Rohfling, I. (2013) "Combining QCA and process tracing in set-theoretic multimethod research," *Sociological Methods and Research*, 42(4), 559–597.

Schoofs, M. (1998) "The Berlin patient," *The New York Times Magazine*, June 21.

Seawright, J. (2016) "The case for selecting cases that are deviant or extreme on the independent variable," *Sociological Methods & Research*, 45(3), 493–525.

Sydes, M. R., Spiegelhalter, D. H., Altman, D. G., Babiker, A. B., and Parmar, M. K. B. (2004) "Systematic qualitative review of the literature on data monitoring committees for randomized controlled trials," *Clinical Trials*, 1(1), 60–79.

Will It Work Here? Using Case Studies to Generate 'Key Facts' About Complex Development Programs

Michael Woolcock

Immersion in the particular proved, as usual, essential for the catching of anything general.

Albert Hirschman[1]

[T]he bulk of the literature presently recommended for policy decisions ... cannot be used to identify "what works here". And this is not because it may fail to deliver in some particular cases [; it] is not because its advice fails to deliver what it can be expected to deliver ... The failing is rather that it is not designed to deliver the bulk of the *key facts* required to conclude that it will work here.

Nancy Cartwright and Jeremy Hardie[2]

5.1 Introduction: In Search of 'Key Facts'

Over the last two decades, social scientists across the disciplines have worked tirelessly to enhance the precision of claims made about the impact of development projects, seeking to formally verify 'what works' as part of a broader campaign for 'evidence-based policy-making' conducted on the basis of 'rigorous evaluations'.[3] In an age of heightened public scrutiny of aid budgets and policy effectiveness, and of rising calls by development

The views expressed in this chapter are those of the author alone, and should not be attributed to the World Bank, its executive directors, or the countries they represent. This chapter refines and updates Woolcock (2013), extending issues with which I have been wrestling for many years. I am grateful for the clarifications, corrections, and insights I have gained over many years from colleagues too numerous to mention, even as, of course, errors of fact and interpretation expressed herein remain solely my own.

[1] Hirschman (1967, p. 3).   [2] Cartwright and Hardie (2012, p. 137); emphasis added.

[3] For present purposes I do not want to engage in philosophical debates about what exactly constitutes a 'fact' (or 'key facts'); such issues are amply discussed in the cases presented in Howlett and Morgan (2010). Here I interpret 'key facts' to mean, pragmatically, "crucially important (but too often overlooked) issues that decision-makers, upon learning that a certain development intervention demonstrably worked 'there', need to take into account when considering whether they too can expect similar results if they adopt this intervention 'here'."

agencies themselves for greater accountability and transparency, it was deemed no longer acceptable to claim success for a project if selected beneficiaries or officials merely expressed satisfaction, if necessary administrative requirements had been upheld, or if large sums had been dispersed without undue controversy. For their part, researchers seeking publication in elite empirical journals, where the primary criteria for acceptance was (and remains) the integrity of one's 'identification strategy' – that is, the methods deployed to verify a causal relationship – faced powerful incentives to actively promote not merely more and better impact evaluations, but methods, such as randomized controlled trials (RCTs) or quasi-experimental designs (QEDs), squarely focused on isolating the singular effects of particular variables. Moreover, by claiming to be adopting (or at least approximating) the 'gold standard' methodological procedures of biomedical science, champions of RCTs in particular could impute to themselves the moral and epistemological high ground as 'the white lab coat guys' of development research.

The heightened focus on RCTs as the privileged basis on which to impute causal claims in development research and project evaluation has been subjected to increasingly trenchant critique,[4] but for present purposes my objective is not to rehearse, summarize, or contribute to these debates per se; it is, rather, to assert that these preoccupations have drained attention from an equally important issue, namely our basis for generalizing any claims about impact from different types of interventions across time, contexts, groups, and scales of operation. If identification and causality are debates about 'internal validity', then generalization and extrapolation are concerns about 'external validity'.[5] It surely matters for the latter that we first have a good handle on the former, but even the cleanest estimation of a given project's impact does not axiomatically provide warrant for confidently inferring that similar results can be expected if that project is scaled up or

---

[4] See, among others, Cartwright (2007), Deaton (2010), Deaton and Cartwright (2018), Pritchett and Sandefur (2015), Picciotto (2012), Ravallion (2009), and Shaffer (2011). Nobel laureate James Heckman has been making related critiques of "randomization bias" in the evaluation of social policy experiments for more than twenty years. And as Achen (Chapter 3, this volume) stresses, RCTs have a long (and not always glorious) history in policy research, the lessons from which most contemporary advocates of RCTs seem completely unaware of.

[5] The distinctions between construct, internal and external validity form, along with replication, the four core elements of the classic quasi-experimental methodological framework of Cook and Campbell (1979). In later work, Cook (2001) was decidedly more circumspect about the extent to which social scientists (of any kind) can draw empirical generalizations. For those engaged in development policy, Williams (2020) argues that rather than focusing on general external validity concerns, the more specific focus should be on identifying how evidence can be used to more accurately discern whether and how a given intervention might be optimally fitted to a novel context.

replicated elsewhere.[6] Yet too often this is precisely what happens: having expended enormous effort and resources in procuring a clean estimate of a project's impact, and having successfully defended the finding under vigorous questioning at professional seminars and review sessions, the standards for inferring that similar results can be expected elsewhere or when 'scaled up' suddenly drop away markedly. The 'rigorous result', if 'significantly positive', slips all too quickly into implicit or explicit claims that 'we know' the intervention 'works' (even perhaps assuming the status of a veritable 'best practice'), the very 'rigor' of 'the evidence' invoked to promote or defend the project's introduction into a novel (perhaps highly uncertain) context. In short, because an intervention demonstrably worked 'there', we all too often and too confidently presume it will also work 'here'.

Even if concerns about the weak external validity of RCTs/QEDs – or, for that matter, any methodology – of development interventions are acknowledged by most researchers, decision-makers still lack a usable framework by which to engage in the vexing deliberations surrounding whether and when it is at least plausible to infer that a given impact result (positive or negative) 'there' is likely to obtain 'here'. Equally importantly, we lack a coherent system-level imperative requiring decision-makers to take these concerns seriously, not only so that we avoid intractable, nonresolvable debates about the effectiveness of entire portfolios of activity ('community health', 'justice reform') or abstractions ('do women's empowerment programs work?'[7]), but, more positively and constructively, so that we can enter into context-specific discussions about the relative merits of (and priority that should be accorded to) roads, irrigation, cash transfers, immunization, legal reform, etc., with some degree of grounded confidence – that is, on the basis of appropriate metrics, theory, experience, and (as we shall see) trajectories and theories of change.

Though the external validity problem is widespread and vastly consequential for lives, resources, and careers, this chapter's modest goal is not to provide a "tool kit" for "resolving it" but rather to promote a broader conversation about how external validity concerns might be more adequately

---

[6] The veracity of extrapolating given findings to a broader population in large part turns on sampling quality; the present concern is with enhancing the analytical bases for making comparisons about likely impact between different populations, scales of operation (e.g., pilot projects to national programs), and across time.

[7] The insightful review of 'community driven development' programs by Mansuri and Rao (2012) emphasizes the importance of understanding context when making claims about the effectiveness of such programs (and their generalizability), though it has not always been read this way.

addressed in the practice of development. (Given that the bar, at present, is very low, facilitating any such conversations will be a nontrivial achievement.) As such, this chapter presents ideas to think with. Assessing the extent to which empirical claims about a given project's impact can be generalized is only partly a technical endeavor; it is equally a political, organizational, and philosophical issue, and as such usable and legitimate responses will inherently require extended deliberation in each instance. To this end, the chapter is structured in five sections. Following this introduction, Section 5.2 provides a general summary of selected contributions to the issue of external validity from a range of disciplines and fields. Section 5.3 outlines three domains of inquiry ('causal density', 'implementation capabilities', 'reasoned expectations') that, for present purposes, constitute the key elements of an applied framework for assessing the external validity of development interventions generally, and 'complex' projects in particular. Section 5.4 considers the role analytic case studies can play in responding constructively to these concerns. Section 5.5 concludes.

5.2 External Validity Concerns Across the Disciplines: A Short Tour

Development professionals are far from the only social scientists, or philosophers or scientists of any kind, who are confronting the challenges posed by external validity concerns.[8] Consider first the field of psychology. It is safe to say that many readers of this chapter, in their undergraduate days, participated in various psychology research studies. The general purpose of those studies, of course, was (and continues to be) to test various hypotheses about how and when individuals engage in strategic decision-making, display prejudice toward certain groups, perceive ambiguous stimuli, respond to peer pressure, and the like. But how generalizable are these findings? In a detailed and fascinating paper, Henrich, Heine, and Norenzayan (2010a) reviewed hundreds of such studies, most of which had been conducted on college students in North American and European universities. Despite the limited geographical scope of this sample, most of the studies they reviewed readily inferred (implicitly or explicitly) that their findings were indicative of 'humanity' or reflected something fundamental about 'human nature'. Subjecting these broad claims of generalizability

---

[8] See, among others, March, Sproull, and Tamuz (1991), Morgan (2012), Ruzzene (2012), and Forrester (2017).

to critical scrutiny (for example, by examining the results from studies where particular 'games' and experiments had been applied to populations elsewhere in the world), Henrich et al. concluded that the participants in the original psychological studies were in fact rather WEIRD – western, educated, industrialized, rich and democratic – since few of the findings of the original studies could be replicated in "non-WEIRD" contexts (see also Henrich, Heine, and Norenzayan 2010b).

Consider next the field of biomedicine, whose methods development researchers are so often invoked to adopt. In the early stages of designing a new pharmaceutical drug, it is common to test prototypes on mice, doing so on the presumption that mouse physiology is sufficiently close to human physiology to enable results for the former to be inferred for the latter. Indeed, over the last several decades a particular mouse – known as 'Black 6' – has been genetically engineered so that biomedical researchers around the world are able to work on mice that are literally genetically identical. This sounds ideal for inferring causal results: biomedical researchers in Norway and New Zealand know they are effectively working on clones, and thus can accurately compare findings. Except that it turns out that in certain key respects mouse physiology is different enough from human physiology to have compromised "years and billions of dollars" (Kolata 2013: A19) of biomedical research on drugs for treating burns, trauma, and sepsis, as reported in a *New York Times* summary of a major (thirty-nine coauthors) paper published in the prestigious *Proceedings of the National Academy of Sciences* (see Seok et al. 2013). In an award-winning science journalism article, Engber (2011) summarized research showing that Black 6 was not even representative of mice – indeed, upon closer inspection, Black 6 turns out to be "a teenaged, alcoholic couch potato with a weakened immune system, and he might be a little hard of hearing." An earlier study published in *The Lancet* (Rothwell 2005) reviewed nearly 200 RCTs in biomedical and clinical research in search of answers to the important question "To whom do the results of this trial apply?" and concluded, rather ominously, that the methodological quality of many of the published studies was such that even their internal validity, let alone their external validity, was questionable. Needless to say, it is more than a little disquieting to learn that even the people who do actually wear white lab coats for a living have their own serious struggles with external validity.[9]

---

[9] It is worth pointing out that the actual "gold standard" in clinical trials requires not merely the random assignment of subjects to treatment and control groups, but that the allocation be 'triple blind' (i.e.,

Consider next a wonderful simulation paper in health research, which explores the efficacy of two different strategies for identifying the optimal solution to a given clinical problem, a process the authors refer to as "searching the fitness landscape" (Eppstein et al. 2012).[10] Strategy one entails adopting a verified 'best practice' solution: you attempt to solve the problem, in effect, by doing what experts elsewhere have determined is the best approach. Strategy two effectively entails making it up as you go along: you work with others and learn from collective experience to iterate your way to a customized 'best fit'[11] solution in response to the particular circumstances you encounter. The problem these two strategies confront is then itself varied. Initially the problem is quite straight forward, exhibiting what is called a 'smooth fitness landscape' – think of being asked to climb an Egyptian pyramid, with its familiar symmetrical sides. Over time the problem being confronted is made more complex, its fitness landscape becoming increasingly rugged – think of being asked to ascend a steep mountain, with craggy, idiosyncratic features. Which strategy is best for which problem? It turns out the 'best practice' approach is best – but only as long as you are climbing a pyramid (i.e., facing a problem with a smooth fitness landscape). As soon as you tweak the fitness landscape just a little, however, making it even slightly 'rugged', the efficacy of 'best practice' solutions fall away precipitously, and the 'best fit' approach surges to the lead. One can over-interpret these results, of course, but given the powerful imperatives in development to identify "best practices" (as verified, preferably, by an RCT/QED) and replicate "what works," it is worth pondering the implications of the fact that the 'fitness landscapes' we face in development are probably far more likely to be rugged than smooth, and that compelling

neither the subjects themselves, the front-line researchers, nor the principal investigators know who has been assigned to which group until after the study is complete), that control groups receive a placebo treatment (i.e., a treatment that looks and feels like a real treatment, but is in fact not one at all), and that subjects cross over between groups mid-way through the study (i.e., the control group becomes the treatment group, and vice versa) – all to deal with well-understood sources of bias (e.g., Hawthorn effects) that could otherwise compromise the integrity of the study. Needless to say, it is hard to imagine that more than handful of policy intervention, let alone development projects, could come remotely close to upholding these standards.

[10] In a more applied version of this idea, Pritchett, Samji, and Hammer (2012) argue for "crawling the design space" as the strategy of choice for navigating rugged fitness environments.

[11] The concept of 'best fit' comes to development primarily through the work of David Booth (2012); in the Eppstein et al. (2012) formulation, the equivalent concept for determining optimal solutions to novel problems in different contexts emerges through what they refer to as 'quality improvement collaboratives' (QICs). Their study effectively sets up an empirical showdown between RCTs and QICs as rival strategies for complex problem solving.

experimental evidence (supporting a long tradition in the history of science) now suggests that promulgating best practice solutions is a demonstrably inferior strategy for resolving them.

Two final studies demonstrate the crucial importance of implementation and context for understanding external validity concerns in development. Bold et al. (2013) deploy the novel technique of subjecting RCT results themselves to an RCT test of their generalizability using different types of implementing agencies. Earlier studies from India (e.g., Banerjee et al. 2007, Duflo, Dupas, and Kremer 2012, Muralidharan and Sundararaman 2010) famously found that, on the basis of an RCT, contract teachers were demonstrably 'better' (i.e., both more effective and less costly) than regular teachers in terms of helping children to learn. A similar result had been found in Kenya, but as with the India finding, the implementing agent was an NGO. Bold et al. took essentially an identical project design but deployed an evaluation procedure in which 192 schools in Kenya were randomly allocated either to a control group, an NGO-implemented group, or a Ministry of Education-implemented group. The findings were highly diverse: the NGO-implemented group did quite well relative to the control group (as expected), but the Ministry of Education group actually performed *worse* than the control group. In short, the impact of "the project" was a function not only of its design but, crucially and inextricably, of its implementation and context. As the authors aptly conclude, "the effects of this intervention appear highly fragile to the involvement of carefully-selected non-governmental organizations. Ongoing initiatives to produce a fixed, evidence-based menu of effective development interventions will be potentially misleading if interventions are defined at the school, clinic, or village level without reference to their institutional context" (Bold et al. 2013: 7).[12]

A similar conclusion, this time with implications for the basis on which policy interventions might be 'scaled up', emerges from an evaluation of a small business registration program in Brazil (see Bruhn and McKenzie 2013). Intuition and some previous research suggests that a barrier to growth faced by small unregistered firms is that their very informality denies them access to legal protection and financial resources; if ways could be found to lower the barriers to registration – for example, by reducing fees, expanding

---

[12] See also the important work of Denizer, Kaufmann, and Kraay (2012), who assess the performance of more than 6,000 World Bank projects from inception to completion, a central finding of which is the key role played by high-quality task team leaders (i.e., those responsible for the project's management and implementation on a day-to-day basis) in projects that are not only consistently rated 'satisfactory' but manage to become 'satisfactory' after a mid-term review deeming their project 'unsatisfactory'.

information campaigns promoting the virtues of registration, etc. – many otherwise unregistered firms would surely avail themselves of the opportunity to register, with both the firms themselves and the economy more generally enjoying the fruits. This was the basis on which the state of Minas Gerais in Brazil sought to expand a business start-up simplification program into rural areas: a pilot program that had been reasonably successful in urban areas now sought to 'scale up' into more rural and remote districts, the initial impacts extrapolated by its promoters to the new levels and places of operation. At face value, this was an entirely sensible expectation, one that could also be justified on intrinsic grounds: one could argue that all small firms, irrespective of location, should as a matter of principle be able to register. Deploying an innovative evaluation strategy centered on the use of existing administrative data, Bruhn and McKenzie found that despite faithful implementation the effects of the expanded program on firm registration were net *negative*; isolated villagers, it seems, were so deeply wary of the state that heightened information campaigns on the virtues of small business registration only confirmed their suspicions that the government's real purposes were probably sinister and predatory, and so even those owners that once might have registered their business now did not. If only with the benefit of hindsight, 'what worked' in one place and at one scale of operation was clearly inadequate grounds for inferring what could be expected elsewhere at a much larger one.[13]

In this brief tour[14] of fields ranging from psychology, biomedicine, and clinical health to education, regulation, and criminology we have compelling empirical evidence that inferring external validity to given empirical results – that is, generalizing findings from one group, place, implementation modality, or scale of operation to another – is a highly fraught exercise. As the opening epigraph wisely intones, evidence supporting claims of a significant impact 'there', *even (or especially) when that evidence is a product of a putatively rigorous research design*, does not "deliver the bulk of the key facts required to conclude that it will work here." What might those missing

---

[13] See also the insightful discussion of the criminology impact evaluation literature in Sampson (2013), who argues strongly for exploring the notion of "contextual causality" as a basis for inferring what might work elsewhere. Lamont (2012) also provides a thoughtful overview of evaluation issues from a sociological perspective.

[14] Econometricians have recently begun to focus more concertedly on external validity concerns (e.g., Allcott and Mullainathan, 2012; Angrist and Fernandez-Val, 2010), though their contributions to date have largely focused on technical problems emergent within evaluations of large social programs in OECD countries (most notably the United States) rather than identifying pragmatic guidelines for replicating or expanding different types of projects in different types of (developing) country contexts.

"key facts" be? Clearly some interventions can be scaled and replicated more readily than others, so how might the content of those "facts" vary between different types of interventions?

In the next section, I propose three categories of issues that can be used to interrogate given development interventions and the basis of the claims made regarding their effectiveness; I argue that these categories can yield potentially useful and usable "key facts" to better inform pragmatic decision-making regarding the likelihood that results obtained 'there' can be expected 'here'. In Section 2.4 I argue that analytic case studies can be a particularly fruitful empirical resource informing the tone and terms of this interrogation, especially for complex development interventions. I posit that this fruitfulness rises in proportion to the 'complexity' of the intervention: the higher the complexity, the more salient (even necessary) inputs from analytic case studies become as contributors to the decision-making process.

5.3   Elements of an Applied Framework for Identifying 'Key Facts'

Heightened sensitivity to external validity concerns does not axiomatically solve the problem of how exactly to make difficult decisions regarding whether, when, and how to replicate and/or scale up (or, for that matter, cancel) interventions on the basis of an initial empirical result, a challenge that becomes incrementally harder as interventions themselves, or constituent elements of them, become more 'complex' (defined below). Even if we have eminently reasonable grounds for accepting a claim about a given project's impact 'there' (with 'that group', at this 'size', implemented by 'these people' using 'this approach'), under what conditions can we confidently infer that the project will generate similar results 'here' (or with 'this group', or if it is 'scaled up', or if implemented by 'those people' deploying 'that approach')? We surely need firmer analytical foundations on which to engage in these deliberations; in short, we need more and better "key facts," and a corresponding theoretical framework able to both generate and accurately interpret those facts.

One could plausibly defend a number of domains in which such "key facts" might reside, but for present purposes I focus on three:[15] 'causal density' (the

---

[15] These three domains are derived from my reading of the literature, numerous discussions with senior operational colleagues, and my hard-won experience both assessing complex development interventions (e.g., Barron, Diprose, and Woolcock, 2011) and advising others considering their expansion/

extent to which an intervention or its constituent elements are 'complex'); 'implementation capability' (the extent to which a designated organizational entity in the new context can in fact faithfully implement the type of intervention under consideration); and 'reasoned expectations' (the extent to which claims about actual or potential impact are understood within the context of a grounded theory of change specifying what can reasonably be expected to be achieved by when). I address each of these domains in turn.

5.3.1   Causal Density

Conducting even the most routine development intervention is difficult, in the sense that considerable effort needs to be expended at all stages over long periods of time, and that doing so may entail carrying out duties in places that are dangerous ('fragile states') or require navigating morally wrenching situations (dealing with overt corruption, watching children die).[16] If there is no such thing as a 'simple' development project, we need at least a framework for distinguishing between different types and degrees of complexity, since this has a major bearing on the likelihood that a project (indeed, a system or intervention of any kind) will function in predictable ways, which in turn shapes the probability that impact claims associated with it can be generalized.

One entry point into analytical discussions of complexity is of course 'complexity theory', a field to which social scientists engaging with policy issues have increasingly begun to contribute and learn,[17] but for present purposes I will create some basic distinctions using the concept of 'causal density' (see Manzi 2012). An entity with low causal density is one whose constituent elements interact in precisely predictable ways: a wrist watch, for example, may be a marvel of craftsmanship and micro-engineering, but its genius actually lies in its relative 'simplicity': in the finest watches, the cogs comprising the internal mechanism are connected with such a degree of precision that they keep near perfect time over many years, but this is possible because every single aspect of the process is perfectly understood.

---

replication elsewhere. In the spirit in which this chapter is written, I remain very open to the possibility that other domains should also be considered.

[16] The idea of causal density comes from neuroscience, computing, and physics, and can be succinctly defined as "the number of independent significant interactions among a system's components" (Shanahan, 2008: 041924).

[17] A sampling of this literature across the disciplines includes Byrne (2013), Byrne and Callighan (2013), Colander and Kupers (2014), Ramalingam (2014), and Room (2011).

Development interventions (or aspects of interventions[18]) with low causal density are ideally suited for assessment via techniques such as RCTs because it is reasonable to expect that the impact of a particular element can be isolated and empirically discerned, and the corresponding adjustments or policy decisions made. Indeed, the most celebrated RCTs in the development literature – assessing deworming pills, textbooks, malaria nets, classroom size, cameras in classrooms to reduce teacher absenteeism – have largely been undertaken with interventions (or aspect of interventions) with relatively low causal density. If we are even close to reaching "proof of concept" with interventions such as immunization and iodized salt it is largely because the underlying physiology and biochemistry *has come to be* perfectly understood, and their implementation (while still challenging logistically) requires relatively basic, routinized behavior on the part of front-line agents (see Pritchett and Woolcock 2004). In short, attaining "proof of concept" means the proverbial 'black box' has essentially been eliminated – everything going on inside the 'box' (i.e., the dynamics behind every mechanism connecting inputs and outcomes) is known or knowable.[19]

Entities with high causal density, on the other hand, are characterized by high uncertainty, which is a function of the numerous pathways and feedback loops connecting inputs, actions, and outcomes, the entity's openness to exogenous influences, and the capacity of constituent elements (most notably people) to exercise discretion (i.e., to act independently of or in accordance with rules, expectations, precedent, passions, professional norms, or self-interest). Parenting is perhaps the most familiar example of a high causal density activity. Humans have literally been raising children forever, but as every parent knows, there are often many factors (known and unknown) intervening between their actions and the behavior of their offspring, who are intensely subject to peer pressure and willfully act in accordance with their own (often fluctuating, seemingly quixotic) wishes. Despite millions of years and billions of 'trials', we have not produced anything remotely like "proof of concept" with parenting, even if there are certainly useful rules of thumb. Each generation produces its own bestselling

---

[18] See Ludwig Kling, and Mullainathan (2011) for a discussion of the virtues of conducting delineated 'mechanism experiments' within otherwise large social policy interventions.

[19] Such knowledge is also readily shareable and cumulative over time. The seminal 2015 paper in physics documenting the existence and weight of the Higgs boson particle, for example, set a "world record" for the number of coauthors: an astounding 5,154 (see Aad et al., 2015). In contrast, books marking the centenary of World War I, perhaps the seminal geopolitical event of the twentieth century, continue to debate lingering points of disagreement, and are mostly written by a single historian.

'manual' based on what it regards as the prevailing scientific and collective wisdom, but even if a given parent dutifully internalizes and enacts the latest manual's every word it is far from certain that his/her child will emerge as a minimally functional and independent young adult; conversely, a parent may know nothing of the book or unwittingly engage in seemingly contrarian practices and yet happily preside over the emergence of a perfectly normal young adult.[20]

Assessing the veracity of development interventions (or aspects of them) with high causal density (e.g., women's empowerment projects, programs to change adolescent sexual behavior in the face of the HIV/AIDS epidemic) requires evaluation strategies tailored to accommodate this reality. Precisely because the 'impact' (wholly or in part) of these interventions often cannot be truly isolated, and is highly contingent on the quality of implementation, any observed impact is very likely to change over time, across contexts, and at different scales of implementation; as such, we need evaluation strategies able to capture these dynamics and provide correspondingly usable recommendations. Crucially, strategies used to assess high causal density interventions are not "less rigorous" than those used to assess their low causal density counterpart; any evaluation strategy, like any tool, is "rigorous" to the extent it deftly and ably responds to the questions being asked of it.[21]

To operationalize causal density we need a basic analytical framework for distinguishing more carefully between these 'low' and 'high' extremes: we can agree that a lawn mower and a family are qualitatively different 'systems', but how can we array the spaces in between?[22] Four questions can be proposed to distinguish between different types of problems in development.[23] First, how many person-to-person transactions are required?[24] Second, how much

---

[20] Such books are still useful, of course, and diligent parents do well to read them; the point is that at best the books provide general guidance at the margins on particular issues, which is incorporated into the larger storehouse of knowledge the parent has gleaned from their own parents, through experience, common sense, and the advice of significant others.

[21] That is, hammers, saws, and screwdrivers are not "rigorous" tools; they become so to the extent they are correctly deployed in response to the distinctive problem they are designed to solve.

[22] In the complexity theory literature, this space is characteristically arrayed according to whether problems are 'simple', 'complicated', 'complex', and 'chaotic' (see Ramalingam and Jones, 2009). There is much overlap in these distinctions with the framework I present herein, but my concern (and that of the colleagues with whom I work most closely on this) is primarily with articulating pragmatic questions for arraying development interventions, which leads to slightly different categories.

[23] The first two questions (or dimensions) come from Pritchett and Woolcock (2004); the latter two from Andrews, Pritchett, and Woolcock (2017).

[24] Producing a minimally educated child, for example, requires countless interactions between teacher and student (and between students) over many years (roughly 1,000 hours per year of instruction); the

discretion is required of front-line implementing agents?[25] Third, how much pressure do implementing agents face to do something other than respond constructively to the problem?[26] Fourth, to what extent are implementing agents required to deploy solutions from a known menu or to innovate in situ?[27] These questions are most useful when applied to specific operational challenges; rather than asserting that (or trying to determine whether) one 'sector' in development is more or less 'complex' than another (e.g., 'health' versus 'infrastructure'), it is more instructive to begin with a locally nominated and prioritized problem (e.g., how can workers in this factory be afforded adequate working conditions and wages?) and asking of it the four questions posed above to interrogate its component elements. An example of an array of such problems within 'health' is provided in Table 5.1; by providing categorical yes/no answers to these four questions we can arrive at five discrete kinds of problems in development: technocratic, logistical, implementation intensive services, implementation intensive obligations, and complex.

So understood, problems are truly 'complex' that are highly transaction intensive, require considerable discretion by implementing agents, yield powerful pressures for those agents to do something other than implement a solution, and have no known (ex ante) solution.[28] The eventual solutions to these *kinds* of problems are likely to be highly idiosyncratic and context

raising or lowering of interest rates is determined at periodic meetings by a handful of designated technical professionals.

[25] Being an effective social worker requires making wrenching discretionary decisions (e.g., is this family sufficiently dysfunctional that I should withdraw the children and make them wards of the state?); reducing some problems to invariant rules (e.g., the age at which young adults are sufficiently mature to drive, vote, or drink alcohol) should in principle make their implementation relatively straightforward by reducing discretion entirely, but as Gupta (2012) powerfully shows for India, weak administrative infrastructure (e.g., no birth certificates or land registers) can render even the most basic demographic questions (age, number of children, size of land holding) matters for discretionary interpretation by front-line agents, with all the potential for abuse and arbitrariness that goes with it.

[26] Virtually everyone agrees that babies should be immunized, that potholes should be fixed, and that children should be educated; professionals implementing these activities will face little political resistance or 'temptations' to do otherwise (except perhaps just not showing up for work). Those enforcing border patrols, regulating firms, or collecting property taxes, on the other hand, will encounter all manner of resistance and 'temptations' (e.g., bribes, kickbacks) to be less than diligent.

[27] Even when a problem is clear and well understood (e.g., sugary foods, a sedentary lifestyle, and smoking are not good for one's health), it may or may not map onto a known, universal, readily implementable solution.

[28] In more vernacular language we might characterize such problems as 'wicked' (after Churchman, 1967).

Table 5.1 Classification of activities in 'health'

	Local discretion?	Transaction intensive?	Contentious; Tempting alternatives?	Known technology?	Type of implementation challenge
Iodization of salt	No	No	No	Yes	*Technocratic* (policy decree + light implementation)
Vaccinations	No	Yes	No	Yes	*Logistical* (implementation intensive, but 'easy')
Ambulatory curative care	Yes	Yes	No(ish)	Yes	*Implementation Intensive Services* (welcomed, expected)
Regulating private providers	Yes	Yes	Yes	Yes	*Implementation Intensive Obligations* (resisted, evaded)
Promoting preventive health	Yes	Yes	No	No	*Complex* (Implementation intensive, motivation hard, solutions require continuous innovation)

Source: Adapted from Pritchett (2013)

specific; as such, and irrespective of the quality of the evaluation strategy used to discern their 'impact', the default assumption regarding their external validity should be, I argue, zero. Put differently, in such instances the burden of proof should lie with those claiming that the result *is* in fact generalizable. (This burden might be slightly eased for 'implementation intensive' problems, but some considerable burden remains nonetheless.) I hasten to add, however, that this does not mean others facing similarly 'complex' (or 'implementation intensive') challenges elsewhere have little to learn from a successful (or failed) intervention's experiences; on the contrary, it may be highly instructive, but its "lessons" reside less in the content of its final design characteristics than in the processes of exploration and incremental understanding by which a solution was proposed, refined, supported, funded, implemented, refined again, and assessed – that is, in the ideas, principles, and inspiration from which, over time, a solution was crafted and enacted. This is the point at which analytic case studies can demonstrate their true utility, as I discuss in the following sections.

5.3.2   Implementation Capability

Another danger stemming from a single-minded focus on a project's design characteristics as the causal agent determining observed outcomes is that implementation dynamics are largely overlooked, or at least assumed to be nonproblematic. If, as a result of an RCT (or series of RCTs), a given conditional cash transfer (CCT) program is deemed to have 'worked',[29] we all too quickly presume that it can and should be introduced elsewhere, in effect ascribing to it "proof of concept" status. Again, we can be properly convinced of the veracity of a given evaluation's empirical findings and yet have grave concerns about its generalizability. If from a 'causal density' perspective our four questions would likely reveal that in fact any given CCT comprises numerous elements, some of which are 'complex', from an 'implementation capability' perspective the concern is more prosaic: how confident can we be that any designated implementing agency in the new country or context (e.g., Ministry of Social Welfare) would in fact have the capability to do so, at the designated scale of operation?

Recent research and everyday experience suggests, again, that the burden of proof should lie with those claiming or presuming that the designated implementing agency in the proposed context is indeed up to the task (Pritchett and Sandefur 2015). Consider the delivery of mail. It is hard to think of a less contentious and 'less complex' task: everybody wants their mail to be delivered accurately and punctually, and doing so is almost entirely a logistical exercise.[30] The procedures to be followed are unambiguous,

---

[29] See, among others, the extensive review of the empirical literature on CCTs provided in Fiszbein and Schady (2009); Baird et al. (2013) provide a systematic review of the effect of both conditional and unconditional cash transfer programs on education outcomes.

[30] Indeed, the high-profile advertising slogan of a large, private international parcel service is "We love logistics."

universally recognized (by international agreement), and entail little discretion on the part of implementing agents (sorters, deliverers). A recent empirical test of the capability of mail delivery systems around the world, however, yielded sobering results. Chong et al. (2014) sent letters to 10 nonexistent addresses in 159 countries, all of which were signatories to an international convention requiring them simply to return such letters to the country of origin (in this case the United States) within 90 days. How many countries were actually able to perform this most routine of tasks? In 25 countries *none* of the 10 letters came back within the designated timeframe; of countries in the bottom half of the world's education distribution the average return rate was 21 percent of the letters. Working with a broader cross-country dataset documenting the current levels and trends in state capability for implementation, Andrews, Pritchett, and Woolcock (2017) ruefully conclude that, by the end of the twenty-first century, only about a dozen of today's low-income countries will have acquired levels of state capability equal to that of today's least-rich OECD countries.[31]

The general point is that in many developing countries, especially the poorest, implementation capability is demonstrably low for 'logistical' tasks, let alone for 'complex' ones. 'Fragile states', almost by definition, cannot readily be assumed to be able to undertake complex tasks (such as responding to medical emergencies after natural disasters) even if such tasks are desperately needed there. And even if they are in fact able to undertake some complex projects (such as regulatory or tax reform), which would be admirable, yet again the burden of proof in these instances should reside with those arguing that such capability to implement the designated intervention does indeed exist (or can readily be acquired). For complex interventions as here defined, high-quality implementation is inherently and inseparably a constituent element of any success they may enjoy (see Honig 2018); the presence in novel contexts of implementing organizations with the requisite capability thus should be demonstrated rather than assumed by those seeking to replicate or expand 'complex' interventions.

5.3.3   Reasoned Expectations

The final domain of consideration, which I call 'reasoned expectations', focuses attention on an intervention's known or imputed trajectory of

---

[31] An applied strategy for responding to the challenges identified therein is presented in Andrews, Pritchett, and Woolcock (2013, 2017).

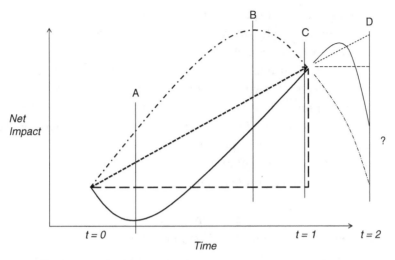

Figure 5.1 Understanding impact trajectories
Source: Woolcock (2013)

change. By this I mean that any empirical claims about a project's putative impact, *independently of the method(s) by which the claims were determined*, should be understood in the light of where we should reasonably expect a project to be by when. As I have documented elsewhere (Woolcock 2009), the default assumption in the vast majority of impact evaluations is that change over time is monotonically linear: baseline data is collected (perhaps on both a 'treatment' and a 'control' group) and after a specified time follow-up data is also obtained; following necessary steps to control for the effects of selection and confounding variables, a claim is then made about the net impact of the intervention, and, if presented graphically, is done by connecting a straight line from the baseline scores to the net follow-up scores. The presumption of a straight-line impact trajectory is an enormous one, however, which becomes readily apparent when one alters the shape of the trajectory (to, say, a step-function or a J-curve) and recognizes that the period between the baseline and follow-up data collection is mostly arbitrary (or chosen in accordance with administrative or political imperatives); with variable time frames and nonlinear impact trajectories, however, vastly different accounts can be provided of whether or not a given project is "working."

Consider Figure 5.1. If one was ignorant of a project impact's underlying functional form, and the net impact of four projects was evaluated "rigorously" at point C, then remarkably similar stories would be told about these projects' positive impact, and the conclusion would be that they all unambiguously "worked." But what if the impact trajectory of these four interventions actually differs markedly, as represented by the four different lines? And what if the evaluation was conducted not at point C but rather at points A or B? At point A one tells four qualitatively different stories about which projects are "working"; indeed, if one had the misfortune to be the team leader on the J-curve project during its evaluation by an RCT at point A, one may well face disciplinary sanction for not merely having "no impact" but for making things worse – as verified by "rigorous evidence"! If one then extrapolates into the future, to point D, it is only the linear trajectory that turns out to yield continued gains; the rest either remain stagnant or decline markedly.

The conclusions reached in an otherwise seminal paper by Casey, Glennerster, and Miguel (2012) embody these concerns. Using an innovative RCT design to assess the efficacy of a 'community driven development' project in Sierra Leone, the authors sought to jointly determine the impact of the project on participants' incomes and the quality of their local institutions. They found "positive short-run effects on local public goods and economic outcomes, but no evidence for sustained impacts on collective action, decision-making, or the involvement of marginalized groups, suggesting that the intervention did not durably reshape local institutions" (2012: 1755). This may well be true empirically, but such a conclusion presumes that incomes and institutions change at the same pace and along the same trajectory; most of what we know from political and social history would suggest that institutional change in fact follows a trajectory (if it has one at all) more like a step-function or a J-curve than a straight line, and that our 'reasoned expectations' against which to assess the effects of an intervention trying to change 'local institutions' should thus be guided accordingly.[32]

Recent work deftly exemplifies the importance of such considerations. Baird, McIntosh, and Özler (2019:182) provide interesting findings from an unconditional cash transfer program in Malawi, in which initially significant declines in teen pregnancy, HIV prevalence, and early marriage turned out, upon a subsequent evaluation conducted two years after the program had concluded, to have dissipated. On the other hand, a conditional cash transfer (CCT) program in the same country offered to girls who were not in school led to "sustained program effects on school attainment, early

---

[32] On the rising (if belated) awareness among senior researchers of the broader importance of incorporating a theory of change into monitoring and evaluation procedures in development, see Gugerty and Karlan (2018).

marriage, and pregnancy for baseline dropouts receiving CCTs. However, these effects did not translate into reductions in HIV, gains in labor market outcomes, or increased empowerment." Same country, different projects, both with variable nonlinear impact trajectories, and thus different conclusions regarding program effectiveness.[33] One surely needs to have several, sophisticated, contextually grounded theories of change to anticipate and accurately interpret such diverse findings at a given point in time – and especially to inform considerations about the programs' likely effectiveness over time in different country contexts. But, alas, this is rarely the case.[34]

Again, the key point here is not that the *empirical* strategy per se is flawed (it clearly is not – in this instance, in fact, it is exemplary); it is that (a) we rarely have more than two data points on which to base any claims about impact, and, when we do, it can lead to rather different interpretations about impact 'there' (and thus its likely variable impact 'here'); and (b) rigorous (indeed all) results must be interpreted against a theory of change. Perhaps it is entirely within historical experience to see no measurable change on institutions for a decade; perhaps, in fact, one needs to toil in obscurity for two or more decades as the necessary price to pay for any 'change' to be subsequently achieved and discerned;[35] perhaps seeking such change is a highly 'complex' endeavor, and as such has no consistent functional form, or has one that is apparent only with the benefit of hindsight, and is an idiosyncratic product of a series of historically contingent moments and processes (see Woolcock, Szreter, and Rao 2011). In any event, the interpretation and implications of "the evidence" from any evaluation of any intervention is never self-evident; it must be discerned in the light of theory and benchmarked against reasoned expectations, especially when that intervention exhibits high causal density and necessarily requires robust implementation capability.[36]

[33] In the 'complex' development space, see Biddulph (2014) on the impact trajectory of a land titling project in Cambodia, which initially showed spectacular results but over time became so contentious that it led to a breakdown in relations between the World Bank and the Government of Cambodia that lasted several years.

[34] In earlier work, these same authors (Baird, McIntosh, and Ozler, 2011) also showed that different ways of measuring the outcome variables also led to very different interpretations of project impact.

[35] Any student of the history of issues such as civil liberties, gender equality, the rule of law, or human rights surely appreciates this; many changes took centuries to be realized, and many clearly remain unfulfilled.

[36] A horticultural analogy can be invoked to demonstrate this point: no one would claim that sunflowers are "more effective" than acorns if we were to test their "growth performance" over a two-month period. After this time the sunflowers would be six feet high and the acorns would still be dormant underground, with "nothing to show" for their efforts. But we know the expected impact trajectory of sunflowers and oak trees: it is wildly different, and as such we judge (or benchmark) their growth

In the first instance this has important implications for internal validity, but it also matters for external validity, since one dimension of external validity is extrapolation over time. As Figure 5.1 shows, the trajectory of change between the baseline and follow-up points bears not only on the claims made about 'impact' but also on the claims made about the likely impact of this intervention in the future. These extrapolations only become more fraught once we add the dimensions of scale and context, as the Braun and McKenzie (2013) and Bold et al. (2013) papers reviewed earlier show. The abiding point for external validity concerns is that decision-makers need a coherent theory of change against which to accurately assess claims about a project's impact 'to date' and its likely impact 'in the future'; crucially, claims made on the basis of a "rigorous methodology" alone do not solve this problem.

5.3.4   Integrating These Domains into a Single Framework

The three domains considered in this analysis – causal density, implementation capability, and reasoned expectations – comprise a basis for pragmatic and informed deliberations regarding the external validity of development interventions in general and 'complex' interventions in particular. While data in various forms and from various sources can be vital inputs into these deliberations (see Bamberger, Rao, and Woolcock 2010; Woolcock 2019), when the three domains are considered as part of a single integrated framework for engaging with 'complex' interventions, it is extended deliberations on the basis of analytic case studies, I argue, that have a particular comparative advantage for eliciting the "key facts" necessary for making hard decisions about the generalizability of those interventions (or their constituent elements). Indeed, it is within the domains of causal density, implementation capability, and reasoned expectations, I argue, that the "key facts" themselves reside.

These deliberations move from the analytical and abstract to the decidedly concrete when hard decisions have to be made about the impact and generalizability of claims pertaining to truly complex development interventions, such as those seeking to empower the marginalized, enhance the legitimacy of justice systems, or promote more effective local government. The Sustainable Development Goals have put issues such as these squarely and

performance over time accordingly. Unfortunately, we have no such theory of change informing most assessments of most development projects at particular points in time; in the absence of such theories – whether grounded in evidence and/or experience – of multiple data points, and of corresponding trajectories of change, we assume linearity (which for 'complex' interventions as defined in this chapter is almost assuredly inaccurate).

Table 5.2 An integrated framework for assessing external validity claims

	Iodization of salt	Vaccinations	Ambulatory curative care	Regulating private providers	Promoting preventive health
Local discretion?	No	No	Yes	Yes	Yes
Transaction intensive?	No	Yes	Yes	Yes	Yes
Contentious; Tempting alternatives?	No	No	No	Yes	No
Known technology?	Yes	Yes	Yes	Yes	Yes
Type of implementation challenge	*Technocratic* Policy decree + light implementation	*Logistical* Implementation intensive, but 'easy'	*Implementation Intensive Services* Welcomed, expected	*Implementation Intensive Obligations* Resisted, evaded	*Complex* Implementation intensive, motivation hard, solutions require continuous innovation
Likelihood impact claims can be scaled, replicated	High				Low
Utility of case studies in external validity deliberations	Low				High

Source: Revised from Woolcock (2013)

formally on the global agenda, and in the years leading up to 2030 there will surely be a flurry of brave attempts to 'measure' and 'demonstrate' that all countries have indeed made 'progress' on them. Is fifteen years (2015–2030) a 'reasonable' timeframe over which to expect any such change to occur? What 'proven' instruments and policy strategies can domestic and international actors wield in response to such challenges? There aren't any, and there never will be, at least not in the way there are now 'proven' ways in which to build durable roads in high rainfall environments, tame high inflation, or immunize babies against polio. But we do have an array of tools in the social science kit that can help us navigate the distinctive challenges posed by truly complex problems – we just need to forge and protect the political space in which they can be ably deployed. Analytic case studies, so understood, are one of those tools.

5.4 Harnessing the Distinctive Contribution of Analytic Case Studies

When carefully compiled and conveyed, case studies can be instructive for policy deliberations across the analytic space set out in Table 5.2. Our focus here is on development problems that are highly complex, require robust implementation capability, and unfold along nonlinear context-specific trajectories, but this is only where the comparative advantage of case studies is strongest (and where, by extension, the comparative advantage of RCTs for engaging with external validity issues is weakest). It is obviously beyond the scope of this chapter to provide a comprehensive summary of the theory and strategies underpinning case study analysis,[37] but three key points bear some discussion (which I provide below): the distinctiveness of case studies as a method of analysis in social science beyond the familiar qualitative/quantitative divide; the capacity of case studies to elicit causal claims and generate testable hypotheses; and (related) the focus of case studies on exploring and explaining mechanisms (i.e., identifying how, for whom, and under what conditions outcomes are observed – or "getting inside the black box").

The rising quality of the analytic foundations of case study research has been one of the underappreciated (at least in mainstream social science) methodological advances of the last few decades (Mahoney 2007). Where everyday discourse in development research typically presumes a rigid and binary 'qualitative' or 'quantitative' divide, this is a distinction many contemporary social scientists (especially historians, historical sociologists, and comparative political scientists) feel does not aptly accommodate their work – if 'qualitative' is primarily understood to mean ethnography, participant observation, and interviews. These researchers see themselves as occupying a distinctive epistemological space, using case studies (across varying units of analysis: countries to firms to events) to interrogate instances of phenomena – with an 'N' of, say, 30, such as revolutions – that are "too large" for orthodox qualitative approaches and "too small" for orthodox quantitative analysis. (There is no inherent reason, they argue, why the problems of the world should array themselves in accordance with

---

[37] Such accounts are provided in the key works of Ragin and Becker (1992), Stake (1995), Burawoy (1998), George and Bennett (2005), Levy (2008), and Yin (2017); see also the earlier work of Ragin (1987) on 'qualitative comparative analysis' and Bates et al. (1998) on 'analytic narratives' (updated in Levy and Weingast, Chapter 11, this volume), and the most recent methodological innovations outlined in Goertz and Mahoney (2012), Gerring (2017), and Goertz (2017).

the bimodal methodological distribution social scientists otherwise impose on them.)

More ambitiously, perhaps, case study researchers also claim to be able to draw causal inferences (see Mahoney 2000; Levy 2008; Cartwright, Chapter 2 this volume). Defending this claim in detail requires engagement with philosophical issues beyond the scope of this chapter,[38] but a pragmatic application can be seen in the law (Honoré 2010), where it is the task of investigators to assemble various forms and sources of evidence (inherently of highly variable quality) as part of the process of building a "case" for or against a charge, which must then pass the scrutiny of a judge or jury: whether a threshold of causality is reached in this instance has very real (in the real world) consequences. Good case study research in effect engages in its own internal dialogue with the 'prosecution' and 'defense', posing alternative hypotheses to account for observed outcomes and seeking to test their veracity on the basis of the best available evidence. As in civil law, a "preponderance of the evidence" standard[39] is used to determine whether a causal relationship has been established. This is the basis on which causal claims (and, needless to say, highly 'complex' causal claims) affecting the fates of individuals, firms, and governments are determined in courts every day; deploying a variant on it is what good case study research entails.

Finally, by exploring 'cases within cases' (thereby raising or lowering the instances of phenomena they are exploring), and by overtly tracing the evolution of given cases over time within the context(s) in which they occur, case study researchers seek to document and explain the processes by which, and the conditions under which, certain outcomes are obtained. (This technique is sometimes referred to as process tracing – or, as noted earlier, assessing the 'causes of effects' as opposed to the 'effects of causes' approach characteristic of most econometric research.) Case study research finds its most prominent place in applied development research and program assessment in the literature on 'realist evaluation',[40] where the abiding focus is exploiting, exploring, and explaining variance (or standard deviations): that is, on identifying what works for whom, when, where, and why.[41] In

---

[38] But see the discussion in Cartwright and Hardie (2012); Freedman (2008) and especially Goertz and Mahoney (2012) are also instructive on this point. On the significance of "one or a few cases" for advancing theory, see Rueschemeyer (2003) and Small (2009).

[39] In criminal law, of course, the standard is higher: the evidence must be "beyond a reasonable doubt."

[40] The foundational text is Pawson and Tilly (1997).

[41] This strand of work can reasonably be understood as a qualitative complement to Ravallion's (2001) clarion call for development researchers to "look beyond averages."

their study of service delivery systems across the Middle East and North Africa, Brixi, Lust, and Woolcock (2015) use this strategy – deploying existing household survey data to 'map' broad national trends in health and education outcomes, complementing it with analytical case studies of specific locations that are positive 'outliers' – to explain how, within otherwise similar (and deeply challenging) policy environments, some implementation systems become and remain so much more effective than others (see also McDonnell 2020). This is the signature role that case studies can play for understanding, and sharing the lessons from, 'complex' development interventions on their own terms, as has been the central plea of this chapter.

5.5   Conclusion

The energy and exactitude with which development researchers debate the veracity of claims about 'causality' and 'impact' (internal validity) has yet to inspire corresponding firepower in the domain of concerns about whether and how to 'replicate' and 'scale up' interventions (external validity). Indeed, as manifest in everyday policy debates in contemporary development, the gulf between these modes of analysis is wide, palpable, and consequential: the fates of billions of dollars, millions of lives, and thousands of careers turn on how external validity concerns are addressed, and yet too often the basis for these deliberations is decidedly shallow.

It does not have to be this way. The social sciences, broadly defined, contain within them an array of theories and methods for addressing both internal and external validity concerns; they are there to be deployed if invited to the table (see Stern et al. 2012). This chapter has sought to show that 'complex' development interventions require evaluation strategies tailored to accommodate that reality; such interventions are square pegs which when forced into methodological round holes yield confused, even erroneous, verdicts regarding their effectiveness 'there' and likely effectiveness 'here'. In the early twenty-first century, development professionals routinely engage with issues of increasing 'complexity': consolidating democratic transitions, reforming legal systems, promoting social inclusion, enhancing public sector management[42] – the list is endless. These types of

---

[42] So et al. (2018) use case studies to explain the array of outcomes associated with efforts to reform the public sector in eight East Asian countries. Such massive, contentious, long-term efforts to modernize administrative systems that enable federal governments to function on a day-to-day basis are quintessentially 'complex': one simply cannot conclude that a singular approach did or did not "work;" it is

issues are decidedly (wickedly) 'complex', and responses to them need to be prioritized, designed, implemented, and assessed accordingly. Beyond evaluating such interventions on their own terms, however, it is as important to be able to advise front-line staff, senior management, and colleagues working elsewhere about when and how the "lessons" from these diverse experiences can be applied. Deliberations centered on causal density, implementation capability, and reasoned expectations have the potential to usefully elicit, inform, and consolidate this process.

References

Aad, G., Abbott, B., Abdallah, J. et al. (2015) "Combined measurement of the Higgs boson mass in pp collisions at sqrt[s]= 7 and 8 TeV with the ATLAS and CMS experiments," *Physical Review Letters*, 114(19), 191803. (This paper has 5,154 coauthors, so for obvious reasons not all are listed here.)

Allcott, H. and Mullainathan, S. (2012) External validity and partner selection bias. Cambridge, MA: National Bureau of Economic Research Working Paper No. 18373.

Andrews, M., Pritchett, L., and Woolcock, M. (2013) "Escaping capability traps through problem-driven iterative adaption (PDIA)," *World Development*, 51(11), 234–244.

Andrews, M., Pritchett, L., and Woolcock, M. (2017) *Building state capability: Evidence, analysis, action* New York: Oxford University Press.

Angrist, J. and Fernandez-Val, I. (2010) Extrapolate-ing: External validity and overidentification in the LATE framework. Cambridge, MA: National Bureau of Economic Research, NBER Working Paper 16566.

Baird, S., Ferreira, F., Özler, B., and Woolcock, M. (2013) "Relative effectiveness of conditional and unconditional cash transfers for schooling outcomes in developing countries: A systematic review," *Campbell Systematic Reviews*, 9(8), 1–124.

Baird, S., McIntosh, C., and Özler, B. (2011) "Cash or condition? Evidence from a cash transfer experiment," *Quarterly Journal of Economics*, 126(4), 1709–1753.

Baird, S., McIntosh, C., and Özler, B. (2019) "When the money runs out: Do cash transfers have sustained effects on human capital accumulation?" *Journal of Development Economics*, 140(September), 169–185.

Bamberger, M., Rao, V., and Woolcock, M. (2010) "Using mixed methods in monitoring and evaluation: Experiences from international development" in Tashakkori, A. and Teddlie, C.

unreasonable to expect such a verdict, and one certainly can't lament that verdicts are "merely anecdotal" because an "RCT" of such reforms wasn't conducted (on such reform it would be neither possible nor desirable to take this approach, even if tiny slices of it perhaps could be so interrogated). Rather, all sorts of contingent events and processes aligned to drive observed outcomes in each case; those contemplating public sector reforms in their own country, we argue, are best served (and prepared) by learning from detailed, analytically informed accounts of the diverse experiences of others with 'similar enough' country/political/administrative characteristics.

(eds.) *Handbook of mixed methods in social and behavioral research* (2nd revised edition). Thousand Oaks, CA: Sage Publications, pp. 613–641.

Banerjee, A. V., Cole, S., Duflo, E., and Linden, L. (2007) "Remedying education: Evidence from two randomized experiments in India," *Quarterly Journal of Economics*, 122(3), 1235–1264.

Barron, P., Diprose, R., and Woolcock, M. (2011) *Contesting development: Participatory projects and local conflict dynamics in Indonesia*. New Haven, CT: Yale University Press.

Bates, R., Greif, A., Levi, M., Rosenthal, J. L., and Weingast, B. R. (eds.) (1998) *Analytic narratives*. Princeton, NJ: Princeton University Press.

Biddulph, R. (2014) Cambodia's land management and administration project. Helsinki: WIDER, Working Paper No. 2014/086.

Bold, T., Kimenyi, M., Mwabu, G., Ng'ang'a, A., and Sandefur, J. (2013) Scaling-up what works: Experimental evidence on external validity in Kenyan education. Washington: Center for Global Development, Working Paper No. 321.

Booth, D. (2012) "Aid effectiveness: Bring country ownership (and politics) back in," *Conflict, Security and Development*, 12(5), 537–558.

Brixi, H., Lust, E., and Woolcock, M. (2015) *Trust, voice and incentives: Learning from local success stories in service delivery in the Middle East and North Africa*. Washington, DC: The World Bank.

Bruhn, M. and McKenzie, D. (2013) "Using administrative data to evaluate municipal reforms: An evaluation of the impact of Minas Fácil Expresso," *Journal of Development Effectiveness*, 5(3), 319–338.

Burawoy, M. (1998) "The extended case method," *Sociological Theory*, 16(1), 4–33.

Byrne, D. (2013) "Evaluating complex social interventions in a complex world," *Evaluation*, 19(3), 217–228.

Byrne, D. and Callighan, G. (2013) *Complexity theory and the social sciences: The state of the art*. London: Routledge.

Cartwright, N. (2007) "Are RCTs the gold standard?" *Biosocieties*, 2(2), 11–20.

Cartwright, N. and Hardie, J. (2012) *Evidence-based policy: A practical guide to doing it better*. New York: Oxford University Press.

Casey, K., Glennerster, R., and Miguel, E. (2012) "Reshaping institutions: Evidence on aid impacts using a pre-analysis plan," *Quarterly Journal of Economics*, 127(4), 1755–1812.

Chong, A., La Porta, R., Lopez-de-Silanes, F., and Shleifer, A. (2014) "Letter grading government efficiency," *Journal of the European Economic Association*, 12(2), 277–298.

Churchman, C. W. (1967) "Wicked problems," *Management Science*, 14(4), 141–142.

Colander, D. and Kupers, R. (2014) *Complexity and the art of social science: Solving society's problems from the bottom up*. Princeton, NJ: Princeton University Press.

Cook, T. D. (2001) "Generalization: Conceptions in the social sciences" in Smelser, N. J., Wright, J., and Baltes, P. B. (eds.) *International encyclopedia of the social and behavioral sciences*. Amsterdam: Elsevier, vol. 9, pp. 6037–6043.

Cook, T. D. and Campbell, D. T. (1979) *Quasi-experimentation: Design and analysis issues for field settings*. Boston, MA: Houghton Mifflin Company.

Deaton, A. (2010) "Instruments, randomization, and learning about development," *Journal of Economic Perspectives*, 48(June), 424–455.

Deaton, A. and Cartwright, N. (2018) "Understanding and misunderstanding randomized controlled trials," *Social Science & Medicine*, 210(2018), 2–21.

Denizer, C., Kaufmann, D., and Kraay, A. (2012) "*Good projects or good countries? Macro and micro correlates of World Bank project performance,*" Washington, DC: The World Bank, Policy Research Working Papers No. 5646.

Duflo, E., Dupas, P., and Kremer, M. (2012) School governance, teacher incentives, and pupil-teacher ratios: Experimental evidence from Kenyan primary schools. NBER Working Paper No. 17939.

Engber, D. (2011) "The mouse trap (part I): The dangers of using one lab animal to study every disease," *Slate*, November 15. Available at: www.slate.com/articles/health_and_science/the_mouse_trap/2011/11/the_mouse_trap.html (accessed January 22, 2020).

Eppstein, M. J., Horbar, J. D., Buzas, J. S., and Kauffman, S. (2012) "Searching the clinical fitness landscape," *PLoS One*, 7(11), e49901.

Fiszbein, A. and Schady, N. (2009) *Conditional cash transfers: Reducing present and future poverty*. Washington, DC: The World Bank.

Forrester, J. (2017) *Thinking in cases*. Cambridge: Polity Press.

Freedman, D. A. (2008) "On types of scientific enquiry: The role of qualitative reasoning" in Box-Steffensmeier, J., Brady, H. E., and Collier, D. (eds.) *The Oxford handbook of political methodology*. New York: Oxford University Press, pp. 300–318.

George, A. and Bennett, A. (2005) *Case studies and theory development in the social sciences*. Cambridge, MA: MIT Press.

Gerring, J. (2017) *Case study research: Principles and practices* (2nd ed.) New York: Cambridge University Press.

Goertz, G. (2017) *Multimethod research, causal mechanisms, and case studies*. Princeton, NJ: Princeton University Press.

Goertz, G. and Mahoney, J. (2012) *A tale of two cultures: Qualitative and quantitative research in the social sciences*. Princeton, NJ: Princeton University Press.

Gugerty, M. K. and Karlan, D. (2018) *The Goldilocks challenge: Right-fit evidence for the social sector*. New York: Oxford University Press.

Gupta, A. (2012) *Red tape: Bureaucracy, structural violence and poverty in India*. Durham and London: Duke University Press.

Henrich, J., Heine, S. J., and Norenzayan, A. (2010a) "The weirdest people in the world?" *Behavioral and Brain Sciences*, 33(2–3), 61–83.

Henrich, J., Heine, S. J., and Norenzayan, A. (2010b) "Beyond WEIRD: Towards a broad-based behavioral science," *Behavioral and Brain Sciences*, 33(2–3), 111–135.

Hirschman, A. O. (1967) *Development projects observed*. Washington, DC: Brookings Institution.

Honig, D. (2018) *Navigation by judgment: Why and when top-down management of foreign aid doesn't work*. New York: Oxford University Press.

Honoré, A. (2010) "Causation in the law," *Stanford Encyclopedia of Philosophy*. Available at http://stanford.library.usyd.edu.au/entries/causation-law/ (accessed March 20, 2013).

Howlett, P. and Morgan, M. (eds.) (2010) *How well do facts travel? The dissemination of reliable knowledge*. New York: Cambridge University Press.

Kolata, G. (2013) "Mice fall short as test subjects for humans' deadly ills," *The New York Times*, February 11, A19.

Lamont, M. (2012) "Toward a comparative sociology of valuation and evaluation," *Annual Review of Sociology*, 38(1), 201–221.

Levy, J. S. (2008) "Case studies: Types, designs and logics of inference," *Conflict Management and Peace Studies*, 25(1), 1–18.

Ludwig, J., Kling, J. R., and Mullainathan, S. (2011) "Mechanism experiments and policy evaluations," *Journal of Economic Perspectives*, 25(3), 17–38.

Mahoney, J. (2000) "Strategies of causal inference in small-N analysis," *Sociological Methods & Research*, 28(4), 387–424.

Mahoney, J. (2007) "Qualitative methodology and comparative politics," *Comparative Political Studies*, 40(2), 122–144.

Mansuri, G. and Rao, V. (2012) *Localizing development: Does participation work?* Washington, DC: The World Bank.

Manzi, J. (2012) *Uncontrolled: The surprising payoff of trial and error for business, politics, and society*. New York: Basic Books.

March, J. G., Sproull, L. S., and Tamuz, M. (1991) "Learning from samples of one or fewer," *Organization Science*, 2(1), 1–13.

McDonnell, E. M. (2020) *Patchwork Leviathan: Pockets of bureaucratic effectiveness in developing states*. Princeton, NJ: Princeton University Press.

Morgan, M. (2012) "Case studies: One observation or many? Justification or discovery?" *Philosophy of Science*, 79(5), 667–677.

Muralidharan, K. and Sundararaman, V. (2010) *Contract teachers: Experimental evidence from India*. San Diego, CA: Mimeo.

Pawson, R. and Tilly, N. (1997) *Realist evaluation*. London: Sage Publications.

Picciotto, R. (2012) "Experimentalism and development evaluation: Will the bubble burst?" *Evaluation*, 18(2), 213–229.

Pritchett, L. (2013) *The folk and the formula: Fact and fiction in development*. Helsinki: WIDER Annual Lecture 16.

Pritchett, L., Samji, S., and Hammer, J. (2012) It's all about MeE: Using structured experiential learning ('e') to crawl the design space. Helsinki: UNU-WIDER Working Paper No. 2012/104.

Pritchett, L. and Sandefur, J. (2015) "Learning from experiments when context matters," *American Economic Review*, 105(5), 471–475.

Pritchett, L. and Woolcock, M. (2004) "Solutions when the solution is the problem: Arraying the disarray in development," *World Development*, 32(2), 191–212.

Pritchett, L., Woolcock, M., and Andrews, M. (2013) "Looking like a state: Techniques of persistent failure in state capability for implementation," *Journal of Development Studies*, 49(1), 1–18.

Ragin, C. C. (1987) *The comparative method: Moving beyond qualitative and quantitative strategies*. Berkeley and Los Angeles: University of California Press.

Ragin, C. C. and Becker, H. (eds.) (1992) *What is a case? Exploring the foundations of social inquiry*. New York: Cambridge University Press.

Ramalingam, B. (2014) *Aid on the edge of chaos: Rethinking international cooperation in a complex world*. New York: Oxford University Press.

Ramalingam, B. and Jones, H. (with Toussaint Reba and John Young) (2009) Exploring the science of complexity: Ideas and implications for development and humanitarian efforts. London: ODI Working Paper No. 285.

Ravallion, M. (2001) "Growth, inequality and poverty: Looking beyond averages," *World Development*, 29(11), 1803–1815.

Ravallion, M. (2009) "Should the randomistas rule?" *Economists' Voice*, 6(2), 1–5.

Room, G. (2011) *Complexity, institutions and public policy: Agile decision-making in a turbulent world*. Northampton, MA: Edward Elgar Publishing.

Rothwell, P. M. (2005) "External validity of randomized controlled trials: 'To whom do the results of this trial apply?'" *The Lancet*, 365(9453), 82–93.

Rueschemeyer, D. (2003) "Can one or a few cases yield theoretical gains?" in Mahoney, J. and Rueschemeyer, D. (eds.) *Comparative historical analysis in the social sciences*. New York: Cambridge University Press, pp. 305–336.

Ruzzene, A. (2012) "Drawing lessons from case studies by enhancing comparability," *Philosophy of the Social Sciences*, 42(1), 99–120.

Sampson, R. (2013) "The place of context: A theory and strategy for criminology's hard problems," *Criminology*, 51(1), 1–31.

Seok, J., Warren, H. S., Cuenca, A. G., et al. (2013) "Genomic responses in mouse models poorly mimic human inflammatory diseases," *Proceedings of the National Academy of Sciences*, 110(9), 3507–3512. (This paper has 39 coauthors, so for obvious reasons not all of them are listed here.)

Shaffer, P. (2011) "Against excessive rhetoric in impact assessment: Overstating the case for randomised controlled experiments," *Journal of Development Studies*, 47(11), 1619–1635.

Shanahan, M. (2008) "Dynamical complexity in small-world networks of spiking neurons," *Physical Review E*, 78(4), 041924.

Small, M. L. (2009) "How many cases do I need? On science and the logic of case selection in field-based research," *Ethnography*, 10(1), 5–38.

So, S., Woolcock, M., April, L., Hughes, C., and Smithers, N. (eds.) (2018) *Alternative paths to public financial management and public sector reform: Experiences from East Asia*. Washington, DC: The World Bank.

Stake, R. E. (1995) *The art of case study research*. Thousand Oaks, CA: Sage Publications.

Stern, E., Stame, N., Mayne, J., Forss, K., Davies, R., and Befani, B. (2012) Broadening the range of designs and methods for impact evaluation. London: DFID Working Paper No. 38.

Williams, M. (2020) "External validity and policy adaptation: From impact evaluation to policy design," *World Bank Research Observer*, 35(2), 158–191.

Woolcock, M. (2009) "Toward a plurality of methods in project evaluation: A contextualized approach to understanding impact trajectories and efficacy," *Journal of Development Effectiveness*, 1(1), 1–14.

Woolcock, M. (2013) "Using case studies to explore the external validity of complex development interventions," *Evaluation*, 19(3), 229–248.

Woolcock, M. (2019) "Reasons for using mixed methods in the evaluation of complex projects" in Nagatsu, M. and Ruzzene, A. (eds.) *Philosophy and interdisciplinary social science: A dialogue*. London: Bloomsbury Academic, pp. 149–171.

Woolcock, M., Szreter, S., and Rao, V. (2011) "How and why does history matter for development policy?" *Journal of Development Studies*, 47(1), 70–96.

Yin, R. K. (2017) *Case study research: Design and methods* (6th ed.) Thousand Oaks, CA: Sage Publications. (First edition published in 1984.)

Part II

Ensuring High-Quality Case Studies

6 Descriptive Accuracy in Interview-Based Case Studies

Jennifer Widner

6.1 Introduction

Social scientists and policy-makers care deeply about their ability to draw clear causal inferences from research – and justifiably so. But descriptive accuracy also matters profoundly for the success of this enterprise. Correctly identifying relevant parties, choice points, and perceptions, for example, strongly impacts our ability to understand sources of influence on development outcomes, successfully disrupt and overcome obstacles, and identify scope conditions. The challenge is how to tease out this kind of information in interview-based qualitative research.

This chapter draws on a decade of experience in developing policy implementation case studies under the auspices of a Princeton University program called Innovations for Successful Societies in order to highlight ways to address some of the most common difficulties in achieving descriptive accuracy. The program responded to a need, in the mid-2000s, to enable people leading public sector reform and innovation in low-income and low-middle-income countries to share experiences and evolve practical wisdom suited to context. To develop reasonably accurate portrayals of the reform process and create accurate after-action reports, the program carried out in-depth interviews with decision-makers, their deputies, and the other people with whom they engaged, as well as critics. The research employed intensive conversation with small-N purposive samples of public servants and politicians as a means of data collection.[1] In the eyes of some, this interview-generated

[1] For a compelling argument about the use of nonprobability sampling in elite interview-based case studies, see Tansey (2007).

information was suspect because it was potentially vulnerable to bias or gloss, fading or selective memory, partial knowledge, and the pressures of the moment. Taking these concerns seriously, the program drew on research about the interaction between survey design and respondent behavior and evolved routines to boost the robustness of the interviews it conducted.

6.2 Background

Accuracy is related to reliability, or the degree of confidence we have that the same description would emerge if someone else reviewed the data available or conducted additional interviews.[2] Our methods have to help us come as close as possible to the "true value" of the actual process used to accomplish something or the perceptions of the people in the room where a decision took place. How do we ensure that statements about processes, decisions, actions, preferences, judgments, and outcomes acquired from interviews closely mirror actual perceptions and choices at the time an event occurred?

In this chapter, I propose that we understand the interview process as an exercise in theory building and theory testing. At the core is a person we ask to play dual roles. On the one hand, our interviewees are a source of facts about an otherwise opaque process. On the other hand, the people we talk to are themselves the object of research. To borrow the words of my colleague Tommaso Pavone, who commented on a draft of this chapter, "The interviewee acts like a pair of reading glasses, allowing us to see an objective reality that is otherwise inaccessible." At the same time, however, we are also interested in that person's own perceptions, and subjective interpretations of events, and motivations. "For example," Pavone said, "we might want to know whether and why a given meeting produced divergent interpretations about its relative collegiality or contentiousness, and we might subsequently probe how the interviewee's positionality, personality, and preferences might have affected their views."

In both instances, there are many potential confounding influences that might blur the view. Some threats stem from the *character of the subject matter* – whether it is comparatively simple or causally dense (in Michael Woolcock's terms, i.e., subject to many sources of influence, interactions, and feedback loops; see Chapter 5, this volume), whether it is socially or politically

---

[2] A good description also represents what it is that we aim to study or report. That is, the measures and facts used are logically linked to the key concepts.

sensitive, or whether the person interviewed is still involved in the activity and has friends and relatives whose careers might be affected by the study. Other threats emanate from the nature of *the interviewee's exposure to the subject matter*, such as the amount of time that has elapsed since the events (memory), the extent of contact (knowledge), and the intensity of engagement at the time of the events. Still other influences may stem from the *interview setting*: rapport with the researcher, the order and phrasing of questions, whether there is a risk of being overheard, and the time available to expand on answers, for example.

Our job as case writers is to identify those influences and minimize them in order to get as close as possible to a true account, much as we do in other kinds of social science. And there are potential trade-offs. A source may be biased in an account of the facts, but, as Pavone suggested in his earlier comments, "he may be fascinating if we treat him as a subjective interpreter," whose gloss on a subject may reveal how decision-makers rationalized intense investment in a particular outcome or how they responded to local norms in the way they cloaked discord.

The following section of this chapter treats the pursuit of descriptive accuracy as an endeavor very closely aligned with the logic used in other types of research. Subsequent sections outline practices we can mobilize to ensure a close match between the information drawn from interviews and objective reality – whether of a process or of a perspective.

6.3   The Interview as Social Science Research

An interview usually aims to take the measure of something, and any time a scientist takes a measurement, there is some risk of error, systematic or random. We can try to reduce this problem by modeling the effects of our instruments or methods on the information generated. The goal is to refine the interview process so that it improves the accuracy and completeness of recall, whether of events and facts or of views.

First, let's step back a bit and consider how theory fuels qualitative interviewing, for even though we often talk about this kind of research as inductive, a good interview is rarely free-form. A skilled interviewer always approaches a conversation self-consciously, with a number of key ideas and hypotheses about the subject and the interviewee's relationship to that subject in mind. The inquiry is exploratory, but it has a strong initial deductive framework.

This process proceeds on three dimensions simultaneously, focused at once on the subject matter; the interviewee's preferences, perceptions, and biases; and the need to triangulate among competing accounts.

Theory and interview focus. The capacity to generate good description draws heavily on being able to identify the general, abstract problem or problems at the core of what someone is saying and to quickly ask about the conditions that likely set up this challenge or the options likely tried. At the outset, the interviewer has presumably already thought hard about the general focus of the conversation in the kinds of terms Robert Weiss outlines in his helpful book, *Learning from Strangers*[3] – for example, describing a process, learning how someone interpreted an event, presenting a point of view, framing hypotheses and identifying variables, etc. In policy-focused case studies, we begin by identifying the broad outcomes decision-makers sought and then consider hypotheses about the underlying strategic challenges or impediments decision-makers were likely to encounter. Collective action? Coordination across institutions? Alignment of interests or incentives (principal–agent problems)? Critical mass? Coordination of social expectations? Capacity? Risk mitigation? Spoilers? All of the above? Others?

Locking down an initial general understanding – "This is a case of what?" – helps launch the conversation: "As I understand it, you faced ___ challenge in order to achieve the outcomes the program was supposed to generate. How would you characterize that challenge? . . . This problem often has a couple of dimensions [fill in]. In what ways were these important here, or were they not so important?" Asking follow-up questions in order to assess each possible impediment helps overcome problems of omission, deliberate or inadvertent. In this sense, accuracy is partly a function of the richness of the dialogue between the interviewer's theoretical imagination, the questions posed, and the answers received.

The interview then proceeds to document the steps taken to address each component problem, and here, again, theory is helpful. The characterization of the core strategic challenges spawns a set of hypotheses. For example, if the key delivery challenge is the need for collective action, then we know we will have to ask questions to help assess whether the outcome sought was really a public good as well as how the decision-maker helped devise a solution, including (most likely) a way to reduce the costs of contributing to the provision of that public good, a system for monitoring contributions, or whether there was one person or organization with an exceptional stake in

[3] Weiss (1994), pp. 9–10.

the outcome and therefore a willingness to bear the costs. In short, the interview script flows in large part from a sense of curiosity informed by theory.

Theory also helps us think about the outcomes we seek to explain in a case study and discuss in an interview. In policy-relevant research we are constantly thinking in terms of measures or indicators, each of which has an imperfect relationship with the overarching development outcome we seek to explain. A skilled interviewer comes to a conversation having thought deeply about possible measures to evaluate the success or failure of an action and asks not only how the speaker, the interviewee, thought about this matter, but also whether any of these plausible measures were mooted, understanding that the public servants or citizens involved in a program may have had entirely different metrics in mind.

Often the outcomes are not that easy to measure. Nonetheless, we want something more concrete than a personal opinion, a thumbs up or thumbs down. To take one example, suppose the aim of a case study is to trace the impact of cabinet management or cabinet design on "ability of factions to work together." This outcome is not easy to assess. Certainly, we want to know how people themselves define "ability to work together," and open-ended questions are initially helpful. Instead of nudging the interviewee's mind down a particular path, the interviewer allows people to organize their own thoughts.[4] But a skilled interviewer then engages the speaker to try to get a better sense of what it was about people's perceptions or behavior that really changed, if anything. In the abstract it is possible to think of several possible measures: how long it took to arrange meetings to coordinate joint initiatives, how often requested meetings actually took place, how often the person interviewed was included in subcabinet deliberations that involved the other political parties, whether the person interviewed felt part of the decision process, whether the deputy minister (always from the other party in this instance) followed through on action items within the prescribed timeframe, whether there was name-calling in the meeting room or fistfights, etc.

An interviewer also wants to figure out whether the theory of change that motivated a policy intervention actually generated the outcomes observed. Again, theory plays a role. It helps to come to an interview with plausible alternative explanations in mind. In the example above, maybe power-sharing had little to do with reducing tension among faction leaders.

---

[4] See Aberbach and Rockman (2002).

Instead, war weariness, a shift in public opinion, a sharp expansion of economic opportunity outside government that reduced the desire to remain in government, the collapse of factional differences in the wake of demographic change, the personality of the head of government – any of these things might also have accounted for the results. A skilled interviewer devises questions to identify whether any of these causal dynamics were in play and which facts would help us understand the relative importance of one explanation versus the others.

Let me add a caveat at this point. Theoretically informed interviewing leads us to the kinds of descriptive detail important for analysis and understanding. However, it is also crucial to remember that our initial frameworks, if too narrowly defined, can cause us to lose the added value that interviews can generate. As Albert Hirschman (1985) noted years ago, paradigms and hypotheses can become becoming a straightjacket ('confirmation bias'), and the unique contribution of interview-based research is that it can foster a dialogue that corrects misimpressions. Openness to ideas outside the interview script is important for this reason

For example, understanding the source of political will is important in a lot of policy research, but sometimes the most important outcome the lead decision-maker wants to achieve is not the one that most people associated with a policy know about or share. Say we want to use interview-based cases to help identify the conditions that prompt municipal public works programs and other city services to invest in changes that would improve access to early childhood development services. It soon becomes clear that the mayors who had made the most progress in promoting this kind of investment and collaboration sought outcomes that went well beyond boosting children's preparedness for preschool, the initial supposition, and, moreover, each wanted to achieve something quite distinctive. For some, the larger and longer-term aim was to reduce neighborhood violence, while for others the ambition was to diminish inequality or boost social capital and build trust. The open-ended question "Why was this program important to you?" helps leverage this insight.

Theory and the interview process . Interviewing employs theory in a second sense as well. To reveal what really happened, we have to weed out the details people have remembered incorrectly while filling in the details some never knew and others didn't consider important, didn't want to highlight, or simply forgot. Therefore, in the context of an interview, it is the researcher's job not only to seek relevant detail about processes, but also to perceive the gaps and silences and use additional follow-up questions or return interviews to secure explanations or elaboration.

In this instance, the researcher navigates through a series of hypotheses about the speaker's relationship to the issue at hand and knowledge of events. A few of the questions that leverage information for assessing or weighting answers include:

- "You had a peripheral role in the early stages of these deliberations/this implementation process, as I understand it. How did you learn about the rationale for these decisions? [Co-workers on the committee? Friends? Briefed by the person who led the committee or kept the minutes? Gleaned this information as you began to participate?] How would you say that joining the deliberation/process/negotiation late colored your view of the issues and shaped your actions, or did it not make much difference?"
- "You were involved in a lot of difficult decisions at the time. How closely involved were you in this matter? Did you spend a lot of time on it? Was it an especially high priority for you, or was it just part of your daily work?" "Given all the difficult matters you had to deal with at the time, how greatly did this issue stand out, or is it hard to remember?" (Level of knowledge helps the interviewer weight the account when trying to integrate it with other information.)
- "The other people involved in this decision/process/negotiation had strong ties to political factions. At least some of them must have tried to influence you. At what stages and in what form did these kinds of pressures arise?" "Were some voices stronger than others?" "How would you say these lobbying efforts affected your decision/work/stance?"
- "As I understand it, you took a decision/action that was unusual/worked against your personal interest/was sure to be unpopular with some important people. How would you characterize your reasons for doing so?"

The information these questions leverage helps the case writer assess the likely accuracy of an account, in at least three ways: First, it helps us understand whether someone was in a position to know or heard about an action secondhand. Second, it helps us assess the integrity of a response – for example, does a statement run contrary to the speaker's obvious personal interests and is it therefore more believable? Third, it can also help spot purely opportunistic spin: Is the view expressed consistent with the speaker's other actions and attitudes, or is at odds with these? Can the person offer a clear story about this divergence, or did this perception or preference evolve in association with a promotion, an election, or some other event that may have influenced behavior?

Theory and ability to arbitrate among competing statements. The third task of interview-based case research is to meld information garnered from different conversations and other types of sources in order to triangulate to the truth. This too is a theory-driven enterprise. Every time there is a clash between two assertions, we ask ourselves the familiar refrain "what could be going on here?" (hypothesis formation, drawn from theory), "how would I know?" (observable measures), and "by what method can I get this information?" (framing a follow-up question, checking a news report, consulting a register, etc.).

We may weigh the account of someone who joined a process late less heavily if it clashes with the information provided by those closer to a process, but it could be that the latecomer is less vulnerable to groupthink, has no reputation at stake, and offers a clearheaded story. Maybe we know the person was brought in as a troubleshooter and carried out a careful review of program data, or that the person is highly ambitious, eager to appear the hero who saved a failing initiative that, in fact, had not performed as badly as stated? Career paths, reputational information, and the written record – for example, longitudinal performance data – can all assist in making sense of disparate accounts.

This thought process may have to take place in the context of an interview as we listen and form follow-up questions, but it can also fuel exit interviews or second conversations designed both to provide another occasion to relate events remembered after the first encounter and to afford a chance to react to divergent information or ideas others may have voiced. This is the task of the exit interview.

To stress that skilled interviewing is theory-driven does not mean social scientists do a better job than journalists. Journalists might call the same kind of thought process "intuition" or "savvy," but, when asked to step back, be self-conscious, and break down the mental exercise involved, the reality of what they do differs little from how social scientists or historians proceed in their work. The editor who tells a cub reporter, "I smell a rat" upon hearing the sketch of a story is positing an alternative hypothesis to test the adequacy of a description. Employing a general model built on experience, the editor pushes the reporter to use evidence to identify what the people described in the reporter's draft are really doing.[5] A reporter's intuition is equivalent to a social scientist's skill in quickly framing plausible hypotheses and crafting a follow-up question that will yield the evidence to arbitrate among conflicting accounts – conducting social science inquiry "on the fly."

Regardless of the interviewer's own background, skilled interviewing places a premium on preparation. Even if the interviewer does not have a full-blown research design, it is crucial to have a preconversation sketch that frames hypotheses about the subject matter of the case and alternative plausible explanations; specifies the role the interviewee played in these events and the level of knowledge or type of gloss that relationship might produce (or at least does so with as much care as possible at this stage); and summarizes what archival sources say about the story line. This practice helps frame the questions that will tease out the evidence that disconfirms, modifies, or corroborates different versions of a story mid-conversation as new facts and observations emerge.

6.4   Improving Recall and Specificity

Solid, substantive preparation alone does not generate the requisite level of detail and accuracy needed in a policy case study. The skilled interviewer also has to overcome barriers to cognition. The people we interview are busy. They often work in a language different from ours. They may not understand what a study is about and what kinds of information the interviewer seeks. Further, like the rest of us, they forget and they tire. As a result, their answers to questions may vary from one interview to the next, making the descriptions we assemble less reliable.

Survey researchers have struggled with these challenges for decades.[6] They have investigated how people answer questions and how to improve accuracy in responses. Their reflections are helpful for those who do qualitative interviews.

---

[5] Although we are often insufficiently self-conscious about this thought process, the practice is broad and has long-standing roots. Just think of the common English phrase "I smell a rat," which signals that the speaker has an alternative, probably more cynical, hypothesis about something a conversational partner has just described than the partner has offered. The origins of the phrase go back to the 1500s. Samuel Johnson defined its meaning as "to be put on the watch by suspicion as the cat by the scent of a rat; to suspect danger." All is not as it seems: Johnson (1755).

[6] For example, Cannell, Miller, and Oksenberg (1981); Wright, Gaskell, and O'Muircheartaigh (1994); and Krosnick (1991).

1. One fairly obvious starting point or maxim is to make sure that the interviewee understands the purpose of the project or study and can perceive the level of detail expected. It is common for someone to ask quizzically, "Why would anyone be interested in what I did?"

Helping a speaker understand the intended audience improves motivation and accuracy. With respect to policy-focused interviews, asking someone to help a peer learn from a program's experience usually changes an interviewee's mental stance, and enables the person to hone in on the kind of subject matter sought and the level of operational detail needed. In the Princeton program we often used the phrase, "The purpose is to help your counterparts in other countries learn from your experience" in the invitation letter and follow-up, as well as in the lead-in to the interview itself. We also emphasized that "the aim of the case study is to profile the reform you helped design, the steps you took to implement the new system, and the results you have observed so that others can learn from you." Periodically, we reiterated these points. When an interviewee can imagine a conversation with the person who will use the information, answers are more likely to be specific. It also becomes easier to induce someone to be compassionate and speak honestly about the real problems that arose during a process, so that the target group of readers don't go astray or fail to benefit from the experience.

2. A second maxim is to ensure questions are clear so the interviewee does not have to struggle with meaning. A long, rambling question that requires energy to parse can sink an interview. By contrast, a simple, open-ended "grand tour" question is often a good place to begin, because many people are natural storytellers, become engaged, and start to focus their comments themselves when given this latitude. In his ethnographic interview classic, for example, Spradely suggests asking "Could you describe what happened that day?" or "Could you tell me how this office works?" Subsequent questions can focus on the elements of special relevance to the subject and may include prompts to reach specific subject matter or the requisite level of detail.[7]

---

[7] Spradely (1979). The people who train investigators or prosecutors to conduct interviews have experimented with interview formats. "Structured interviews" usually begin with an open question and then focus on particular points raised. Instructions to "remember back to____" can trigger improved recall as well. Adding "yes/no" questions can generate additional information (and sometimes aide in detecting prevarication).

3. In framing questions, we try to avoid ambiguous or culturally loaded terms that increase the amount of mental calculation an answer requires.[8] How much is "usually" or "regularly"? "Big"? How many years is "young" or "recently"? It may be better to ask, "About how often did that happen during that year?" or "How many times did that happen that year?" Novice interviewers often refer to seasons as they pinpoint the time of an action, but of course these vary globally, so the references merely confuse (moral: benchmark to events or national holidays).

Similarly, we try to eliminate questions that require the interviewee to talk about two different things – the "double-barreled question" or compound question. "Did that step reduce error?" is clear, but "Did that process reduce error and delay?" asks about two dimensions that may not be related, yet it seems to require one answer. In this instance, it does not take much effort to sort out the two dimensions and in an interview context, as opposed to a survey, that is feasible. However, a speaker will have a slightly tougher time with a compound question about a preference, motivation, or interaction: "Was the main challenge to compensate those who would have to alter their farming practices and to help the community monitor illegal deforestation?" "Was this group an obstacle to winning the vote in the legislature and a source of public backlash?" Simple questions and quick follow-ups usually elicit better information than complex questions that ask for views on two or more things at once.

4. The passage of time influences the ability to remember information and potentially also makes it hard to check the reliability of a description. In the 1980s, studies of physician recall found that memory of specific patient visits decayed very rapidly, within two weeks of a visit.[9] Norma Bradburn and her colleagues reported that about 20 percent of critical details are irretrievable by interviewees after a year and 60 percent are irretrievable after 5 years.[10] The ability to remember distant events interacts with the salience or importance of the events to the interviewee and with social desirability. A well-received achievement that occurred two years earlier may be easier to remember than something that did not work very well or was not considered important at the time. Using "probes," or questions that fill in a little detail from archival research, can help break the mental logjam.

Phrasing that takes the interviewee carefully back in time and provides reminders of the events that occurred or the locations in which they occurred

---

[8] Wright, Gaskell, and O'Muircheartaigh (1994).   [9] Cannell, Miller, and Oksenberg (1981) p. 397.
[10] Bradburn, Rips, and Shevell (1986) p. 158.

may improve recall. Specific dates rarely have the same effect (imagine trying to remember what you were doing in August three years ago). Recall can improve during the course of an interview or after the interviewer has left.

The passage of time may also alter perceptions. Views change, and the interviewee may subconsciously try to harmonize interests, attitudes, or opinions. As in a historical account, what the principal actors knew at the time they recognized a problem and decided what to do is very important to capture accurately, and it may take some extra effort to trigger memory of initial perceptions and how these changed. Here is an example from a series of cases on the 2014 West Africa Ebola Outbreak Response.[11]

Example: Effects of time on accuracy (two interviews conducted in late 2015 about the Ebola response):

Interview 1: Question: "How useful was the US military response to improving logistics capability?" "The US timing was all wrong. The military built emergency treatment centers that were never used because the epidemic ended by the time the centers were ready. The US military action was irrelevant."

Interview 2: Question: "Let's go back to August and September 2014 when the outbreak escalated dramatically in Liberia. Could you talk about the impact of the US military on logistics?" "In September 2014, the models said the number of people infected would rise to over a million. The US military prepared for that eventuality. Later the epidemic declined and the ETUs [emergency treatment units] weren't used, but in the end what seemed to matter to the public was the visible sign that a big power cared, which generated a psychological boost. We hoped the military would be more useful in moving lab materials around but they had instructions not to enter areas where an outbreak had occurred so they just dropped us at the edges of these areas and then we made our way from there."

There is some truth to both statements but the timestamp in the second question elicited a more complete answer that helped resolve tensions among accounts.

5. Memory of actions taken in a crisis atmosphere, when people may have worked intensely on many different fronts, tends to be less good, emerges in a highly fragmented form with high levels of error, or acquires a gloss. Said one ISS interviewee who had worked intensely on a disaster response, "As we talk, I can feel PTSD [post-traumatic stress disorder] coming back." Words tumbled out, and the interviewer had to piece together the order in which actions occurred.

In these circumstances, it is helpful to plan one or more return interviews. Between sessions, people will tend to remember more, though their

---

[11] See Widner (2019a and 2019b).

memories may also start to embellish or spin the account. Questions that contain specific information about the circumstances and ask for a reaction may help alleviate that problem. For the researcher, the challenge then becomes integrating the different versions of an event to ensure that they synchronize accurately.

6. Research on how respondents react to surveys suggests that question order can make a big difference in the responses people offer.[12] Although there is not parallel research on long-form qualitative interviews, it stands to reason that some of the same issues arise in this slightly different context, although it is easier for the interviewer to circle back and ask for views a second time than it might be in a survey, providing a possible corrective.

In designing and modifying the informal script that structures the interviews, it may help to consider how the sequence or juxtaposition of particular questions might influence what people say by inadvertently priming a particular response. For example, if one question focuses attention on the influence an interest group brought to bear on a decision, the answer to an unrelated question may place heavier emphasis on interest groups than it would have in a different question lineup. Sometimes the best cure for this type of spillover is to acknowledge it directly: "We have talked a lot about interest group influence. I want to change the topic and focus on ____, now. Although there may have been some interest group influence, most likely other things were important too, so I encourage you to step back and think about what shaped this decision, more broadly." An alternative is to shift to a different, more minor topic – or recommend a brief break – before returning to the line of questioning.

In policy research, political or social sensitivity may lead to self-censorship. To lessen this response, while also respecting the risks a speaker faces, it is sometimes possible to sequence questions so that they enable the speaker to articulate a problem in a diplomatic way, threading the needle: "I imagine that people who had invested in that land were upset that the city wanted to build a road there. Did any of those people ever speak about this problem in public? Did any of them ever come here to express their views? I see in the newspapers that politician X owned some land in that area – was he part of the group that objected? Did the program change after this point?"

Pacing sensitive questions may necessitate extra care in order to prevent the interviewee from calling an end to the conversation or from shifting to highly abbreviated responses. If the point of an interview is to acquire

---

[12] For example, see Zaller and Feldman (1992) and Schwarz, Oyserman, and Peytcheva (2010).

information about a particular stage of a negotiation, then it may be better to proceed to that point in the conversation before posing sensitive questions about earlier matters – and then loop back to these other sensitive issues when asking about results or reflections toward the conclusion of the conversation. By that point the interviewer has had a chance to build credibility and signal facility with some of the technical details, making it more likely the speaker feels s/he has had a fair chance to explain actions and views, while also realizing the interviewer is unlikely to be satisfied with a stock answer. Ethics rules that require returning to the speaker for permission to use quotes or identifying information can also assist willingness to speak, provided the speaker trusts that the interviewer will indeed live up to this commitment. (Note that this research ethics commitment runs counter to the standards in journalism, where the emphasis is on conveying publicly important information in real time and not allowing the holders of that information to act as censors.)

Ending on a more positive note is also helpful, both for the well-being of the interviewee and for maintaining the goodwill that makes it possible to return to the conversation later: "You accomplished __, ___, and ____. When you think back on this episode are there other things that make you especially proud/happy/satisfied with the work/____?"

7. Offer the right kinds of rewards. Because it takes a lot of mental energy to respond to questions and because there is no immediate tangible reward, an interview has to generate and sustain motivation. Usually, helping someone understand the important purpose and specific focus increases interest. Most people also want some sense that they are responding with useful information. If they don't have this sense, they will drop out.

There is a fine line between leading, on the one hand, and nondirective feedback that merely sustains a conversation. A leading question suggests correct answers or reveals the researcher's point of view. This type of feedback reduces accuracy. By contrast, there are neutral forms of feedback that can motivate and lead the interviewee to persist in answering questions. Cannell, Miller, and Oksenberg (1981: 409–411) suggest a set of four responses that ISS has also found helpful:

- "Thanks, that's useful, OK."
- "I see. This is the kind of information we want."
- "Thanks, you have mentioned ___ things . . ."
- "Thanks, we are interested in details like these . . ."

Speakers often model the length of their responses on the interviewer's behavior. Rewarding specificity in a response to an open-ended question early in the interview with "Thanks, we are interested in details like these" can send the right signal (assuming detail is in fact what we want).

6.5   Integrating Streams of Evidence, Arbitrating Differences

In survey research, social scientists aggregate data from multiple respondents by analyzing central tendencies, assessing variance, and then evaluating the influence of causal factors on responses to questions using some type of regression analysis. Although less concerned with central tendencies and average effects, qualitative case study research also has to integrate multiple streams of information from interviews – information about views as well as processes. This stage of the research can catch and reconcile discrepancies or spin, but it can also become a source of error if the researcher incorrectly judges one account to be more truthful than another, with little basis in fact or little transparency about the reasons for privileging a particular point of view.

Arbitrating among conflicting streams of evidence takes place in journalism every day, and the adages journalists follow are equally applicable in social science research. Editors and reporters term the failure to resolve a contradiction or a clash of perspectives as "he said, she said" journalism.[13] Columbia University journalism professor Jay Rosen, who led the charge against "he said, she said" reporting, offered an illustration. In this instance, a US National Public Radio reporter described a controversy over new reproductive health regulations and said that one group portrayed the rules as "common sense" while another saw them as designed to drive clinics out of business. The reporter laid out each group's claims and moved on. Rosen cried foul and said the reporter had an obligation to offer a more complete description that gave the reader some sense of the evidence underlying the seemingly disparate claims. This imperative has grown stronger as quality journalism has tried to combat disinformation.

Rosen's remedies were exactly those his social science counterparts would have offered: hypothesis formation, measurement, and follow-up questions. In this instance, Rosen said, the reporter could have compared the new regulations to those already in place for similar procedures in the same state and to regulations in other jurisdictions so the reader could see whether

---

[13] Rosen (2011).

the claim that the new rules were "common sense" had some basis in fact. The reporter could have read the safety report to see whether the accident or infection rates were especially high compared to related procedures. In short, Rosen argues, the researcher's obligation to the reader is to resolve discrepancies when they involve matters that affect the reader's ability to make a judgment about the core subject matter of the case. The reader's mind should not buzz with further questions, and the description must have all the components necessary to understand the intervention described, including those an expert would consider fundamental.

Discrepancies in streams of interview evidence can arise from many sources, including differences regarding when two people became involved in a process, the roles they played and the knowledge available to them in each of these roles, and the life experiences or technical skills they brought to the job. That is, disagreements do not always arise from deliberate spin. Here are three examples of descriptive or reporting challenges drawn from ISS case study research and the intellectual process these challenges triggered.

One: Superficially discrepant timelines (case about the Liberian Ebola Outbreak response coordination[14]):

Question: When did Liberia adopt an incident management system for responding to the Ebola outbreak?

Interview 1: CDC Director Tom Frieden persuaded President Ellen Sirleaf to support an incident management system for coordinating the Ebola response. (From archival record: This meeting took place on or around August 24, 2014, on Frieden's visit to the country.)

Interview 2: A CDC team visited Monrovia the third week in July 2014 and began to work with officials to set up an incident management system. (From archival record: The president appointed Tolbert Nyenswah head of the incident management system on August 10.)

Thought Process: The interviewer seeks accuracy in describing a sequence of events. At first blush it might seem that one subject just remembered a date incorrectly, but the archival evidence suggests that the dates of the events cited are indeed different. What else could be going on? One hypothesis is that something happened in between the two periods that required the president to revisit the choice of approach. An interviewer in strong command of the timeline might then frame a follow-up for interviewee 1: "Could you clarify the situation for me? I thought that the president had earlier appointed someone to head an incident management system. Did the first

---

[14] Widner (2019a and 2019b).

effort to launch the system fail or flounder?" For interviewee 2: "I understand that later the president and the head of the CDC discussed whether to continue the system in late August. Did anything happen in mid-August to shake the president's confidence that the IMS was the right approach?"

Two: Superficially discrepant information about states of mind or relationships: (case on cabinet coordination in a power-sharing government[15])

Interview 1 (with someone who was in the meeting): "The dialogue process helped resolve stalemates and we emerged from these sessions in a better position to work together."

Interview 2 (with a knowledgeable observer who was not in the meeting): "The dialogue process just helped the parties delay taking steps to meet the goals they had jointly agreed to. The leaders argued for long periods."

Thought Process: In this instance, the researcher wants to know whether tensions among political parties in a unity government were lower, about the same, or higher after resort to an externally mediated "dialogue" mechanism. There are three challenges. First, few people were in the room and the perceptions may vary with knowledge. Second, "tension" or "trust" among political parties is something that is "latent" or hard to measure. Third, delay and levels of distrust could be related in a wide variety of ways. Delay might have increased trust or decreased it.

In this instance, the researcher would likely have to return to the people interviewed with follow-up questions. One might venture several hypotheses and ask what evidence would allow us to rule out each one, then frame questions accordingly. Did the number of matters referred to mediation go down over time? Did the number of days of mediation required diminish over time? Did deputy ministers perceive that it became easier or harder to work with colleagues from the other party during this period? Did progress toward pre-agreed priorities stall or proceed during this period?

If what went on in the mediation room is confidential, then the researcher has to frame questions that rely on other types of information: "Comparing the period before the mediation with the weeks after the mediation, would you say that you had more purely social conversations with people in the opposite party, fewer, or about the same? Was there a new practice introduced after the mediation that affected your ability to have these conversations?"

Three: Insufficient detail; "the mind does not come to rest" and the reader is left with an obvious, big, unanswered question. This challenge arises frequently. For example, the Princeton ISS program ran into this issue in trying to document the introduction of a public service delivery tracking system in the Dominican Republic.[16]

---

[15] Schreiber (2016).   [16] Cameron (2016).

Interview 1 (with an officer responsible for tracking action items in a ministry): "At first we added data to the tracking system each month but after a few months everything slowed down and we added information only every three or four months."

Interview 2 (with an officer responsible for overseeing the central recording process): "Some ministries didn't report at all. They never added information to the tracking system."

Thought process: There is a discrepancy between the two statements, but in both instances it is clear that work had ground to a halt. The issue is when and why. Was the new system unworkable in all ministries or just some? Further, was the system impossible for most to use, or was there something else going on? One could ask a general question, "Why did that happen?" – an approach that often yields surprising answers. But hypotheses and follow-ups might also help winnow out plausible from less-plausible explanations. Did a few ministries try to report and then give up and join the others in noncompliance, or did a few continue to report? Then to the rationale: Was there no progress to report? Was there no penalty for not reporting? Was it hard to find the time to file the report? Did the software break down, or was there limited electrical power to run the system? Was someone designated to acquire and upload the information, or was no one really in charge of that function? Were the instructions hard to follow? Did the minister care or say anything when reporting slowed or halted? Did anyone from the president's office/delivery unit call to ask why the report was slow? Was there pressure to delay the reports? Why?

If there are no data available to resolve a contradiction or settle a logical subsidiary question, then the researcher can say so. Andrew Bennett has proposed valuing evidence from different interviews according to kind of schedule of plausibility.[17] Attach an estimate or "prior" to the possible motives of each interviewee who provides evidence and weigh the evidence provided accordingly. If someone offers evidence that clearly does not make that person "look good," one might have more confidence in the other information offered. "Social psychologists have long noted that audiences find an individual more convincing when that person espouses a view that is seemingly contrary to his or her instrumental goals," Bennett suggests; "For similar reasons, researchers should follow established advice on considering issues of context and authorship in assessing evidence. Spontaneous statements have a different evidentiary status from prepared remarks. Public

---

[17] Bennett and Checkel (2015: 24–25).

statements have a different evidentiary status from private ones or from those that will remain classified for a period of time."

6.6 Selection Bias

The protocols used to select interviewees are always a potential source of error, whether in survey research or in qualitative interviewing. In process-tracing case studies, we choose the people to interview instrumentally. That is, we want information from people who have direct knowledge of a process. But there is a consequent risk of interviewing only people from a single political party; from the group tasked with the daily work of carrying out a program; or from one ethnic, religious, or economic group affected. This problem may not always be damning. It may be partly contingent on the question asked: for example, there may be circumstances when the only people who are in a position to know about a series of actions are indeed people from the same small group. However, if the aim is to know how others perceived a decision or a program, or whether people thought a process was representative – or whether beneficiaries viewed the program in the same way policy-makers did – it goes without saying that we need the views of a broader group of people.

Avoiding selection bias in interview-based research can prove challenging, especially in less open societies. At ISS, which has focused on governmental reform, researchers typically spend much of their time securing an accurate description of a change in structure or practice and its implementation. Usually the only people with that information are those in government who actually carried out the daily legwork. In some settings, these people are likely to have a party affiliation and come only from one political party. They also may not know how the "clients" – the country's citizens – view what they do. Because of this, the research program made it standard practice to include in its interview lists:

- people most likely to be critical of the reforms we profile (we try to identify such people by looking at local newspaper editorials and headlines, speaking on background with journalists, etc.)
- counterparts from another political party where these exist (predecessors in the same role, for example)
- civic leaders or university researchers who work closely with the intended beneficiaries or clients

- public servants who worked on the project in different locations
- the "victors" and the "vanquished" – the people whose views prevailed and those whose views did not.

Where there are few civic groups it may be particularly difficult to identify people who are close to the views of clients and users and can generalize reliably about perceptions and experiences.

Problem: Critics won't speak (case study on extension of civilian oversight of the military)

Interview 1: The defense minister in the political party that recently came to power says, "We retrenched several thousand soldiers and gave them severance pay. There was no serious objection to the new policy. Some of the senior military officers believed the policy was the right thing to do and supported it."

Missing Interview: From archival sources we know that a political party led a protest against this very policy. Neither the officers of that political party nor the identifiable leaders of the protest assented to an interview, however.

Remedy: There are some partial solutions for countering selection bias that arises from this sort of "missing actor" problem. One is to try to induce people who will speak on the record to be self-reflective. For example, Jeffrey Berry suggests that the researcher "ask the subject to critique his own case – Why aren't Democrats buying this?" or to say, "I'm confused on one point; I read …."[18] Another approach is to draw on the publications the critics have authored. These may not get at the real reasons for the criticisms the groups raise, but they may provide enough information to represent the view, and enough detail for the researcher to use to seek a reaction from those who will go on the record.

Another kind of selection bias can arise in new democracies or more authoritarian political systems: self-censorship. In this situation, because of concerns about vulnerability or because of traditions that discourage openly critical comments, everyone interviewed offers a "careful" or biased response. The question is how to break through the reserve without jeopardizing any participant's safety. One possibility is to identify fractures within the political party – a committee or wing or leadership group that genuinely wants to know how well something works and is willing to talk about suspected problems. We can then use these to frame questions that don't require an interviewee to criticize but instead just ask for steps taken when X happened. Phrasing questions so that they don't force one person to impugn another can also help: "If you had to do this over again, what would you do

---

[18] Berry (2002), p. 680.

differently?" "If you could advise your counterpart in another country how to do _____, what special advice or tips would you want to convey?"

The act of "getting in the door" can create selection bias problems too.[19] The first people to respond favorably to requests to interviews may be people who are distinctive in some way – those who feel empowered, younger people, people who have aspirations in electoral politics and see a way to lend some credibility to their campaigns. To guard against this kind of bias, it is important to step back periodically and to ensure that the list of those who responded favorably to interview invitations includes people who were involved with what we seek to document but don't have the same profile as others.

6.7 Conclusion

Qualitative case studies are a form of empirical research. Facts are the currency in which they trade. As such they are potentially vulnerable to the same kinds of problems that bedevil quantitative research, from low measurement validity to data collection techniques that bias the views or accounts surveyed or introduce error. This chapter offers a schema for thinking about these challenges in the context of preparing interview-based process-tracing case studies, along with a few partial solutions to some common problems.

One implication of the observations offered here is that careful interview preparation yields a high return with respect to the accuracy and completeness of a process-tracing case study. That means 1) knowing the subject well enough to frame thoughtful hypotheses and measures in advance, and to build these into draft questions; 2) establishing a timeline and "prestory" from news sources, operations reports, or preliminary "informant" interviews; 3) learning about the backgrounds of the people central to the policy initiative; 4) identifying representatives of the beneficiary groups as well as likely critics or people who had special vantage points; and 5) understanding options tried in other, similar settings or in other periods. This background preparation then shapes the development of interview scripts, useful for thinking hard about clarity, narrative flow, question sequence, and other matters that impinge on the quality of the information elicited. Although the interview itself is a conversation, not (usually) a series of survey questions read off a schedule, the development of the written script sharpens the

---

[19] Goldstein (2002), p. 669.

interviewer's ability to elicit the information required, while maintaining a positive rapport with the speaker.

A second implication is that we have to be transparent about the basis for arbitrating differences that emerge across interviews. Sometimes the prose can say what the reader needs to know: "Staff members involved at the beginning of the project, when the initial pilot failed, remembered that ____. But those who joined later, after the first results of the revised program started to emerge and neighborhood resistance had dissipated, had a different view of the challenges the government faced." In other instances, a discursive footnote of the sort that Andrew Moravcsik (Chapter 8, this volume) proposes may be the best way to help the reader understand the judgments the author made.

A third implication of this analysis is that the purported differences in ability to rely on quantitatively analyzed survey data, on the one hand, and qualitative interview data, on the other, are vastly overstated. The main difference between the two has more to do with whether frequencies or distribution of perspectives across populations matter to the aim of the project. If they do, then survey data may have greater value. But if the aim is to elicit understanding of strategic interaction or a process, then purposive interviewing will tell us more. In both contexts, however, the same concerns about eliciting accurate responses apply and some of the same remedies prove useful.

References

Aberbach, J. and Rockman, B. (2002) "Conducting and coding elite interviews," *PS: Political Science and Politics*, 35 (4), 673–676.

Bennett, A. and Checkel, J. T. eds. (2015) *Process tracing: From metaphor to analytic tool.* New York: Cambridge University Press.

Berry, J. (2002) "Validity and reliability issues in elite interviewing," *PS: Political Science & Politics.* 35 (4), 679–682.

Bradburn, N. M., Rips, L. J., and Shevell, S. K. (1986) "Answering autobiographical questions: The impact of memory and inference on surveys," *Science*, 236, 158.

Cameron, B. (2016) "Delivering on promises: The Presidential Goals System in the Dominican Republic, 2012–2016," Innovations for Successful Societies, Princeton University, accessed December 13, 2021 at https://successfulsocieties.princeton.edu/publications/delivering-promises-presidential-goals-system-dominican-republic-2012%E2%80%932016.

Cannell, C., Miller, P., and Oksenberg, L. (1981) "Research on interviewing techniques" in Leinhardt, S. ed., *Sociological methodology.* San Francisco: Jossey-Bass, pp. 389–437.

Gerring, J. (2012) "Mere description," *British Journal of Political Science*, 42 (4), 721–746.

Goldstein, K. (2002) "Getting in the door: Sampling and completing elite interviews," *PS: Political Science & Politics*, 35 (4), 669–672.

Hirschman, A. O. (1985) *A bias for hope: Essays on development and Latin America*. Boulder: Westview Press.

Johnson, S. (1755) "Smell a rat." In *A dictionary of the English language: A digital edition of the 1755 classic by Samuel Johnson*. Edited by B. Besalke. Last modified: March 26, 2012. https:// johnsonsdictionaryonline.com/smell-a-rat/.

Krosnick, J. (1991) "Response strategies for coping with the cognitive demands of attitude measures in surveys," *Applied Cognitive Psychology*, 5, 213–236.

Leech, B. (2002) "Asking questions: Techniques for semistructured interviews," *PS: Political Science and Politics*, 35 (4), 666.

Rosen, J. (2011) "We have no idea who's right: Criticizing 'he said, she said' journalism at NPR." Accessed December 13, 2021 at https://pressthink.org/2011/09/we-have-no-idea-whos-right-criticizing-he-said-she-said-journalism-at-NPR/.

Schreiber, Leon. "Making power sharing work: Kenya's Grand Coalition Cabinet, 2008–2013," Innovations for Successful Societies, Princeton University, 2016 accessed December 13, 2021 at https://successfulsocieties.princeton.edu/publications/kenya-powersharing-cabinet.

Schwarz, N., Oyserma, D., and Peytcheva, E. (2010) "Cognition, communication, and culture: Implications for the survey response process," in *Survey methods in multinational, multi-regional, and multicultural contexts*, edited by J. A. Harkness et al., John Wiley & Sons, Inc., pp. 175–190.

Spradley, J. (1979) *The ethnographic interview*. New York: Holt, Rinehart and Winston.

Tansey, O. (2007) "Process tracing and elite interviewing: A case for non-probability sampling," *PSOnline*, pp. 765–772. Accessed December 13, 2021 at www.cambridge.org/core/ journals/ps-political-science-and-politics/article/process-tracing-and-elite-interviewing-a-case-for-nonprobability-sampling/8EE25765F4BF94599E7FBD996CBFDE74.

Weiss, R. S. (1994) *Learning from strangers: The art and method of qualitative interview studies*. New York: Free Press.

Widner, J. (2019a) "All hands on deck: The US response to West Africa's Ebola crisis, 2014–2015," Innovations for Successful Societies, Princeton University, accessed December 13, 2021 at https://successfulsocieties.princeton.edu/sites/successfulsocieties/files/JW_Ebola_ USResponse_Final_June%2028%202018_JRG_0-3_1.pdf.

Widner, J. (2019b) *Responding to global health crises: Lessons from the US response to the 2014–2016 West Africa Ebola outbreak*. IBM Center for the Business of Government, accessed December 13, 2021, at www.businessofgovernment.org/report/responding-global-health-crises-lessons-us-response-2014-2016-west-africa-ebola-outbreak.

Wright, D., Gaskell, G., and O'Muircheartaigh, C. (1994) "How much is 'quite a bit?' Mapping between numerical values and vague quantifiers." *Applied Cognitive Psychology*, 8, 479–496.

Zaller, J. and Feldman, S. (1992) "A simple theory of the survey response: Answering questions versus revealing preferences," *American Journal of Political Science*, 36 (3), 579–616.

7 Selecting Cases for Comparative Sequential Analysis

Novel Uses for Old Methods

Tommaso Pavone

7.1 Introduction

In the lead article of the first issue of *Comparative politics*, Harold Lasswell posited that the "scientific approach" and the "comparative method" are one and the same (Lasswell 1968: 3). So important is comparative case study research to the modern social sciences that two disciplinary subfields – comparative politics in political science and comparative-historical sociology – crystallized in no small part because of their shared use of comparative case study research (Collier 1993; Adams, Clemens, and Orloff 2005: 22–26; Mahoney and Thelen 2015). As a result, a first-principles methodological debate emerged about the appropriate ways to select cases for causal inquiry. In particular, the diffusion of econometric methods in the social sciences exposed case study researchers to allegations that they were "selecting on the dependent variable" and that "selection bias" would hamper the "answers they get" (Geddes 1990). Lest they be pushed to randomly select cases or turn to statistical and experimental approaches, case study researchers had to develop a set of persuasive analytic tools for their enterprise.

I would like to thank Jennifer Widner and Michael Woolcock for the invitation to write this chapter, and Daniel Ortega Nieto for pointing me to case studies conducted by the World Bank's Global Delivery Initiative that I use as illustrative examples, as well as Jack Levy, Hillel Soifer, Andrew Moravcsik, Cassandra Emmons, Rory Truex, Dan Tavana, Manuel Vogt, and Killian Clarke for constructive feedback.

It is unsurprising, therefore, that there has been a profusion of scholarship discussing case selection over the years.[1] Gerring and Cojocaru (2015) synthesize this literature by deriving no less than five distinct types (representative, anomalous, most-similar, crucial, and most-different) and eighteen subtypes of cases, each with its own logic of case selection. It falls outside the scope of this chapter to provide a descriptive overview of each approach to case selection. Rather, the purpose of the present inquiry is to place the literature on case selection in constructive dialogue with the equally lively and burgeoning body of scholarship on process tracing (George and Bennett 2005; Brady and Collier 2010; Beach and Pedersen 2013; Bennett and Checkel 2015). I ask a simple question: Should our evolving understanding of causation and our toolkit for case-based causal inference courtesy of process-tracing scholars alter how scholars approach case selection? If so, why, and what may be the most fruitful paths forward?

To propose an answer, this chapter focuses on perhaps the most influential and widely used means to conduct qualitative research involving two or more cases: Mill's methods of agreement and difference. Also known as the "most-different systems/cases" and "most-similar systems/cases" designs, these strategies have not escaped challenge – although, as we will see, many of these critiques were fallaciously premised on case study research serving as a weaker analogue to econometric analysis. Here, I take a different approach: I argue that the traditional use of Millian methods of case selection can indeed be flawed, but rather because it risks treating cases as static units to be synchronically compared rather than as social processes unfolding over time. As a result, Millian methods risk prematurely rejecting and otherwise overlooking (1) ordered causal processes, (2) paced causal processes, and (3) equifinality, or the presence of multiple pathways that produce the same outcome. While qualitative methodologists have stressed the importance of these processual dynamics, they have been less attentive to how these factors may problematize pairing Millian methods of case selection with within-case process tracing (e.g., Hall 2003; Tarrow 2010; Falleti and Mahoney 2015). This chapter begins to fill that gap.

Taking a more constructive and prescriptive turn, the chapter provides a set of recommendations for ensuring the alignment of Millian methods of case selection with within-case sequential analysis. It begins by outlining how

---

[1] See, for example, Przeworski and Teune (1970), Lijphart (1971), Eckstein (1975), Yin (1984), Geddes (1990), Collier (1993), Faure (1994), George and Bennett (2005), Flyvbjerg (2006), Levy (2008), Seawright and Gerring (2008), Gerring (2007), Brady and Collier (2010), and Tarrow (2010).

the deductive use of processualist theories can help reformulate Millian case selection designs to accommodate ordered and paced processes (but not equifinal processes). More originally, the chapter concludes by proposing a new, alternative approach to comparative case study research: *the method of inductive case selection*. By making use of Millian methods to select cases for comparison after a causal process has been identified within a particular case, the method of inductive case selection enables researchers to assess (1) the generalizability of the causal sequences, (2) the logics of scope conditions on the causal argument, and (3) the presence of equifinal pathways to the same outcome. In so doing, scholars can convert the weaknesses of Millian approaches into strengths and better align comparative case study research with the advances of processualist researchers.

Organizationally, the chapter proceeds as follows. Section 7.2 provides an overview of Millian methods for case selection and articulates how the literature on process tracing fits within debates about the utility and short-comings of the comparative method. Section 7.3 articulates why the traditional use of Millian methods risks blinding the researcher to ordered, paced, and equifinal causal processes, and describes how deductive, processualist theorizing helps attenuate some of these risks. Section 7.4 develops a new inductive method of case selection and provides a number of concrete examples from development practice to illustrate how it can be used by scholars and policy practitioners alike. Section 7.5 concludes.

7.2   Case Selection in Comparative Research

7.2.1   Case Selection Before the Processual Turn

Before "process tracing" entered the lexicon of social scientists, the dominant case selection strategy in case study research sought to maximize causal leverage via comparison, particularly via the "methods of agreement and difference" of John Stuart Mill (1843 [1974]: 388–391).

In Mill's method of difference, the researcher purposively chooses two (or more) cases that experience different outcomes, despite otherwise being very similar on a number of relevant dimensions. Put differently, the researcher seeks to maximize variation in the outcome variable while minimizing variation amongst a set of plausible explanatory variables. It is for this reason that the approach also came to be referred to as the 'most-similar systems' or 'most-similar cases' design – while Mill's nomenclature highlights variation in the outcome of interest, the alternative terminology highlights minimal variation amongst a set of possible explanatory factors. The underlying logic of this case selection strategy is that because the cases are so similar, the researcher can subsequently probe for the explanatory factor that actually does exhibit cross-case variation and isolate it as a likely cause.

Mill's method of agreement is the mirror image of the method of difference. Here, the researcher chooses two (or more) cases that experience similar outcomes despite being very different on a number of relevant dimensions. That is, the researcher seeks to minimize variation in the outcome variable while maximizing variation amongst a set of plausible explanatory variables. An alternative, independent variable-focused terminology for this approach was developed – the 'most-different systems' or 'most-different cases' design – breeding some confusion. The underlying logic of this case selection strategy is that it helps the researcher isolate the explanatory factor that is similar across the otherwise different cases as a likely cause.[2]

Mill's method of difference / most-similar cases design

	DV / Outcome	IV1 / Event1	IV2 / Event2	IV3 / Event3	IV4 / Event4
Case 1:	1	1	1	1	1
Case 2:	0	1	1	1	0

IV1-IV3 d/n covary w/ outcome   IV4 covaries w/ outcome
→ Rejected as causally insufficient   → Identified as likely cause

Mill's method of agreement / most-different cases design

	DV / Outcome	IV1 / Event1	IV2 / Event2	IV3 / Event3	IV4 / Event4
Case 1:	1	1	0	1	1
Case 2:	1	0	1	0	1

IV1-IV3 d/n covary w/ outcome   IV4 covaries w/ outcome
→ Rejected as causally unnecessary   → Identified as likely cause

Figure 7.1   Case selection setup under Mill's methods of difference and agreement

[2] Some scholars, such as Faure (1994), distinguish Mill's dependent-variable driven methods of agreement and difference from the independent-variable driven most-similar and most-different systems designs, suggesting they are distinct. But because, as Figure 7.1 shows, Mill's dependent-variable driven methods also impose requirements on the array of independent variables to permit causal inference via exclusion, this distinction is not particularly fertile.

Mill himself did not believe that such methods could yield causal inferences outside of the physical sciences (Mill 1843 [1974]: 452). Nevertheless, in the 1970s a number of comparative social scientists endorsed Millian methods as the cornerstones of the comparative method. For example, Przeworski and Teune (1970) advocated in favor of the most-different cases design, whereas Lijphart (1971) favored the most-similar cases approach. In so doing, scholars sought case selection techniques that would be as analogous as possible to regression analysis: focused on controlling for independent variables across cases, maximizing covariation between the outcome and a plausible explanatory variable, and treating cases as a qualitative equivalent to a row of dataset observations. It is not difficult to see why this contributed to the view that case study research serves as the "inherently flawed" version of econometrics (Adams, Clemens, and Orloff 2005: 25; Tarrow 2010). Indeed, despite his prominence as a case study researcher, Lijphart (1975: 165; 1971: 685) concluded that "because the comparative method must be considered the weaker method," then "if at all possible one should generally use the statistical (or perhaps even the experimental) method instead." As Hall (2003: 380; 396) brilliantly notes, case study research

was deeply influenced by [Lijphart's] framing of it ... [where] the only important observations to be drawn from the cases are taken on the values of the dependent variable and a few explanatory variables ... From this perspective, because the number of pertinent observations available from small-N comparison is seriously limited, the analyst lacks the degrees of freedom to consider more than a few explanatory variables, and the value of small-N comparison for causal inference seems distinctly limited.

In other words, the predominant case selection approach through the 1990s sought to do its best to reproduce a regression framework in a small-N setting – hence Lijphart's concern with the "many variables, small number of cases" problem, which he argued could only be partially mitigated if, *inter alia*, the researcher increases the number of cases and decreases the number of variables across said cases (1971: 685–686). Later works embraced Lijphart's formulation of the problem even as they sought to address it: for example, Eckstein (1975: 85) argued that a "case" could actually be comprised of many "cases" if the unit of analysis shifted from being, say, the electoral system to, say, the voter. Predictably, such interventions invited retorts: Lieberson (1994), for example, claimed that Millian methods' inability to accommodate probabilistic causation,[3] interaction effects, and multivariate analysis would remain fatal flaws.

7.2.2   Enter Process Tracing

It is in this light that 'process tracing' – a term first used by Hobarth (1972) but popularized by George (1979) and particularly George and Bennett (2005), Brady and Collier (2010), Beach and Pedersen (2013), and Bennett and Checkel (2015) – proved revolutionary for the ways in which social scientists conceive of case study research. Cases have gradually been reconceptualized not as dataset observations but as concatenations of concrete historical events that produce a specific outcome (Goertz and Mahoney 2012). That is, cases are increasingly treated as social processes, where a process is defined as "a particular type of sequence in which the temporally ordered events belong to a single coherent pattern of activity" (Falleti and Mahoney 2015: 214). Although there exist multiple distinct conceptions of process tracing – from Bayesian approaches (Bennett 2015) to set-theoretic approaches (Mahoney et al. 2009) to mechanistic approaches (Beach and Pedersen 2013) to sequentialist approaches (Falleti and Mahoney 2015) – their overall *esprit* is the same: reconstructing the sequence of events and interlinking causal logics that produce an outcome – isolating the 'causes of effects' – rather than probing a variable's mean impact across cases via an 'effects of causes' approach.[4]

For this intellectual shift to occur, processualist social scientists had to show how a number of assumptions underlying Millian comparative methods – as well as frequentist approaches more generally – are usually inappropriate for case study research. For example, the correlational approach endorsed by Przeworski and Teune (1970), Lijphart (1971), and Eckstein (1975) treats observational units as homogeneous and independent (Hall 2003: 382; Goertz and Mahoney 2012). Unit homogeneity means that "different units are presumed to be fully identical to each other in all relevant respects except for the values of the main independent variable," such that each observation contributes equally to the confidence we have in the

---

[3] In Mill's method of difference, factors present in both cases are eliminated for being insufficient for the outcome (in the method of agreement, factors that vary across the cases are eliminated for being unnecessary).

[4] Note that Mill himself distinguished between deductively assessing the average "effect of causes" and inductively retracing the "causes of effects" using the methods of agreement and disagreement (Mill 1843 [1974], pp. 449, 764).

accuracy and magnitude of our causal estimates (Brady and Collier 2010: 41–42). Given this assumption, more observations are better – hence, Lijphart (1971)'s dictum to "increase the number of cases" and, in its more recent variant, to "increase the number of observations" (King, Keohane, and Verba 1994: 208–230). By independence, we mean that "for each observation, the value of a particular variable is not influenced by its value in other observations"; thus, each observation contributes "new information about the phenomenon in question" (Brady and Collier 2010: 43).

By contrast, practitioners of process tracing have shown that treating cases as social processes implies that case study observations are often interdependent and derived from heterogeneous units (Goertz and Mahoney 2012). Unit heterogeneity means that not all historical events, and the observable evidence they generate, are created equal. Hence, some observations may better enable the reconstruction of a causal process because they are more proximate to the central events under study. Correlatively, this is why historians accord greater 'weight' to primary than to secondary sources, and why primary sources concerning actors central to a key event are more important than those for peripheral figures (Trachtenberg 2009; Tansey 2007). In short, while process tracing may yield a bounty of observable evidence, we seek not to necessarily increase the number, but rather the quality, of observations. Finally, by interdependence we mean that because time is "fateful" (Sewell 2005: 6), antecedent events in a sequence may influence subsequent events. This "fatefulness" has multiple sources. For instance, historical institutionalists have shown how social processes can exhibit path dependencies where the outcome of interest becomes a central driver of its own reproduction (Pierson 1996; Pierson 2000; Mahoney 2000; Hall 2003; Falleti and Mahoney 2015). At the individual level, processual sociologists have noted that causation in the social world is rarely a matter of one billiard ball hitting another, as in Hume's (1738 [2003]) frequentist concept of "constant conjunction." Rather, it hinges upon actors endowed with memory, such that the micro-foundations of social causation rest on individuals aware of their own historicality (Sewell 2005; Abbott 2001; 2016).

At its core, eschewing the independence and unit homogeneity assumptions simply means situating case study evidence within its spatiotemporal context (Hall 2003; Falleti and Lynch 2009). This commitment is showcased by the language which process-sensitive case study researchers use when making causal inferences. First, rather than relating 'independent variables' to 'dependent variables', they often privilege the contextualizing language of relating 'events' to 'outcomes' (Falleti and Mahoney 2015). Second, they prefer to speak not of 'dataset observations' evocative of cross-sectional analysis, but of 'causal process observations' evocative of sequential analysis (Brady and Collier 2010; Goertz and Mahoney 2012). Third, they may substitute the language of 'causal inference via concatenation' – a terminology implying that unobservable causal mechanisms are embedded within a sequence of observable events – for that of 'causal inference via correlation', evocative of the frequentist billiard-ball analogy (Waldner 2012: 68). The result is that case study research is increasingly hailed as a "distinctive approach that offers a much richer set of observations, especially about causal processes, than statistical analyses normally allow" (Hall 2003: 397).

7.3   Threats to Processual Inference and the Role of Theory

While scholars have shown how process-tracing methods have reconceived the utility of case studies for causal inference, there remains some ambiguity about the implications for case selection, particularly using Millian methods. While several works have touched upon this theme (e.g., Hall 2003; George and Bennett 2005; Levy 2008; Tarrow 2010), the contribution that most explicitly wrestles with this topic is Falleti and Mahoney (2015), who acknowledge that "the application of Millian methods for sequential arguments has not been systematically explored, although we believe it is commonly used in practice" (Falleti and Mahoney 2015: 226). Falleti and Mahoney argue that process tracing can remedy the weaknesses of Millian approaches: "When used in isolation, the methods of agreement and difference are weak instruments for small-N causal inference ... small-N researchers thus normally must combine Millian methods with process tracing or other within-case methods to make a positive case for causality" (2015: 225–226). Their optimism about the synergy between Millian methods and process tracing leads them to conclude that "by fusing these two elements, the comparative sequential method merits the distinction of being the principal overarching methodology for [comparative-historical analysis] in general" (2015: 236).

Falleti and Mahoney's contribution is the definitive statement of how comparative case study research has long abandoned its Lijphartian origins and fully embraced treating cases as social processes. It is certainly true that process-tracing advocates have shown that some past critiques of Millian methods may not have been as damning as they first appeared. For example,

Lieberson's (1994) critique that Millian case selection requires a deterministic understanding of causation has been countered by set-theoretic process tracers who note that causal processes can indeed be conceptualized as concatenations of necessary and sufficient conditions (Goertz and Mahoney 2012; Mahoney and Vanderpoel 2015). After all, "at the individual case level, the ex post (objective) probability of a specific outcome occurring is either 1 or 0" (Mahoney 2008: 415). Even for those who do not explicitly embrace set-theoretic approaches and prefer to perform a series of "process tracing tests" (such as straw-in-the-wind, hoop, smoking gun, and doubly-decisive tests), the objective remains to evaluate the deterministic causal relevance of a historical event on the next linkage in a sequence (Collier 2011; Mahoney 2012). In this light, Millian methods appear to have been thrown a much-needed lifeline.

Yet processualist researchers have implicitly exposed new, and perhaps more damning, weaknesses in the traditional use of the comparative method. Here, Falleti and Mahoney (2015) are less engaged in highlighting how their focus on comparing within-case sequences should push scholars to revisit strategies for case selection premised on assumptions that process-tracing advocates have undermined. In this light, I begin by outlining three hitherto underappreciated threats to inference associated with the traditional use of Millian case selection: potentially ignoring (1) ordered and (2) paced causal processes, and ignoring (3) the possibility of equifinality. I then demonstrate how risks (1) and (2) can be attenuated deductively by formulating processualist theories and tweaking Millian designs for case selection.

Risk 1: Ignoring Ordered Processes

Process-sensitive social scientists have long noted that "the temporal order of the events in a sequence [can be] causally consequential for the outcome of interest" (Falleti and Mahoney 2015: 218; see also Pierson 2004: 54–78). For example, where individual acts of agency play a critical role – such as political elites' response to a violent protest – "reordering can radically change [a] subject's understanding of the meaning of particular events," altering their response and the resulting outcomes (Abbott 1995: 97).

An evocative illustration is provided by Sewell's (1996) analysis of how the storming of the Bastille in 1789 produced the modern concept of "revolution." After overrunning the fortress, the crowd freed the few prisoners held within it; shot, stabbed, and beheaded the Bastille's commander; and paraded his severed head through the streets of Paris (Sewell 1996: 850).

When the French National Assembly heard of the taking of the Bastille, it first interpreted the contentious event as "disastrous news" and an "excess of fury"; yet, when the king subsequently responded by retreating his troops to their provincial barracks, the Assembly recognized that the storming of the Bastille had strengthened its hand, and proceeded to reinterpret the event as a patriotic act of protest in support of political change (Sewell 1996: 854–855). The king's reaction to the Bastille thus bolstered the Assembly's resolve to "invent" the modern concept of revolution as a "legitimate rising of the sovereign people that transformed the political system of a nation" (Sewell 1996: 854–858). Proceeding counterfactually, had the ordering of events been reversed – had the king withdrawn his troops before the Bastille had been stormed – the National Assembly would have had little reason to interpret the popular uprising as a patriotic act legitimating reform rather than a violent act of barbarism.

Temporal ordering may also alter a social process's political outcomes through macro-level mechanisms. For example, consider Falleti's (2005, 2010) analysis of the conditions under which state decentralization – the devolution of national powers to subnational administrative bodies – increases local political autonomy in Latin America. Through process tracing, Falleti demonstrates that when fiscal decentralization precedes electoral decentralization, local autonomy is increased, since this sequence endows local districts with the monetary resources necessary to subsequently administer an election effectively. However, when the reverse occurs, such that electoral decentralization precedes fiscal decentralization, local autonomy is compromised. For although the district is being offered the opportunity to hold local elections, it lacks the monetary resources to administer them effectively, endowing the national government with added leverage to impose conditions upon the devolution of fiscal resources.

For our purposes, what is crucial to note is not simply that temporal ordering matters, but that in ordered processes it is not the presence or absence of events that is most consequential for the outcome of interest. For instance, in Falleti's analysis both fiscal and electoral decentralization occur. This means that a traditional Millian framework risks dismissing some explanatory events as causally irrelevant on the grounds that their presence is insufficient for explicating the outcome of interest (see Figure 7.2).

The way to deductively attenuate the foregoing risk is to develop an ordered theory and then modify the traditional Millian setup to assess the effect of ordering on an outcome of interest. That is, deductive theorizing

Ordered process revealed via process tracing

Case 1:   Outcome   ⬅ Event4 ⬅ Event3 ⬅ Event2 ⬅ Event1

Case 2:   No Outcome ⬅ Event3 ⬅ Event4 ⬅ Event2 ⬅ Event1

The order of Events 3 & 4 is causally consequential

How a traditional Millian setup risks treating the above process

Case 1:	Outcome	Event4	Event3	Event2	Event1
Case 2:	No Outcome	Event4	Event3	Event2	Event1

Events 1–4 do not covary w/ outcome
→ Rejected as causally insufficient

Figure 7.2   How ordered processes risk being ignored by a Millian setup

	Outcome	IV1 = Event1	IV2 = Event2	IV3 = Event3	**IV4 = Event1→Event2**
Case 1:	1	1	1	1	1
Case 2:	0	1	1	1	0

presence of Events 1–3 d/n covary w/ outcome   *sequencing of Events 1 & 2 covaries w/ outcome*
→ rejected as causally insufficient   *→ identified as likely cause*

Figure 7.3   Deductively incorporating ordered processes within a Millian setup

aimed at probing the causal effect of ordering can guide us in constructing an appropriate Millan case selection design, such as that in Figure 7.3. In this example, we redefine the fourth independent variable to measure not the presence or absence of a fourth event, but rather to measure the ordering of two previously defined events (in this case, events 1 and 2). This case selection setup would be appropriate if deductive theorizing predicts that the outcome of interest is produced when event 1 is followed by event 2 (such that, unless this specific ordering occurs, the presence of events 1 and 2 is insufficient to generate the outcome). In other words, if Millian methods are to be deductively used to select cases for comparison, the way to guard against prematurely dismissing the causal role of temporal ordering is to explicitly theorize said ordering *a priori*. If this proves difficult, or if the researcher lacks sufficient knowledge to develop such a theory, it is advisable to switch to the more inductive method for case selection outlined in the next section.

Risk 2: Ignoring Paced Processes

Processualist researchers have also emphasized that, beyond temporal order, "the speed or duration of events ... is causally consequential" (Falleti and Mahoney 2015: 219). For example, social scientists have long distinguished an "eventful temporality" (Sewell 1996) from those "big, slow moving" incremental sequences devoid of rapid social change (Pierson 2003). For historical institutionalists, this distinction is illustrated by "critical junctures" – defined as "relatively short periods of time during which there is a substantially heightened probability that agents' choices will affect the outcome of interest" (Capoccia and Kelemen 2007: 348; Capoccia 2015: 150–151) – on the one hand, and those "causal forces that develop over an extended period of time," such as "cumulative" social processes, sequences involving "threshold effects," and "extended causal chains" on the other hand (Pierson 2004: 82–90; Mahoney and Thelen 2010).

An excellent illustration is provided by Beissinger (2002)'s analysis of the contentious events that led to the collapse of the Soviet State. Descriptively, the sequence of events has its origins in the increasing transparency of Soviet institutions and freedom of expression accompanying Gorbachev's Glasnost (Beissinger 2002: 47). As internal fissures within the Politburo began to emerge in 1987, Glasnost facilitated media coverage of the split within the Soviet leadership (2002: 64). In response, "interactive attempts to contest the state grew regularized and began to influence one another" (2002: 74). These challenging acts mobilized around previously dormant national identities, and for the first time – often out of state incompetence – these early protests were not shut down (2002: 67). Protests reached a boiling point in early 1989 as the first semicompetitive electoral campaign spurred challengers to mobilize the electorate and cultivate grievances in response to regime efforts to "control nominations and electoral outcomes" (2002: 86). By 1990 the Soviet State was crumbling, and "in many parts of the USSR demonstration activity ... had become a normal means for dealing with political conflict" (2002: 90).

Crucially, Beissinger stresses that to understand the causal dynamics of the Soviet State's collapse, highlighting the chronology of events is insufficient. The 1987–1990 period comprised a moment of "thickened history" wherein "what takes place ... has the potential to move history onto tracks otherwise unimaginable ... all within an extremely compressed period of time" (2002: 27). Information overload, the density of interaction between diverse social actors, and the diffusion of contention engendered "enormous confusion and division within Soviet institutions," allowing the hypertrophy of challenging acts to play "an increasingly significant role in their own causal structure" (2002: 97, 27). In this light, the temporal compression of a sequence of events can bolster the causal role of human agency and erode the constraints of social structure. Proceeding counterfactually, had the exact same sequence of contentious events unfolded more slowly, it is doubtful that the Soviet State would have suddenly collapsed.

Many examples of how the prolongation of a sequence of events can render them invisible, and thus produce different outcomes, could be referenced. Consider, for example, how global climate change – which is highlighted by Pierson (2004: 81) as a prototypical process with prolonged time horizons – conditions the psychological response of social actors. As a report from the American Psychological Association underscores, "climate change that is construed as rapid is more likely to be dreaded," for "people often apply sharp discounts to costs or benefits that will occur in the future … relative to experiencing them immediately" (Swim et al. 2009: 24–25; Loewenstein and Elster 1992). This logic is captured by the metaphor of the "boiling frog": "place a frog in a pot of cool water, and gradually raise the temperature to boiling, and the frog will remain in the water until it is cooked" (Boyatzis 2006: 614).

What is important to note is that, once more, paced processes are not premised on the absence or presence of their constitutive events being causally determinative; rather, they are premised on the duration of events (or their temporal separation) bearing explanatory significance. Hence the traditional approach to case selection risks neglecting the causal impact of temporal duration on the outcome of interest (see Figure 7.4).

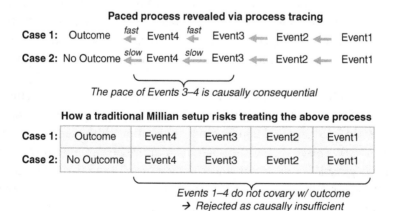

Figure 7.4   Paced processes risk being ignored by a Millian setup

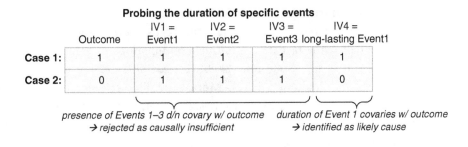

Figure 7.5   Deductively incorporating paced processes within a Millian setup

Here, too, the way to deductively assess the causal role of pacing on an outcome of interest is to explicitly develop a paced theory before selecting cases for empirical analysis. On the one hand, we might theorize that it is the duration of a given event that is causally consequential; on the other hand, we might theorize that it is the temporal separation of said event from other events that is significant. Figure 7.5 suggests how a researcher can assess both theories through a revised Millian design. In the first example, we define a fourth independent variable measuring not the presence of a fourth event, but rather the temporal duration of a previously defined event (in this case, event 1). This would be an appropriate case selection design to assess a theory predicting that the outcome of interest occurs when event 1 unfolds over a prolonged period of time (such that if event 1 unfolds more rapidly, its mere occurrence is insufficient for the outcome). In the second example, we define a fourth independent variable measuring the temporal separation between two previously defined events (in this case, events 1 and 2). This would be an appropriate case selection design for a theory predicting that the outcome of interest only occurs when event 1 is temporally distant to event 2 (such that events 1 and 2 are insufficient for the outcome if they are proximate). Again, if the researcher lacks *a priori* knowledge to theorize how a paced process may be generating the outcome, it is advisable to adopt the inductive method of case selection described in Section 7.4.

Risk 3: Ignoring Equifinal Causal Processes

Finally, researchers have noted that causal processes may be mired by equifinality: the fact that "multiple combinations of values ... produce the same outcome" (Mahoney 2008: 424; see also George and Bennett 2005; Goertz and Mahoney 2012). More formally, set-theoretic process tracers account for equifinality by emphasizing that, in most circumstances, "necessary" conditions or events are actually INUS conditions – individually necessary components of an unnecessary but sufficient combination of factors (Mahoney and Vanderpoel 2015: 15–18).

One of the reasons why processualist social scientists increasingly take equifinality seriously is the recognition that causal mechanisms may be context-dependent. Sewell's work stresses that "the consequences of a given act ... are not intrinsic to the act but rather will depend on the nature of the social world within which it takes place" (Sewell 2005: 9–10). Similarly, Falleti and Lynch (2009: 2; 11) argue that "causal effects depend on the interaction of specific mechanisms with aspects of the context within which these mechanisms operate," hence the necessity of imposing "scope conditions" on theory building. One implication is that the exact same sequence of events in two different settings may produce vastly different causal outcomes. The flip side of this conclusion is that we should not expect a given outcome to always be produced by the same sequence of events.

For example, consider Sewell's critique of Skocpol (1979)'s *States and Social Revolutions* for embracing an "experimental temporality." Skocpol deploys Millian methods of case selection to theorize that the great social revolutions – the French, Russian, and Chinese revolutions – were caused by a conjunction of three necessary conditions: "(1) military backwardness, (2) politically powerful landlord classes, and (3) autonomous peasant communities" (Sewell 2005: 93). Yet to permit comparison, Skocpol assumes that the outcomes of one revolution, and the processes of historical change more generally, have no effect on a subsequent revolution (Sewell 2005: 94–95). This approach amounts to "cutting up the congealed block of historical time into artificially interchangeable units," ignoring the fatefulness of historical sequences (Sewell 2005). For example, the Industrial Revolution "intervened" between the French and Russian Revolutions, and consequently one could argue that "the revolt of the Petersburg and Moscow proletariat was a necessary condition for social revolution in Russia in 1917, even if it was not a condition for the French Revolution in 1789" (Sewell 2005: 94–95). What

Sewell is emphasizing, in short, is that peasant rebellion is an INUS condition (as is a proletariat uprising), rather than a necessary condition.

Another prominent example of equifinality is outlined by Collier's (1999: 5–11) review of the diverse pathways through which democratization occurs. In the elite-driven pathway, emphasized by O'Donnell and Schmitter (1986), an internal split amongst authoritarian incumbents emerges; this is followed by liberalizing efforts by some incumbents, which enables the resurrection of civil society and popular mobilization; finally, authoritarian incumbents negotiate a pacted transition with opposition leaders. By contrast, in the working-class-driven pathway, emphasized by Rueschemeyer, Stephens, and Stephens (1992), a shift in the material balance of power in favor of the democracy-demanding working class and against the democracy-resisting landed aristocracy causes the former to overpower the latter, and via a democratic revolution from below a regime transition occurs. Crucially, Collier (1999: 12) emphasizes that these two pathways need not be contradictory (or exhaustive): the elite-driven pathway appears more common in the Latin American context during the second wave of democratization, whereas the working-class-driven pathway appears more common in Europe during the first wave of democratization.

What is crucial is that Millian case selection is premised on there being a single cause underlying the outcome of interest. As a result, Millian methods risk dismissing a set of events as causally irrelevant ex ante in one case simply because that same set of events fails to produce the outcome in another case (see Figure 7.6). Unlike ordered and paced processes, there is no

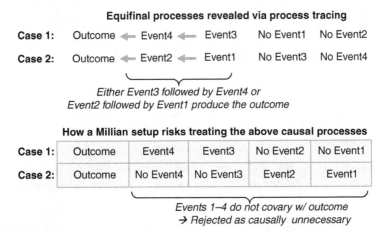

Figure 7.6   Equifinal causal processes risk being ignored by a Millian setup

clear way to leverage deductive theorizing to reconfigure Millian methods for case selection and accommodate equifinality. However, I argue that the presence of equifinal pathways can be fruitfully probed if we embrace a more inductive approach to comparative case selection, as the next section outlines.

7.4   A New Approach: The Method of Inductive Case Selection

If a researcher wishes to guard against ignoring consequential temporal dynamics but lacks the *a priori* knowledge necessary to develop a processual theory and tailor their case selection strategy, is there an alternative path forward? Yes, indeed: I suggest that researchers could wield most-similar or most-different cases designs to (1) probe causal generalizability, (2) reveal scope conditions, and (3) explore the presence of equifinality.[5] To walk through this more inductive case selection approach, I engage some case studies from development practice to illustrate how researchers and practitioners alike could implement and benefit from the method.

7.4.1   Tempering the Deductive Use of Millian Methods

To begin, one means to ensure against a Millian case selection design overlooking an ordered, paced, or equifinal causal process (in the absence of deductive theorizing) is to be wary of leveraging the methods of agreement and difference to eliminate potential explanatory factors (Falleti and Mahoney 2015: 225–226). That is, the decision to discard an explanatory variable or historical event as causally unnecessary (via the method of agreement) or insufficient (via the method of difference) may be remanded to the process-tracing stage, rather than being made *ex ante* at the case selection stage.

Notice how this recommendation is particularly intuitive in light of the advances in process-tracing methods. Before this burgeoning literature existed, Millian methods were called upon to accomplish two things at once: (1) provide a justification for selecting two or more cases for social inquiry, and (2) yield causal leverage via comparison and the elimination of potential explanatory factors as unnecessary or

---

[5] The proposed approach bears several similarities to Soifer's (2020) fertile analysis of how "shadow cases" in comparative research can contribute to theory-building and empirical analysis.

insufficient. But process-tracing methodologists have showcased how the analysis of temporal variation disciplined via counterfactual analysis, congruence testing, and process-tracing tests renders within-case causal inference possible even in the absence of an empirical comparative case (George and Bennett 2005; Gerring 2007; Collier 2011; Mahoney 2012; Beach and Pedersen 2013; Bennett and Checkel 2015; Levy 2015). That is, the ability to make causal inferences need not be primarily determined at the case selection stage.

The foregoing implies that if a researcher does not take temporal dynamics into account when developing their theory, the use of Millian methods should do no more than to provisionally discount the explanatory purchase of a given explanatory factor. The researcher should then bear in mind that as the causal process is reconstructed from a given outcome, the provisionally discounted factor may nonetheless be shown to be of causal relevance – particularly if the underlying process is ordered or paced, or if equifinal pathways are possible.

Despite these limitations, Millian methods might fruitfully serve additional functions from the standpoint of case selection, particularly if researchers shift (1) when and (2) why they make use of them. First, Millian methods may be as – if not more – useful *after* process tracing of a particular case is completed rather than to set the stage for within-case analysis. Such a chronological reversal – process tracing followed by Millian case selection, instead of Millian case selection followed by process tracing – inherently embraces a more inductive, theory-building approach to case study research (Falleti and Mahoney 2015: 229–231) which, I suspect, is far more commonly used in practice than is acknowledged. I refer to this approach as *the method of inductive case selection*, wherein "theory-building process tracing" (Beach and Pedersen 2013: 16–18) of a single case is subsequently followed by the use of a most-similar or most-different cases design.

7.4.2   Getting Started: Selecting the Initial Case

The method of inductive case selection begins by assuming that the researcher has justifiable reasons for picking a particular case for process tracing and is subsequently looking to contextualize the findings or build a theory outwards. Hence, the first step involves picking an initial case. Qualitative methodologists have already supplied a number of plausible logics for selecting a single case, and I describe three nonexhaustive possibilities here: (1) theoretical or historical importance; (2) policy relevance and salience; and (3) empirically puzzling nature.

First, an initial case may be selected due to its theoretical or historical importance. Eckstein (1975), for example, defines an idiographic case study as a case where the specific empirical events/outcome serve as a central referent for a scholarly literature. As an illustration, Gerring and Cojocaru (2015: 11) point to North and Weingast (1989)'s influential study of how the Glorious Revolution in seventeenth-century Britain favorably shifted the constitutional balance of power for the government to make credible commitments to protecting property rights (paving the way for the financial revolution of the early eighteenth century). Given that so much of the scholarly debate amongst economic historians centers on the institutional foundations of economic growth, North and Weingast's case study was "chosen (it would appear) because of its central importance in the [historical political economy] literature on the topic, and because it is ... a prominent and much-studied case" (Gerring and Cojocaru 2015: 11). In other words, North and Weingast (1989)'s study is idiographic in that it "aim[s] to explain and/or interpret a single historical episode," but it remains "theory-guided" in that it "focuses attention on some theoretically specified aspects of reality and neglects others" (Levy 2008: 4).

While the causes of the Glorious Revolution are a much-debated topic amongst economic historians, they have less relevance to researchers and practitioners focused on assessing the effects of contemporary public policy interventions. Hence, a second logic for picking a first case for process tracing is its policy relevance and salience. George and Bennett (2005: 263–286) define a policy-relevant case study as one where the outcome is of interest to policy-makers and its causes are at least partially amenable to policy manipulation. For example, one recent World Bank case study (El-Saharty and Nagaraj 2015) analyzes how HIV/AIDS prevalence amongst vulnerable subpopulations – particularly female sex workers – can be reduced via targeted service delivery. To study this outcome, two states in India – Andhra Pradesh and Karnataka – were selected for process tracing. There are three reasons why this constitutes an appropriate policy-relevant case selection choice. First, the outcome of interest – a decline in HIV/AIDS prevalence amongst female sex workers – was present in both Indian states. Second, because India accounts for almost 17.5 percent of the world population and has a large population of female sex workers, this outcome was salient to the government (El-Saharty and Nagaraj

2015: 3). Third, the Indian government had created a four-phase National AIDS Control Program (NACP) spanning from 1986 through 2017, meaning that at least one set of possible explanatory factors for the decline in HIV/AIDS prevalence comprised policy interventions that could be manipulated.[6]

A third logic for picking an initial case for process tracing is its puzzling empirical nature. One obvious instantiation is when an exogenous shock or otherwise significant event/policy intervention yields a different outcome from the one scholars and practitioners expected.[7] For example, in 2004 the federal government of Nigeria partnered with the World Bank to improve the share of Nigeria's urban population with access to piped drinking water. This partnership – the National Urban Water Sector Reform Project (NUWSRP1) – aimed to "increase access to piped water supply in selected urban areas by improving the reliability and financial viability of selected urban water utilities" and by shifting resources away from "infrastructure rehabilitation" that had failed in the past (Hima and Santibanez 2015: 2). Despite $200 million worth of investments, ultimately the NUWSRP1 "did not perform as strongly on the institutional reforms needed to ensure sustainability" (Hima and Santibanez 2015). Given this puzzling outcome, the World Bank conducted an intensive case study to ask why the program did "not fully meet its essential objective of achieving a sustainable water delivery service" (Hima and Santibanez 2015).[8]

The common thread of these three logics for selecting an initial case is that the case itself is theoretically or substantively important and that its empirical dynamics – underlying either the outcome itself or its relationship to some explanatory events – are not well understood. That being said, the method of inductive case selection merely presumes that there is some theoretical, policy-related, empirical, or normative justification to pick the initial case.

---

[6] This study found that the expansion of clinical services into government facilities embedded in the public health system, the introduction of peer educators, and the harmonization of large quantities of public health data underlay the timing and breadth of the decline in HIV/AIDS amongst female sex workers.

[7] What Levy (2008:13) calls a "deviant" case – which "focus[es] on observed empirical anomalies in existing theoretical propositions" – would also fit within the category of a puzzling case.

[8] Process tracing revealed that a conjunction of factors – management turnover and a lackluster culture of staff performance at the state level, inadequate coordination at the federal level, premature disbursement of funds, and citizen aversion to the commercialization of the public water supply – underlay the initially perplexing underperformance of the urban water delivery project.

7.4.3   Probing Generalizability Via a Most-Similar Cases Design

It is after picking an initial case that the method of inductive case selection contributes novel guidelines for case study researchers by reconfiguring how Millian methods are used. Namely, how should one (or more) additional cases be selected for comparison, and why? This question presumes that the researcher wishes to move beyond an idiographic, single-case study for the purposes of generating inferences that can travel. Yet in this effort, we should take seriously process-tracing scholars' argument that causal mechanisms are often context-dependent. As a result, the selection of one or more comparative cases is not meant to uncover universally generalizable abstractions; rather, it is meant to contextualize the initial case within a set or family of cases that are spatiotemporally bounded.

That being said, the first logical step is to understand whether the causal inferences yielded by the process-traced case can indeed travel to other contexts (Goertz 2017: 239). This constitutes the first reconfiguration of Millian methods: the use of comparative case studies to assess generalizability. Specifically, after within-case process tracing reveals a factor or sequence of factors as causally important to an outcome of interest, the logic is to select a case that is as contextually analogous as possible such that there is a higher probability that the causal process will operate similarly in the second case. This approach exploits the context-dependence of causal mechanisms to the researcher's advantage: Similarity of context increases the probability that a causal mechanism will operate similarly across both cases. By "context," it is useful to follow Falleti and Lynch (2009: 14) and to be

concerned with a variety of contextual layers: those that are quite proximate to the input (e.g., in a study of the emergence of radical right-wing parties, one such layer might be the electoral system); exogenous shocks quite distant from the input that might nevertheless effect the functioning of the mechanism and, hence, the outcome (e.g., a rise in the price of oil that slows the economy and makes voters more sensitive to higher taxes); and the middle-range context that is neither completely exogenous nor tightly coupled to the input and so may include other relevant institutions and structures (the tax system, social solidarity) as well as more atmospheric conditions, such as rates of economic growth, flows of immigrants, trends in partisan identification, and the like.

For this approach to yield valuable insights, the researcher focuses on 'controlling' for as many of these contextual explanatory factors (crudely put, for as many independent variables) as possible. In other words, the researcher selects a most-similar case: if the causal chain similarly operates in

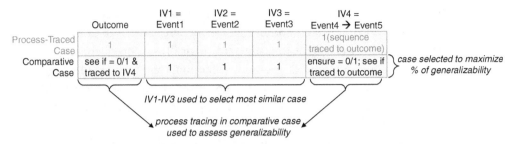

Figure 7.7   Probing generalizability by selecting a most-similar case

the second case, this would support the conclusion that the causal process is likely at work across the constellation of cases bearing 'family resemblances' to the process-traced case (Soifer 2020). Figure 7.7 displays the logic of this design:

As in Figure 7.7, suppose that process tracing of Case 1 reveals that some sequence of events (in this example, event 4 followed by event 5) caused the outcome of interest. The researcher would then select a most-similar case (a case with similar values/occurrences of other independent variables/events (here, IV1–IV3) that might also influence the outcome). The researcher would then scout whether the sequence in Case 1 (event 4 followed by event 5) also occurs in the comparative case. If it does, the expectation for a minimally generalizable theory is that it would produce a similar outcome in Case 2 as in Case 1. Correlatively, if the sequence does not occur in Case 2, the expectation is that it would not experience the same outcome as Case 1. These findings would provide evidence that the explanatory sequence (event 4 followed by event 5) has causal power that is generalizable across a set of cases bearing family resemblances.

For example, suppose a researcher studying democratization in Country A finds evidence congruent with the elite-centric theory of democratization of O'Donnell and Schmitter (1986) described previously. To assess causal generalizability, the researcher would subsequently select a case – Country B – that is similar in the background conditions that the literature has shown to be conducive to democratization, such as level of GDP per capita (Przeworski and Limongi 1997; Boix and Stokes 2003) or belonging to the same "wave" of democratization via spatial and temporal proximity (Collier 1991; Huntington 1993). Notice that these background conditions in Case B have to be at least partially exogenous to the causal process whose generalizability is being probed – that is, they cannot constitute the events that directly comprise the causal chain revealed in Case A. One way to think about them is as factors that in Case A appear to have been necessary, but less proximate and important, conditions for the outcome. Here, importance is determined by the "extent that they are [logically/counterfactually] present only when the outcome is present" (Mahoney et al. 2009: 119), whereas proximity is determined by the degree to which the condition is "tightly coupled" with the chain of events directly producing the outcome (Falleti and Mahoney 2015: 233).

An example related to the impact of service delivery in developmental contexts can be drawn from the World Bank's case study of HIV/AIDS interventions in India. Recall that this case study actually spans across two states: Andhra Pradesh and Karnataka. In a traditional comparative case study setup, the selection of both cases would seem to yield limited insights. After all, they are contextually similar: "Andhra Pradesh and Karnataka ... represent the epicenter of the HIV/AIDS epidemic in India. In addition, they were early adopters of the targeted interventions"; and they also experience a similar outcome: "HIV/AIDS prevalence among female sex workers declined from 20 percent to 7 percent in Andhra Pradesh and from 15 percent to 5 percent in Karnataka between 2003 and 2011" (El-Saharty and Nagaraj 2015: 7; 3). In truth, this comparative case study design makes substantial sense: had the researchers focused on the impact of the Indian government's NACP program only in Andhra Pradesh or only in Karnataka, one might have argued that there was something unique about either state that rendered it impossible to generalize the causal inferences. By instead demonstrating that favorable public health outcomes can be traced to the NACP program in both states, the researchers can support the argument that the intervention would likely prove successful in other contexts to the extent that they are similar to Andhra Pradesh and Karnataka.

One risk of the foregoing approach is highlighted by Sewell (2005: 95–96): contextual similarity may suggest cross-case interactions that hamper the ability to treat the second, most-similar case as if it were independent of the process-traced case. For example, an extensive body of research has underscored how protests often diffuse across proximate spatiotemporal contexts through mimicry and the modularity of repertoires of contention (Tilly 1995; Tarrow 1998). And, returning to the World Bank case study of HIV/AIDS interventions in Andhra Pradesh and Karnataka, one concern is that because these states share a common border, cross-state learning or other interactions might limit the value-added of a comparative design over a single case study, since the second case may not constitute truly new data. The researcher should be highly sensitive to this possibility when selecting and subsequently process tracing the most-similar case: the greater the likelihood of cross-case interactions, the lesser the likelihood that it is a case-specific causal process – as opposed to cross-case diffusion mechanism – that is doing most of the explanatory work.

Conversely, if the causal chain is found to operate differently in the second, most-similar case, then the researcher can make an argument for rejecting the generalizability of the causal explanation with some confidence. The conclusion would be that the causal process is *sui generis* and requires the "localization" of the theoretical explanation for the outcome of interest (Tarrow 2010: 251–252). In short, this would suggest that the process-traced case is an exceptional or deviant case, given a lack of causal generalizability even to cases bearing strong family resemblances. Here, we are using the 'strong' notion of 'deviant': the inability of a causal process to generalize to similar contexts substantially decreases the likelihood that "other cases" could be explained with reference to (or even in opposition to) the process-traced case.

There is, of course, the risk that by getting mired in the weeds of the first case, the researcher is unable to recognize how the overall chronology of events and causal logics in the most-similar case strongly resembles the process-traced case. That is, a null finding of generalizability in a most-similar context calls on the researcher to probe whether they have descended too far down the "ladder of generality," requiring more abstract conceptual categories to compare effectively (Sartori 1970; Collier and Levitsky 1997).

7.4.4 Probing Scope Conditions and Equifinality Via a Most-Different Cases Design

A researcher that has process-traced a given case and revealed a factor or sequence of factors as causally relevant may also benefit from leveraging a most-different cases approach. This case selection technique yields complementary insights to the most-similar cases design described in the previous section, but its focus is altogether different: instead of uncovering the degree to which an identified causal process travels, the objective is to try to understand where and why it fails to travel and whether alternative pathways to the same outcome may be possible.

More precisely, by selecting a case that differs substantially from the process-traced case in background characteristics, the researcher maximizes contextual heterogeneity and the likelihood that the causal process will not generalize to the second case (Soifer 2020). Put differently, the scholar would

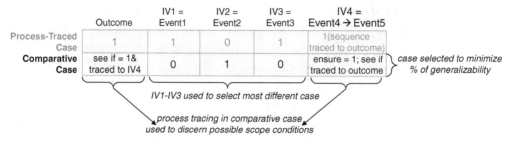

Figure 7.8   Probing scope conditions by selecting a most-different case

be selecting a least-likely case for generalizability, because the context-dependence of causal mechanisms renders it unlikely that the same sequence of events will generate the same outcome in the second case. This would offer a first cut at establishing "scope conditions" upon the generalizability of the theory (Tarrow 2010: 251) by isolating which contextual factors prevented the process from producing the outcome in the most-different case.

Figure 7.8 provides a visual illustration of what this design could look like. Suppose, once more, that process tracing in Case 1 has revealed that some event 4 followed by event 5 generated the outcome of interest. To maximize the probability that we will be able to place scope conditions on this finding, we would select a comparative case that is most different to the process-traced case (a case with different values/occurrences of other independent variables/events [denoted as IV1–IV3 in Figure 7.8] that might also influence the outcome) but which also experienced the sequence of event 4 followed by event 5. Given the contextual differences between these two cases, the likelihood that the same sequence will produce the same outcome in both is low, which then opens up opportunities for the researcher to probe the logic of scope conditions. In this endeavor, temporality can serve as a useful guide: a means for restricting the set of potential contextual factors that prevented the causal process from reproducing the outcome in Case 2 is to identify at what chronological point the linkages between events 4 and 5 on the one hand and the outcome of interest on the other hand branched off from the way they unfolded in Case 1. The researcher can then scout which contextual factors exuded the greatest influence at that temporal location and identify them as central to the scope conditions to be placed upon the findings.

To provide an example for how this logic of inquiry can work, consider a recent case study focused on understanding the effectiveness of Mexico's conditional cash transfer program – *Opportunitades*, the first program of its kind – in providing monetary support to the female heads of Indigenous households (Alva Estrabridis and Ortega Nieto 2015). The program suffered from the fact that Indigenous beneficiaries dropped out at higher rates than their non-Indigenous counterparts. In 2009 the World Bank spearheaded an Indigenous Peoples Plan (IPP) to bolster service delivery of cash transfers to Indigenous populations, which crucially included "catering to indigenous peoples in their native languages and disseminating information in their languages" (Alva Estrabridis and Ortega Nieto 2015: 2). A subsequent impact evaluation found that "[w]hen program messages were offered in beneficiaries' mother tongues, they were more convincing, and beneficiaries tended to participate and express themselves more actively" (Alva Estrabridis and Ortega Nieto 2015; Mir et al. 2011).

Researchers might well be interested in the portability of the foregoing finding, in which case the previously described most-similar cases design is appropriate – for example, a comparison with the *Familias en Accion* program in Colombia may be undertaken (Attanasio et al. 2005). But they might also be interested in the limits of the policy intervention – in understanding where and why it is unlikely to yield similar outcomes. To assess the scope conditions upon the "bilingualism" effect of cash transfer programs, a most-different cases design is appropriate. Thankfully, conditional cash transfer programs are increasingly common even in historical, cultural, and linguistic contexts markedly different from Mexico, most prominently in sub-Saharan Africa (Lagarde et al. 2007; Garcia and Moore 2012). Selecting a comparative case from sub-Saharan Africa should prove effective for probing scope conditions: the more divergent the contextual factors, the less likely it is that the policy intervention will produce the same outcome in both contexts.

On the flip side, in the unlikely event that part or all of the causal process is nonetheless reproduced in the most-different case, the researcher would obtain a strong signal that they have identified one of those rare causal explanations of general scope. In coming to this conclusion, however, the researcher should be wary of "conceptual stretching" (Sartori 1970: 1034), such that there is confidence that the similarity in the causal chain across the most-different cases lies at the empirical level and is not an artificial by-product of imprecise conceptual categories (Bennett and Checkel 2015: 10–11). Here process tracing, by pushing researchers to not only specify a sequence of "tightly-coupled" events (Falleti and Mahoney 2015: 233), but also to collect observable implications about the causal mechanisms concatenating these events, can guard against conceptual stretching. By opening the "black box" of causation through detailed within-case analysis, process tracing limits the researcher's ability to posit "pseudo-equivalences" across contexts (Sartori 1970: 1035).

Selecting a most-different case vis-à-vis the process-traced case is also an excellent strategy for probing equifinality – for maximizing the likelihood that the scholar will be able to probe multiple causal pathways to the same outcome. To do so, it is not sufficient to merely ensure divergence in background conditions; it is equally necessary to follow Mill's method of agreement by ensuring that the outcome in the process-traced case is also present in the second, most-different case. By ensuring minimal variation in outcome, the scholar guarantees that process tracing the second case will lead to the desired destination; by ensuring maximal variation in background conditions, the scholar substantially increases the likelihood that process tracing will reveal a slightly or significantly different causal pathway to said destination. Should an alternative route to the outcome be found, then its generalizability could be assessed using the most-similar cases approach described previously.

Figure 7.9 visualizes what this case selection design might look like. Here, as in previous examples, suppose process tracing in Case 1 provides evidence that event 4 followed by event 5 produced the outcome of interest. The researcher then selects a case with the same outcome, but with different values/occurrences of some independent variables/events (in this case, IV1–IV3) that may influence the outcome. Working backwards from the outcome to reconstruct the causal chain that produced it, the researcher then probes whether (i) the sequence (event 4 followed by event 5) also occurred in Case 2, and (ii) whether the outcome of interest can be retraced to said sequence. Given the contextual dissimilarities between these most-different cases, such a finding is rather unlikely, which would subsequently enable to the researcher to probe whether some other factor (perhaps IV2/event 2 in the example of Figure 7.9) produced the outcome in the comparative case instead, which would comprise clear evidence of equifinality.

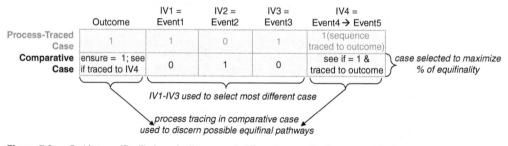

Figure 7.9   Probing equifinality by selecting a most-different case with the same outcome

To return to the concrete example of Mexico's conditional cash transfer program's successful outreach to marginalized populations via bilingual service provision, an alternative route to the same outcome might be unearthed if a cash transfer program without bilingual outreach implemented in a country characterized by different linguistic, gender, and financial decision-making norms proves similarly successful in targeting marginalized populations. Several factors – including recruitment procedures, the size of the cash transfers, the requirements for participation, and the supply of other benefits (Lagarde et al. 2007: 1902) – could interact with the different setting to produce similar intervention outcomes, regardless of whether multilingual services are provided. Such a finding would suggest that these policy interventions can be designed in multiple ways and still prove effective.

To conclude, the method of inductive case selection complements within-case analysis by supplying a coherent logic for probing generalizability, scope conditions, and equifinality. To summarize, Figure 7.10 provides a roadmap of this approach to comparative case selection.

In short, if the researcher has the requisite time and resources, a multistage use of Millian methods to conduct four comparative case studies could prove

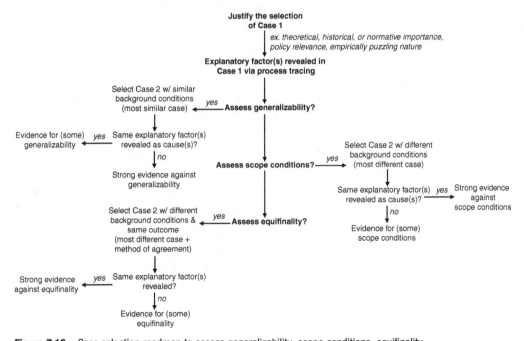

Figure 7.10   Case selection roadmap to assess generalizability, scope conditions, equifinality

very fertile. The researcher would begin by selecting a second, most-similar case to assess causal generalizability to a family of cases similar to the process-traced case; subsequently, a third, most-different case would be selected to surface possible scope conditions blocking the portability of the theory to divergent contexts; and a fourth, most-different case experiencing the same outcome would be picked to probe equifinal pathways. This sequential, four-case comparison would substantially improve the researcher's ability to map the portability and contours of both their empirical analysis and their theoretical claims.[9]

7.5 Conclusion

The method of inductive case selection converts process tracing meant to simply "craft a minimally sufficient explanation of a particular outcome" into a methodology used to build and refine a causal theory – a form of "theory-building process-tracing" (Beach and Pedersen 2013: 16–18). Millian methods are called upon to probe the portability of a particular causal process or causal mechanism and to specify the logics of its relative contextual-dependence. In so doing, they enable theory-building without presuming that the case study researcher holds the *a priori* knowledge necessary to account for complex temporal dynamics at the deductive theorizing stage. Both of these approaches – deductive, processualist theorizing on the one hand, and the method of inductive case selection on the other hand – provide some insurance against Millian methods leading the researcher into ignoring the ordered, paced, or equifinal structure that may underlie the pathway(s) to the outcome of interest. But, I would argue, the more inductive approach is uniquely suited for research that is not only process-sensitive, but also open to novel insights supplied by the empirical world that may not be captured by existing theories.

Furthermore, case study research often does (and should!) proceed with the scholar outlining why an outcome is of interest, and then seeking ways to not only make inferences about what produced said outcome (via process tracing) but situating it within a broader empirical and theoretical landscape (via the method of inductive case selection). This approach pushes scholars to answer that pesky yet fundamental question – why should we care or be interested in this case/outcome? – before disciplining their drive for

---

[9] Many thanks to Rory Truex for highlighting this implication of the roadmap in Figure 7.5.

generalizable causal inferences. After all, the deductive use of Millian methods tells us nothing about why we should care about the cases selected, yet arguably this is an essential component of any case selection justification. By deploying a most-similar or most-different cases design after an initial case has been justifiably selected due to its theoretical or historical importance, policy relevance, or puzzling empirical nature, the researcher is nudged toward undertaking case study research yielding causal theories that are not only comparatively engaged, but also substantively interesting.

The method of inductive case selection is most useful when the foregoing approach constitutes the *esprit* of the case study researcher. Undoubtedly, deductively oriented case study research (see Lieberman 2005; 2015) and traditional uses of Millian methods will continue to contribute to social scientific understanding. Nevertheless, the perils of ignoring important sequential causal dynamics – particularly in the absence of good, processualist theories – should caution researchers to proceed with the greatest of care. In particular, researchers should be willing to revise both theory building and research design to its more inductive variant should process tracing reveal temporal sequences that eschew the analytic possibilities of the traditional comparative method.

References

Abbott, A. (1995) "Sequence analysis: New methods for old ideas," *Annual Review of Sociology*, 21(1995), 93–113.

Abbott, A. (2001) *Time matters: On theory and method*. Chicago, IL: University of Chicago Press.

Abbott, A. (2016) *Processual sociology*. Chicago, IL: University of Chicago Press.

Adams, J., Clemens, E., and Orloff, A. S. (2005) "Introduction: Social theory, modernity, and the three waves of historical sociology" in Adams, J., Clemens, E., and Orloff, A. S. (eds.) *Remaking modernity: Politics, history, and sociology*. Durham, NC: Duke University Press, pp. 1–72.

Alva Estrabridis, C. and Ortega Nieto, D. (2015) "How to overcome communication and cultural barriers to improve service provision to indigenous populations." World Bank Global Delivery Initiative Case Study (Sept. 2015). Washington, DC: The World Bank.

Attanasio, O., Battistin, E., Fitzsimons, E., Mesnard, A., and Vera-Hernandez. M. (2005) How effective are conditional cash transfers? Evidence from Colombia. *Institute for Fiscal Studies Briefing Notes*, 54(2005), 1–9.

Beach, D. and Pedersen, R. B. (2013) *Process-tracing methods: Foundations and guidelines*. Ann Arbor: University of Michigan Press.

Beissinger, M. (2002) *Nationalist mobilization and the collapse of the Soviet State*. New York: Cambridge University Press.

Bennett, A. (2015) "Appendix: Disciplining our conjectures: Systematizing process tracing with Bayesian analysis" in Bennett, A. and Checkel, J. T. (eds.) *Process tracing: From metaphor to analytic tool*. New York: Cambridge University Press, pp. 276–298.

Bennett, A. and Checkel, J. T. (eds). (2015) *Process tracing: From metaphor to analytic tool*. New York: Cambridge University Press.

Boix, C. and Stokes, S. C. (2003) "Endogenous democratization," *World Politics*, 55(4), 517–549.

Boyatzis, R. E. (2006) "An overview of intentional change from a complexity perspective," *Journal of Management Development*, 25(7), 607–623.

Brady, H. and Collier, D. (2010) *Rethinking social inquiry: Diverse tools, shared standards* (2nd ed.). New York: Rowman & Littlefield.

Collier, D. (1991) "The comparative method: Two decades of change" in Rustow, D. A. and Erickson, K. P. (eds.) *Comparative political dynamics: Global research perspectives*. New York: Harper Collins, pp. 7–31.

Collier, D. (1993) "The comparative method," in Finifter, A. W. (ed.), *Political science: The state of the discipline II*, Washington, DC: American Political Science Association, pp. 105–119.

Collier, D. (2011) "Understanding process tracing," *PS: Political Science and Politics*, 44(4), 823–830.

Collier, D. and Levitsky, S. (1997) "Democracy with adjectives: Conceptual innovation in comparative research," *World Politics*, 49(3), 430–451.

Collier, R. B. (1999) *Paths toward democracy: The working class and elites in Western Europe and South America*. New York: Cambridge University Press.

Capoccia, G. (2015) "Critical junctures and institutional change" in Mahoney, J. and Thelen, K. (eds.) *Advances in comparative-historical analysis*. New York: Cambridge University Press, pp. 147–179.

Capoccia, G. and Kelemen, R. D. (2007) "The study of critical junctures: Theory, narrative and counterfactuals in historical institutionalism," *World Politics*, 59(3), 341–369.

Eckstein, H. (1975) "Case study and theory in political science" in Greenstein, F. I. and Polsby, N. W. (eds.) *Handbook of political science, vol. 7. Political science: Scope and theory*. Reading, MA: Addison-Wesley, pp. 79–138.

El-Saharty, S. and Nagaraj, B. A. (2015) "Reducing the risk of HIV/AIDS among female sex workers in India." World Bank Global Delivery Initiative Case Study (Oct. 2015). Washington, DC: The World Bank.

Falleti, T. (2005) "A sequential theory of decentralization: Latin American cases in comparative perspective," *American Political Science Review*, 99(3), 327–346.

Falleti, T. (2010) *Decentralization and subnational politics in Latin America*. New York: Cambridge University Press.

Falleti, T. and Lynch, J. (2009) "Context and causal mechanisms in political analysis," *Comparative Political Studies*, 42(9), 1132–1166.

Falleti, T. and Mahoney, J. (2015) "The comparative sequential method," in Mahoney, J. and Thelen, K. (eds.) *Advances in comparative-historical analysis*. New York: Cambridge University Press, pp. 211–239.

Faure, A. D. (1994) "Some methodological problems in comparative politics," *Journal of Theoretical Politics*, 6(3), 307–322.

Flyvbjerg, B. (2006) "Five misunderstandings about case-study research," *Qualitative Inquiry*, 12(2), 219–245.

Garcia, M. and Moore, C. M. T. (2012) *The cash dividend: The rise of cash transfer programs in sub-Saharan Africa*. Washington, DC: The World Bank.

Geddes, B. (1990) "How the cases you choose affect the answers you get: Selection bias in comparative politics," *Political Analysis*, 2, 131–150.

George, A. L. (1979) "Case studies and theory development: The method of structured, focused comparison," in Lauren, P. G. (ed.) *Diplomacy: New approaches in history, theory, and policy*. New York: Free Press, pp. 43–68.

George, A. L. and Bennett, A. (2005) *Case studies and theory development in the social sciences*. Cambridge, MA: MIT Press.

Gerring, J. (2007) *Case study research: Principles and practices*. New York: Cambridge University Press.

Gerring, J. and Cojocaru, L. (2015) "Case-selection: A diversity of methods and techniques." Working paper, Boston University.

Goertz, G. (2017) *Multimethod research, causal mechanisms, and case studies: An integrated approach*. Princeton, NJ: Princeton University Press.

Goertz, G. and Mahoney, J. (2012). *A tale of two cultures: Qualitative and quantitative research in the social sciences*. Princeton, NJ: Princeton University Press.

Hall, P. A. (2003) "Aligning ontology and methodology in comparative politics" in Mahoney, J. and Rueschemeyer, D. (eds.) *Comparative historical analysis in the social sciences*. New York: Cambridge University Press, pp. 373–404.

Hima, H. and Santibanez, C. (2015) "How to shape an enabling environment for sustainable water service delivery in Nigeria." World Bank Global Delivery Initiative Case Study (Sept. 2015). Washington, DC: The World Bank.

Hobarth, R. (1972) Process tracing in clinical judgment: An analytic approach (Unpublished PhD Dissertation). Chicago, IL: University of Chicago.

Hume, D. 1738 [2003] *A treatise of human nature*. Mineola, NY: Dover.

Huntington, S. (1993) *The third wave: Democratization in the late twentieth century*. Norman, OK: University of Oklahoma Press.

King, G., Keohane, R. O., and Verba, S. (1994) *Designing social inquiry: Scientific inference in qualitative research*. Princeton, NJ: Princeton University Press.

Lagarde, M., Haines, A., and Palmer, N. (2007) "Conditional cash transfers for improving uptake of health interventions in low- and middle-income countries: A systematic review," *Journal of the American Medical Association*, 298(16), 1900–1910.

Lasswell, H. D. (1968) "The future of the comparative method," *Comparative Politics*, 1(1), 3–18.

Levy, J. S. (2008) "Case studies: Types, designs, and logics of inference," *Conflict Management and Peace Science*, 25(2008), 1–18.

Levy, J. S. (2015) "Counterfactuals, causal inference, and historical analysis," *Security Studies*, 24(3), 378–402.

Lieberman, E. S. (2005) "Nested analysis as a mixed-method strategy for comparative research," *American Political Science Review*, 99(3), 435–452.

Lieberman, E. S. (2015). "Nested analysis: Toward the integration of comparative-historical analysis and other social science methods" in Mahoney, J. and Thelen, K. (eds.) *Advances in comparative-historical analysis*. New York: Cambridge University Press, pp. 240–263.

Lieberson, S. (1994) "More on the uneasy case for using Mill-type methods in small-n comparative studies," *Social Forces*, 72(4), 1225–1237.

Lijphart, A. (1971) "Comparative politics and the comparative method," *American Political Science Review*, 65(3), 682–693.

Lijphart, A. (1975) "The comparable-cases strategy in comparative research," *Comparative Political Studies*, 8(2), 158.

Loewenstein, G. and Elster, J. (1992) *Choice over time*. New York: Russell Sage.

Mahoney, J. (2000) "Path dependence in historical sociology," *Theory and Society*, 29(4), 507–548.

Mahoney, J. (2008) "Toward a unified theory of causality," *Comparative Political Studies*, 41(4/5), 412–436.

Mahoney, J. (2012) "The logic of process tracing tests in the social sciences," *Sociological Methods and Research*, 41(4), 570–597.

Mahoney, J., Kimball, E., and Koivu, K. (2009) "The logic of historical explanation in the social sciences," *Comparative Political Studies*, 42(1), 114–146.

Mahoney, J. and Thelen, K. (2010) "A theory of gradual institutional change" in Mahoney, J. and Thelen, K. (eds.) *Explaining institutional change: Ambiguity, agency, and power*. New York: Cambridge University Press, pp. 1–37.

Mahoney, J. and Thelen, K. (eds.) (2015) *Advances in comparative-historical analysis*. New York: Cambridge University Press.

Mahoney, J. and Vanderpoel, R. S. (2015) "Set diagrams and qualitative research," *Comparative Political Studies*, 48(1), 65–100.

Mill, J. S. 1843 [1974]. *A system of logic ratiocinative and inductive: Being a connected view of the principles of evidence and the methods of scientific investigation*. Toronto: University of Toronto Press.

Mir, C., Gámez, H., Loyola, D., Martí, C., and Veraza, A. (2011) *Informe de los Resultados del Estudio de Acompañamiento de los Procesos Operativos en el Esquema de Micro Zonas*. Mexico City: Instituto Nacional de Administración Pública.

North, D. C. and Weingast, B. R. (1989) "Constitutions and commitment: The evolution of institutions governing public choice in seventeenth-century England," *Journal of Economic History*, 49(4), 803–832.

O'Donnell, G. and Schmitter, P. (1986) *Transitions from authoritarian rule: Tentative conclusions about uncertain democracies*. Baltimore, MD: Johns Hopkins University Press.

Pierson, P. (1996) "The path to European integration: A historical institutionalist analysis," *Comparative Political Studies*, 29(2), 123–163.

Pierson, P. (2000) "Increasing returns, path dependence, and the study of politics," *American Political Science Review*, 94(2), 251–267.

Pierson, P. (2003) "Big, slow-moving, and … invisible: Macrosocial processes in the study of comparative politics" in Mahoney, J. and Rueschemeyer, D. (eds.) *Comparative-historical analysis in the social sciences*. New York: Cambridge University Press, pp. 177–207.

Pierson, P. (2004) *Politics in time: History, institutions, and social analysis*. Princeton, NJ: Princeton University Press.

Przeworski, A. and Limongi, F. (1997) "Modernization: Theories and facts," *World Politics*, 49(2), 155–183.

Przeworski, A. and Teune, H. (1970) *The logic of comparative social inquiry*. New York: John Wiley.

Rueschemeyer, D., Stephens, E. H., and Stephens, J. D. (1992) *Capitalist development and democracy*. Chicago, IL: University of Chicago Press.

Sartori, G. (1970) "Concept misformation in comparative politics," *American Political Science Review*, 64(4), 1033–1053.

Seawright, J. and Gerring, J. (2008) "Case-selection techniques in case study research: A menu of qualitative and quantitative options," *Political Research Quarterly*, 61(2), 294–308.

Sewell, W. (1996) "Historical events as transformations of structures: Inventing revolution at the Bastille," *Theory and Society*, 25(6), 841–881.

Sewell, W. H. (2005) *Logics of history: Social theory and social transformation*. Chicago, IL: University of Chicago Press.

Skocpol, T. (1979) *States and social revolutions: A comparative analysis of France, Russia, and China*. New York: Cambridge University Press.

Soifer, H. (2020) "Shadow cases in comparative research," *Qualitative & Multi-Method Research*, 18(2), 9–18.

Swim, J. et al. (2009) *Psychology & global climate change: Addressing a multifaceted phenomenon and set of challenges*. American Psychological Association. Available at: www.apa.org/science/about/publications/climate-change-booklet.pdf

Tansey, O. (2007) "Process tracing and elite interviewing: A case for non-probabilistic sampling," *PS: Political Science and Politics*, 40(4), 765–772.

Tarrow, S. (1998) *Power in movement: Social movements, collective action, and politics*. New York: Cambridge University Press.

Tarrow, S. (2010) "The strategy of paired comparison: Toward a theory of practice," *Comparative Political Studies*, 43(2), 230–259.

Tilly, C. (1995) *Popular contention in Great Britain, 1758–1834*. New York: Routledge.

Trachtenberg, M. (2009) *The craft of international history: A guide to method*. Princeton, NJ: Princeton University Press.

Waldner, D. (2012) "Process tracing and causal mechanisms" in Kincaid, H. (ed) *Oxford handbook of philosophy of social science*. New York: Oxford University Press, pp. 65–84.

Yin, R. K. (1984) *Case study research: Design and methods*. Beverly Hills, CA: Sage.

8 The Transparency Revolution in Qualitative Social Science

Implications for Policy Analysis

Andrew Moravcsik

8.1 Introduction

A transparency revolution is sweeping the social sciences.[1] The failure to replicate existing findings, a suspicious absence of disconfirming results, the proliferation of uninformative or inaccurate citations, and broader concerns about a media environment that privileges "fake news" and sensationalism over rigorously grounded facts have all raised concerns about the legitimacy and credibility of academic scholarship. Journals, professional associations, funders, politicians, regulators, and colleagues now press researchers to open their data, analysis, and methods to greater scrutiny.[2] Qualitative researchers who conduct case studies, collect archival or interview data, and do ethnography, participant observation, or other types of nonquantitative studies are no exception. They have been developing specific standards and techniques for enhancing transparency, including some that exploit digital technology. Reputable research now requires more than solid empirical evidence, state-of-the-art theory, and sophisticated methods: It must be transparent.[3]

Yet the transparency of qualitative analysis by practitioners in governmental, intergovernmental, and civil society institutions lags behind. In recent

---

[1] This paper draws on numerous articles published over the past decade, especially Moravcsik (2014, 2016). I thank Tommaso Pavone for helping draft an earlier version,; Mareike Kleine, Robert Keohane and colleagues at the Qualitative Data Repository at Syracuse University for their comments; and the volume editors for their patience and encouragement.
[2] See Wiener (2005), Wright and Armstrong (2008), Goodstein (2010), and Rekdal (2014).
[3] On general advances in qualitative methods, see King, Keohane, and Verba (1994), Van Evera (1997), and Brady and Collier (2010).

years, practitioners have pushed policy-makers to improve governmental transparency, yet, ironically, the data, analysis, methods, and other elements of their own research lack a similar openness.[4] The data and analysis in policy case studies and histories, after-action reports, and interview or focus-group analyses are often opaque. This is troubling, since the justifications for enhancing transparency in academic research apply equally, or even more so, to research by practitioners in governments, think tanks, and international organizations. To them, moreover, we can add numerous and pressing justifications for greater transparency specific to the policy world. Safeguarding the clarity, accessibility, and integrity of policy-relevant research helps ensure that decision-makers avoid basing costly policy interventions on flawed analysis or incomplete information. Transparency helps guard against potential conflicts of interest that might arise in research or policy implementation. Most importantly, it opens up public assessment and evaluation to proper official and public deliberation – thus according them greater legitimacy.

This chapter offers a brief background on the basic logic and practice of transparency in qualitative social science and reviews the cost-effectiveness of the available practical options to enhance it – both in the academy and in the policy world. Section 8.2 defines three dimensions of research transparency and explores some of the distinctiveness of qualitative research, which suggests various reasons why the applied transparency standards in qualitative research may differ from those employed in quantitative research. Section 8.3 examines three commonly discussed strategies to enhance transparency. It argues that in most cases it is infeasible and inappropriate – and, at the very least, insufficient – for qualitative policy analysts to employ conventional footnotes, hyperlinks to web-based sources, or, as some suggest by analogy to statistical research, centralized "datasets" to store all of a project's qualitative source material. Section 8.4 introduces a new strategy to enhance qualitative research transparency that is emerging as a "best practice." This is "Active Citation" (AC) or "Annotation for Transparency Initiative" (ATI): a digitally enabled open-source discursive annotation system that is flexible, simple, and compatible with all existing online formats.[5] For practitioners, as for scholars, AC/ATI is likely to be the most practical and broadly applicable means to enhance the transparency of qualitative research and reporting.

---

[4] On these issues, see Brown, De Jong, and Lessidrenska (2009), Cuervo-Cazurra (2014), Stiglitz (2003), Woods (2001), and World Bank (1992).

[5] https://qdr.syr.edu/ati/ati-initiative.

8.2   Research Transparency in the Social Sciences

Transparency is a norm that mandates that "researchers have an ethical obligation to facilitate the evaluation of their evidence-based knowledge claims."[6] This is a foundational principle of all scientific work. Scholars embrace it across the full range of epistemological commitments, theoretical views, and substantive interests. It enjoys this status because nearly all researchers view scholarship as a collective enterprise: a conversation among scholars and often extending to those outside academia.[7] Researchers who conduct transparent work enhance the ability of others to engage in the conversation through productive evaluation, application, critique, debate, and extension of existing work. Without transparent data, theory, and methods, the conversation would be impoverished. A research community in which scholars can read, understand, verify, and debate published work when they choose should foster legitimate confidence in results. A research community in which analysts accept findings because of the prominence of the author or the apparent authority of big data, copious citations, clever arguments, or sophisticated "gold standard" methods should not inspire trust.

Research transparency has three broad dimensions.[8] The first, *data transparency*, stipulates that researchers should publicize the data and evidence on which their research rests. This helps readers apprehend the richness and diversity of the real-world political activity scholars study and to assess for themselves to what extent (and how reliably) that evidence of that activity confirms particular descriptive, interpretive, or causal interpretations and theories linked to it. The second dimension, *analytic transparency*, stipulates that researchers should publicize how they interpret and analyze evidence in order to generate descriptive and causal inferences. In social research, evidence does not speak for itself but is analyzed to infer unobservable characteristics such as preferences, identities, beliefs, rationality, power, strategic intent, and causality. For readers to understand and engage with research, they must be able to assess how the author purports to conceptualize and

---

[6] American Political Science Association (2012, pp. 9–10); also available in Lupia and Elman (2014).

[7] The celebrated physicist Richard Feynman (1974: 11) locates the essence of scientific investigation in an "integrity . . . that corresponds to a kind of utter honesty," which he defines in terms of transparency: "The idea is to try to give all of the information to help others to judge the value of your contribution; not just the information that leads to judgment in one particular direction or another."

[8] Lupia and Elman (2014), appendices A and B.

measure behavior, draw descriptive and causal inferences from those measures, determine that the results are conclusive vis-à-vis alternatives, and specify broader implications. The third dimension, *production transparency*, stipulates that social scientists should publicize the broader set of design choices that underlie the research. Decisions on how to select data, measure variables, test propositions, and weight overall findings – before, during, and after data analysis – often drive research results by defining the particular combination of data, theories, and methods they use for empirical analysis. Researchers are obliged, to the extent possible, to afford readers all three types of research transparency.

These three elements of research transparency underlie all scientific research communities, including those in fields such as history, law, ethnography, policy assessment, and discourse analysis.[9] Yet its form varies by research method. The appropriate rules and standards of applied transparency in qualitative research, for example, differ from those governing quantitative research. An ideal-typical qualitative case study of public policy has three distinctive characteristics. It focuses intensively on only one or a few cases. It employs primarily textual evidence, such as documents, transcripts, descriptions, and notes (though visual and numerical evidence may sometimes also be used). And, finally, it is generally reported and written up as a temporal, causal, or descriptive narrative, with individual pieces of evidence (and interpretation) inserted at specific points in the story. Different types of data and inference should generate subtly different transparency norms.

Qualitative research methods – intensive, text-based narrative studies of individual cases – are indispensable. They play a critical role in a healthy and balanced environment of research and policy evaluation – not just in the academy, but in the policy world as well. In both contexts, qualitative research enjoys distinct comparative advantages. For policy-makers, one of the most important is that qualitative analysis permits analysts to draw inferences from and about single cases (see Cartwright, Chapter 2 this volume). Detailed knowledge and insights about the characteristics of a single case, rather than average outcomes, are often what policy-makers

---

[9] Even the eminent philosopher of history R. J. Collingwood (1946: 252), a defender of the radical view that historians should contextually interpret and even reenact past subjective experiences, nonetheless argued: "History has this in common with every other science: that the historian is not allowed to claim any single piece of knowledge, except where he can justify his claim by exhibiting . . . to anyone else who is both able and willing to follow his demonstration, the grounds upon which it is based [and] what the evidence at his disposal proves about certain events."

and analysts most need. This may be because some types of phenomena are intrinsically rare, even unique. If only a limited number of cases exist, a case study may be the best way to inform policy.[10] The demand for precise knowledge about a single case may arise also because policy-makers are focused on designing a particular intervention at a specific time and geographical location. Even if solid quantitative generalizations exist, policy-makers often want to know exactly what mix of factors is at work in that case – that is, whether the case before them is a typical case or an outlier. If, for example, after-action reports show that a promising program design recently failed when implemented in Northern India, does that mean it is less likely to succeed if launched in Bolivia? Answering this type of everyday policy problem in real time often requires detailed knowledge of important contextual nuances of the local culture, politics, and economics. This, in turn, implies that, in order to be useful, the original after-action report may want to consider detailed evidence of incentives, perceptions, and inclinations as revealed by actions, documents, and statements. For similar reasons, case studies often enjoy a comparative advantage in situations where analysts possess relatively little prior knowledge and seek to observe and theorize previously unknown causal mechanisms, social contexts, and outcomes in detail, thus contributing to the development of new and more accurate explanations and theories.[11]

8.3   Practical Options for Enhancing Qualitative Transparency

By what means can we best render qualitative research more transparent? Social scientists generally possess some inkling of the research transparency norms governing statistical and experimental research. When we turn to qualitative research, however, many analysts remain unaware that explicit standards for transparency of data, analysis, or methods exist, let alone what

---

[10] This assumes also that analysts cannot easily disaggregate the phenomenon into many internal actions that can be studied using high-N or experimental techniques. This seems a reasonable assumption with regard to many macrosocial phenomena, such as government transitions, civil wars, revolutions, unusual forms of government, new trends in social organization, and hybrid institutions, as well as new issues or rapidly changing circumstances.

[11] Such situations may be the norm. In general, controlled studies of prediction in policy studies reveal that experts whose analyses are informed by "eclectic" and "inductive" theories and the detailed "situational facts of each historical episode" (a mode in which qualitative analysis excels) tend to predict future events considerably better than those using average tendencies and internally consistent abstract theory (hallmarks of quantitative and formal analysis). In Tolstoy's famous metaphor, "foxes" consistently outperform "hedgehogs." See Tetlock (2017).

they are. In recent years, qualitative social scientists have moved to establish stronger norms of transparency. Building on the American Political Science Association's initiative on Data Access and Research Transparency (APSA/DA-RT) in the US field of political science, a team of scholars has developed specific applied transparency guidelines for qualitative research.[12] A series of conferences, workshops, journal articles, and foundation projects are further elaborating how best to implement qualitative transparency in practice.[13] The National Science Foundation (NSF) has funded a Qualitative Data Repository (QDR) based at Syracuse University, as well as various projects demonstrating new transparency standards and instruments that use new software and internet technologies.[14]

Scholars have thereby generated shared knowledge and experience about this issue. They have learned that qualitative research poses distinctive practical problems due to factors such as human subject protection, intellectual property law, and logistical complexity, and distinctive epistemological problems, which arise from its unique narrative form. These must be kept in mind when assessing alternative proposals to enhance transparency.

Four major options exist: conventional footnotes, hyperlinks to online sources, archiving textual data, and digitally enabled discursive notes. A close examination of these options reveals, first, that the practical and epistemological distinctiveness of qualitative research implies a different strategy than is employed in quantitative research, and, second, that the optimal strategy is that of creating digital entries containing annotated source material, often called Active Citation or the Annotation for Transparency Initiative. We consider each of these four options in turn.

8.3.1 Conventional Footnotes

The simplest and most widespread instruments of transparency used today in social science are citations found in footnotes, endnotes, and the text itself. Yet the current state of citation practice demonstrates the flaws in this approach. Basic citations in published work are often incomplete or incorrect, particularly if they appear as brief in-text "scientific citations" designed for a world in which most (quantitative) analysts use footnotes to acknowledge other researchers rather than cite evidence. Such citations do not provide

---

[12] American Political Science Association (2013).

[13] American Political Science Association (2013), for guidance on qualitative methods.

[14] Qualitative Data Repository (QDR), Center for Qualitative and Multi-Method Inquiry, Syracuse University: www.qdr.org.

either data access or analytic transparency. Scientific citations are often incomplete, leaving out page numbers and failing to specify the concrete textual reference within an article or on a page that the author considers decisive. Even if a citation is precise, most readers will be deterred by the need to locate each source at some third location, perhaps a library or an archive – and, in many cases, as with interviews and records of focus groups, the source material may not be available at all.[15] Even more troubling, conventional citations offer no analytical transparency whatsoever: the reader knows what is cited, but generally much less about why.

In theory, an attractive solution would be to return to the traditional method of linking evidence and explanation in most scholarly fields: long discursive footnotes containing extended quotations with interpretive annotations. Discursive footnotes of this kind remain widespread in legal academia, history, some humanities, and a few other academic disciplines that still prize qualitative transparency. In legal academia, for example, where fidelity to the precise text and rigorous interpretation are of great academic and practical value, articles may have dozens, even hundreds, of such discursive footnotes – a body of supplementary material many times longer than the article itself. The format evolved because it can enhance all three dimensions of transparency. The researcher is often obliged to insert extensive quotations from sources (data access); annotate those quotations with extensive interpretation of how, why, and to what extent they support a claim made in the text and how they fit into the broader context (analytic transparency); and discuss issues of data selection and opposing evidence (production transparency). At a glance, readers can scan everything: the main argument, the citation, the source material, the author's interpretation, and information about how representative the source is. In many ways, discursive footnotes remain the "best practice" instruments for providing efficient qualitative transparency.

Yet recent trends in formatting social science journals – in particular, the advent of so-called scientific citations and ever-tighter word limits – have all but banished discursive footnotes. This trend is not methodologically neutral: it privileges quantitative research that employs external datasets and cites secondary journals rather than data, while blocking qualitative research from citing and interpreting texts in detail. As a result, in many social sciences, we see relatively little serious debate about the empirics of

---

[15] Systematic replication results from highly regarded political science research suggest that levels of error and omission total 20–30 percent of citations.

qualitative research. Replication or reanalysis is extremely difficult, and extension or secondary analysis almost impossible.[16] Given the economics of social science journals, this trend is unlikely to reverse. Practitioners and policy analysts face similar constraints, because they often aim their publications, at least in part, at nonexperts. Memos and reports have been growing shorter. Long discursive footnotes pose a visual barrier, both expanding the size of a text, and rendering it less readable and accessible. In sum, conventional footnotes and word limits are part of the problem, not the solution.

8.3.2   Hyperlinks to Online Sources

Some suggest that a simple digital solution would be to link articles and reports to source documents already posted online. Many government reports, journalistic articles, contemporary scholarship, and blogs often do just this. Yet this offers an inadequate level of research transparency, for three basic reasons. First, much material simply cannot be found online: Most primary field research evidence (e.g., interviews) is not there, and despite the efforts of archives to digitalize, we are far from having all documents online even in the most advanced industrial democracies, let alone elsewhere. Even journalistic articles and secondary scholarly works are unevenly available, with much inaccessible online (or hidden behind paywalls), in foreign languages, or buried within longer documents. Second, links to outside sources are notoriously unstable, and subject to "link rot" or removal.[17] Attempts to stabilize links to permit cross-citation have proven extremely challenging even when they focus on a very narrow range of documents (e.g., academic medical journals), and it is nearly impossible to do so if one is dealing, as policy analysts do, with an essentially unlimited range of contemporary material of many types and in many languages. Third, even when sources are available online – or when we place them online for this purpose – hyperlinks provide only data transparency, not analytical and process transparency. We learn what source a scholar cited but not why, let alone how he or she interpreted, contextualized, and weighed the evidence. This

---

[16] Even quantitative social and natural scientists now employ online appendices, sometimes many times longer than the articles, to convey such background information.

[17] Web pages migrate or disappear surprisingly often when periodicals and book series switch owners, formats, or archiving systems or when government agencies, private firms, or civil society groups reorganize. For example, this occurred in 2009 to the entire flagship series of US government documents on foreign policy (US Department of State, *Foreign Relations of the United States*).

undermines one of the distinctive epistemological advantages of qualitative research.

8.3.3   Archiving Evidence in a Centralized Database

For many from other research traditions, data archiving may seem at first glance the most natural way to enhance transparency. It is, after all, the conventional solution employed by statistical researchers, who create centralized, homogeneous "datasets" where all evidence is stored, connected to a single set of algorithms used to analyze it. Moreover, data repositories do already exist for textual material, notably the Qualitative Data Repository for social science materials recently established with NSF funding at Syracuse University.[18] Data archiving is admittedly essential, especially for the purpose of preserving complete collections of new field data drawn from interviews, ethnographic notes, primary document collections, and web-searches of manageable size that are unencumbered by human subject or copyright restrictions.[19] Archiving full datasets can also help create a stronger bulwark against selection bias ("cherry-picking" or constructing biased case studies by selecting only confirming evidence) by obliging qualitative scholars to archive "all" their data.

Yet, while data archiving can be a useful ancillary technique in selected cases, it is unworkable as a general "default" approach for assuring qualitative research transparency because it is both impractical and inappropriate. Archiving is often *impractical* because ethical, legal, and logistical constraints limit the analyst's ability to reveal to readers all the interviews, documents, or notes underlying qualitative research. Doing so often threatens to infringe the confidentiality of human subjects and violates copyright law limiting the reproduction of published material.[20] Sanitizing all the interviews, documents, and notes (i.e., rendering them entirely anonymous and consistent with confidentiality agreements) is likely to impose a prohibitive logistical burden on many research projects. These limitations become much greater

---

[18] QDR: www.qdr.org; Henry Murray Data Archive at Harvard University: www.murray.harvard.edu/.

[19] See Elman, Kapiszewski, and Vinuela (2010); Qualitative Data Repository (2012).

[20] This is one reason why, in many cases of quantitative research, the precise reproducible primary data used to define variables, and the way in which they were coded, often remains confidential – or is, as in medical research, subject to extremely complex and onerous confidentiality procedures not replicable in most social scientific settings. Even where no such constraints exist, it is often conceptually unclear what data a qualitative analyst should reveal: all evidence the analyst thought was important, or all evidence the analyst consulted, or all evidence the analyst *might have* consulted? The latter is the only way to truly discipline cherry picking, but in most cases it is almost certainly neither legal nor feasible.

when the researcher seeks to archive comprehensive sets of complete documents, as opposed to just releasing quotations or summaries, as some other transparency strategies require. This is often particularly problematic for policy practitioners, perhaps more so than scholars, because policy case studies and histories, after-action reports, and interview or focus-group analyses so commonly contain sensitive information.

Archiving is also *inappropriate* because it dilutes the distinctive epistemological advantages of qualitative research. The notion that archiving documents in one large collection generates transparency overlooks a distinctive quality of case study analysis. A qualitative analyst does not treat the data as one undifferentiated mass, analyzing all of it at once using a centralized algorithm, as in a statistical study. Instead, he or she presents and interprets individual pieces of data one at a time, each linked to a single step in the main narrative.[21] Qualitative analysts enjoy considerable flexibility to assign a different location, role, relative weight, reliability, and exact meaning to each piece of evidence, depending on its logical position in a causal narrative, the specific type of document it is, and the textual content of the quotation within that document. This type of nuanced and open-ended, yet rigorous and informed, contextual interpretation of sources is highly prized in fields such as history, law, anthropology, and the humanities. Any serious effort to enhance qualitative transparency must thus make clear to the reader how the analyst interprets each piece of data and exactly where in the narrative it fits. Simply placing all the evidence in a single database, even where it is logistically and legally feasible, does not help the reader much.[22] Links from citations to archived material are, at best, cumbersome. Moreover, as with hyperlinks and conventional citations, archiving fails to specify particular passages and provides little analytic transparency, because it fails to explain why each source supports the underlying argument at that point in the narrative. To achieve qualitative transparency, a less costly approach is required – one that reveals the inferential connection between each datum and the underlying analytical point in the narrative.

---

[21] These are termed "causal process observations" – that is "an insight or piece of data that provides information about context or mechanism and contributes a different kind of leverage in causal inference. It does not necessarily do so as part of a larger, systematized array of observations . . . A causal-process observation may be like a 'smoking gun'. It gives insight into causal mechanisms, insight that is essential to causal assessment and is an indispensable alternative and/or supplement to correlation-based causal inference" Brady and Collier (2010, pp. 252–253). See also Mahoney and Goertz (2012, pp. 230–231) and Van Evera (1997).

[22] An analogy would be for a quantitative scholar to provide a replication website with raw data but no code.

8.3.4   Active Citation/ATI: A "Best Practice" Standard of Qualitative Transparency

Given the practical and epistemological constraints outlined above, social scientists have recently agreed that the best way to enhance transparency is to exploit recent innovations in internet formatting and software engineering. These technologies permit us to create new digital formats that can reestablish the high levels of qualitative transparency afforded by discursive footnotes in a more efficient and flexible way. Active Citation (AC) and Annotation for Transparency Initiative (ATI) are two related, digitally enhanced transparency standards designed do just this. They are practical and epistemologically appropriate to qualitative research.

AC/ATI envisages a digitally enabled appendix to research publications and reports. Rather than being an entirely separate document, however, the appendix embeds each source and annotation in an entry linked to a specific statement or citation in the main narrative of a research article or report. These may take the form of numbered hyperlinks from the article to an appendix or, in the ATI version, a set of annotations that overlay the article using a separate but parallel software platform. Unlike modern in-text footnotes, hyperlinks, and archiving, AC/ATI reinforces the epistemological link between narrative, data, and interpretation central to qualitative research. This author-driven process of annotation and elaboration via a separate document assures the same (or greater) levels of data, analytical, and production transparency as discursive footnotes, but with greater flexibility and no constraint on overall length. Moreover, it reduces the logistical difficulties by leaving the existing format of basic digital or paper articles and reports completely unchanged. Indeed, AC/ATI has the advantage that some audiences can simply skim or read the article without any additional materials, while those with a desire for more information can activate the additional materials.

Two ways exist to implement the AC/ATI standards. One, initially proposed by advocates of AC, obliges authors to design standardized entries that promote realistic levels of data, analytic, and production transparency in a relatively structured way. Accordingly, AC prescribes that researchers link each annotation that concerns an "empirically contestable knowledge claim" to a corresponding appendix entry. Of course, this still leaves tremendous leeway to the author(s), who decide (as with any footnote or citation) what is sufficiently "empirical" or "contestable" to merit further elaboration. Once an author decides that further elaboration is required, each entry would contain three mandatory elements and room for one more optional one – though, again, the author would decide how detailed and lengthy this elaboration needs to be.

An examination of the four elements in an AC entry shows how, in essence, this system simply updates the centuries-old practice of discursive footnoting in a flexible, author-driven, and electronic form appropriate to a digital age.[23] The four elements that can be in each entry are:

1) *A textual excerpt from the source.* This excerpt is presumptively 50–100 words long, though the length is ultimately up to the author. It achieves basic qualitative data transparency by placing the essential textual source material that supports the claim "one click away" from the reader. Sources subject to human subject or copyright restrictions can be replaced with a sanitized version, a summary, or a brief description, as is feasible. This provides a modest level of prima facie data transparency, while minimizing the logistical demands on authors, the ethical threats to subjects, and the potential legal liability.

2) *An annotation.* This length of interpretive commentary explains how, why, to what extent, and with what certainty the source supports the underlying claim in the main text. This provides basic analytic transparency, explaining how the author has interpreted the source. In this section, the author may raise not just the analysis of a given source, but its interpretive context, its representativeness of a broader sample, the existence of counterevidence, how it should be read in broader context, how it was translated, etc. This annotation can be of any length the author believes is justified.

3) *A copy of the full footnote citation, sufficient to locate the document.* This is critical because authors may seek to use the appendices independently of the text – for example, in a bibliography or database. Also, it assures that, whatever the format being employed in the main report, a genuine full citation exists somewhere, which is far from true today.

4) *An <u>optional</u> link to (or scan of) the full source.* A visual copy of the source would provide more context and unambiguous evidence of the source, as well as creating additional flexibility to accommodate nontraditional sources such as maps, charts, photographs, drawings, video, recordings, and so on. This option can be invoked, however, only if the author has the right to link or copy material legally and the ability to do so cost effectively, which may not always be the case – and doing so at all remains at the discretion of the author.

---

[23] For discussions of Active Citation, see Moravcsik (2014, 2016).

Of course, the de facto level of transparency that an author chooses to provide in any specific case will still reflect other important constraints. One constraint is *ethical*. The active citations cannot make material transparent that would harm research subjects or that is subject to confidentiality agreements. Ethical imperatives obviously override transparency.[24] A second constraint is *legal*. The content of the entries must respect intellectual property rights. Fortunately, small citations of most published material (except artistic or visual products) can be cited subject to "fair use" or its equivalent in almost all jurisdictions – but in cases of conflict, legal requirements override transparency. A third constraint is *logistical*. The amount of time and effort required to provide discursive notes of the type AC envisages is surely manageable, since discursive footnotes with roughly the same content were the norm in some academic disciplines and were widely used in the social sciences until a generation ago – and still appear in many published books. Today, the advent of electronic scanning and word processing make the process far easier. One can readily imagine situations in which that would create excessive work for the likely benefit. This is yet another reason why the decision of how many annotations to provide and how long they are remains primarily with individual authors, subject to guidance from relevant research communities, as is currently the case with conventional citations. Ultimately, the number of such entries, and their length and content, remain essentially up to the author, much as the nature of footnotes is today.

ATI offers the slightly different prospect of a more flexible, open-ended standard. ATI's major innovation is to use innovative software provided by the nonprofit firm *hypothesis*.[25] In lieu of storing the annotated source entries in a conventional appendix (akin to existing practice with formal and quantitative research) and hyperlinking individual entries to selected citations, as AC initially recommended, ATI allows the annotations to be written at will, stored in a separate program, and seamlessly layered on top of a PDF article by running the two programs simultaneously. ATI software makes the annotated sections appear as highlighted portions of the article, and when one clicks on a section of highlighting, the additional material appears in a box alongside the article. ATI provides a particularly efficient and manipulable means of delivering these source

[24] Sometimes researchers can square the circle by, for example, citing anonymous sources or by giving subjects a bounded time period of anonymity. One useful by-product of active citation would be more discussion of these options.
[25] For a discussion of how this works, with examples from recent conferences in which scholars employ this format, see https://qdr.syr.edu/ati and https://web.hypothes.is/blog/qdr-ati/.

material and annotations, and it provides almost infinite flexibility to authors. In trials, authors use the software to add annotations as they see fit. This type of software option also allows for separate commentary by readers. One might imagine the social sciences moving forward for a time with a set of such experiments that recommend no specific set of minimum standards for transparency but permit authors to define their own digital options. In a number of large test studies, dozens of younger scholars have tried ATI out with considerable enthusiasm, and this approach is in the process of adoption by major university presses that publish journals. This, it seems, is the future.

8.4   Conclusion: Qualitative Transparency in the Future

Qualitative social science journals, publishers, and scholars, having inadvertently undermined traditional qualitative transparency in recent decades, appear now to be moving back toward the higher levels practiced by researchers in history, law, and the humanities. An approach such as AC/ATI offers a more attractive trade-off between enhanced research transparency and the imperatives of ethics/confidentiality, intellectual property rights, and logistics than that offered by any existing alternative, even if data archives, conventional citations, and hyperlinks to existing web sources can occasionally be useful. These new digital standards are logistically efficient, flexible in the face of competing concerns, and remain firmly decentralized in the hands of researchers themselves. Over the next decade, journals and research communities are likely to adopt levels and strategies of qualitative transparency that differ in detail but all move in this direction, not least because funders and their fellow scholars are coming to expect it. Thus, while it remains to be seen precisely how standards for qualitative transparency will evolve in the future, it seems likely that digital means will be deployed more intensively to enhance research transparency. This is true not just because it renders social science research richer and more rigorous, but because society as a whole is moving in that direction. As digital transparency that clicks through to more detailed source material has become the norm in journalism, government messaging, business, and entertainment, the notion that researchers should not follow suit seems increasingly anachronistic. The same is true, of course, for practitioners and policy analysts who work on the major international challenges of our time.

References

American Political Science Association. (2012) *A guide to professional ethics in political science*, 2nd ed. Washington, DC: American Political Science Association.

American Political Science Association. (2013) *Guidelines for qualitative transparency*. Washington, DC: American Political Science Association.

Brady, H. and Collier, D. (2010) *Rethinking social inquiry: Diverse tools, shared standards*. Lanham, MD: Rowman & Littlefield.

Brown, H. S., De Jong, M., and Lessidrenska, T. (2009) "The rise of the global reporting initiative: A case of institutional entrepreneurship," *Environmental Politics*, 18(2), 182–200.

Collingwood, R. G. (1946) *The idea of history*. Oxford: Oxford University Press.

Cuervo-Cazurra, A. (2014) "Transparency and corruption" in Forssbæck, J. and Oxelheim, L. (eds.) *The Oxford handbook of economic and institutional transparency*. New York: Oxford University Press, p. 323.

Elman, C., Kapiszewski, D., and Viñuela, L. (2010) "Qualitative data archiving: Rewards and challenges," *PS: Political Science & Politics*, 43(1), 23–27.

Feynman, R. P. (1974) "Cargo cult science: Caltech 1974 commencement address," *Engineering and Science*, 37(7), 10–13.

Goodstein, D. (2010) *On fact and fraud: Cautionary tales from the front lines of science*. Princeton, NJ: Princeton University Press.

King, G., Keohane, R. O., and Verba, S. (1994) *Designing social inquiry: Scientific inference in qualitative research*. Princeton, NJ: Princeton University Press.

Lupia, A. and Elman, C. (2014) "Openness in political science: Data access and research transparency," *PS: Political Science & Politics*, 47(1), 19–42.

Mahoney, J. and Goertz, G. (2012) *A tale of two cultures: Qualitative and quantitative research in the social sciences*. Princeton, NJ: Princeton University Press.

Moravcsik, A. (2014) "Trust, but verify: The transparency revolution and qualitative international relations," *Security Studies*, 23(4), 663–688.

Moravcsik, A. (2016) "Qualitative transparency: Pluralistic, humanistic and policy-relevant," *International History and Politics*, 1(2), 17–23.

Qualitative Data Repository. (2012) *A guide to sharing qualitative data*. Syracuse, NY: Syracuse University, Qualitative Data Repository Project.

Rekdal, O. B. (2014) "Academic citation practice: A sinking sheep?" *Libraries and the Academy*, 14(4), 567–585.

Stiglitz, J. E. (2003) "Democratizing the International Monetary Fund and the World Bank: Governance and accountability," *Governance*, 16(1), 111–139.

Tetlock, P. E. (2017) *Expert political judgment: How good is it? How can we know?* Princeton, NJ: Princeton University Press.

Van Evera, S. (1997) *Guide to methods for students of political science*. Ithaca, NY: Cornell University Press.

Wiener, J. (2005) *Historians in trouble: Plagiarism, fraud and politics in the ivory tower* New York: New Press.

Woods, N. (2001) "Making the IMF and the World Bank more accountable," *International Affairs*, 77(1), 83–100.

World Bank (1992) *Governance and development*. Washington, DC: The World Bank.

Wright, M. and Armstrong, J. S. (2008) "The ombudsman: Verification of citations: Fawlty towers of knowledge?" *INFORMS Journal of Applied Analytics*, 38(2), 125–132.

Part III

Putting Case Studies to Work: Applications to Development Practice

Process Tracing for Program Evaluation

Andrew Bennett

9.1 Introduction

In recent years, the "replication crisis," or the finding that many attempts to replicate prominent published studies have failed to reproduce their original results, has roiled the medical, social science, public policy, and development research communities (Ioannidis 2005).[1] This has led to efforts to change both procedures and cultures in carrying out and publishing research, including a de-emphasis of p-values in statistical research, preregistration of studies using experimental designs or observational statistics, and, in some journals, preacceptance of studies based on their designs rather than their results.

Although many of the projects whose results could not be replicated were experimental studies, one response in the program evaluation community has been to increase the emphasis on experiments. Done well, these research designs, including field experiments and natural experiments as well as lab and survey experiments, remain powerful tools in program evaluation. Yet experiments impose demanding methodological requirements (Cook 2018; Deaton and Cartwright 2018), they face challenges of external validity, and in some policy domains they are not practical for fiscal or ethical reasons. In addition, evaluators are often called upon to evaluate programs that were not set up as experiments, including programs instituted quickly to address pressing needs.

---

[1] It is important to note that failure to replicate a study's findings does not necessarily mean the study's results are false; some studies cannot be replicated, for example, because it is no longer possible to replicate their particular context or sample.

Thus, a second response in the evaluation community has been increased interest in "process tracing," a method of causal inference that is applicable to single observational case studies (Bamanyaki and Holvoet 2016; Barnett and Munslow 2014; Befani and Mayne 2014; Befani and Stedman-Bryce 2017; Busetti and Dente 2017; Mendoza and Woolcock 2014; Punton and Welle 2015; Schmitt and Beach 2015; Stern et al. 2012; Wauters and Beach 2018). Process tracing has been common in political science for decades and has been the subject of recent methodological innovations, most notably the explicit use of Bayesian logic in making inferences about the alternative explanations for the outcomes of cases. Process tracing and program evaluation, or contribution analysis, have much in common, as they both involve causal inference on alternative explanations for the outcome of a single case (although process tracing can be combined with case comparisons as well). Evaluators are often interested in whether one particular explanation – the implicit or explicit theory of change behind a program – accounts for the outcome. Yet they still need to consider whether exogenous nonprogram factors (such as macroeconomic developments) account for the outcome, whether the program generated the outcome through some process other than the theory of change, and whether the program had additional or unintended consequences, either good or bad. Process tracing can address these questions, and it is also useful in assessing the validity of the assumptions behind natural, field, and lab experiments.

This chapter outlines the logic of process tracing and the ways in which it can be useful in program evaluation. It begins with a short discussion of the philosophy of science underlying process tracing and a definition of process tracing. It then turns to the role of process tracing in single case studies and in checking the underlying assumptions of experiments, field experiments, and natural experiments. Next, the chapter provides practical advice on process tracing for causal inference in individual cases and discusses the special considerations that arise in the use of process tracing in program evaluation. Finally, the chapter outlines an important recent development in process tracing methods: the explicit and transparent application of Bayesian logic to process tracing. It concludes that explicit Bayesian process tracing holds promise, but not yet proof, of improving the use of process tracing in causal inference and program evaluation.

9.2   The Philosophy of Science of Causal Mechanisms and Process Tracing

The increased interest in process tracing across the social and policy sciences is related to the turn in the philosophy of science over the last few decades toward a focus on causal mechanisms as the locus of causal explanation. Earlier, philosophers hoped that either "laws" or observed relations of statistical conditional dependence – analogous to what the philosopher David Hume called "constant conjunction" – would provide satisfactory accounts of causation and causal inference. The attempt to explain outcomes by reference to "laws" or "covering laws" foundered, however, when its advocates, including Carl Hempel, failed to come up with a justification or warrant for laws themselves (Salmon 1998, 69). In addition, Hempel's approach, known as the "Deductive-Nomological (D-N) Model," had difficulty distinguishing between causal and accidental regularities. In a common example, a barometer's readings move up and down with changes in the weather, but they do not cause the weather. Rather, changes in air pressure, which are measured by a barometer, combine with changes in temperature and other factors (topography, humidity, ocean currents, etc.) to cause the weather. But the D-N model has trouble distinguishing between a barometer and a causal explanation of the weather, as the barometer readings exhibit strong law-like correlations with the weather.

In an effort to address these problems, philosopher of science Wesley Salmon attempted to work out a defensible schema of explanation based on conditional dependence, or, in Salmon's terms, "statistical relevance." After encountering several paradoxes and dead-ends in this effort, he ultimately concluded that "statistical relevance relations, in and of themselves, have no explanatory force. They have significance for scientific explanation only insofar as they provide evidence for causal relations ... causal explanation, I argued, must appeal to such mechanisms as causal propagation and causal interactions, which are not explicated in statistical terms" (Salmon 2006, 166).

Many philosophers and social and other scientists thus turned to exploring the role of causal mechanisms and causal processes in causal explanation and the roles of different research methods (experiments, observational statistics, case studies, etc.) in uncovering evidence about the ways in which causal mechanisms work and the contexts in which they do and do not operate. Within philosophy, the discussion of causal mechanisms has generally gone under the label of "scientific realism" (related but not necessarily identical approaches include "causal realism" and "critical realism"). This is the school of thought that Ray Pawson, Nick Tilley, and others in the evaluation community have drawn upon in their discussions of "realist evaluation" (Astbury and Leeuw 2010; Dalkin et al. 2015; Pawson and Tilley 1997).

A detailed analysis of scientific realism and causal mechanisms, and of debates surrounding their definitions, is beyond the scope of the present chapter, but a brief summary will suffice. Realism argues that there is an ontological world independent of the mind of the observer or scientist, and causal mechanisms ultimately reside in that ontological world. Scientists have theories about how causal mechanisms work, and, to the extent that those theories are accurate, they can explain outcomes. In one widely cited formulation, causal mechanisms are "entities and activities, organized such that they are productive of regular changes from start or set-up to finish or termination conditions" (Machamer, Darden, and Craver 2000, 3). In another definition that also emphasizes a kind of regularity, mechanisms are processes that cannot be "turned off" through an intervention (Waldner 2012). Fire happens, for example, whenever there is combustible material, oxygen, and a sufficient ignition temperature; we can intervene on the presence of oxygen or materials or the temperature, but we cannot intervene on the mechanism of fire happening when the requisite materials and conditions exist.

Mechanisms are in the world, and theories about mechanisms are cognitive or social constructs in our heads. Scientists make inferences about the accuracy and explanatory power of theories about mechanisms by outlining the observable implications of these theories and testing them against evidence. In frequentist studies, the observable implications of theorized mechanisms lie at the population level, such as the correlations one would expect to find if a theory were true. In contrast, process tracing gets closer to mechanisms where they actually operate: in individual cases. The operation and interaction of causal mechanisms is realized in specific cases and contexts, and scientists and evaluators are interested in building theoretical understandings of the conditions under which mechanisms are activated or deactivated and the ways in which they interact with other mechanisms.

In studying individual cases, process tracers focus not just on the values of the independent and dependent variables, but on diagnostic evidence of sequences and processes that lie in the temporal space between the independent variables and the observed outcome. Process tracing uses this evidence to make inferences about which theories most likely offer true explanations of a case's outcome, sometimes called "inference to the best explanation." Process tracers continually ask "What should be true about the sequence of events between the independent variables and the dependent variable if a theory is a true explanation of the outcome of a case?" In the social sciences, this often takes the form of asking "Who should have

conveyed what information to whom, when, and with what effect at each
stage in the process if this explanation is true?" Diagnostic evidence, ideally,
is information that allows inferences about which processes are in operation,
but that does not itself represent an additional variable that independently
affects the operation or outcome of these processes. Diagnostic evidence, in
other words, is not an "intervening variable" in a process, as the term
"variable" implies an independent entity with its own potential causal effects.

9.3   Definition of Process Tracing

Process tracing is "the analysis of evidence on processes, sequences, and
conjunctures of events within a case for the purposes of either developing
or testing hypotheses about causal mechanisms that might causally explain
the case" (Bennett and Checkel 2015, 7).[2] Process tracing is a within-case
form of analysis: that is, it seeks to explain the outcomes of individual cases
(sometimes called "historical explanation" or "token explanation"). At the
same time, process tracing can be combined with cross-case comparisons or
other methods. Researchers can use process tracing, for example, to assess
whether differences between most-similar cases might account for these
cases' different outcomes. The theoretical explanations of case outcomes
assessed through process tracing can be about individual mechanisms or
processes, or combinations of mechanisms and processes. They can include
structural mechanisms, agent-based mechanisms, or any combinations
thereof.

A key difference between process tracing and frequentist statistical analysis
is that statistical analysis faces the "ecological inference" problem: even if
a statistical correlation correctly captures an average causal effect for
a population, it does not necessarily explain the outcome for any particular
case in that population. Process tracing, in contrast, focuses directly on the
causal explanation of individual cases. It may or may not uncover strong
evidence leading to a confident explanation of a case, but it does aspire to
develop directly the strongest explanation of the case that the evidence
allows. Rather than facing an ecological inference problem, process tracing
explanations, even when strong, face challenges regarding the external validity or generalizability of findings from individual cases. As Chapter 4 argues,
the challenges of generalizing the results of case studies, while real, are often

---

[2] The term "causal chain" analysis refers to methods quite similar to process tracing.

misunderstood. The explanation of an individual case can indeed prove generalizable: a new understanding of how a causal mechanism works, derived from the study of an individual case, can give strong clues about the scope conditions in which we should expect that mechanism to operate.

While process tracing is most often focused on the explanation of case study outcomes, the logic of process tracing can also be used in interrogating the validity of the strong assumptions necessary for experiments, field experiments, and natural experiments. In lab experiments, in addition to carrying out various balance tests on the treatment and control groups, researchers can use process tracing to check the procedures through which individuals were assigned to one group or the other, to assess the ways in which and reasons for which individuals opted to drop out of one group or the other, and to check on the possible presence of unmeasured confounders. Similarly, in field and natural experiments, where there is less control over assignment to treatment and control groups, researchers can use process tracing to assess whether the actual assignment or election into treatment and control groups was "as if random," and to evaluate evidence on whether the hypothesized process does indeed account for differences between the outcomes of the treatment and control groups (Dunning 2015).

Process tracing is much like detective work: the researcher is seeking an explanation of one case, and they can use both deductive and inductive inferences to find the best explanation. Deductively, the researcher starts with some "suspects" – the theories that have typically been applied to the outcome of interest. In program evaluation, this includes the theory of change explicitly or implicitly adopted by a program's designers and managers, but it also includes alternative explanations that relate to variables exogenous to the theory of change, such as macroeconomic trends, demographic change, local and national political developments, wars, natural disasters, etc. The researcher then looks for evidence on the deductively derived observable implications of each potential theoretical explanation of the outcome of the case. Just as a detective can reason forward from suspects and backward from a crime to connect possible causes and consequences, researchers can trace processes in both directions. A researcher can trace sequences forward from the independent variables, asking whether each caused the next step in the hypothesized chain leading to the outcome, and the step after that, and so on to the outcome. She or he can also trace backward from the outcome, asking about the most proximate step in the process that caused the outcome, and the step prior to that, back to the independent variables.

Deductively derived implications of a theory are one type of "clue," but researchers also gather other kinds of evidence or clues that they stumble upon inductively as they investigate or "soak and poke" in their cases. Inductively discovered evidence might point to an existing social science theory that the researcher had not identified as a possible explanation of the case, or it may lead to the development of an entirely new theory as a potential explanation of the case. It is possible that an inductively identified piece of evidence, even evidence for an entirely new theory or explanation, can be so strong – so uniquely consistent with one explanation and so inconsistent with all other explanations – that this theory could become the most likely explanation for the outcome even without further corroboration. This cuts against the common but erroneous intuition that a theory developed from a case can never be considered to have undergone a severe test from the evidence that led to the theory. Anyone who has done their own amateur home or car repairs knows the experience of finding physical evidence that not only suggests but makes highly likely a heretofore untheorized explanation for why a switch, appliance, or part is not working.

In addition, our confidence in a newly derived or newly added potential explanation of a case can be strengthened if the explanation entails additional observable implications within the same case that are then corroborated by additional evidence. This contravenes the frequent claim that one cannot develop a theory from a case and test it against the same case. We can develop a theory from a case and test it against *different evidence* from the same case that is independent of the evidence that gave rise to the theory. It would be illogical, for example, for a doctor to diagnose a rare illness in a patient based on an unexpected test result, and then insist on testing the diagnosis on a different patient, rather than on an additional diagnostic test in the first patient.

9.4   Practical Advice on Traditional Process Tracing

The general approach of process tracing is fairly intuitive as it follows a kind of inferential process that has been around as long as humankind. Yet despite its seeming simplicity and familiarity, researchers do not always do process tracing well, and, as the final section of this chapter argues, even trained researchers make common mistakes in employing the Bayesian logic that underlies process tracing. So how can we do process tracing well? Elsewhere I have elaborated with my co-author Jeffrey Checkel on ten best practices for

> # Box 9.1 Best practices in process tracing
>
> 1. Cast the net widely for alternative explanations.
> 2. Be equally tough on the alternative explanations.
> 3. Consider the potential biases of evidentiary sources.
> 4. Take into account whether the case is most or least likely for alternative explanations.
> 5. Make a justifiable decision on when to start.
> 6. Be relentless in gathering diverse and relevant evidence, but make a justifiable decision on when to stop.
> 7. Combine process tracing with case comparisons when useful for the research goal and feasible.
> 8. Be open to inductive insights.
> 9. Use deduction to ask "If the explanation is true, what will be the specific process leading to the outcome?"
> 10. Remember that conclusive process tracing is good, but not all good process tracing is conclusive.
>
> Source: Bennett and Checkel (2015)

being a good traditional process-tracing detective; here, I introduce these practices briefly and elaborate on the considerations of each that are most relevant to program evaluation (Bennett and Checkel 2013, 20–31). In the final section of this chapter I address how to carry out the more formal Bayesian variant of process tracing.

9.4.1 Cast the Net Widely for Alternative Explanations

One of the most common mistakes in case study research designs is the omission of a potentially viable explanation. It is important to consider a wide range of potential explanations, as the omission of a viable explanation can skew the interpretation of evidence on all the other explanations that a researcher does consider. Explanations for program outcomes need not be – and usually should not be – single-variable explanations. Rather, they can include combinations of interacting variables. There are four main sources of potential alternative explanations of program outcomes. The first is the program's explicit or implicit theory of change, which should be evident in program documents and interviews with program managers. In practice, individuals may differ in how they view the theory of change or interpret its implications for how they administer the program, so it may be necessary to process trace different variants of the theory of change. As it is essential to not unduly privilege the theory of change, a second source of explanations includes those offered by other stakeholders (beneficiaries, government officials, members of communities who experience knock-on effects, etc.), as well as the implicit or explicit explanations news reporters give for program outcomes. A third range of candidate explanations consists of social science theories that researchers have typically applied to the kind of program or outcome in question. As there is a wide range of such theories, a useful checklist is to consider both explanations focused on variations among agents (their interests, capacities and resources, networks, ideas, etc.) and those focused on social structures (norms, institutional rules and transactions costs, and actors' relative material resources).[3] Fourth, it is useful to consider the standard list of potential confounding explanations for program outcomes and to do process tracing on any that are relevant. These include:[4]

History: exogenous events (economic cycles, elections, natural disasters, wars, etc.) during the program period that can affect outcomes.

Maturation: program beneficiaries might go through aging processes that improve or degrade outcomes over time.

Instrumentation: changes in measurement instruments or technologies during the program can affect the assessment of outcomes.

Testing: exposure to testing or assessment can change the behavior of stakeholders.

Mortality: there may be selection bias regarding which stakeholders or recipients drop out of the program.

Sequencing: the order in which program treatments are implemented may affect outcomes.

Selection: if acceptance into the program is not random – for example, if the program chooses to address the easiest cases first (low-hanging fruit) or the hardest cases first (triage), there can be selection bias.

Diffusion: if stakeholders interact with each other due to the program, this can affect results.

Design contamination: competition among stakeholders can affect outcomes; those not selected as beneficiaries might try harder to improve

---

[3] For a taxonomy of twelve common types of social science theories based on different types of agentic and structural interactions, and approaches to explanations focused on material power, institutional transactions costs, and ideas and social relations, see Bennett (2013).

[4] Many of these are discussed in Shadish, Cook, and Campbell (2002).

their own outcomes, or they might become demoralized and not try as hard to succeed.

Multiple treatments: if governments or other organizations are administering programs targeted at similar outcomes, or if the program being evaluated includes multiple treatments, this can affect outcomes.

There can also be potential interactions among these factors that merit process tracing.

9.4.2   Be Equally Tough on the Alternative Explanations

Being fair to alternative explanations is an obvious goal for evaluation and causal inference, but it can be difficult to achieve in practice given the cognitive propensity for confirmation bias. A key contribution of rigorous research methods, whether qualitative, quantitative, or experimental, is to make it harder to engage in the well-known heuristics and biases through which individuals often make faulty inferences. Process tracing methods aim to achieve this by requiring that we consider not only what evidence would be consistent with each explanation, but also what other explanations might be equally or more consistent with that same evidence. They also require that we consider what evidence would be inconsistent with each explanation, and the degree to which other explanations would be (in)consistent with that evidence. This can prevent the temptation to focus mostly on affirming evidence for one explanation and to neglect how that same evidence could also fit other explanations. A common mistake occurs when researchers do deep process tracing on one theory, such as the theory of change, and only cursory process tracing on alternative explanations. An unbiased estimate of how likely it is that a theory is a good explanation of the outcome of a case requires that the alternative explanations receive scrutiny as well. Process tracing proceeds not only by finding evidence that fits one explanation better than the others, but also by eliminative induction of alternative explanations that do not fit the evidence. The discussion of Bayesianism in Section 9.5 gives a more formal assessment of how the relative likelihood of evidence given alternative explanations should affect the confidence we invest in those explanations.

9.4.3   Consider the Potential Biases of Evidentiary Sources

The potential biases of stakeholders are sometimes fairly clear, but they can depend on institutional and contextual factors. A government official might want to cast a program in a good or bad light, for example, depending on their party affiliation. Program managers generally want to show that their program is succeeding, but they might be tempted to downplay the baseline achievements they inherited from their predecessors. It is important as well to consider not only motivated biases, but also unmotivated biases that can arise from the selective information streams to which individuals are exposed, or from procedures through which some documents are maintained and made accessible and others are discarded.

9.4.4   Take Into Account Whether the Case is Most or Least Likely for Alternative Explanations

This consideration applies to the ability to generalize the findings of a program evaluation to other contexts in which the program might be instituted. When a program succeeds in its least hospitable conditions, this can provide a warrant for arguing that it is likely to succeed in a wide range of conditions. When it fails in its most favorable context, this suggests a program is unlikely to succeed anywhere. For additional discussion, see Chapter 4.

9.4.5   Make a Justifiable Decision on When to Start

An obvious point in time at which to start an evaluation or establish a baseline is often at the initial implementation of a program. Different parts of a program may have started at different times, however, or they may have started at different times in different regions or for different groups of stakeholders. There can also be time lags between the proposal, approval, and implementation of a program, and during each period stakeholders might start to change their behavior in ways that either enhance or undermine program performance. For example, actors might try to corner the local market and increase the prices of local goods, properties, or services that will be in greater demand once a program starts. In addition, stakeholders may have had incentives to boost or depress some of a program's indicators or measures to try to get initial baseline measures that suit their purposes. When such anticipatory behaviors are possible, it makes sense to consider beginning the evaluation period at the first point in time when actors became aware of the program (which might include private leaks of information, and rumors and misinformation, even before a program is publicly announced).

9.4.6   Be Relentless in Gathering Diverse and Relevant Evidence, but Make a Justifiable Decision on When to Stop

The Bayesian logic outlined at the end of this chapter gives rationales for why diverse evidence is important and for deciding on when it is reasonable to stop gathering additional evidence. Essentially, when we assess a particular kind of evidence, each successive piece of this evidence has less potential to strongly change our confidence in different explanations of a case. We will have already updated our views based on the earlier pieces of the same kind of evidence, so each new piece of this kind of evidence is less likely to surprise us, and at some point our time would be better spent looking at a different kind of evidence or a different observable implication of a potential explanation.

At the same time, the appropriate "stopping rule" for looking at a particular kind of evidence depends not just on whether each successive piece of evidence is consistent with the story told by each previous piece, but also on how unexpected that story is in the first place. As the philosopher David Hume wrote, "No testimony is sufficient to establish a miracle, unless the testimony be of such a kind, that its falsehood would be more miraculous than the fact which it endeavors to establish" (Hume 1748, chp. 10).[5] We would thus demand more voluminous, consistent, and diverse evidence to be convinced that a program had an astonishingly strong or weak effect than to be convinced that it does not.

A third consideration for determining a stopping rule for policy-relevant process tracing concerns the question of what is at stake. The higher the consequences of a type I (false positive) or type II (false negative) inference on whether the program worked, the higher the degree of confidence we will seek to establish based on the evidence. It makes sense, for example, to demand more conclusive evidence for medical treatments where lives are at stake than for programs that might at best modestly improve incomes or at worst leave them unchanged.

9.4.7   Combine Process Tracing with Case Comparisons when Useful for the Research Goal and Feasible

Process tracing is a within-case form of analysis, but it can be combined with cross-case comparisons to strengthen inferences. In a "most-similar" case

---

[5] The astronomer Carl Sagan popularized a pithier formulation: "extraordinary claims require extraordinary evidence."

comparison, for example, a researcher selects two cases that are, ideally, similar in the values of all but one independent variable and that have different outcomes on the dependent variable. Before–after comparisons, which compare a preprogram baseline to postprogram outcomes, can be most-similar comparisons if important nonprogram variables do not change in the same time period. The goal in most-similar comparisons is to make an inference on whether the difference on the independent variable – or, here, the program intervention – accounts for the difference on the dependent variable. The key limitation of this design is that even if all but one of the independent variables are closely matched, there may be other untheorized differences between the two cases, including exogenous variables that change in the time period between the inception and the evaluation of a program, that might account for the difference in their outcomes. It is thus important to do process tracing on the independent variable that differs, or the program intervention, to show that it created a causal chain leading up to the outcome. The researcher should also process trace the hypothesized effects of any other potential independent variables that differ between the comparison cases, and to the extent that this reveals that they can be ruled out as causes of the cases' differing outcomes, we can be more confident that the program's theory of change generated the outcome.[6]

9.4.8   Be Open to Inductive Insights

Because the omission of a viable candidate explanation can undermine inferences about a case, it is important to watch for potentially causal variables that were omitted from the initial list of candidate explanations. The feeling of surprise at discovering an unexpected potential causal factor is something to be savored rather than feared, as it signals that there may be something new to be learned about the process that led to the outcome. Cases where the outcome was surprisingly good or unexpectedly poor, or "deviant" or "outlier" cases, are good candidates for process tracing that puts added emphasis on inductive soaking and poking to identify and assess variables whose omission from researchers' or practitioners' prior theories might explain why one or both communities were surprised by the outcome.

---

[6] Similarly, researchers can use process tracing on "least-similar cases" comparisons, or comparisons among cases with similar measures on only one independent variable and similar outcomes. Here, the researcher can process trace from the common independent variable to the common outcome, and also process trace on any other potential independent variables that are similar to see if they might also account for the outcome.

9.4.9   Use Deduction to Ask "If the Explanation Is True, What Will Be the Specific Process Leading to the Outcome?"

Researchers need to think concretely about specific hypothesized processes in order to do process tracing well. Social science theories are usually stated in general terms, and it is necessary to adapt them to the case and circumstances at hand and ask what specific sequences and events they would predict if they were to constitute an adequate explanation for the outcome.

Consider the example of microfinance. On one level, the hypothesized mechanism through which such loans work (if they do) is simple: microloans give credit to businesses too small or informal to have access to conventional loans. Yet depending on the details of the microfinance program, several different mechanisms may be at work. In the process of applying for a microloan, applicants might receive feedback that improves their business plans, and those that receive loans may receive further monitoring and advice. Being accepted as a loan recipient might be seen as an indicator of the quality of the applicant's business plan, opening the door to additional credit, whether from social networks or formal financial institutions. If the savings that provide the funds for loans come from local actors who also decide on which loans to make, as in solidarity lending, this can create social pressures – and social resources – for the business to succeed and for loan repayment. Transactions costs, interest rates, inflation, macroeconomic trends, and other factors can affect whether and how microloans work as well. It is necessary to specify concretely how each of these possible mechanisms might have worked in the case at hand, and to outline the observable implications for each, in order to carry out process tracing.

Educational programs provide another example of the importance of thinking concretely about how projects actually work. University scholarship programs aim to provide opportunities for students who could not otherwise afford higher education. It is relatively easy to measure inputs (how many scholarships were given out) and outputs (how many scholarship recipients graduated), but the challenge is to assess how such a program actually works and what its actual effects are compared to the counterfactual world in which the program did not exist. On what basis does it select students for funding? How does it establish and verify the criterion of financial need? Does it also advise students on how to apply to universities and how to prepare for and succeed once they begin attending? Does it get students into programs they would not otherwise attend, or to which they would not even apply without the possibility of a scholarship? What programs were students contemplating or applying to before and after they heard of the scholarship? Might the same students have received scholarships or loans that would allow them to get a university education at the same institutions? Does the scholarship lead to a higher rate of program completion for funded students compared to students who nearly won funding? Were funds provided in a timely way in each semester, or did delay cause dropouts or registration difficulties? Did scholarship students expand the capacities of universities and the numbers of students they accepted, or merely take the place of other students who then had to go to other universities? Did accepting the scholarship open up other funds or resources that the student would have used, creating opportunities for yet other students (including siblings, cousins, etc.)? Such concrete questions get us closer to assessing the actual outcomes that arose and the ways in which they came about.

9.4.10   Remember That Conclusive Process Tracing Is Good, but Not All Good Process Tracing Is Conclusive

When the evidence from a case sharply discriminates among alternative hypotheses – that is, when it is likely to be true under one hypothesis but very unlikely under the alternatives – this allows strong claims that the one hypothesis consistent with the evidence is a strong explanation of the outcome in the case. The evidence is not always strongly conclusive, however, and it is important not to overstate the certainty that the evidence allows. The evidence may be weak or mixed, and it is important to convey how strong the evidence is and how strong the inferences are that the evidence allows. As discussed later in this chapter, this can be expressed in informal terms, such as "smoking gun" versus "straw in the wind" evidence, and "high confidence" or "likely" explanations, or it can be conveyed in numerical point or range estimates of probabilities ranging from zero to one.

In addition, often a combination of factors rather than one factor alone explains the outcome of a case, and it can be difficult to figure out process tracing tests that discriminate among all the possible interactions of the variables of interest. For example, in a particular case of microfinance, it may be that expanded credit alone was sufficient for the outcome, or it may be that this together with business advice from the lender generated the outcome. To distinguish among these, an evaluator would have to think of observable implications that would be consistent with the "credit alone" explanation but not the "both together" explanation, and vice versa.

A third reason to be careful to not overstate the certitude that the evidence allows is that it is always possible that the outcome is due to an explanation that the evaluator did not consider. As discussed later in this chapter, the Bayesian logic in which process tracing is rooted requires exhaustive and mutually exclusive explanations in order to function completely, and it is never possible to know with certitude that one has considered all the possible explanations. This is one reason that Bayesians do not allow for 100 percent certitude in any inferences.

9.5   Program Evaluation Process Tracing versus Social Science Process Tracing

There is one key difference between program evaluation process tracing and social science process tracing, and it generates both advantages and challenges for program evaluators. This is the fact that the experts who design policy interventions have the opportunity to outline in advance diagnostic indicators that will later provide evidence on whether a program is working as its theory of change suggests. Moreover, officials can require that program implementers begin gathering and reporting evidence on these indicators from the inception of the program or even the preprogram baseline. If the indicators are well designed, and if they also include data on alternative causal processes that might affect program outcomes, this greatly eases the task of program evaluation. Social scientists, in contrast, usually have to devise their own process tracing tests and gather the relevant evidence themselves after the events under study have already taken place.

Predesignation of program indicators can present challenges as well, however. First, indicators may be poorly designed and fail to provide strong evidence on the mechanisms through which the theory of change is expected to operate. Program outcomes can be difficult to conceptualize and measure, which can create a tendency to rely on measuring inputs or outputs instead of outcomes (Castro 2011; Markiewicz and Patrick 2016; Van der Knaap 2016). Diagnostic process tracing evidence is not the same as measures of outputs or outcomes, as it focuses on hypothesized causal mechanisms and processes, but it can overlap with output measures. There can also be a temptation to focus on diagnostic measures that are easy to measure rather than those that provide strong evidence for causal inference.

Second, there is a risk that program managers and other stakeholders will "game" the measurement and reporting of indicators to slant them toward their desired evaluation results. It can be difficult to devise diagnostic measures that provide strong evidence on the causes of program outcomes and that are not also susceptible to gaming. Essentially, this requires devising diagnostic measures that program implementers cannot achieve unless they actually are faithfully carrying out the program in accordance with its theory of change. This can lead to another problem, however: if diagnostic measures are too demanding and detailed, or if program implementers think (rightly or wrongly) that the theory of change is imperfect and that their experience and skills (or changed circumstances) give them better ideas on how to achieve the program's goals, these program managers will face unpleasant choices between following micromanaging guidelines that they think are inappropriate or departing from the prescribed practices and measures. This raises the classic dilemmas concerning how much authority and flexibility to delegate in principal–agent relations, how to monitor agents through management information systems, and whether and how to allow for changes in the middle of program implementation (Honig 2018). While there is no perfect solution to these dilemmas, consulting stakeholders and program managers on the design of appropriate diagnostic measures and putting in place procedures and decision-making processes for modification or adaptation of these measures can minimize the trade-offs between too much and too little delegation and oversight (Gooding et al. 2018).

Perhaps a more common challenge, however, arises when program designers had an under-specified theory of change or gave insufficient attention to developing and gathering evidence on indicators that would make later process tracing and program evaluation easy. Even when a theory of change is well specified, evaluators need to assess its coherence and consider alternative explanations that program managers may not have considered or on which they did not gather evidence. In this regard, program evaluators are often in a position similar to that of social scientists who design and gather evidence on alternative explanations only after the events of interest have taken place.

9.6   Bayesian Logic and Process Tracing

The best practices outlined earlier address the "traditional" process tracing that characterizes almost all published research and completed program evaluations to date. In the last few years, however, methodologists have begun to explore the possibility of applying more explicitly and formally the Bayesian logic that underlies process tracing. There are as yet few applications of this approach to empirical research, and there are strong pragmatic reasons why full formal Bayesian analysis of evidence from case studies is not appropriate in most research settings. Still, it is useful to understand the formal Bayesian logic that informs more informal process tracing practices, as this can lead to better implementation of these less formal practices. In addition, it may be useful to apply more formal Bayesian analysis to a few of the most important pieces of evidence in a study even if it is unduly cumbersome to do so for most of the evidence. While a full discussion of the Bayesian logic of process tracing is beyond the scope of this chapter, the brief outline that follows provides an introduction to the topic.[7]

In Bayesian analysis, probability is conceived of as the degree of belief or confidence that we place in alternative explanations. This is quite different from the standard frequentist statistical conception of probability as representing the likelihood that a sample is or is not representative of a population. In Bayesian analysis of individual case studies, the analyst starts with a "prior," or an initial guess regarding the likelihood that alternative explanations are true regarding the outcome of the case. The analyst uses the logic of the explanations, or of their underlying theories, to estimate how likely particular kinds of evidence are in the possible worlds represented by each explanation. The analyst then uses the laws of conditional probability to translate the likelihood of evidence given alternative explanations into the likelihood of alternative explanations given the evidence. This new, updated estimate of the likelihood that alternative explanations are true is called the "posterior" probability, or simply the posterior.[8]

Bayesianism provides a formal language for discussing the relative strength or probative value of different pieces of evidence. We already have an informal language for this: "smoking gun" evidence strongly supports one

---

[7] The most complete discussion of Bayesian process tracing to date is Fairfield and Charman (2017). For discussion of Bayesian process tracing in the context of program evaluation, see Befani and Stedman-Bryce (2017).

[8] Using the symbols of probability theory, this paragraph relates to the following version of Bayes Theorem:

$$Pr(P|k) = pr(P)pr(k|P) \qquad pr(P)pr(k|P) + pr(\sim P)pr(k|\sim P)$$

Notation:

$Pr(P|k)$ is the posterior or updated probability of proposition P given (or conditional on) evidence k

$pr(P)$ is the prior probability that proposition P is true

$pr(k|P)$ is the likelihood of evidence k if P is true (or conditional on P)

$pr(\sim P)$ is the prior probability that proposition P is false

$pr(k|\sim P)$ is the likelihood of evidence k if proposition P is false (or conditional on $\sim P$)

explanation, but the absence of such evidence does not necessarily reduce confidence in that explanation. Passing a "hoop test" is asymmetrical in the other direction: an explanation is strongly undermined if it fails a hoop test, but we do not necessarily greatly increase our confidence in an explanation that passes a hoop test. These informal examples are points on a continuum: the "likelihood" of evidence taking on a certain value if a theory or an explanation is true can range from 0 to 1, and when we compare the likelihood of evidence under one explanation to its likelihood under an alternative – that is, when we divide the likelihoods – this ranges from 0 to infinity. The more likely evidence is under one explanation, and the less likely it is under the alternatives, the more strongly the discovery of that evidence affirms the one explanation it fits. It is the *relative* likelihood of the evidence under the alternative explanations, or the "likelihood ratio," that matters, not the absolute likelihood that the evidence or data will take on a certain value if one explanation is true.[9]

Bayesian inference, however, is only as good as the information that informs the analysis, which raises the obvious question: How do we estimate the priors and likelihoods? The prior, or our initial guess on the likelihood that a particular theory correctly explains the outcome of a case, in principle represents all of our "background knowledge," or all of our conclusions and intuitions from previous research and experience. In some situations, such as when we have mountains of data, we can use well-informed priors, just as life insurance companies do when they use the ample data at their disposal to estimate life expectancies given a person's age, health habits, and health indicators. Most of the time in social science settings, however, we lack a strong evidentiary basis for estimating priors. One option here is to use uninformed priors – that is, to give each alternative explanation an equal prior (such as a prior of 1/3 if there are three candidate explanations). Another option is to try the analysis with different priors to see how sensitive the conclusions are to the choice of the prior; if the evidence is strong, the estimate of the prior

---

[9] This relates to the "odds form" of Bayes Theorem, which is mathematically equivalent to the version in the previous footnote but in some ways is more intuitive and easier to work with:

Posterior = Likelihood. Prior Odds
Odds Ratio   Ratio   Ratio
Or, in the notation of probability:
$$Pr(P|k) = pr(k|P). pr(P)$$
$$Pr(\sim P|k) \quad pr(k|\sim P) \quad pr(\sim P)$$

might not matter much to the estimate of the posterior (Bayesians call this the "washing out of priors"). A third approach that case study methodologists are beginning to assess is to "crowd source" estimates of priors, whether among subject matter experts or nonexperts.

Estimating likelihoods of evidence is challenging as well. This requires "inhabiting the world" of each hypothesis – that is, assuming that the hypothesis is true and then assessing the likelihood of a piece of evidence given the truth of the hypothesis. Estimating likelihood ratios requires performing this task for multiple hypotheses. On the other hand, it can be easier to assess the relative likelihood of evidence – to ask which of two hypotheses makes the evidence more likely, and even to estimate the ratio of these likelihoods – than to estimate the absolute likelihood of evidence given each hypothesis. As with estimating priors, researchers can try crowd-sourcing estimates of likelihoods.

A third challenge is arranging the alternative explanations, as Bayesian inference requires, in such ways that they are mutually exclusive and exhaustive. This includes explanations that combine several interacting theoretical variables or causal mechanisms, such as agents, institutions, norms, etc. In principle, this is possible for any group of hypotheses. To take a simple example, a criminal investigator might divide the explanations for a murder into four possibilities: the murder could have been committed by suspect A alone, by suspect B alone, by both A and B colluding together, or by neither A nor B. The next step is a bit more complex: the investigator has to think of the likelihood of different pieces of evidence under all these possible explanations, and, ideally, to find evidence that strongly discriminates among the explanations. This can be difficult for murder investigations: the detective has to ask what evidence would point to collusion that would not also be consistent with A or B acting alone. It is arguably even more challenging for social science researchers who are evaluating various combinations of structural, normative, macroeconomic, managerial, and other factors that can contribute to the success or failure of development programs.

A final difficulty with formal Bayesian analysis is that the calculations it requires become tedious and lengthy to write up and to read even for a small number of pieces of evidence and alternative explanations, and much more so for multiple pieces of evidence and explanations. For this reason, even the methodologists who have begun to explore formal Bayesian process tracing argue against trying to implement it fully for all the evidence (Fairfield and Charman 2017).

Still, it can be useful to do formal Bayesian analysis on one or a few of the pieces of evidence that a researcher judges to be most powerful in discriminating among alternative explanations, as this can make the analysis more transparent. Specifically, understanding the Bayesian logic of process tracing can contribute to better process tracing practices in at least four ways. First, Bayesian logic provides a clear philosophical warrant for much of the practical advice methodologists have given regarding traditional process tracing, including the ten best practices of traditional process tracing discussed earlier. One reason to initially consider a wide range of alternative explanations, for example, is that failing to consider a viable explanation can bias the estimates of the likelihoods, and thus the posterior estimates, of all the explanations the analyst does consider. Bayesianism also gives a clear explication of what constitutes strong evidence, of why diverse and independent evidence is important, of the trade-offs involved in stopping too soon or too late in gathering and analyzing evidence, and of why we should never be 100 percent confident in any explanation.

Second, Bayesianism leads to counterintuitive insights. Evidence that is consistent with an explanation, for example, can actually make that explanation less likely to be true if the same evidence is even more consistent with an alternative explanation. Also, numerous pieces of weak evidence (or what might be called "circumstantial evidence" in a court), if they all or mostly point in the same direction, can jointly constitute strong evidence that considerably changes our confidence in alternative explanations.

Third, formal Bayesian analysis, even if it is done only on a few key pieces of evidence, provides a transparent form of inference that allows researchers and their readers or critics to identify exactly why their inferences diverge when they disagree on how to update their confidence in explanations in light of the evidence. Researchers and their readers can disagree about their priors, the likelihood of evidence under alternative explanations, and the interpretation or measurement of the evidence itself. Leaving estimates and interpretation of each of these ambiguous obscures where authors and readers agree and disagree. Making judgments on each of these clear, in contrast, can prompt researchers and their critics to reveal the background information that underlies their judgments, which can narrow areas of disagreement.

The fourth, and perhaps strongest, rationale for learning Bayesian analysis is that it illuminates the logic that traditional process tracers have used informally all along in order to make causal inferences form individual cases, and it can help them to use it better. Research on the psychology of decision-making indicates that people often make mistakes when they try to be intuitive

Bayesians or first attempt formal Bayesian analysis (Casscells, Schoenberger, and Grayboys 1978). Other research shows that deeper training in Bayesian analysis can help improve forecasting (Tetlock and Gardner 2015). Additional research indicates that a few simple practices consistent with Bayesian process tracing, such as actively considering alternative explanations, can help debias judgments (Hirt and Markman 1995).

9.7 Conclusion

Process tracing and program evaluation, especially forms of evaluation that emphasize contribution analysis, have much in common. Both involve inferences on alternative explanations of outcomes of cases. It is not accidental that the evaluation community has taken a growing interest in process tracing, or that process tracing methodologists have become interested in program evaluation. The best practices developed in traditional social science process tracing are applicable, with modest adaptations, to the task of program evaluation. The biggest difference is that in contrast to researchers doing process tracing in the social sciences, program evaluators may have the opportunity to designate in advance, and to require reporting upon, diagnostic indicators about alternative processes as well as measures of inputs, outputs, and outcomes. This can make later evaluation easier, but it can also introduce potential distortions and biases as program managers and stakeholders might "game the system" once they know what measures will be tracked. Program designers and evaluators need to be creative and flexible in designing indicators that are useful in subsequent program evaluations, that cannot be achieved without also achieving the desired results at which a program aims, and that do not become a straightjacket on program managers when modifications to a program can better achieve its goals.

Program evaluators can benefit as well from exploring the emerging literature on formal Bayesian process tracing. This literature clarifies the logic behind traditional process tracing methods, and it is beginning to explore and outline new practices, such as crowd-sourcing of estimates of priors and likelihood ratios, that might further strengthen process tracing. Although formally analyzing the weight of every piece of evidence is impractical, it can be useful to formally assess a few of the strongest pieces of evidence. This can contribute to more logically consistent and analytically transparent assessments of alternative explanations of program outcomes.

References

Astbury, B. and Leeuw, F. L. (2010) "Unpacking black boxes: Mechanisms and theory building in evaluation," *American Journal of Evaluation*, 31(3), 363–381.

Bamanyaki, P. A. and Holvoet, N. (2016) "Integrating theory-based evaluation and process tracing in the evaluation of civil society gender budget initiatives," *Evaluation*, 22(1), 72–90.

Barnett, C. and Munslow, T. (2014) "Process tracing: The potential and pitfalls for impact evaluation in international development," Summary of a workshop held on May 7, 2014, IDS Evidence Report 102, Brighton: IDS.

Befani, B. and Mayne, J. (2014) "Process tracing and contribution analysis: A combined approach to generative causal inference for impact evaluation," *IDS Bulletin*, 45(6), 17–36.

Befani, B. and Stedman-Bryce, G. (2017) "Process tracing and Bayesian updating for impact evaluation," *Evaluation*, 23(1), 42–60.

Bennett, A. (2013) "The mother of all isms: Causal mechanisms and structured pluralism in international relations theory," *European Journal of International Relations*, 19(3), 459–481.

Bennett, A. and Checkel, J. (2015) "Process tracing: From philosophical roots to best practices" in Bennett, A. and Checkel, J. (eds.) *Process tracing: From metaphor to analytic tool.* Cambridge: Cambridge University Press, pp. 3–37.

Busetti, S. and Dente, B. (2017) "Using process tracing to evaluate unique events: The case of EXPO Milano 2015," *Evaluation*, 23(3), 256–273.

Casscells, W., Schoenberger, A., and Grayboys, T. B. (1978) "Interpretation by physicians of clinical laboratory results," *The New England Journal of Medicine*, 299(1978), 999–1001.

Castro, M. F. (2011) "Defining and using performance indicators and targets in Government M and E systems." Washington, DC: The World Bank. PREM Notes and Special series on the Nuts and Bolts of Government M&E Systems; No. 12.

Cook, T. D. (2018) "Twenty-six assumptions that have to be met if single random assignment experiments are to warrant 'gold standard' status: A commentary on Deaton and Cartwright," *Social Science & Medicine*, 210(2018), 37–40.

Dalkin, S. M., Greenhalgh, J., Jones, D. et al. (2015) "What's in a mechanism? Development of a key concept in realist evaluation," *Implementation Science*, 10(49), 1–7.

Deaton, A. and Cartwright, N. (2018) "Understanding and misunderstanding randomized controlled trials," *Social Science & Medicine*, 210(2018), 2–21.

Dunning, T. (2015) "Improving process tracing: The case of multi-method research" in Bennett, A. and Checkel, J. (eds.) *Process tracing: From metaphor to analystic tool.* Cambridge: Cambridge University Press, pp. 211–236.

Fairfield, T. and Charman, A. (2017) "Explicit Bayesian analysis for process tracing: Guidelines, opportunities, and caveats," *Political Analysis*, 25(3), 363–380.

Gooding, K., Makwinja, R., Nyirenda, D. et al. (2018) "Using theories of change to design monitoring and evaluation of community engagement in research: Experiences from a research institute in Malawi," *Wellcome Open Research* 3(8), available at https://wellcomeopenresearch.org/articles/3-8 (accessed November 22, 2019).

Hirt, E. R. and Markman, K. D. (1995) "Multiple explanation: A consider-an-alternative strategy for debiasing judgments," *Journal of Personality and Social Psychology*, 69(6), 1069–1086.

Honig, D. (2018) *Navigation by judgment: Why and when top down management of foreign aid doesn't work*. New York: Oxford University Press.

Hume, D. (1748) *An enquiry concerning human understanding*. New York: Oxford University Press. Posthumous edition 1777; edited with introduction by L. A. Selby-Bigg, 1902, reproduced through Project Gutenberg. Accessed at www.gutenberg.org/files/9662/9662-h/9662-h.htm.

Ioannidis, J. P. A. (2005) "Why most published research findings are false," *PLOS Med*, 2(8), e124. Available at https://doi.org/10.1371/journal.pmed.0020124 (accessed November 22, 2019).

Machamer, P., Darden, L., and Craver, C. F. (2000) "Thinking about mechanisms," *Philosophy of Science*, 67(1), 1–25.

Markiewicz, A. and Patrick, I. (2016) *Developing monitoring and evaluation frameworks*. Thousand Oaks, CA: Sage.

Mendoza, A. A. and Woolcock, M. (2014) Integrating qualitative methods into investment climate impact evaluations. World Bank Policy Research Working Paper No. 7145. Available at https://elibrary.worldbank.org/doi/abs/10.1596/1813-9450-7145 (accessed November 22, 2019).

Pawson, R. and Tilley, N. (1997) *Realistic evaluation*. Thousand Oaks, CA: Sage.

Punton, M. and Welle, K. (2015) "Straws-in-the-wind, hoops and smoking guns: What can process tracing offer to impact evaluation?" Centre for Development Impact Practice Paper 10, Brighton: IDS, 1–8.

Salmon, W. (1998) "Scientific explanation: Causation and unification" in Salmon, W. (ed.) *Causality and explanation*. New York: Oxford University Press.

Salmon, W. (2006) *Four decades of scientific explanation*. Pittsburgh: University of Pittsburgh Press.

Schmitt, J. and Beach, D. (2015) "The contribution of process tracing to theory-based evaluations of complex aid instruments," *Evaluation*, 21(4), 429–447.

Shadish, W., Cook, T., and Campbell, D. T. (2002) *Experimental and quasi-experimental designs for generalized causal inference*. Boston, MA: Houghton Mifflin.

Stern, E., Stame, N., Mayne, J. et al. (2012) Broadening the range of designs and methods for impact evaluations. London: DFID Working Paper 38.

Tetlock, P. and Gardner, D. (2015) *Superforecasting: The art and science of prediction*. New York: Broadway Books.

Van der Knaap, P. (2016) "Responsive evaluation and performance management: Overcoming the downsides of policy objectives and performance indicators," *Evaluation*, 12(3), 278–293.

Waldner, D. (2012) "Process tracing and causal mechanisms" in Kincaid, H. (ed.) *The Oxford handbook of philosophy of social science*. New York: Oxford University Press.

Wauters, B. and Beach, D. (2018) "Process tracing and congruence analysis to support theory-based impact evaluation," *Evaluation*, 24(3), 284–305.

10 Positive Deviance Cases: Their Value for Development Research, Policy, and Practice

Melani Cammett

10.1 Introduction

Case studies can contribute valuably to the study of development generally and to the implementation of development policy in particular. Case studies are uniquely well situated to identify and disentangle causal complexity and to interrogate the role of contextual factors in shaping outcomes, among other strengths. In this chapter, I focus on the potential insights that can be derived from the study of a particular kind of case – the deviant case – and, more specifically, on anomalies that exceed expectations, or "positive deviant" cases. I argue that the study of positive deviance can offer two distinct types of benefits for development policy. The first is methodological: Building on the literature on case selection in the social sciences, I emphasize the value of deviant cases for hypothesis generation and for the analysis of causal heterogeneity. The second potential contribution is less technical. Deviant cases can play an important inspirational role, signaling to practitioners, policy-makers, and local development actors that improvement is possible, even in resource-constrained environments. At the same time, the celebration of positive deviant cases must proceed with caution, not only because idiosyncratic factors may deter the replication of their experiences to other units or contexts, but also because other actors operating in the same sectors or communities may feel undermined if they are implicitly judged vis-à-vis similar institutions or actors deemed to be more successful.

In Section 10.2, I elaborate on the concept of positive deviance and highlight the potential value of positive deviant cases for development policy.

The discussion focuses on both the methodological strengths and limits of positive outliers and on the value and risks of using such cases as sources of inspiration for local actors and development practitioners. The section identifies ways of selecting positive deviant cases in systematic and less systematic ways. In the subsequent section of the chapter, I illustrate the value of positive deviant cases for several projects on the quality of social service delivery in the Middle East and North Africa to which I have contributed. Section 10.3 summarizes the main arguments and raises additional issues related to the pros and cons of using positive deviance as a way to formulate and propel beneficial reforms in development policy.

10.2   What Can Development Policy Learn From Positive Deviance?

The analysis of high-performing outliers is a promising approach for the formulation and implementation of development policy on both technical and nontechnical grounds. The literature on case studies in the social sciences highlights the methodological value-added of positive deviant cases in research designs. An additional, nontechnical merit of the approach emphasizes the role of such cases in encouraging greater performance from other actors and institutions operating in the same field. In this section, I define positive deviance and review these distinct justifications for the study of positive deviance.

10.2.1   What are Positive Deviant Cases?

Positive deviant cases are outliers that exhibit superior performance than the predictions of a model would hold. In technical terms, this refers to cases selected to maximize $|Y_i - \hat{Y}_i|$, or the difference between the actual value and the fitted value in a regression (Gerring, 2007: 89; Seawright, 2016: 16). In order to qualify as cases of positive deviance, however, cases must be more than ephemeral outliers operating in an environment conducive to good performance. Rather, examples of positive deviant organizations or other types of collective actors must exhibit sustained high performance in a context in which good results are uncommon.

Writing from the perspective of organizational behavior in the management literature, Spreitzer and Sonenshein (2004) present a somewhat distinct definition and operationalization of positive deviance that is especially useful when thinking about the role that deviant cases can play in the formulation and implementation of development policy. Their definition emphasizes a normative component of positive deviance, depicting the construct as behavior that departs from established norms in a referent group "in honorable ways" (Spreitzer and Sonenshein, 2004: 832). This understanding differs from the more neutral statistical perspective in which deviance – whether positive or negative – represents behavior that diverges from average or normal experiences (Spreitzer and Sonenshein, 2004: 830). In their analysis of positive deviance in agricultural development, Pant and Hambly Odame (2009: 160), too, describe positive deviants as those who break from prevailing norms to promote positive change, which in their study is measured by the facilitation of agricultural knowledge creation and application in the instances they highlight. As I hope to show, an understanding of positive deviance that incorporates a technical, statistical definition while including attention to deviation from prevailing norms and practices in a given sociopolitical context is essential if we view positive deviant cases in both methodological and inspirational terms.[1]

10.2.2 Methodological Justifications

The literature on research design in the social sciences identifies a range of case selection strategies and highlights the pros and cons of each type for distinct research goals (Collier and Mahoney, 1996; Eckstein, 2009; Geddes, 1990; Gerring, 2007; Przeworski and Teune, 1970; Seawright, 2016; Seawright and Gerring, 2008). What, if anything, can be learned from positive deviance in the context of development policy?

The consensus view on the role of deviant cases is that they are most useful for exploratory purposes or discovery. Anomalous cases, whether positive or negative, are valuable for theory building exercises and to search for new but as yet unspecified explanations (Odell, 2001: 166; Seawright, 2016; Seawright and Gerring, 2008: 302). They can also generate insights into the identification and operation of causal mechanisms not examined in the existing literature (George and Bennett, 2005: 20; Gerring, 2007: 89; Seawright and Gerring, 2008: 303). In the case of positive deviance, then, these outliers can show how specific causal mechanisms propelled high performance, indicating how specific values on a previously unexplored variable propel superior outcomes.[2]

---

[1] Put differently: the ends do not justify the means. A case that is a positive deviant in an empirical sense is not 'positive' if it became so as a result of unscrupulous processes.

[2] Seawright (2016: 23) also shows how deviant cases can be used to illuminate the sources of measurement error in the outcome variable.

Deviant cases are well suited to pinpoint sources of causal heterogeneity (Seawright, 2016: 21, 25). This goal is particularly relevant for development policy because it is increasingly recognized that social context affects the implementation and results of the same types of interventions and policies (Pritchett and Sandefur, 2013). Policy interventions that have been validated through experimental research in one country or subnational unit often do not yield the same results in another place, limiting the broader value of studies based on experimental designs for development policy (Pritchett and Sandefur, 2013; Rodrik, 2008: 26–27). An advantage of a qualitative approach to studying positive deviance is that contextual factors can be identified and integrated into an analysis of what has or has not worked in a given unit (Bradley et al., 2009: 3). As a result, it is possible to study the way that social norms within an organization or in the community where it is embedded may affect the behavior of relevant actors and, hence, the performance of the organization as a whole.

At the same time, deviant cases have inbuilt limitations. By virtue of their status as outliers, they are obviously not useful for identifying the causal pathways of average or on-the-line cases. In addition, as Seawright (2016: 21) argues, they may not be as useful for identifying omitted variables as some have suggested (Bennett and Elman, 2006). Furthermore, as is true for other types of case studies, deviant cases cannot on their own refute a theory. However, when a theory is based on a deterministic proposition, deviant cases can also be used to disconfirm a theory (Seawright and Gerring, 2008: 302), although this is a less common causal premise in mainstream social science research.

It is also important to stress that identifying cases of positive deviance by selecting cases with exceptionally high values on the outcome of interest is subject to the usual pitfalls of selecting on the dependent variable (King, Keohane, and Verba, 1994). If we only study cases of high performers, we are liable to falsely ascribe their success to factors that may also be present in less successful cases as well. For this reason, the convention in qualitative research is to select on the independent variable whenever possible. But analyses of positive deviant cases among a field of otherwise similar cases that operate in the same context or area can be a valuable way to identify potential explanatory variables for exceptional performance. The hypothesized explanatory variables can then be incorporated in subsequent quantitative or qualitative studies in which their effects are evaluated more generally.

Despite these words of caution, taking a positive deviance approach has the potential to change the way researchers or development practitioners think about the phenomenon or outcome in question because the goal of analyzing outliers is to identify factors that explain why it does not fit the general pattern. From a statistical perspective, the ultimate goal of analyzing deviant cases is to aid in the development of a new model or the revision of an existing model so that the variable responsible for the anomalous value of a case is incorporated. The insights generated from a close analysis of the positive (or negative) deviant case can then be can tested more generally in a broader set of cases. To the extent that this model works, the deviant case is no longer deviant (Seawright and Gerring, 2008: 302–303). Deviant cases, then, can play an important role in revising the conventional wisdom on the determinants of a particular development outcome.

Positive deviant cases can yield especially valuable insights when situated in a larger mixed methods approach. In particular, if a qualitative analysis of high performers precedes a quantitative study, this affords the possibility of identifying previously unconsidered hypotheses or of devising measures that can tap into potentially important constructs. Process tracing is a valuable technique for identifying the factors that explain deviant performance (George and Bennett, 2005, p. 215), which can then be assessed in a larger sample. For example, in their discussion of learning from positive deviance in health care delivery, Bradley et al. (2009) present an approach that entails (a) the identification of organizations that have consistently demonstrated high performance on a clear set of indicators, (b) intensive analysis using qualitative methods to generate hypotheses about the specific practices and policies that led to exceptional performance, (c) the use of statistical tests in a larger, representative sample of organizations to assess the broader applicability of the hypothesized explanatory factors, and (d) the dissemination of best practices to other organizations operating in the same field. The discussion of a multistep research project on the determinants of quality in social service provision in Jordan, which was led by the World Bank, is another example of this approach (see Section 10.3.1).

10.2.3 Inspirational Justifications

A less technical perspective highlights a distinct potential benefit of focusing on deviant cases, and especially positive deviant cases, with notable benefits for development policy. The identification and exploration of high performers can be motivating in and of itself through a signaling effect. In the context of low-resource environments, which development policy tends to target, cases of success against the odds indicate to others that there is hope. When the prospects for advancement seem dim, examples of high performers signal that it is possible to break, or at least start to weaken, development traps.

Actors embedded within resource-constrained communities may regard the experiences of other actors or organizations in similar contexts as applicable to their own circumstances, increasing the probability that they will seek to emulate their practices. This dynamic may facilitate the diffusion of best practices, in the same way that activists in the Arab region or in other regional waves of mass mobilization emulated the strategies and tactics of first movers because they perceived that they faced similar opportunities and constraints in their own countries (Patel, Bunce, and Wolchik, 2014). In this sense, positive outliers can help to stimulate a sense of "cognitive liberation" (McAdam, 1999), whereby practitioners and policy-makers come to believe that change is not only desirable, but possible. The mere act of shedding feelings of resignation and hopelessness can propel positive change by motivating greater effort and stimulating collaboration toward shared community goals.[3]

In the day-to-day design and implementation of development policy, highlighting examples of positive deviance is likely to play a far more constructive role than pinpointing instances of underperformance or negative deviance. Positive incentives can be a source of motivation, potentially inducing greater effort and commitment to problem-solving among stakeholders, whereas sanctions may have a deterrent effect by increasing the sense of resentment and hostility to change (Ryan and Deci, 2000). Thus, just as emphasizing instances of success may galvanize positive change, policy-makers and development practitioners must tread lightly when advertising success stories lest others in the community resent the fact that they, too, were not the objects of praise. As I note below, this is precisely the reason why Moroccan officials were hesitant to include identifying information in a short case study of high-performing public health centers included in a World Bank report (Belkâab and Cammett, 2014; Brixi, Lust, and Woolcock, 2015). For these reasons, *how* the lessons of positive deviance are shared can affect the probability that other organizations will adopt them. If the management of organizations with less-distinguished records feels threatened or marginalized when learning of the exceptional performance of others, then it will be difficult to foster acceptance of the identified best practices. If, on the other

---

[3] Of course, the results of diffusion are not foreordained and activists can easily overestimate the potential for success in their own contexts of strategies implemented elsewhere (Weyland, 2012). This point is relevant for the questions at hand because it underscores the importance of ensuring that similar underlying conditions operate in contexts or organizations to which best practices may be disseminated.

hand, others can be made to feel as if they are partners in the identification and scale-up of effective strategies, then dissemination may be more likely.

In short, in development practice it is imperative to distinguish between the empirical identification of positive deviant behavior for methodological purposes and the inspirational role of positive deviant actors or organizations in driving beneficial outcomes. Positive deviants in the context of development policy and outcomes may be more than statistically anomalous cases. From the standpoint of effecting tangible change in public goods provision or other development policy goals, they may be actors or groups who drive innovation and bring about solutions to problems that are not well addressed under the status quo; alternatively, they may just be those who, on an everyday basis, seek to find ways to manage existing resources in a way that yields strong performance against the odds. As such, an analysis of deviant cases can serve at least two roles. First, a close analysis of the actions and behaviors of deviant actors, and especially the identification of causal pathways linking these to outcomes, provides explanations for why a handful of cases exceeded expectations. Second, in the design and implementation of development policies and programs, positive deviants can play an important signaling role by demonstrating to others who toil under equally challenging circumstances that success (or at least improvement) is possible.

10.2.4   Selecting Cases of Positive Deviance

A systematic approach to the selection of positive deviance cases is important to avoid biases that can result in missed lessons or misleading interpretations of the causal factors leading to exceptional performance. Under ideal circumstances, case selection must occur with reference to a broader population of cases that are identified based on a general causal model. This approach, however, is contingent on the availability and validity of information on the population – a condition that is often hard to meet in some countries, whether due to lack of information or lack of transparency – and on the quality and nature of the model (Gerring, 2007: 106; Seawright, 2016).

Given a conventional understanding of the determinants of the outcome of interest, then, positive deviant cases can be selected because they are off the regression line in the direction corresponding to high performance, or outcomes that imply beneficial or honorable behavior or outcomes (Spreitzer and Sonenshein, 2004). Yet positive deviant cases are more than just outliers. Rather, to qualify as examples of positive deviance, high performers must excel in a context in which most other comparable units do not perform well. To pinpoint such cases, case selection might proceed in a two-stage process in which the research first highlights low performers in a high-deviance region and then identifies high performers in an area characterized by low overall results (Woolcock, 1998). At the same time, such exceptional performance in a field of otherwise poor results must be sustained lest it arises due to chance, ephemeral factors, or particular circumstances.

As with any model, the utility of a regression line approach to selecting positive deviant cases also depends on the ways in which the outcome of interest is conceptualized and measured. Many goals central to development policy are multidimensional. A case or unit may perform exceptionally well with regard to some aspects of an outcome but may exhibit average or inferior values with respect to others. For example, in analyses of the quality of health care, the empirical focus of the examples discussed in the next section, dependent variables can focus on the infrastructural, process-oriented, or health outcome aspects of quality (Donabedian, 1988). Which aspects of quality are emphasized may be self-evident if there is a professional consensus on which dimensions are the key drivers of human development outcomes, or the choice may depend on the objectives of the researcher or development program.

In practice, it may be impossible to employ such a systematic approach to case selection due to a lack of data or restrictions on access to data. Should case studies of positive deviance then be abandoned? Not necessarily. It may be possible to identify actors or organizations that are deemed to be high performers in a less rigorous way by drawing on insights from local officials or community members. These actors know the terrain exceptionally well because they are embedded in the communities where policies or programs are implemented and have implicit or explicit rankings of local actors with respect to performance on development outcomes. Feedback from local actors can be elicited through interviews or by the administration of a survey, depending on resource availability.

That said, the measurement of positive deviance based on the reports of key informants is obviously vulnerable to a host of biases, even when respondents have the best of intentions. For example, officials or other stakeholders may inadvertently provide invalid information due to recall biases or because they wish to highlight favored actors or organizations at the expense of others. At a minimum, when cases are selected purposively, it is important to choose cases for in-depth analysis from a diverse sample that includes organizations varying in size, resource endowments, geographic location, and other factors that might affect performance (Bradley et al.,

2009: 3). As an alternative or supplemental approach, researchers may draw on findings and insights derived from studies in other, comparable settings to use as a benchmark for the determination of high-performing organizations or actors.

10.3   Examples: What Explains High-Performance Service Delivery in Jordan and Morocco?

In this section, I aim to flesh out the potential contributions and limitations of case studies of apparent positive deviance with reference to two studies carried out in preparation for a World Bank report highlighting local success stories in service delivery in the Middle East and North Africa (Belkâab and Cammett, 2014; Brixi et al., 2015; Rabie et al., 2014). The first entailed a case study of high-performing public health centers in Jordan and evolved in two stages. The first part of the study was based on in-depth, qualitative analyses of the drivers of high performance at the facility level. The second stage of the research built on the findings of the case study to design a quantitative study based on a nationally representative sample. The Jordanian case therefore shows how a case study of positive deviance can fit into a larger mixed methods research design. The second study also focused on the drivers of high-quality health care through a case study of high-performing public health centers in provincial and semirural areas of Morocco. By describing the methods and findings of case studies of positive deviance in Jordan and Morocco, and detailing how they have contributed to larger-scale projects in the two countries, I hope to illustrate the value and limitations of this approach for development policy.

10.3.1   Jordan

In March 2014, I was part of a team of researchers that visited six health centers in four of Jordan's twelve governorates, collecting data for a case study of positive deviance in the delivery of primary health care in the Jordanian public health system. The first order of business was to identify a set of indicators against which high performance would be assessed. A growing body of research emphasizes that several process-oriented aspects of health care quality, such as provider effort and human resource management at the facility level, are key factors contributing to the poor quality of health care in developing countries, with consequences for health outcomes (Das and Hammer, 2014; Dieleman, Gerretsen, and van der Wilt, 2009; Harris, Cortvriend, and Hyde, 2007: 450–452). At the same time, the quality of physical infrastructure may enhance or inhibit the ability of health workers to fulfill their professional obligations, and therefore it was also imperative to collect data on the availability and condition of medical equipment and supplies.[4]

In order to identify appropriate cases, we aimed to benchmark the performance of the selected centers in the past three to five years against others *within the same urban or rural region* with similar socioeconomic profiles. Given the limitations of time, resources, and existing data on service quality, case selection faced significant challenges. In the end, the choice of facilities relied heavily on insights provided by the Ministry of Health and referrals made by the Health Care Accreditation Council (HCAC),[5] a nonprofit organization in Jordan that implemented an accreditation program funded by USAID. As a result of its role in identifying appropriate health centers to undergo the accreditation process, HCAC staff members had collected a database on a sample of high-performing facilities in the public health system and were willing to advise us on case selection even though they were not permitted to share the full database with us. Input from the HCAC was especially valuable for the purposes of carrying out case studies of positive deviance because the participating facilities had been selected in the first place due to a longer record of high performance, which was enhanced after completing the accreditation program.

During site visits, the team carried out a series of open-ended interviews with the chief medical officers, doctors, nurses, administrative staff, and, where applicable, the members of local health councils to gather information on multiple indicators of health care quality and to probe the underlying drivers of the quality of care. In conjunction with administrative data provided by the Ministry of Health and the centers themselves and with interviews with local, regional, and national government officials, the data collected during these visits provided the information used to write the case studies. Given that the accreditation process itself was an important driver of quality, the team was careful to collect data illuminating

---

[4] We did not focus on health outcomes, in part because it is difficult to isolate the impact of health care as opposed to an array of social determinants on health indicators (Marmot and Wilkinson, 2005).

[5] The HCAC was established in 2007 as a private, not-for-profit organization that oversees and implements the accreditation of health care facilities in Jordan (see www.hcac.jo).

performance on quality indicators prior to and following participation in the program.

The findings of in-depth studies of the selected health centers yielded a variety of insights about the determinants of high performance in the delivery of primary health services in Jordan. The fact that the accreditation program was implemented in a nonrandom fashion and the design of the study prevented an analysis of the independent effects of participation in the program. However, in-depth interviews at the facility level clearly demonstrated that the act of preparing for and undergoing the evaluation for accreditation drove major improvements in the quality of care, even at facilities that already performed above their peers. In particular, the findings indicated that preparation for accreditation in and of itself provides one mechanism for improving administrative procedures and the quality of service delivery. The procedures and requirements of the accreditation process helped to establish clear rules and regulations, increase transparency to clients and staff, develop more effective staff monitoring, and give greater voice to and participation for staff within facilities as well as communities.

Beyond adherence to externally imposed standards and practices, leadership emerged as a key factor improving the operation of facilities. Indeed, strong, proactive chief medical officers at the health centers multiplied the positive outcomes from reforms implemented for accreditation or for other purposes. The head of one health center emphasized that he set clear expectations for his employees, fostered a collaborative work environment, and ensured that adequate feedback mechanisms existed for staff members to convey their concerns. Conversely, administrative reforms were less effective under weak leaders. For instance, the chief medical officer in one center noted that staff meetings were not held, since people came on different days and the assumption was that "everyone knows their job."

A third finding pointed to the role of social networks in facilitating voice and participation and potentially for improving the extent and quality of service provision. Personal ties, whether among family or friends and neighbors, are particularly valuable for establishing priorities, extending public health outreach in the community, and mobilizing resources to support the activities and development of health centers. Interviews with staff and members of local committees at the selected facilities indicated that shared identity, especially a common tribal affiliation, was especially valuable in rural areas but somewhat less relevant in urban centers, where people from diverse regions and backgrounds intermingle and many residents do not come from the major Transjordanian tribal families. In particular, when members of local health committees and local residents hail from the same tribes, the staff and governing board of a given center had an inbuilt channel through which to reach the community with vaccination and other health campaigns and to encourage greater compliance with medical advice. At one center, members of the local health committee claimed that the center's public outreach initiatives are relatively successful because they come from the same families as the targeted beneficiaries.[6] Beyond family ties, we also found that social networks and linkages to important local social institutions such as mosques, youth centers, and local schools also assist health workers to accomplish their tasks. This insight provides a clear example of the ways in which case studies of positive deviance can generate new variables and causal pathways.

The information gathered through the case study of successful facilities helped to inform a subsequent quantitative study that the team undertook in Jordan. Based on a national sample of 100 health centers, the analysis aimed to explain variation in standard measures of provider effort, including absenteeism, adherence to clinical practice guidelines, rights-based practice, and time spent with provider. The main independent variables captured various aspects of within-facility governance, a neglected variable in the public health literature on quality and, more generally, in research on governance and the quality of service delivery. These included indicators to capture the presence of various management practices at the health center, including monitoring of professional staff, sanctions for underperformance, and financial and nonfinancial rewards for good performance. The main control variables tried to address both top-down monitoring and a limited component of citizen engagement, notably the presence of a community health committee within the local primary health center (PHC). Many other factors were not measured, however, due to a lack of resources and time. The findings indicated that monitoring is the most consistent predictor of improved provider effort, including adherence to clinical practice guidelines, the provision of rights-based and responsive care, and time spent with patients in clinical examinations. When considered independently, sanctions were either not associated with provider effort or were associated with worse provider effort, a finding that fits with existing studies in the management

---

[6] Strong social ties may also complicate the work of the health center. For example, it may make sensitive issues such as domestic violence more difficult to address and, where strong social ties largely consist of blood ties, and where they promote intermarriage and consanguinity, they can also increase the prevalence of chronic diseases.

literature on the importance of positive work environments (Edmondson, 2003) and accords with what we saw at high-performing facilities in the case studies. The use of nonfinancial rewards to recognize good performance was not associated with provider effort, but this result likely obtained because the usage of this approach was too infrequent to be able to detect an effect.

Due to resource constraints, the study could not incorporate much attention to the impact of social context on the quality of service delivery. However, insights on the role of social ties in driving higher-quality health care derived from the case study of positive deviance facilities in Jordan have informed subsequent projects that my collaborators and I have undertaken. Thus, while we were not able to fully capitalize on the findings from deviant cases in the quantitative study in Jordan in order to build a new, more comprehensive model, we aim to do so in future research in relevant contexts.

10.3.2 Morocco

In May 2014, I traveled to Morocco to carry out a parallel case study of positive deviance primary health centers for the aforementioned World Bank report (Brixi et al., 2015). Initially, the strategy for case selection adopted a systematic approach by identifying positive outliers from data collected through a quantitative, nationally representative sample of the quality of primary health care in public centers carried out by the World Bank and the Ministry of Health (MOH). Given time constraints, it was not possible to visit all the centers I initially requested and, instead, I selected centers in several provinces with guidance from national and regional MOH officials. Although the sampling procedures were nonrandom, several systematic criteria guided the choice of facilities. First, half of the facilities participated in the *Concours Qualité* (CQ), a program introduced by the MOH to set up province-level competitions between public health facilities to be recognized for exceptional performance.[7] Second, they exhibited notable and sustained improvements in one or more key dimensions of the quality of health care

---

[7] Launched in 2007 and now in its sixth round, the CQ aims to improve quality based on the logic that competition and recognition of good work motivate people to seek improvement. Provincial MOH officials select centers to participate based on the motivation of the team, their openness to change and willingness to adopt new procedures, and their prospects for winning. In return for enrolling in the CQ, employees have greater access to supplemental training programs, and centers may become eligible to receive new equipment or even to receive funds for renovation.

provision in the last five years. Third, the centers were not located in major urban areas, where quality tends to be somewhat higher.

A consistent array of factors was observed at well-performing Moroccan public health centers, including larger patient loads; reasonable wait times despite high demand; good management and availability of stocks, consumables, and equipment; and detailed and regular maintenance of patient medical records, among other factors. Based on interviews with staff members at the facilities and MOH officials from multiple administrative jurisdictions, at least five factors seemed to be associated with improvements in the quality of care. First, the presence of dynamic, energetic, and visionary leadership helped to motivate staff members to carry out their duties competently and thoroughly, introduce new procedures and management systems, institute a "culture of quality" among staff members, inspire confidence in the community and local government officials, and attract additional resources to the facility. Second, a sense of a shared mission and collaborative ethic helped to motivate the staff and ensure that all staff members know and fulfill their responsibilities. Like leadership, a team spirit and a relatively flat organizational culture are especially important in the context of resource scarcity, in which staff members are required to make do with less.

Third, meetings with staff members from facilities that had and had not previously competed in the national CQ program demonstrated that the initiative has had a clear, positive effect on the management and administration of participating centers. The mere act of enrolling in the program generates significant transfer of knowledge and the adoption of new procedures within participating health centers. At the same time, it became clear that the program may be unsustainable because it requires a major investment on the part of staff members, taking them away from their primary professional duties, and has the paradoxical effect of increasing pressures on the successful facilities by boosting their patient load.

Fourth, effective coordination between the head doctor and local health officials was critical for the health centers to meet the needs of the populations in their catchment areas. Regular exchanges between the administrators of facilities and officials from the provincial delegation help to ensure that stock-outs of medications and equipment do not occur, that facilities receive resources when available, that local solutions are developed for local problems, and that good administrative and management practices are disseminated. Finally, partnerships with nearby groups, organizations, and prominent individuals help health centers to meet the needs of their surrounding communities more effectively. These findings were elaborated in a case study of positive deviance in the Moroccan primary health sector (Belkâab and Cammett, 2014). It is important to note that MOH officials explicitly requested that we refrain from naming specific health centers that performed exceptionally well in order to avoid resentment among staff members at other facilities not featured in the case study.

10.3.3   The Contributions of Positive Deviance Case Studies in Jordan and Morocco for Mixed Methods Research Designs

Case studies of high-performing health centers in two countries in the Middle East and North Africa suggest that, even in different sociopolitical contexts, some common factors at the facility and community levels affect the quality of service delivery. For example, leadership and management practices were important proximate determinants of quality in both contexts. This finding helped to inform a subsequent quantitative study in Jordan centered on the factors within facilities that incentivize greater provider effort.

Perhaps more interesting are the findings that facility health committees composed of elites, who hold either formal or informal positions of influence at the local level, and the extent and nature of social ties may have important causal effects on the quality of social services. From the perspective of the large body of social science research on clientelism and elite capture (Bardhan and Mookherjee, 2012; Dasgupta and Beard, 2007; Khemani, 2015; Platteau, 2004), the potentially constructive role of elites in driving improved process and outcome-based measures of health care quality may be surprising and deserves greater investigation. This finding raises questions about the conditions under which elites are likely to exert efforts to improve the quality of services and, more generally, to play a positive role in promoting inclusive access to services for local communities and to encourage citizens to adopt more health-seeking behavior. They also call for additional research into the nature of social ties and how they may mediate the effects of different types of interventions on the quality of social services. In both Jordan and Morocco, at least some local elites appear to have leveraged their influence to improve the quality of care delivered and to ensure that nonelites take greater responsibility for their own well-being.

10.4   Conclusion: Can Positive Deviance Inform Development Policy?

In this chapter, I have argued that positive deviant cases have the potential to contribute in important ways to the formulation and execution of development policy in at least two overarching ways. First, building on insights from the methodological literature on case selection in the social sciences, I reiterate the value of deviant cases – whether positive or negative – for identifying previously overlooked factors that may help to explain a phenomenon and distinct causal pathways that account for causal heterogeneity. At the same time, it is critical to add the caution that potential causal factors identified through small-N research based on selection on the dependent variable must be assessed more broadly before informing development policy and practice. In particular, follow-up studies, whether qualitative or quantitative, which select on the hypothesized explanatory variable would be a valuable complementary component of a larger research strategy.

Second, deviant cases, and especially *positive* deviant cases, can serve an important inspirational function for multiple audiences, whether development practitioners, policy-makers, or organizational staff and citizens who experience and shape development policy on a quotidian basis. By signaling that beneficial reforms or outcomes are possible, even in a resource-constrained environment, positive deviant cases can provide hope, empowering others to pursue similar approaches or outcomes. At the same time, the depiction and dissemination of lessons from positive deviant cases must proceed with caution in order to avoid inducing resentment on the part of similar actors or organizations that were not singled out for commendation.

Ultimately, the potential value of the study of positive deviant cases for development policy is contingent on a number of factors, only some of which are in the control of the researchers. Given data availability and consensus over the indicators that enable the classification of high performance, researchers can and should follow systematic principles of case selection by identifying and choosing positive outliers in carefully specified models that build on the state of knowledge on the outcome of interest.

In practice, however, many real-world factors, which are largely out of the control of researchers, may impede adherence to best practices in case selection. First and foremost, officials or other gatekeepers must be willing to share data or facilitate the collection of data that enables the identification of positive deviance. Once the cases have been identified and the lessons extracted from their experiences, other conditions must be in place to ensure that these examples spur reforms or constructive outcomes. In particular, other actors or organizations that have not distinguished themselves must be ready to experiment with new approaches or systems. If they are resistant to adopting lessons generated from more successful peer institutions, then the dissemination of best practices based on positive deviance will be hindered. Furthermore, government officials and other stakeholders must exhibit the political will to promote the dissemination of such practices.

The very fact that the lessons of positive deviance are derived from outlier cases raises the question of whether their experiences are idiosyncratic or can be generalized. For example, case studies of high-performing health centers in Jordan and Morocco underscored the value of strong and effective leadership at the facility level for high-quality service provision. If leaders are born and not made, or at least not easily cultivated, then this finding is less useful for generating policy prescriptions. In this case, the best that development practitioners and government officials can hope for is to recruit and retain employees with demonstrated and appropriate leadership skills. In most cases, however, policy lessons will not be so specific to individual personality traits or other idiosyncratic factors. Furthermore, factors that seem difficult to replicate may be less idiosyncratic than they appear; as studies of leadership attest (Nohria and Kurana, 2011), even this quality can be fostered.

To the extent that context matters, the same practices often do not have the same effects in different places, potentially limiting the generalizability of the lessons of positive deviance for development policy. Fortunately, the case study method itself may compensate for this potential drawback. Because case studies enable deep attention to context, it is possible to identify the factors that facilitated success and to adapt the lessons to other contexts or to identify similar contexts where the lessons may apply more readily. Attention to context also avoids a cookie-cutter or "best practices" approach to development policy by pointing to the ways in which local factors may moderate or completely alter the effects of a particular policy prescription and must be harnessed to design appropriate policy interventions.

References

Bardhan, P. and Mookherjee, D. (2012) Political clientelism and capture: Theory and evidence from West Bengal, India. Helsinki: UNU-WIDER Working Paper No. 2012/97.

Belkâab, N. and Cammett, M. (2014) *Mission report: Governance and the quality of primary health care in Morocco*. Washington, DC: The World Bank.

Bennett, A. and Elman, C. (2006) "Complex causal relations and case study methods: The example of path dependence," *Political Analysis*, 14(3), 250–267.

Bradley, E. H., Curry, L. A., Ramanadhan, S., Rowe, L., Nembhard, I. M., and Krumholz, H. M. (2009) "Research in action: Using positive deviance to improve quality of health care," *Implementation Science*, 4(1), 25.

Brixi, H., Lust, E., and Woolcock, M. (2015) *Trust, voice and incentives: Learning from local success stories in service delivery in the Middle East and North Africa*. Washington, DC: The World Bank.

Collier, D. and Mahoney, J. (1996) "Insights and pitfalls: Selection bias in qualitative research," *World Politics*, 49(1), 56–91.

Das, J. and Hammer, J. (2014) "Quality of primary care in low-income countries: Facts and economics," *Annual Review of Economics*, 6(1), 525–553.

Dasgupta, A. and Beard, V. A. (2007) "Community driven development, collective action and elite capture in Indonesia," *Development and Change*, 38(2), 229–249.

Dieleman, M., Gerretsen, B., and van der Wilt, G. J. (2009) "Human resource management interventions to improve health workers' performance in low and middle income countries: A realist review," *Health Research Policy and Systems*, 7(7), 1–13.

Donabedian, A. (1988) "The quality of care: How can it be assessed?" *Journal of the American Medical Association*, 26(12), 1743–1748.

Eckstein, H. (2009) "Case study and theory in political science" in Gomm, R., Hammersley, M., and Foster, P. (eds.) *Case study method*. Thousand Oaks, CA: Sage Publications, pp. 79–137.

Edmondson, A. C. (2003) "Speaking up in the operating room: How team leaders promote learning in interdisciplinary action teams," *Journal of Management Studies*, 40(6), 1419–1452.

Geddes, B. (1990) "How the cases you choose affect the answers you get: Selection bias in comparative politics," *Political Analysis*, 2(1), 131–150.

George, A. L. and Bennett, A. (2005) *Case studies and theory development in the social sciences*. Cambridge, MA: MIT Press.

Gerring, J. (2007) *Case study research: Principles and practices*. Cambridge: Cambridge University Press.

Harris, C., Cortvriend, P., and Hyde, P. (2007) "Human resource management and performance in healthcare organisations," *Journal of Health Organization and Management*, 21(4–5), 448–459.

Khemani, S. (2015) "Buying votes vs. supplying public services: Political incentives to under-invest in pro-poor policies," *Journal of Development Economics*, 117 (November): 84–93.

King, G., Keohane, R. O., and Verba, S. (1994). *Designing social inquiry: Scientific inference in qualitative research*. Princeton, NJ: Princeton University Press.

Marmot, M. and Wilkinson, R. (eds.) (2005) *Social determinants of health* (2nd ed.). Oxford: Oxford University Press.

McAdam, D. (1999) *Political process and the development of black insurgency, 1930–1970* (2nd ed.). Chicago, IL: University of Chicago.

Nohria, N. and Kurana, R. (eds.) (2011) *The handbook for teaching leadership*. New York: Sage Publications.

Odell, J. S. (2001) "Case study methods in international political economy," *International Studies Perspectives*, 2(2), 161–176.

Pant, L. P. and Odame, H. H. (2009) "The promise of positive deviants: Bridging divides between scientific research and local practices in smallholder agriculture," *Knowledge Management for Development Journal*, 5(2), 160–172.

Patel, D., Bunce, V., and Wolchik, S. (2014) "Diffusion and demonstration" in Lynch, M. (ed.) *The Arab uprisings explained: New contentious politics in the Middle East*. New York: Columbia University Press, pp. 57–74.

Platteau, J-P. (2004) "Monitoring elite capture in community-driven development," *Development and Change*, 35(2), 223–246.

Pritchett, L. and Sandefur, J. (2013) "Context matters for size: Why external validity claims and development practice do not mix," *Journal of Globalization and Development*, 4(2), 161–197.

Przeworski, A. and Teune, H. (1970) *The logic of comparative social inquiry*. New York: Wiley-Interscience.

Rabie, T. S., Lust, E., Clark, C., Cammett, M., and Linnemann, H. (2014) Improving quality of care against all odds: A local success story in Jordan. *Voices and Views: Middle East and North Africa*, July 22 [online]. Available at: http://blogs.worldbank.org/arabvoices/improving-quality-care-against-all-odds-local-success-story-jordan.

Rodrik, D. (2008) "The new development economics: We shall experiment, but how shall we learn?" in Cohen, J. and Easterly, W. (eds.) *What works in development? Thinking big and thinking small*. Washington, DC: The Brookings Institution, pp. 24–54.

Ryan, R. M. and Deci, E. L. (2000) "Intrinsic and extrinsic motivations: Classic definitions and new directions," *Contemporary Educational Psychology*, 25(1), 54–67.

Seawright, J. (2016) "The case for selecting cases that are deviant or extreme on the independent variable," *Sociological Methods & Research*, 45(3), 493–525.

Seawright, J. and Gerring, J. (2008) "Case selection techniques in case study research: A menu of qualitative and quantitative options," *Political Research Quarterly*, 61(2), 294–308.

Spreitzer, G. M. and Sonenshein, S. (2004) "Toward the construct definition of positive deviance," *American Behavioral Scientist*, 47(6), 828–847.

Weyland, K. (2012) "The Arab Spring: Why the surprising similarities with the revolutionary wave of 1848?" *Perspectives on Politics*, 10(4), 917–934.

Woolcock, M. (1998) *Social theory, development policy and poverty alleviation: A historical-comparative analysis of group-based banking in developing economies* (Published PhD dissertation, Sociology), Brown University. Available at www.proquest.com/docview/304434170?pq-origsite=gscholar&fromopenview=true.

11 Analytic Narratives and Case Studies

Margaret Levi and Barry R. Weingast

11.1 Introduction

Analytic narratives (Bates et al., 1998, 2000; Levi, 2002, 2004) involve selecting a problem or puzzle, then building a model to explicate the logic of an explanation for the puzzle or problem, often in the context of a unique case. The method involves several steps. First, the use of narrative to elucidate the principal players, their preferences, the key decision points and possible choices, and the rules of game, all in a textured and sequenced account. Second, building a model of the sequence of interaction, including predicted outcomes. And, third, the evaluation of the model through comparative statics and the testable implications the model generates. The analytic narrative approach is most useful to scholars who seek to evaluate the strength of parsimonious causal mechanisms in the context of a specific and often unique case. The requirement of explicit formal theorizing (or at least theory that could be formalized) compels scholars to make causal statements and to identify a small number of variables as central to understanding the case.

Case studies abound in the study of development. A weakness of case studies per se is that there typically exist multiple ways to interpret a given case. How are we to know which interpretation makes most sense? What gives us confidence in the particular interpretation offered? This problem is particularly difficult where the uniqueness of the situation precludes the collection of a data set that encompasses multiple cases. Many scholars augment their case study with a model. The model adds some discipline to the account. For example, observed choices must be consistent with the assumption about preferences in the model. A model is necessary, but not sufficient: that is, a model alone does not an analytic narrative make.

The analytic narrative approach provides a means to help get around these questions. The essence of many cases is unique, including the French Revolution, the American Civil War, or the surprising and quick development of Spain following the death of long-time dictator, Francisco Franco, in 1975. Analytic narratives deal with these cases by building a model that has multiple implications, and then testing an implication of the model that provides the possibility for both confidence in the claims and comparison across cases.

For example, Weingast's (1998) case study of the American Civil War builds on a unique feature of American institutions to explain long-term political stability – namely, the "balance rule": the idea that both Northern free states and Southern slave states would be admitted in pairs, giving each set of states a veto over national policy. This institution fell apart in the 1850s. Weingast tests his account of this failure by using game theory to reveal a path not taken, given the interest calculations of those making choices about what path to take. This enabled him to estimate a counterfactual involving what would have happened had a contingency in the case study not occurred. Thus, the main thesis of the case – the balance rule – is unique and cannot be tested directly, but other implications of the approach can be tested so as to give confidence in the overall account.

A second example addresses the effect on public goods provision of a 2004 decentralization reform in postconflict Sierra Leone (Clayton et al. 2015). The specificities of most laws are unique; even when the words are replicated, implementation varies across and within countries. In this instance, the narrative reveals the key stakeholders at the local level: elected councilors and paramount chiefs. The interests of the former should lead them to prefer successful implementation, ceteris paribus; but in some localities they conceded to the paramount chiefs, who preferred the status quo. Given other reforms that increased the power of the councilors and reduced that of the chiefs, the question becomes why the councilors deferred. What are the relevant comparative statics? This question produced a series of testable implications. The case, although unique, sheds light on the more general problem of the variation in the impact of decentralization on the delivery of health and education services.

This chapter proceeds as follows. In Section 11.2, we discuss criteria for case section. Section 11.3 discusses identifying processes and mechanisms, while Section 11.4 discusses the limitations of the approach. In Section 11.5, we briefly discuss the implications of the approach for the development context. Our take-aways follow.

11.2 Criteria for Case Selection

The analytic narrative approach combines a commitment to rational choice, a deep interest in a particular case, a method for devising a generalizable model of the case, and a means of providing empirical evidence, even in unique cases.

The combination also entails an aim most area specialists lack: to go beyond detailing the case to elaborate more general conditions for the problem or puzzle. This exercise requires criteria for selection of cases other than their intellectual appeal as puzzles demanding solutions. Standard approaches to case selection emphasize the bases for choice among a sample of cases which are informative about the causal chain of interest, because of the absence, presence, or extreme values of key variables. One traditional method advocates pairs of cases that are either "most similar," hopefully allowing the analyst to identify similar mechanisms in the two cases, or "most different," hopefully allowing the analyst the ability to isolate a mechanism that accounts for the differences. These traditional methods fail when more than one causal variable is relevant.

Bearing similarities to the analytic narratives approach is process tracing (George and Bennett 2005; Collier 2011; Bennett, Chapter 4, this volume), which shares an emphasis on both sequencing and fine-grained description as means for making causal inferences. Process tracing also shares a concern with generating testable implications, but its emphasis is on key variables rather than the key actors, their interaction, and their strategies. This makes game-theoretic analysis largely irrelevant to process tracing.

Analytic narratives include features that make the cases amenable to modeling, which not all puzzles or problems are. Essential to the model building is the choice of cases in which the key actors interact strategically. That is, the choices of one actor depend on the choices of the other. In addition, analytic narratives consider situations that can be modeled as an extensive-form game, which generates a subgame perfect equilibrium.

Another necessary feature of an analytic narrative is the opportunity to get at an important process or mechanism not easily accessible through other means. For example, the extensive-form game allows the analysis to demonstrate the existence of a self-enforcing institution that often solves an important economic or political problem through creating a credible commitment. The advantage of the game is that it reveals the logic of why, in equilibrium, it is in the interest of the players to fulfill their threats or promises against those who leave the equilibrium path.

The formalization itself is not a requirement of a successful analytic narrative; indeed, in some cases, there are too many actors and no benefit from reducing the multiple players to the small number required for a game-theoretical model. Levi's case on conscription (Bates et al. 1998) illustrates how one can still use the logic of extended form games to assess the strategies and actions – and paths not taken – without formalization. Another example is Ferrara's (2003) analytic narrative of the Burmese uprising in 1988 as a means to understand both a particular historical event and the more general question of the relationship between coercion and protest.

The final expectation of an analytic narrative is that the causal mechanisms and the structures or relationships must be generalizable to other cases under specifiable conditions. We deal with this issue below.

11.3 Identifying Sequence and Mechanisms

Analytics, in this approach, refer to the building of models derived from rational choice, particularly the theory of extensive-form games.[1] The steps toward building the model include:

- First, extracting from the narratives the key actors, their goals, the sequence of options available to an actor at a given moment, and the effective rules that influence actors' behaviors.
- Second, elaborating the strategic interactions that produce an equilibrium that constrains some actions and facilitates others. By making clear and explicit the assumptions about who the key actors and their preferences are, it is possible to challenge the assumptions to produce new insights and competitive interpretations of the data.
- Third, the equilibrium analysis leads to comparative static predictions that produce testable implications even if they're not the main assertion of the case.

---

[1] In principle, the rational choice component can be replaced with decision-making criteria from behavioral economics, although we have not pursued that path.

We emphasize this third criterion. An important advantage of relying on game theory is that this method often produces comparative statics – that is, predictions about how the equilibrium shifts in response to changes in the exogenous variables. This approach allows the analyst to identify the reasons for the shift from one equilibrium to another. It therefore produces expectations of behaviors in the form of testable implications if the key actors are staying on the equilibrium path and if they are not. A case study that includes a model may involve the first two criteria, but generally not the third. This is especially true for unique cases where it is hard to test the model directly. Both authors have written many case studies of this type. These cases may provide insights, but they are not analytical narratives (see, e.g., Levi 1988; Weingast 2004). Analytic narratives require testable implications derived from the comparative statics that the narrative helps reveal.

The narrative of analytic narratives establishes the principal players, their goals, and their preferences while also illuminating the effective rules of the game, constraints, and incentives. Narrative is the story being told but as a detailed and textured account of context and process, with concern for sequence, temporality, and key events. By meeting these criteria, the narrative offers a means to arbitrate among possible explanations for observational equivalences – that is, two distinct processes that lead to the same outcome.

Comparative statics are crucial for comparative research because they generate hypotheses of what could have taken place under different conditions. Comparative statics therefore clarify the relationship between the key endogenous and exogenous variables. Moreover, the consideration of "off-the-equilibrium-path" behavior typically reveals reasons and reasoning for why actors took one path and not another. Indeed, what actors believe will happen were they to make a different choice typically influences the choices they do make. As Niall Ferguson (1999) observed in his study of the causes of World War I, to understand why Britain entered what would otherwise have been a continental war, we need to know what the British believed would happen had they not entered the war. Another important aspect of the game-theoretic approach is that the off-the-path behavior of an equilibrium disciplines each player's beliefs, for they must be consistent with all the other player's strategies (see Weingast 1996).

For example, consider the illustrative "deterrence game" in the appendix of *Analytic narratives* (Bates et al. 1998). Two countries interact: the home country and an opponent. The home country maintains a large, expensive army; the opponent does not attack. Is the large army the reason for peace as it deters the opponent from attacking? Or is it a waste of resources because the

opponent has no interest in attacking? These two hypotheses are observation-
ally equivalent: both offer explanations for why the opponent does not attack,
yet they differ dramatically as to the reason for the observation. Different
people have different beliefs that can only be understood contextually:

> [T]he observationally equivalent interpretations rest on markedly different theories
> of behavior. To settle upon an explanation, we must move outside the game and
> investigate empirical materials. We must determine how the opponent's beliefs
> shape their behavior. This blend of strategic reasoning and empirical investigation
> helps to define the method of analytic narratives. (Bates et al. 1998: 241)

This approach provides the researcher with some discipline. As the deterrence game illustrates, absent a game and an equilibrium structure, it is
possible to posit a wide range of beliefs that motivate action. How do we
choose among these different accounts? In the context of a game, beliefs
about another player's actions are part of the equilibrium. Not just any sets of
beliefs will work. In the deterrence game, the opponent must have a belief
about how the home country will react to an attack; and, in equilibrium, this
belief must hold in practice.

This form of explicit theory provides criteria to enable the researcher to
distill the narrative and ensure that the explanation need not rely too much
on factors outside the model.

11.4 Overcoming the Limits of Analytic Narratives

The analytic narrative approach, at least in its original formulation, had
several potential limitations, some recognized by the authors and others
revealed by various critiques.

11.4.1 Generalizing

The Achilles' heel of analytic narratives – as with any approach to case
studies – is in the capacity to generalize, given that each narrative represents
an effort to account for a particular puzzle in a particular place and time with
a model and theory tailored to that situation. Even so, it is possible to use the
cases to make some more general points.

Although the approach is not straightforwardly deductive, it nonetheless
relies on rational choice, which is a general theory of how structures shape
individual choices and, consequently, collective outcomes. Rational choice,

particularly in its game-theoretic form, highlights certain properties of the structure and strategic choices that arise. Although the specific game may not be portable, it may yield explanations that can be tested in the form of collective action problems, principal–agent issues, credible commitments, veto points, and the like. Analytic narratives provide a way to suggest the characteristics of situations to which these apply and in what ways. For example, the models of federalism, as initially developed by William Riker (1964) and further developed by Weingast and his collaborators (Weingast 1995; Montinola, Qian, and Weingast 1995), are useful in explicating a large number of problems in a wide range of countries, including the case Weingast (1998) addresses in his *Analytic narratives* chapter.

Moreover, the analytic narrative approach also demands identification of causal mechanisms. A wide range of mechanisms, such as emotions, resentment, and other aspects of behavioral economics, can offer a fine-grained explanation of the link between actions and alternatives (Elster 1998, 1999). Others have fruitfully made these links in such situations as insurgency in El Salvador (Wood 2001) and violence in Eastern Europe and the Balkans (Petersen 2002, 2011) while meeting the requirement that they "generate new predictions at the aggregate or structural level" (Stinchcombe 1991: 385).

11.4.2   Surprise, Contingency, and Conjunction

Daniel Carpenter's (2000) critique of *Analytic narratives* raised several issues that the approach needed to confront to fulfill its promise. Carpenter worried that we narrowed the conceptualization of narrative in a way that was likely to neglect the surprises history offers, the contingencies that affect outcomes, and the conjunctures that make parsimony so difficult. The first and last are easiest to address since nothing about the method precludes either. The approach actually makes it possible to take surprises into account since they often take the form of events that would change comparative static outcomes. De Figueiredo, Rakove, and Weingast (2006) illustrate one means by which game-theoretic models can be generalized to encompass surprises. Those American colonists already suspicious of Britain were apt to believe the worst interpretation of any British act and to believe that large-scale rebellion was inevitable. The result was a self-confirming equilibrium to explain the surprise element in the eruption of the American Revolution. Nothing is foreordained by an analytic narrative, which, on the contrary, often reveals factors as significant that we might not otherwise have noted. For example, in Gretchen Helmke's (2005) analysis of courts in autocratic regimes, her counterintuitive finding is that a nonindependent judiciary has the power, under certain circumstances, to rule against its government.

Carpenter also raises conjunctural analysis: the idea that multiple, interlacing factors occur at once – say, a war and a depression – so that the causal factors are difficult to disentangle. Carpenter's concern (2000: 657–658) is that "[i]f one changes the values of two variables at once, or renders the values of one variable dependent on those of another – precisely as historians who rely on conjunctures tend to do – then the embedded independence assumption comes, well, with high costs." Skocpol (2000) and Katznelson and Milner (2002) share Carpenter's concern.

Conjunctures are a problem for every form of analysis, not just analytic narratives. Moreover, by relying on game theory, analytic narratives may be uniquely suited to addressing conjunctures. By providing a specific model of events, a game-theoretic model helps disentangle conjunctures by potentially making predictions about what would have happened had only one of the conjoining events occurred instead.

Carpenter claims that contingency disappears from the analytic narrative approach because, as he perceives it, there is less likelihood of multiple equilibria – that is, alternative stable states of the world. He goes on to say that "[i]t would have been theoretically appealing for the authors to give examples where history in some way 'selects' some equilibria and makes others impossible (kind of like a trembling hand, or stability, or coalition-proofness criterion)" Carpenter (2000, 657).

But this criticism reflects a misreading of the analytic narrative approach. The use of game theory means that in many instances multiple equilibria will arise. Hence, the existence of multiple equilibria is part of the analytic narrative approach even if the case studies in the original volume do not make that evident. Contingency in the form of multiple equilibria is therefore a feature of the approach.

Even when there are clear focal points and strategies, factors in the situation can change unexpectedly. Some contextual changes may have clear and significant consequences, others have butterfly effects, and still others have little or no effect. The narrative is crucial here for sorting out what matters for what. In Rosenthal's *Analytic narratives* chapter, the potential birth of a Catholic heir to James II affects the calculations of both monarch and elites, but its importance lies in how it changes the strategies of the elites even unto the point of revolution (Rosenthal 1998: 92). Why elites resorted to revolution rather than peaceful institutional change becomes apparent through the narrative and the associated model.

Uncertainty and lack of information are prevalent features of the unraveling of events in history, and they are major bases of contingency. Ahlquist and Levi's work on leadership illustrates the effect of uncertainty (Ahlquist and Levi 2011, 2013). They find that followers, members, and citizens are very concerned to have competent representation; followers, members, and citizens therefore do their best to figure out who will be a good leader based on the track record of potential candidates. Nonetheless, unknowns remain, often in the form of other variables that are uncertain. For example, no one can know for sure how opponents will react to a given leader, what the economy will do, or how leaders will respond under circumstances distinctive from those in which they were selected. This uncertainty has direct consequences for other facets of the organization, such as its governance arrangements and mechanisms of accountability. If members knew and understood all the implications of their original choice, they might make a different one – if they could. Yet, uncertainty instead leads them to coordinate around a specific leader and leadership style, and they may well continue to maintain that person in office for years.

Analytic narratives must include problems of randomness or contingency, but not if they are too extreme. The example of unions makes the point. Members address their leadership problem in the face of uncertainty about the occurrence of strikes and only partial information about the reaction of employers to their demands. Because the interactions between unions and managers involve unpredictable elements, and because leaders cannot always deliver what they promise, leadership turnover may result. However, as Ahlquist and Levi (2013) show, this turnover is not only relatively rare but also highly delimited by the organizational culture and governance arrangements that ensure new leaders will share many of the characteristics of their predecessors.

The analytic narrative approach rests on cases where there is some, but hardly complete, contingency in the path of history, cases that the model helps in understanding what was likely to happen. Nothing about the approach, however, limits it to cases of determinateness or low contingency. Extensive-form games have long proved useful in studying settings of high uncertainty and contingency.

11.5   Analytic Narratives for Use in Development Policy and Practice

In this section we turn, briefly, to suggest the implications of the analytic narrative approach to problems of development.

Economists have long proposed an economic role for political institutions, such as the market infrastructure embodied in the provision of secure property rights, enforcement of contracts, and, generally, the provision of justice and the rule of law (Weingast 1995). Governments that use violence against minorities and opponents, confiscate citizens' wealth, and create economic privileges (such as dispensing monopoly rights) fail to provide adequate market infrastructure. As Adam Smith recognized more than two centuries ago, the risk of violence and of plunder leads men to avoid hard work, initiative, and investment. In discussing settings in which "the occupiers of land in the country were exposed to every sort of violence," Smith argued that "men in this defenceless state naturally content themselves with their necessary subsistence; because to acquire more might only tempt the injustice of their oppressors" (Smith 1776: III.iii.12:405). Further, a "person who can acquire no property, can have no other interest but to eat as much, and to labour as little as possible" (Smith 1776: III.ii.9:387–88).

But, if secure property rights, enforcement of contracts, and the provision of justice are necessary for economic development, how are such institutions built and, especially, sustained?

North and Weingast (1989) developed the hypothesis of credible commitments to answer this question. Governments seeking to implement the economists' prescriptions for political institutions had to commit to honoring rights of citizens and to use agreed upon political procedures to make political decisions. They developed their hypothesis in the context of a unique case: the English Glorious Revolution of 1688–1689. Although this revolution and its institutional consequences were unique to that case, North and Weingast provided some important evidence favoring their larger, general argument about credible commitments. Focusing on public finance, they showed that the ability of the English government to borrow money changed dramatically. Government debt had never been much above 5 percent of estimated GDP in the seventeenth century. But in the eight years following the Glorious Revolution, it rose by nearly an order of magnitude, to 40 percent of estimated GDP. Because debt repayment depends critically on credible commitments, the massive increase in debt in a short time suggests that a new mechanism for making credible commitments had emerged.

Sure enough, subsequent studies have identified some of the devices used to create credible commitments and have leant support to the hypothesis.[2] First, Cox (2012) has shown that a number of other variables also increased dramatically, consistent with the credible commitment hypothesis. Specifically, per the North and Weingast narrative, Cox demonstrates that parliament gained control over taxation and the issuance of public debt. Similarly, the ministerial responsibility system emerged: while parliament faced difficulties in holding the king accountable for public decisions, they could hold the king's ministers accountable, forcing them to honor parliament's interests. Second, scholars have undertaken a range of studies of public debt at similar events. For example, Summerhill (2015) has shown that nineteenth-century imperial Brazil provided the institutions for credible commitment to public debt, yet it failed to provide the institutional foundations for private financial markets and hence this fundamental basis for economic development. Mo and Weingast (2013: ch 4) reveal the means by which the South Korean regime under President Park Chung provided credibility to its promises to honor property rights and a range of other programs, such as education, underpinning that country's economic development.

As a second illustration, consider political stability, another element widely agreed as important for economic development. Coups, civil wars, ethnic conflict, and other forms of disorder cripple a country's ability to develop. Cox, North, and Weingast (2019) show that disorder in the form of violent takeover of regimes occurs surprisingly often in the developing world: the median regime of the poorest half of countries lasts only seven years. Just how do a minority of countries provide for political stability?

Mittal and Weingast (2012) provide three conditions for political stability, one of which they call the "limit condition": the idea that all successful constitutions reduce the stakes of power, for example, by providing incentives for political officials to honor a range of citizen rights. Limited government does not imply small government (as modern political debate suggests), but a government that can honor restrictions on its behavior, such as abiding by election results, refraining from the use of violence to repress enemies, and, generally, honoring citizen rights.

The logic of the limit condition is that high stakes make it much more likely that people who feel threatened by the government will support coups. For example, landowners in Chile under the presidency of Salvadore Allende

---

[2] While a number of studies have criticized the North and Weingast thesis and evidence (Sussman and Yafeh, 2007; Pincus and Robinson, 2014), none have argued against the debt-credibility hypothesis; and, further, we believe Cox (2012) and related work provides the latest review and statement of the evidence.

supported the military coup in 1973 to protect themselves. Similar events led to disorder in Spain (1936–1939) and Kenya (2007–2008). One way that constitutions reduce the stakes of politics is through various forms of countermajoritarian institutions.

Mittal and Weingast develop their hypothesis in the context of the American case, where the institutional features of the US Constitution are unique. Subsequent work has revealed similar features in a range of cases of stable constitutions. Countermajoritarian provisions serve two valuable roles in preserving political stability. First, they often aid in the instantiation of democracy. When groups see themselves as potentially worse off under democracy, they are likely to resist democratization. The reality is that powerful – and sometimes inimical – groups often have the power to hold up democratization, such as slaveholders in the early American Republic, Whites in South Africa in the 1990s, the supporters of the authoritarian regime of Francisco Franco in Spain following the death of the dictator in 1975, the military dictatorship in Chile in the late 1980s and early 1990s, and the communist regime in Poland in 1989. In each of these cases, countermajoritarian provisions to protect powerful groups aided democratization and, eventually, the lightening of the relevant constraints. Similarly, electoral laws often bias elections in favor of constituencies that favor the previous regime (Chile and Spain). These provisions also become part of the limit condition once democracy has been initiated.

Others have also used analytic narratives to discuss the difficulties of achieving transitions to democracy. Ferrara (2003) suggests conditions under which widespread protest and uprising has little effect, given the strategic use of coercion. His case is Burma, but the implications are more general. On the other hand, Nalepa (2010) considers the conditions under which pacts and negotiated settlements among elites facilitate the transition from autocracy to more open access regimes. She finds that the transition will prove unstable (if it even takes place) unless a specific type of limit condition holds: namely, that key players receive credible commitments that the "skeletons in their closets" will not be revealed or that they will receive amnesty for politically problematic behavior during the old regime. Her analytic narrative focuses on Eastern Europe but is applicable to a wide range of cases where transitional justice is at issue.

Analytic narrative approaches are also useful in understanding why some reforms succeed while others do not in countries experiencing development. Methodologically, this demands explicit recognition of the comparative statics, on the one hand, and the off-the-path-behavior, on the other. These features distinguish analytic narratives from other case studies, enabling them to reveal processes and causal mechanisms that might otherwise go undetected and to provide the bases for generalizations that might otherwise not be possible. Some authors already self-consciously attempt analytic narratives (e.g., Hosman 2009 on Nigeria's failed oil policies), but many do not. Even so, we could get additional leverage on reform by transforming existing case studies into analytic narratives.

Among the many accounts of reform, we have selected two categories of cases where analytic narratives clearly increase explanatory power for the particular instance as well as making the findings transportable to other situations.

The first set is where the same laws have different effects in different places. The study of the Sierra Leone decentralization reforms (Clayton, Noveck, and Levi 2015) display not only varying impact but also reasons for that variation. Sierra Leone has a long history of tension among elites at different levels of government and a more recent history of tensions among key local elites. This case explores the consequences of the latter for effective public service delivery once decentralization is introduced.

A rich literature (cited in the case study) reveals contradictory expectations of the effects of local interelite dynamics. The narrative reveals considerable county-level variations in power sharing between the traditional power-holders, the paramount chiefs, and the newer power-holders, the elected councilors. This variation provides an opportunity to derive expectations specific to the case and then assess their plausibility. Indeed, from the narrative the authors hypothesized that competitive relationships among the two improve services while collusion reduces their quality.

The first challenge was to offer a measure of elite dynamics to be used in a statistical investigation of the implications of differences. To test the impact of this relationship required, first, a measure of the nature of their interaction. The probability of collusion was operationalized by using data that reports on the following direct relationships: the median number of times councilors report having contacted a chief in the previous month, the percentage of councilors that report having had a dispute with a chief during the past month, and the percentage of councilors that report that they are related to a Paramount Chief either through blood or marriage.

But what accounts for the distinctiveness of power-sharing arrangements? The strategic interaction underlying the implementation of the reforms reveals two possible equilibria of collusion and competition. Digging deeper uncovers factors that possibly change the strategic interactions among the key actors and, thus, the comparative statics. The authors considered the gender, age, and party of the councilors as well as the degree of electoral competition. But the most telling explanatory factor was one that could only be known by knowing the case in depth: the proportion of councilors who were in the Civilian Defense Force (CDF) during the war. Former CDF councilors were likely to have forged deep ties with the paramount chiefs who were the primary sources of funding.

The next step was to determine the extent to which these different kinds of power-sharing arrangements – and the probable causes of them – actually influenced service delivery. Drawing out testable implications that could in fact be explored with the available survey material enabled the authors to provide additional confidence in the hypotheses they had derived. Further statistical tests indeed suggested that collusion, particularly that produced by the proportion of councilors who had been in the CDF, leads to far poorer service delivery than does competition.

Bangladesh, Honduras, China, and the United States all have similar labor laws on their books but very distinctive actual protection and enforcement of labor protections in the supply chains of global brands. Berliner et al. (2015a, 2015b) investigate the clusters of stakeholders and what transforms the relations of power among them. To do this, they consider the strategic interactions among key players and what transforms the current equilibrium or status quo. Using the logic of game theory but not formalizing it, they are aware that it is off the equilibrium path for workers to organize and make demands unless they are assured that they will not be punished for their actions by losing their jobs or being sent to jail.[3] That only happens when brands find it in their interest to improve worker rights and benefits, and this only occurs if government is upholding its laws or the reputation of brands among consumers is being threatened.

Unfortunately, both of these circumstances are most likely to occur when there is an unexpected (if predictable) catastrophe such as a major fire or building collapse where workers' lives are tragically lost. Reflecting comparative statics, such a shift leads to reform, but whether the commitments are credible depends on the creation of legal institutions that are hard to change and that incorporate sufficient administrative capacity to implement the rules. The testable implications may differ among the cases, but they are the organizing principles of the cases. The findings are not promising for

---

[3] Golden (1997) makes similar observations in the European context.

labor rights. Honduras and Bangladesh lack the government capacity to maintain a positive labor rights regime over a long period of time. In China, the government has the capacity but not the will to establish meaningful labor rights, although it does ensure some protections. The United States, which once had both the will and capacity, now lacks the first and possibly the second and so has undergone a reversal. The result in all these instances is that the pressure on brands to discipline their supply chains is episodic or nonexistent.

The second set of cases document instances where societal interests come to trump private interests, making it possible to actually implement policies that will serve the population as a whole. As we saw with the labor illustration, it is difficult enough to ensure the protection of the interests of a neglected group within the society. It is arguably harder to protect general interests, as the case of corruption in Indonesia (Kuris 2012a, 2012b) documents. And it is arguably harder still to implement policies where the interests of the world at large are at issue, as the case of deforestation in Brazil (Jackson 2014, 2015) details.

Of course, in each of these cases a range of stakeholders are the beneficiaries or losers from policy change. To transform past practice required some combination of leadership, interests, expert knowledge disseminated widely, trust relationships, monitoring, new forms of direct enforcement, credible commitments, and mobilizations that changed the incentives of both government officials and recalcitrant stakeholders. All of these features are documented in these cases, and documented well. Lacking is a structure to the accounts that makes it possible to observe the causal mechanisms and derive testable implications. The comparative statics are not sufficiently explicit. While the Sierra Leone decentralization and labor standards cases do not provide an actual formalization of the game, the presentation of the material makes it possible not only to derive but also to test implications that enhance confidence in the claims of the authors and make them generalizable to other cases.

11.6 Creating Take-Aways

Multiple interpretations are inherent in the traditional case study method. Moving beyond traditional approaches, analytic narratives provide two methods for establishing the generalizability of findings from case studies. First, the model in an analytic narrative often affords a range of explanations and predictions. Although the main account of a unique case may not be testable, the model may yield other predictions that can be tested, either in this case or in other cases. Second, as with other methods, out-of-sample tests constitute an important route to generalization. The presumption today in social science research is that the authors will provide those tests themselves. However, seldom does the level of knowledge for the out of sample case rival the detailed understanding of the original case that puzzled the author. The demonstration of generalizability must rest on a larger community of scholars who take the findings applicable to one place and time to illuminate a very different place and time. Each case then becomes a case among many that are grist for the mill of scholars, experts on particular countries and sectors, and policy-makers who must work collaboratively to sort out the lessons learned.

In this chapter, we have outlined the analytic narrative approach and, in Section 11.5, suggested the potential value of the approach for problems of development. Reflecting the interest of the authors employing the approach, the applications tend to focus on political issues, such as political stability and violence. The approach also applies to case studies of particular economic reforms, and we believe it will produce valuable results in this area.

In summary, the goal of analytic narratives is to provide several forms of discipline on the structure of case studies, such as a game, with emphasis on comparative statics and on off-the-path-behavior, and on predictions that can be tested on aspects of the case even if the main assertion about the case cannot.

References

Ahlquist, J. S. and Levi, M. (2011) "Leadership: What it means, what it does, and what we want to know about it,"*Annual Review of Political Science*, 14, 1–24.

Ahlquist, J. S. and Levi, M. (2013) *In the interests of others: Organizations and social activism.* Princeton, NJ: Princeton University Press.

Bates, R., Greif, A., Levi, M., Rosenthal, J. L., and Weingast, B. R. (eds.) (1998) *Analytic narratives*. Princeton, NJ: Princeton University Press.

Bates, R. H., Greif, A., Levi, M., Rosenthal, J. L., and Weingast, B. R. (2000) "Reply, analytic narratives revisited," *Social Science History*, 24(Winter), 685–696.

Berliner, D., Greenleaf, A. R., Lake, M., Levi, M., and Noveck, J. (2015a) *Labor standards in international supply chains: Aligning rights and incentives.* Northampton, MA: Edward Elgar.

Berliner, D., Greenleaf, A. R., Lake, M., Levi, M., and Noveck, J. (2015b) "Governing global supply chains: What we know (and don't) about improving labor rights and working conditions," *Annual Review of Law and Social Science*, 11(2015), 193–209.

Carpenter, D. P. (2000) "What is the marginal value of analytic narratives?" *Social Science History*, 24(4), 653–668.

Clayton, A., Noveck, J., and Levi, M. (2015) When elites meet: Decentralization, power-sharing and public goods provision in post-conflict Sierra Leone. Policy Research Working Paper No. 7335. Washington, DC: The World Bank.

Collier, D. (2011) "Understanding process tracing," *PS: Political Science and Politics*, 44(4), 823–830.

Cox, G. W. (2012) "Was the glorious revolution a watershed?" *Journal of Economic History*, 72(3), 567–600.

(2019). "The Violence Trap: A Political-Economic Approach To the Problems of Development" **Journal of Public Finance and Public Choice** 34(1): 3–19.

Cox, G. W., North, D. C., and Weingast, B. R. (2015). "The violence trap." Stanford, CA: Working Paper, Hoover Institution, Stanford University.

de Figueiredo, R. J. P. Jr., Rakove, J., and Weingast, B. R. (2006) "Rationality, inaccurate mental models, and self-confirming equilibrium: A new understanding of the American revolution," *Journal of Theoretical Politics*, 18 (October), 384–415.

Elster, J. (1998) "Emotions and economic theory," *Journal of Economic Literature*, 36(1), 47–74.

Elster, J. (1999) *Alchemies of the mind: Rationality and the emotions*. New York: Cambridge University Press.

Ferguson, N. (1999) *The pity of war: Explaining World War I*. New York: Basic Books.

Ferrara, F. (2003) "Why regimes create disorder: Hobbes's dilemma during a rangoon summer," *The Journal of Conflict Resolution*, 47(3), 302–325.

George, A. and Bennett, A. (2005) *Case study and theory development in the social sciences*. Cambridge, MA: MIT Press.

Golden, M. A. (1997) *Heroic defeats: The politics of job loss*. New York: Cambridge University Press.

Helmke, G. (2005) *Ruling against the rulers: Court executive relations in Argentina under dictatorship and democracy*. New York: Cambridge University Press.

Hosman, L. (2009) "Dividing the oils: Dynamic bargaining as policy formation in the Nigerian petroleum industry," *Review of Policy Research*, 26(5), 609–632.

Jackson, R. (2014) "Controlling deforestation in the Brazilian amazon: Alta forest works toward sustainability, 2008–13." Princeton, NJ: Princeton University: Innovations for Successful Societies. www.princeton.edu/successfulsocieties (accessed August 15, 2016).

Jackson, R. (2015) "A credible commitment: Reducing deforestation in the Brazilian amazon, 2003–2012." Princeton, NJ: Princeton University: Innovations for Successful Societies. https://successfulsocieties.princeton.edu/publications/credible-commitment-reducing-deforestation-brazilian-amazon-2003%E2%80%932012 (accessed August 15, 2016).

Katznelson, I. and Milner, H. (eds.) (2002) *Political science: State of the discipline*. New York: Norton.

Kuris, G. (2012a) "Inviting a tiger into your home: Indonesia creates an anti-corruption commission with teeth, 2002–2007." Princeton, NJ: Princeton University: Innovations for

Successful Societies. https://successfulsocieties.princeton.edu/publications/inviting-tiger-your-home-indonesia-creates-anti-corruption-commission-teeth-2002-%E2%80%93-2007 (accessed August 15, 2016).

Kuris, G. (2012b) "Holding the high ground with public support: Indonesia's anti-corruption commission digs in, 2007–11." Princeton, NJ: Princeton University: Innovations for Successful Societies. https://successfulsocieties.princeton.edu/publications/holding-high-ground-public-support-indonesias-anti-corruption-commission-digs-2007-%E2%80%93 (accessed August 15, 2016).

Levi, M. 1988. *Of rule and revenue.* New York: Cambridge University Press.

Levi, M. 2002. "Modeling complex historical processes with analytic narratives" in Mayntz, R. (ed.) *Akteure, mechanismen, modelle: Zur theoriefahigkeit makrosozialer analyse.* Frankfurt/Main: Campus Verlag, pp. 108–127.

Levi, M. (2004) "An analytic narrative approach to puzzles and problems" in Shapiro, I., Smith, R., and Masoud, T. (eds.) *Problems and methods in the study of politics.* New York: Cambridge University Press, pp. 201–226.

Mittal, S. and Weingast, B. R. (2012) "Self-enforcing constitutions: With an application to democratic stability in America's first century," *Journal of Law, Economics, and Organization*, 29(2), 278–302.

Mo, J. and Weingast, B. R. (2013) *Korean political and economic development: Crisis, security, and institutional rebalancing.* Cambridge, MA: Harvard University Asia Center.

Montinola, G., Qian, Y., and Weingast, B. R. (1995) "Federalism, Chinese style: The political basis for economic success in China," *World Politics*, 48(October), 50–81.

Nalepa, M. (2010) "Captured commitments: An analytic narrative of transitions with transitional justice," *World Politics*, 62(2), 341–380.

North, D. C. and Weingast, B. R. (1989) "Constitutions and commitment: The evolution of institutions governing public choice in seventeenth-century England," *Journal of Economic History*, 49(4), 803–832.

Petersen, R. (2002) *Understanding ethnic violence: Fear, hatred, and resentment in twentieth-century Eastern Europe.* New York: Cambridge University Press.

Petersen, R. (2011) *Western Intervention in the Balkans: The Strategic Use of Emotion in Conflict.* New York: Cambridge University Press.

Pincus, S. C. A. and Robinson, J. (2014) "What really happened during the glorious revolution?" in Galieni, S. and Sened, I. (eds.) *Institutions, property rights and growth: The legacy of Douglass North.* New York: Cambridge University Press, pp. 192–222.

Riker, W. H. (1964) *Federalism: Origin, operation, significance.* Boston, MA: Little Brown.

Rosenthal, J. L. (1998) "The political economy of absolutism reconsidered," in Bates, R., Greif, A., Levi, M., Rosenthal, J. L., and Weingast, B. R. (eds.), *Analytic narratives.* Princeton, NJ: Princeton University Press, pp. 64–108.

Skocpol, T. (2000) "Commentary: Theory tackles history," *Social Science History*, 24(4), 669–676.

Smith, A. (1776). *An inquiry into the nature and causes of the wealth of nations.* London: Printed for W. Strahan and T. Cadell.

Stinchcombe, A. L. (1991) "On the conditions of fruitfulness of theorizing about mechanisms in the social science," *Philosophy of the Social Sciences*, 21(2), 367–388.

Summerhill, W. R. (2015) *The inglorious revolution: Political institutions, sovereign debt, and financial underdevelopment in imperial Brazil.* New Haven, CT: Yale University Press.

Sussman, N. and Yafeh, Y. (2007) "Institutional reforms, financial development and sovereign debt: Britain 1690–1790," *Journal of Economic History*, 66(4), 1–30.

Weingast, B. R. (1995) "The economic role of political institutions: Market-preserving federalism and economic development," *Journal of Law, Economics, and Organization*, 11(Spring), 1–31.

Weingast, B. R. (1996) "Off-the-path behavior: A game-theoretic approach to counterfactuals and its implications for political and historical analysis" in Tetlock, P. E. and Belkin, A. (eds.) *Counterfactual thought experiments in world politics.* Princeton, NJ: Princeton University Press, pp. 230–244.

Weingast, B. R. (1998) "Political stability and civil war: Institutions, commitment, and American democracy" in Bates, R., Greif, A., Levi, M., Rosenthal, J. L., and Weingast, B. R. (eds.), *Analytic narratives.* Princeton, NJ: Princeton University Press, pp. 148–193.

Weingast, B. R. (2004) "Constructing self-enforcing democracy in Spain" in Morris, I., Oppenheimer, J., and Soltan, K. (eds.) *Politics from anarchy to democracy: Rational choice in political science.* Stanford, CA: Stanford University Press, pp. 161–195.

Wood, E. J. (2001) "The emotional benefits of insurgency in El Salvador" in Goodwin, J., Jasper, J. M., and Polletta, F. (eds.) *Passionate politics: Emotions and social movements.* Chicago, IL: University of Chicago Press, pp. 267–281.

12 Using Case Studies for Organizational Learning in Development Agencies

Sarah Glavey, Oliver Haas, Claudio Santibanez, and Michael Woolcock

12.1 Introduction

This chapter considers how different types of development-focused organizations have introduced case studies into their operations, and explores the lessons from these experiences for other development organizations interested in using case studies to enhance their own implementation effectiveness.[1] At one level, of course, case studies will be used differently depending on the organizational context; as such, to fully exploit a case study's potential it must align with an organization's specific reality: its history, mission, mandate, and capability. Actually doing this, however, requires undertaking the complex task of integrating cases into idiosyncratic organizational structures, rules, regulations and processes, and aligning it with a corporate culture that, at least initially, may or may not be favorably disposed to 'learning' in this way. In the sections that follow, we provide a comparative analysis of how this task has been conducted in four different development organizations, focusing in particular on how they select, prepare, and utilize case studies for collective learning.

A concern from the outset, and one that some regard as a pervasive weakness of case studies, is how to prepare cases that are both faithful to the unique particularities of each intervention and yet potentially usable by practitioners working elsewhere, perhaps even in different sectors, regions,

---

[1] To this end, the chapter draws on our respective experiences with facilitating organizational learning in different institutional contexts, as well as formal interviews with several colleagues within and beyond our respective organizations.

and scales of operation. Indeed, "But how generalizable is that?" is a common critique levelled against case studies as a research method, where the concern is that the case itself is neither randomly selected nor "representative" of a larger population, but rather "cherry picked" to support predetermined conclusions. As methodological and empirical issues, these concerns are addressed elsewhere in this volume.[2] For present purposes, we consider case studies not as "qualitative evaluations" nor as small-scale "impact assessments" of projects, but focus instead on their roles as diagnostic and pedagogical instruments within (and between) development agencies. In this sense, we consider how case studies are prepared and read in ways akin to their use in medicine, law, and public policy – which is to say, as instances of broader phenomena, wherein professionals use their seasoned experience (and, where appropriate, scientific knowledge) to learn from specific instance of *how, why, where,* and *for whom* particular outcomes emerged over the course of a project's or policy's implementation. If formal impact evaluations are concerned with assessing the "effects of causes" (e.g., Did this rice subsidy, on average, benefit the poor? Did that text message invoking sacred precepts increase credit card repayments?), then in this instance case studies primarily seek to discern the "causes of effects" (How was this village able to solve its water disputes so much more effectively than others? Why did that program for improving child nutrition fare so much better with younger mothers than older ones? Where were the weakest and strongest links in the implementation chain of this immunization program? Why do some development organizations seemingly learn more effectively than others?).[3] It is in responding to these latter concerns that case studies have a distinctive comparative advantage; in this sense they should be seen as a key complement to, not a substitute for, more familiar evaluation tools used to engage with and learn from development interventions.

In this spirit, our concern here is to work backwards from broader concerns about the conditions under which development organizations 'learn' (or seek to learn), with a view to considering the role that case studies play in this process. Our discussion proceeds as follows. Section 12.2 considers four broad factors that seem especially important for understanding how organizations (not just their individual staff members) learn – that is,

---

[2] For more formal discussions of this issue in this volume, see the chapters by Bennett (Chapter 4) and Woolcock (Chapter 5).

[3] For further discussion on the distinction between studying the "effects of causes" and the "causes of effects" – a contrast first made in the nineteenth century by John Stuart Mill – see Goertz and Mahoney (2012).

modify and/or improve their procedures and products in the light of experience and evidence. Section 12.3 then considers how these four factors have been deployed in case studies as used by four different organizations engaged with development issues: the World Bank, Germany's GIZ (Gesellschaft für Internationale Zusammenarbeit), the Brookings Institution, and China's Ministry of Finance. Section 12.4 concludes by categorizing how these different organizations are using case studies to learn across four organizational levels.

12.2 Organizational Learning Within Development Organizations

How do development organizations learn? A reading of the literature suggests that four broad factors seem to be especially important for understanding whether and how such learning takes place: motivation, environment, knowledge type, and practical use. We explore each of these factors by responding to four related questions.

12.2.1 Do Development Agencies Have the Motivation to Learn?

What motivates organizations to learn and invest in learning, and why might case studies be a suitable tool for doing so? For private sector organizations operating in today's globalized economy, the motivation is clear: they must 'adapt or die' – that is, they must continually change in response to their fast-moving environments or risk becoming irrelevant. Indeed, in business theory and practice, an organization's capacity to learn, and to apply and communicate knowledge, is considered a key strategic capability and is thus fundamental to its ability to produce value through innovation, improved quality, and efficiency (Drucker 1994). Management specialist Peter Senge (1990) goes so far as to argue that the rate at which organizations learn may become the only sustainable source of competitive advantage; to capture this, he introduced the idea of a 'learning organization' – namely, an organization which actively cultivates certain characteristics to harness value from continuous learning.

For the most part, however, development organizations tend to be mission- or impact-driven rather than profit-driven. As such, they operate in a somewhat different environment and are influenced by different forces. These organizations may not 'die' if they do not adapt – the fate of large development agencies whose mandates derive from nation-states, for example, is ultimately determined by political criteria. As such, and because their very existence serves the purposes of different powerful groups, public and nonprofit development agencies are unlikely to decline, at least in the short term, no matter what their level of "performance" is deemed to be. However, if a key driver of learning in organizations is typically to improve performance (Fiol and Lyles 1985), this can be a source of motivation common to all development organizations – mission-driven as well as profit-driven. So understood, for development agencies performance can be broadly defined by its key functions (e.g., client services, advocacy, distribution of funding, direct service delivery).

Factors both external and internal to the organization can help generate a strong need for learning which acts as an important motivator for action within an organization. Such a need generates the motivation to go from contentment (passive) to curiosity (actively seeking knowledge). A perceived need is therefore the antecedent to new learning (Scott 2011). For development organizations in the current environment, there are many factors that may generate a learning 'need'. External forces, including large global political agendas such as meeting the Sustainable Development Goals, may motivate a learning need as the organization considers how to respond; similarly, the emergence of influential new rival agencies, such as the New Development Bank, may create pressures where previously there were none. Internal factors may also generate a need: the desire to improve communication; to share lessons, build relationships and communicate; or to build a culture that is open to discussing challenges.

12.2.2   Is the Organization's Environment Conducive to Learning?

Any learning initiative will take place in the wider context of the organization's approach to learning and knowledge management. The capacity and openness to learn must be designed into the organization and, in turn, be reflected across its structures, functions, and processes. To do this, an organization, and especially its key managers, must first be open to "unlearning" established ways (Hedberg 1981); indeed, Inkpen and Crossan (1995: 596) argue that "a rigid set of managerial beliefs associated with an unwillingness to cast off or unlearn past practices can severely limit the effectiveness of organization learning" (see also Nonaka and Konna 1998). More positively, Zack (1999: 135) defines a firm's knowledge strategy "as the overall approach an organization intends to take to align its knowledge resources and capabilities to the intellectual requirements of its strategy."

While knowledge may transfer in the normal course of activities, organizations often introduce processes and knowledge management systems that actively facilitate the key processes of knowledge creation, transfer, and retention (Argote, Beckman, and Epple 1990). Schein (1990) suggested that a group's learning over time becomes encapsulated as the group's culture: in other words, it is both internalized as a set of assumptions and externalized as group norms or values.

The use of case studies should therefore be considered in the context of the organization's learning intent, strategy, and culture, and as one of a number of possible organizational learning tools or methods. The production of a case study involves not just a product but also a process which in itself can provoke learning at multiple levels of the organization. Key characteristics of such a process include:

- *Individual learning:* Individuals have generated knowledge through their practices and they have learned how to overcome challenges. Organizations are motivated to capture the tacit knowledge held within individuals in the system and to share this knowledge. Case studies are one tool which can be used to approach this task.
- *Group learning:* Group engagement with producing a case study. Case studies can be used to engage individuals within a group in reflecting together, capturing the group's knowledge and generating shared insights.
- *Organizational learning:* Retention of knowledge within the organization. The case study process is a way of attempting to codify and share knowledge. Members of the organization can then access this knowledge through the case studies, which can be used to initiate and inform discussion. Learning at the organizational level typically requires support from the organization's authorities.
- *Interorganizational learning:* Case studies are shared between organizations to foster the collective learning of a wider community of practice. Knowledge is transferred through a learning network by the development of shared processes/systems. Creating a network expands the reach of any particular initiative.

We will categorize this multilevel learning as IGOIL (individual, group, organizational and interorganizational learning), where different institutions may operate actively on one or more levels relevant to their learning strategy.

12.2.3   What Types of Knowledge are Captured by Case Studies?

Drawing on the early work of Polanyi (1966), Nonaka (1994) distinguishes between two types of knowledge: explicit knowledge, which is easily identified and codified; and tacit knowledge, which is what we know but cannot easily describe, and relates to both cognitive capability ('know what') and action ('know how'). Explicit knowledge can be shared and integrated via reports, databases, and lectures, whereas sharing tacit knowledge occurs through dialogue and practice. One can acquire and convey explicit knowledge about a bicycle (its wheels, frame, etc.) through study, but one only acquires the tacit knowledge required to ride the bicycle by persistent practice (i.e., by falling over many times until one's brain figures out how to stay upright).

There is a lot of technical knowledge within development organizations, and a corresponding familiarity with discussing and recording what was done in a given situation in an attempt to discern and capture 'best practice'. The case studies discussed in this chapter intend instead to capture knowledge about the way that things are done: 'the how' of implementation rather than 'the what' of end results. This type of knowledge is often held within an individual (or team) who has implemented or supported implementation of a program. From the social constructionist perspective on learning, Cook and Brown (1999) suggest that this type of knowledge is acquired "as people wrestle with the intricacies of real world challenges and improvise a way to a solution" (Brown 2011: 6). From this perspective, learning depends on social interaction and collaboration: one person's knowledge is co-dependent on the contributions of peers and must be negotiated with them. Knowledge about 'the how' is often tacit, context specific, and complex; factors relating to behavior, politics, and institutions influence the process. This is difficult to capture as the more we try to codify tacit knowledge the more it loses its context; perhaps it can only be recorded to a degree. Case studies attempt to capture some of this type of knowledge through alternative devices (such as via narrative form and personalization).

The cases discussed in this chapter are written with a specific focus on 'delivery challenges' (see Box 12.1); they describe situations where groups wrestle with and sometimes overcome delivery challenges. By sharing this type of knowledge, it is thought that others in the organization may gain inspiration for wrestling with their own real-world challenges. The organization's culture will influence the openness of its members to capturing and discussing this type of knowledge – that is, knowledge relating to challenges and failures rather than just success stories.

> ## Box 12.1 Defining 'Delivery Challenges'
>
> Delivery challenges are the nontechnical problems that hinder development interventions and that prevent practitioners from translating technical solutions into results on the ground. They are intimately related to development challenges, how interventions are implemented, and organizational issues. Delivery challenges should be the answer to the following questions: Why did intervention X, aimed at solving the development challenge Y, not work or not achieve its full potential? What were the main obstacles that intervention X faced during its implementation?

12.2.4   How Do Development Organizations Enhance the Practical Use of Case Studies?

It is widely accepted that learning requires changes in both cognition (knowing) and behavior (doing) (Argyris 1977; Crossan, Lane, and White 1999; Garvin 1993; Hedberg 1981; Stata and Almond 1989). As such, the practical value of using case studies lies not just in documenting the end product (what was achieved) but also the processes involved in getting there (how the end product was achieved). An advantage of the type of case study described in this chapter is that it remains close to practice. The cases capture stories of practice and should assist practitioners in implementing their work, thereby helping the organization achieve its mission.

Case studies can provide direct learning opportunities for practitioners to gain understanding of specific types of implementation challenges and how they were tackled, and/or to increase knowledge about specific development contexts. They aim to provide knowledge in a context-sensitive manner (unlike 'best practices'). Since this type of knowledge is often best shared in person, additional value can be gained from the case study by using it as a catalyst to spark dialogue around implementation issues between practitioners within and between both sectors and organizations. As the focus is on challenges encountered during implementation, use of this type of case study may also contribute to wider discussions in an organization about challenges, including failures, and how to learn from them. Dissemination and promotion of engagement with case studies are therefore important activities that should take into consideration the specific audience, organizational context, and culture. Knowledge management systems which incorporate the compiling and coding of cases are a useful resource; however, it may not be sufficient to just share a case study with colleagues. Instead, learning platforms and opportunities should be designed with the intended audience in mind; for example, structured discussions and learning events may be appropriate mechanisms to translate knowledge into practice.

12.3 Using Case Studies for Organizational Learning in Four Development Agencies

Organizations have different ways of curating, documenting, and mobilizing knowledge. Generating and using case studies as a tool for organizational learning requires a considerable investment of an organization's time and resources, and different organizations have deployed different approaches. This section presents the experiences of four different organizations engaged with development issues – a multilateral agency (the World Bank), a major bilateral agency (Germany's GIZ), a leading think tank (Brookings Institution), and a key national ministry of a large developing country (China's Ministry of Finance) – as they have developed their use of case studies within their individual contexts. Reflecting on the experience of these different types of organizations may assist other organizations in their decisions about whether and how best to incorporate case studies.

The organizations were selected on the basis of their participation in the Global Delivery Initiative (more on this below) as well as the type of organization they represent. They were assessed via oral interviews as well as complementary desktop research of secondary material. Based on this assessment, the chapter will now examine how the motivation for organizational learning, managing knowledge, and the use of case studies in managing knowledge can vary among different types of development organizations.

All of the four organizations are linked through their involvement in the Global Delivery Initiative (GDI; described below – see Box 12.2) and all have developed case studies and shared them through the GDI network, which allows for some comparison between methods and approaches used.

12.3.1 Motivation for Using Case Studies for Organizational Learning

The motivation for using case studies varies widely across all assessed organizations, depending on organizational objectives, structures, and processes. For example, instead of focusing on 'best practices', China's Ministry of Finance (MoF) seeks to tell the story of China's development over the past decades in ways that capture insights to inform and possibly adapt planned or ongoing interventions in other countries (as well as in China) – the MoF

Table 12.1 Overview of the four development organizations

Name of Organization	Purpose of the Organization	Type of Organization
World Bank	To end extreme poverty (decreasing to 3% the number of people living on less than $1.90 per day) and promote shared prosperity (fostering the income growth of the bottom 40% in every country)	Multilateral finance institution
Deutsche Gesellschaft für Internationale Zusammenarbeit (GIZ) GmbH (Government of Germany)	To contribute to sustainable development through services and approaches such as capacity development, sectoral and policy advice and change management, project management and logistics, network facilitation and mediation, and event management	Bilateral implementing agency
Brookings Institution (Center for Universal Education, Millions Learning Project)	To conduct in-depth research that leads to new ideas for solving problems facing a society at the local, national, and global levels	Nonprofit public policy organization
Ministry of Finance (MoF) of the People's Republic of China	MoF is one of the ministries of State Council which is responsible for financial affairs of the People's Republic of China	National government

invests in case studies because they are perceived as a suitable product for knowledge-sharing between China and the rest of the world. A case study is considered an additional product in documenting project results and hence will be disclosed and distributed publicly. More formally, the MoF's objective(s) when producing case studies are to:

- Shed light on underexplored projects that China has conducted together with the World Bank, producing implementation knowledge on *how* these projects were carried out.
- Identify a platform and adequate tools to document its development experiences in order to share these with the world, especially with other developing countries as part of a "South–South Cooperation" agenda.

Box 12.2 Case studies and the Global Delivery Initiative

The Global Delivery Initiative (GDI) was a joint effort by multiple organizations to create a collective and cumulative evidence base on the ways in which challenges encountered during the delivery of development interventions are addressed. The GDI supported the science of delivery[4] by building on the experience of its partners; connecting perspectives, people, and organizations across sectors and regions; and ensuring that staff and clients have the knowledge they need for effective implementation (see Gonzalez and Woolcock 2015). From the outset, the GDI deployed analytical case studies as its primary tool for acquiring, assessing, and disseminating knowledge on implementation dynamics: how particular teams, often implementing complex projects in difficult circumstances, successfully identify, prioritize, and resolve the problems that inherently accompany delivery.

In addition to producing case studies (and sharing them through its Global Delivery Library), the GDI convened partners to facilitate sharing of experiences and lessons learned on delivery; provided support to practitioners in member organizations as needed; trained prospective case writers; and identified common delivery challenges to provide support to practitioners. The goal was not to identify prescriptive universal 'best practice' solutions, but rather to share particular instances of how common problems were solved, with the expectation that these solutions could be adapted elsewhere as necessary by those who face similar challenges. Knowing that others have faced and overcome similar challenges can also be an important source of ideas and inspiration. Indeed, all professional communities – from brain surgeons to firefighters – have forums of one kind or another for sharing their experiences and soliciting the advice of colleagues as new challenges emerge; similarly, managers and front-line implementers of development projects should have ready access to people and materials that can help enhance their skills and effectiveness.

The steps by which a GDI case study was prepared emerged through an iterative process. The common principles underpinning the preparation of a GDI case study centered on treating it as an instance of applied research: beginning with a thorough desk review (documenting the project's history, objectives, and performance to date); using this to generate specific questions pertaining to implementation challenges that formal documents cannot answer; and then outlining a pragmatic methodology whereby particular stakeholders (project staff, recipients, senior government counterparts, etc.) were interviewed and additional data generated. The case study was then prepared on the basis of this material (Global Delivery Initiative 2015). Unique to the GDI case study methodology was that it evolved around development and delivery challenges. Instead of focusing on (project and/or program) objectives, case studies were built

---

[4] "The Science of Delivery is the collective and cumulative knowledge base of delivery know-how that helps practitioners make more informed decisions and produce consistent results on the ground. It is emerging from the recognition that not only sound technical knowledge is critical for effective interventions that impact people's lives – we also need to improve our ability to combine technical expertise with on-the-ground delivery know how; and develop a more systematic, collaborative, and cumulative understanding not just of what to deliver, but also of how to deliver" (Global Delivery Initiative, 2016a).

around challenges that were cross-sectoral and allowed for learning across sectoral disciplines. The assumption was that this approach would spark a discussion on nontechnical matters amongst technical experts as well as related stakeholders (e.g., governments). This approach varied considerably from general practice in development organizations, wherein learning was focused on project reports, excluding knowledge on the "how to."

The Millions Learning Program at the Center for Universal Education (Brookings Institution) decided that case studies were an appropriate strategy for capturing and sharing the process behind how education interventions around the world went to scale. In order to do so, the Millions Learning team globally scanned for programs and policies initiated by state and nonstate actors that demonstrated a measurable improvement in learning among a significant number of children or youth.

GIZ's interest in case studies is to primarily address specific delivery challenges by first characterizing the most important failure in not closing the delivery gap, specifically the so-called "last mile delivery gap" for the poor. For example, in the case of water and sanitation programs, it is the missing access to clean water; in the case of the energy program, it is missing access to at least one important energy service. Case studies address more complex issues at the governance level, such as the functioning of public administration systems overseeing police forces. They also deal with more institutional/political types of failure, such as the missing rights-based approach to public administration (South Caucasus) or political interventions in police reforms (Central America). Success is therefore always presented as a substantive response to an identified failure in public service delivery.

GIZ's motivation in curating knowledge via case studies has varied depending on the case study in question. Some examples follow:

- Starting a more general reflection process on specific program approaches (Water/Sanitation; Community Policing)
- Promoting an innovative intervention with proven scale-up (Prison Reform/Bangladesh)
- Presenting a proven technical/organizational innovation (Metering System Bangladesh)
- Supporting regional learning processes (Community Policing, Administration Law South Caucasus)
- Marketing program approaches (Cashew Initiative; Energizing Development).

12.3.2   Organizational Learning Environment

Work on case studies is usually embedded in organizational contexts such as units explicitly dealing with organizational learning and/or knowledge management. These linkages are of high importance to ensure that case studies reach their intended target audiences within each organization. Organizational culture – or in this case, learning culture – is the "breeding ground" that highly impacts how case studies are perceived and acknowledged.

For China's MoF, promoting adaptive learning is the core rationale for producing case studies; as such, case studies should at best include stories of successful interventions as well as course correction. However, changing the perspective from focusing on success to challenges has not always been easy for case writers in this context. To openly identify, assess, document, and communicate failure poses a distinct challenge in China's otherwise "success-driven" environment.

Brookings' Millions Learning project was initially interested in learning from case study "success stories" as well as from interventions that did not achieve their intended outcomes. However, the team quickly realized how challenging it was to publish "failure cases," as people are often hesitant to publicly admit to failure. That is why in the project's calls for case studies, the wording is highly important. For example, the team's use of the term "failure" caused resistance, whereas the terms "challenges" and/or "course corrections" resulted in greater sharing among case study partners. Apart from semantics, the change in wording also strongly enhances the emphasis on learning and jointly improving from experiences (such as how challenges have been overcome).

To openly discuss challenges as well as failure is nothing new at GIZ, which for many years has been actively fostering a culture permitting failure to be openly addressed. Strategic evaluations, for example, are done with openness, highlighting deficits and failure. However, discussing failure and limitations is not yet a mainstreamed management attitude. GIZ acknowledged several common challenges to the process of writing case studies, as follows:

- Identifying an appropriate delivery challenge
- Updating the existing literature by internet research, and not just relying on existing institutional documents or reports
- Identifying the most important causal mechanisms
- Lack of recognition of the importance of governance structures/aspects at the national level

- Comparative case studies require a different methodological approach. They are not an extension of a single case study
- The process of organizing a case study depends on the specific demand and should not be too predetermined. (It is not the written document which counts, but the use of the knowledge that emerges by doing case studies.)

Unlike China's MoF or the Millions Learning project at Brookings, the scope of GIZ's case studies depends on the demand of its partner organizations and program managers. Consequently, GIZ's approach to learning from case studies and its integration into corporate learning has several specific objectives:

- To document the tacit implementation knowledge of different program interventions with different partner organizations. As a contribution to an internal reflection process, this type of case study needs a clear mandate from an internal network or community of practice and relies on the motivation of senior advisors to make their implicit knowledge explicit.
- To introduce innovative approaches focused on a specific delivery gap at the country level, but also at regional or international levels. This type of case study is neither a policy document with general recommendations nor a detailed story of a specific program intervention at the country level. The case attempts to understand the most important causal mechanism responsible for the identified delivery challenge and to explain why and how the presented response to the delivery challenge has been effective.
- To present a proven organizational or technical solution to an identified delivery gap mainly at the local or micro-level starts by explaining why the established approach has not been effective in closing the delivery gap. Such case studies usually focus on the incentive structure, in particular on incentives and behavioral attitudes of clients and partner organizations.

At the World Bank, the Independent Evaluation Group (IEG) has embarked on a series of reports to better understand how the Bank learns from its operations, embedded knowledge, and experiences (see IEG 2014, 2015). As a general conclusion, these reports state that the World Bank can do much better in learning from the knowledge it produces and that flows through its practice.[5] The Bank agrees it needs a more strategic approach to learning, and that such strategy should adapt to the different learning needs

---

[5] In many respects these reports are a more recent follow-up to the famous Wapenhans Report of 1992 (World Bank 1992), which explicitly sought to show that effective implementation was key to attaining

identified by these reports (needs related to operational policies and procedures, human resources policies and practices, and promoting an institutional
environment with incentives and accountability to foster knowledge and
learning).

As part of a recent full-fledged institutional change management process,
the World Bank has created different sectoral responsibilities to manage
learning and knowledge to help overcome development challenges. The
new arrangement aims to build capacity for staff and to encourage clients to
learn, share, and use knowledge derived from experience in addressing
operational challenges, including assessing whether and how such experiences can be adapted elsewhere and scaled. One of these institutional
responsibilities resided in the Global Delivery Initiative, which sought to
package such knowledge and lessons into case studies and generate
methods to develop such case studies for use within and between development organizations. For GDI, case studies on delivery provided a clearer
understanding of the sequence of events and balanced the perspectives of
key actors, helping us untangle cause and effect. More specifically, such case
studies sought to outline how interventions were implemented. They
provided insights into the results and challenges of implementation, and
helped to identify why a particular outcome occurred. They explored
interventions in their contexts, and described what was done, why, how,
for whom, and with what results.

12.3.3   Types of Knowledge Curated Via Case Studies

Case studies are an appropriate tool to capture knowledge in a structured yet
context-sensitive manner, allowing for narratives to unfold and implementation processes to be revealed without over-simplifying. The type of knowledge curated via case studies, however, varies according to each organization
assessed.

Guidelines produced by the World Bank were used as the methodological
backbone of all case study work initiated by China's MoF. However, the
Ministry would like to maintain a certain flexibility regarding its case studies
that allows experienced case writers to add their individual styles and additional details. This is because China's MoF strives to capture knowledge
through case studies that informs the design of new interventions (projects)

development impact (and which argued that the World Bank was far from being a learning
organization).

in China, as well as to inform the implementation of ongoing interventions (scaling up). Therefore, the selection criteria for case studies are primarily based on the quality of the project the case study will focus on, and whether it entails concrete experiences that are worth sharing within and beyond China. In a small number of cases, the MoF also selects case studies based on research interest.

Apart from publishing a final report and upcoming stand-alone case studies, the Millions Learning team periodically blogs about its case studies, report findings, and topics. The team is planning to release a series of two-minute videos that feature voices of case study partners to bring each featured case study to life. The Millions Learning team also disseminates a quarterly newsletter, tweets daily, and presents its report and case study findings at international events and conferences every few months. The vast majority of the case studies (80 percent) contained empirical findings from fieldwork and were not limited to desk research only. Fieldwork was conducted by staff at the Center for Universal Education at the Brookings Institution and consultants via in-person or phone interviews. The same people who undertook the field visits and data collection wrote the case studies (in-house researchers as well as external consultants). What is required of case writers is familiarity with the case study methodology as well as the topic of the case, the specific intervention, and the country.

GIZ has broad experience in using case studies and uses an existing methodology. One of the main learnings is that case studies are only valid in specific contexts and that knowledge cannot be directly transferred from one context to another. For instance, once a case study is developed, its results are only used by a couple of colleagues to feed into the development of specific programs. At times meta-evaluations are carried out for specific topics, but these do not always lead to changes in action as the conclusions tend to be fairly general. This has led to the understanding in GIZ that case studies are a necessary tool for specific programs but that generalization of results is tricky and obtaining evidence is highly resource-intensive and often impractical. Use of case studies falls outside the default reporting procedures at GIZ. Reporting requirements are linked to specific program cycles and implementation processes, whereas case studies take a broader view of the social and political context as well as behavioral and institutional aspects. They usually cover a greater period than a program cycle, as they focus on how delivery gaps have been closed (and not only on the impact of a given program intervention).

At the World Bank, the current objective is to gain in-depth and systematic knowledge on the causal mechanisms that explain development results. Based on systematizing casual mechanisms (which includes the identification of the key factors and enabling conditions) that explain the pathway to change, the Bank can identify lessons learned that may usefully inform decision-making in other contexts and scales. The case study method is useful for hypothesis generation: drilling deep into experiences and tracing the casual mechanisms of change (see Gerring 2017) helps to systematize the mechanisms behind implementation process.

GDI's cases, then, worked with a focus on the 'how to' of implementation. The type of knowledge curated revolved around those factors and pathways of change that explain a particular development result. The purpose of gathering such knowledge was to provide practitioners with evidence that can help them inform their own decision-making. As stated in GDI's fact sheets,

The case study method encourages researchers to ask questions about underexplored complex delivery problems and processes that development stakeholders routinely grapple with: what they are, when they arise, and how they might be addressed, including detailed accounts of delivery techniques, strategies, and experiences of the twists and turns of the implementation process. Systematically investigating delivery in its own right will make it possible to distill the common delivery challenges – the institutional, political, behavioral, logistical, and other issues that affect the delivery of specific interventions. It will also inform practitioners when they are faced with similar delivery challenges in their own programs and projects. (Global Delivery Initiative, 2016b)

12.3.4 Use of Case Studies for Organizational Learning

Apart from disseminating case studies via the Global Delivery Library of GDI, China's MoF intends to publish all its case studies via the library of the Shanghai University of Finance and Economics, which is one of the partner universities of MoF China. Conferences and events organized by local government officials are equally important channels for dissemination of insights gained via case studies. For instance, the Ningbo government is planning to include the Wetland project case study in a book about Ningbo's experience in implementing World Bank projects, and it will be shared with participants at a conference hosted by the Ningbo government.

Additionally, all case studies by the MoF will be disseminated via the internal online platform to all bureaus and agencies affiliated with the Ministry. It is too soon to provide evidence on whether case studies have been used by decision-makers and officers in government. However, there has been strong interest by project managers in China to use and learn from these case studies. The MoF does not foresee any resistance or challenges in disseminating case studies. Even so, it has adapted its approach following feedback from a GDI training course so that now a selected group of dedicated academics will produce all case studies; this has significantly increased the quality of the cases.

The explicit objective of the Millions Learning project is to use case studies to provide a picture of the players, processes, and drivers behind the scaling process in education. It is evident that the project is interested in leveraging knowledge in education across organizational and national borders. The project also intends to learn from and build on research on scaling up which may be relevant across sectors – for example, health and nutrition, as well as other disciplines. It has been clear from the start that the project did not intend to publish a compendium of case studies, but instead preferred to focus on patterns across case studies that should be documented and shared. Case studies are referred to in order to provide examples. The team was also clear from the project's inception that documentation of knowledge is more a means to an end than a final product. Therefore, the Millions Learning report is considered to be the starting point for knowledge-sharing, dialogue, and, ideally, action around selected topics and areas in education. Hence, it is outward facing, inviting organizations and individuals to share information and contribute to further shaping the debate around global education. To achieve this, the initiative continuously reaches out to organizations, agencies, and individuals from around the world to contribute to and feed into the process through interviews, conventions, and draft report reviews. The Millions Learning team also published stand-alone case studies in 2016, providing a deeper dive into the individual case studies discussed in the Millions Learning report.

To date, ten case studies using the GDI methodology have been developed by GIZ. There has been exchange across organizational boundaries, but not yet at scale. However, regional programs have used case studies for reflection processes across boundaries. Selected case studies have been presented at regional seminars and used as reference material in the formation of new interventions. Coming back to the different types of case studies GIZ has developed, the following lessons can be derived from experiences in writing and using case studies so far:

- Case studies presenting innovative approaches focus first on design and analyze the real implementation issues related to the chosen design. The context is more related to regional or international experiences in the area or issues presented, and the country context is mainly taken into account for understanding the differences with other experiences. Comparison is more important than detailed understanding of specific case-related aspects of implementation and management. The main focus is on understanding similarities and differences due to specific country conditions.
- Case studies which summarize implementation knowledge focus more on implementation than on design since the design has been proven effective under different conditions and situations. Thus, the main interest is to understand what works under which conditions and what kind of tacit knowledge should be taken into account when approaches have to be transferred and adapted to a "new" context.
- Case studies which present a proven organizational/technical solution to a delivery gap at the local level focus on the "how" of the incentive structure. Therefore, feedback loops with clients and real-time impact monitoring are important tools.

At the World Bank, the GDI was one of the most interesting and productive initiatives using case studies as a learning source. The model of case studies for the GDI provided comprised a critical body of knowledge with insights from the implementation process that helped practitioners identify those causal mechanisms explaining results in particular contexts. An understanding of the critical factors and enabling conditions in achieving results helped to inform projects operating outside the specific context of the case. The cases were also used as part of training sessions to develop the capacity of practitioners to use cases to inform their own practice and to populate the GDI's case study repository, now managed by the Global Partnership for Effective Development Cooperation.[6] At the same time, the training agenda acted as a capacity building "train the trainers" strategy, with the aim of creating a global cadre of suitably qualified practitioners that not only gained skills as case writers but also benefited their own practice. Internally at the World Bank, the GDI trialed some case studies that were used as learning

---

[6] The GDI's case studies are hosted in an online and open platform on delivery knowledge; they are available under the "Resource Type" category at www.effectivecooperation.org/search/resources.

exercises for newcomer staff, in which they simulated how staff approach clients in different contexts and for different development problems.

12.4   Lessons Learned in Aligning Case Studies with an Organizational Learning Agenda

In the previous section we noted that case studies on development practice are used in different ways and with different levels of systematization for the purpose of organizational learning. Here we can make use of our IGOIL categorization to explain how case studies from these different organizations tap into different levels of learning.

As we see from Table 12.2, different organizations use case studies for learning purposes, but such purposes serve different objectives. We can use the MoF of China and the World Bank as two examples with different purposes. For China's MoF, learning is external facing, with partners that want to learn from the experiences captured in the Chinese case studies. This external interest may come typically from other governments that want to learn how the Chinese government dealt with a particular development challenge. Learning is done mainly at the interorganizational level: the MoF selects and systematizes experiences to be disseminated, and this external demand is what guides the capture and systematization of knowledge by the MoF.

The World Bank's approach is also very much about interorganizational learning, by sharing experiences among institutions on how to address development challenges. However, at the same time there is a specific focus on knowledge retention and organizational learning, with the goal of interpreting and using the knowledge collected through the case studies to support the organization's business practices and improve performance. The GDI approach focused on contacting particular partners and using group discussion to advance this learning agenda; it also provided training for practitioners to not only become case writers, but to develop capacity at the individual level for transformational change by better understanding the change process.

Table 12.2 also points to some of the different motivations for using case studies as a learning tool. In the case of MoF China and Brookings, for instance, case studies are shown as exemplars of how to do things or 'what and how things work' in the spirit of sharing such knowledge outside the boundaries of the organization. At GIZ the focus is to provide practitioners, within and outside the organization, with examples of good practices. Finally,

Table 12.2 How different organizations use case studies for learning purposes

Learning Category	MoF, China	GIZ, Germany	Brookings – Millions Learning Initiative	World Bank –GDI
Individual		X		X
Group				X
Organizational		X	X	X
Interorganizational	X		X	X

GIZ understands itself as a convener of experiences on transformational processes, with the role of promoting dialogue not only at the practitioner level but also across organizations and countries.

Table 12.2 and the preceding discussion shows that case studies do not need to use the same knowledge-sharing strategy or audience to inform development processes. Case studies can be used as a learning tool to improve performance and implementation in internal practices. They may never be shared directly with other practitioners or stakeholders outside of that organization, but this approach may still spread lessons indirectly through changes in behavior and practices as a consequence of insights captured in the case study. On the other hand, case studies can be used directly to inform counterparts of experiences that provide insights on what works and how. In this instance cases may have more impact on an external organization receiving such knowledge.

Finally, the use of case studies as a learning tool also generates some knowledge value in the process of developing the case study itself, in addition to the output. As has been shown with MoF China, the GDI, and to some extent GIZ, case writers are trained to focus on a problem-driven approach to tackle case studies. These case writers are also practitioners involved in development projects who may be keen to incorporate this approach in future development practices. Further capacity building at an individual level may also take place among the key stakeholders involved. As a case study's interviewees, they play a role in articulating their experiences, which are captured as knowledge on the "how to" of implementation. As experienced through the preparation of case studies by the four organizations discussed in this chapter, such engagement provides these key stakeholders with a new perspective on how to tackle challenges throughout the implementation cycle, and in the process perhaps generates a change of mindset.

References

Argote, L., Beckman, S. L., and Epple, D. (1990) "The persistence and transfer of learning in industrial settings," *Management Science*, 36(2), 140–154.

Argyris, C. (1977) "Double loop learning in organizations," *Harvard Business Review*, 55(5), 115–125.

Cook, S. D. and Brown, J. S. (1999) "Bridging epistemologies: The generative dance between organizational knowledge and organizational knowing," *Organization Science*, 10(4), 381–400.

Crossan, M. M., Lane, H. W., and White, R. E. (1999) "An organizational learning framework: From intuition to institution," *Academy of Management Review*, 24(3), 522–537.

Drucker, P. F. (1994) *The theory of business.* Boston, MA: Harvard Business Review.

Fiol, C. M. and Lyles, M. A. (1985) "Organizational learning," *Academy of Management Review*, 10(4), 803–813.

Garvin, D. A. (1993) "Building a learning organization," *Harvard Business Review*, 71(4), 78–91.

Gerring, J. (2017) *Case study research: Principles and practices* (2nd edition). New York: Cambridge University Press.

Global Delivery Initiative. (2015) "Delivery case study guidelines." Mimeo, World Bank.

Global Delivery Initiative. (2016a) *Fact sheet on Global Delivery Initiative FAQ.* Mimeo, World Bank.

Global Delivery Initiative. (2016b) *Fact sheet on delivery case studies.* Mimeo, World Bank.

Goertz, G. and Mahoney, J. (2012) *A tale of two cultures.* Princeton, NJ: Princeton University Press.

Gonzalez, M. and Woolcock, M. (2015) *Operationalizing the science of delivery agenda to enhance development results.* Washington, DC: The World Bank.

Hedberg, B. (1981) "How organizations learn and unlearn" in Nystrom, C. and Starbuck, W. (eds.) *Handbook of organizational design.* New York: Oxford University Press, pp. 18–27.

Independent Evaluation Group (IEG). (2014) *Learning and results in World Bank operations: How the bank learns. Evaluation 1.* The World Bank: Independent Evaluation Group.

Independent Evaluation Group (IEG). (2015) *Learning and results in World Bank operations: Toward a new learning strategy. Evaluation 2.* The World Bank: Independent Evaluation Group.

Inkpen, A. C. and Crossan, M. M. (1995) "Believing is seeing: Joint ventures and organization learning," *Journal of Management Studies*, 32(5), 595–618.

Nonaka, I. (1994) "A dynamic theory of organizational knowledge creation," *Organization Science*, 5(1), 14–37.

Nonaka, I. and Konno, N. (1998) "The concept of 'Ba': Building a foundation for knowledge creation," *California Management Review*, 40(3), 40–54.

Polanyi, M. (1966) *The tacit dimension* New York: Doubleday.

Schein, E. H. (1990) "Organizational culture," *American Psychologist*, 45(2), 109–119.

Scott, B. B. (2011) "Organizational learning: A literature review." Queens University, Canada: IRC Research Program Discussion Paper #2011-02.

Senge, P. M. (1990) *The fifth discipline: The art and practice of the learning organization.* New York: Doubleday.

Stata, R. and Almond, P. (1989) "Organizational learning: The key to management innovation" in Schneier, C. E., Russell, C. J., Beatty, R. W., and Baird, L. S. (eds.) *The training and development sourcebook.* Amherst, MA: Human Resource Development Press, pp. 31–42.

World Bank (1992) *Effective implementation: Key to development impact.* Report of the World Bank's Portfolio Management Task Force. Washington, DC: The World Bank.

Zack, M. H. (1999) "Developing a knowledge strategy," *California Management Review,* 41(3), 125–145.

13 Connecting Case Studies to Policy and Practice

Practical Lessons from Operational Experience

Maria Gonzalez de Asis and Jennifer Widner

13.1 Introduction

Former UK prime minister Tony Blair once said: "The problem isn't vision. Often we know what to do. The real problem is getting things done."[1] In 2013, the World Bank Group embraced this challenge as a part of a new "science of delivery" initiative championed by its president,[2] building on an ambition that Sir Michael Barber articulated in the service of the Blair government, manifest most conspicuously in his deployment of dedicated delivery units (see Barber, 2015). At issue was whether organizations could develop and formalize reliable guidance about how best to translate good ideas into real impact.

As part of this effort to improve implementation, the qualitative case study has a special place. Randomized controlled trials and other tools used to assess program design or evaluate the effectiveness of specific interventions provide little leverage or practical insight when the breakdown between ideas and impact lies in the *hows* – the specific steps taken to deliver a service or change an institution. A case study can help improve the translation of policy

---

[1] Blair spoke these words at several meetings. For example, see his speech at a forum sponsored by the Center for Global Development in December 17, 2010. "The vision thing is often the easy part. Where you need to get to, is reasonably obvious. What is really hard is getting there and doing it. It is the nuts and bolts of policy. It is strategy. It is performance management. It is delivery. It is the right expertise in the right place. It is ministers who can focus. It is organizing and communicating it." Available at www .cgdev.org/article/speech-text-tony-blair-making-government-work-will-transform-africa

[2] See Behn (2017) for a brief history of the term 'science of delivery' and a critique of the idea. Kim (2013) provides an outline of how the World Bank's president (at the time) envisioned a 'science of delivery' would function in a multilateral agency.

into results by tracing these pathways, illuminating the effects of context, process, politics, and capacities on intermediate achievements and broader outcomes.

But practitioners can also use case studies to improve performance in a variety of other ways. While previous chapters have laid out a social scientific rationale for the use of qualitative case studies, proposed standards for assessing rigor, and offered examples, this chapter focuses on employing case studies for adaptation and learning, especially in governments or organizations that seek to promote economic growth and development. It proposes that case studies useful for this purpose have seven specific qualities, though they may differ widely in other respects. Additionally, it offers a brief user's guide for policy planners, managers, and instructors.

Our observations build on insights from two programs: the World Bank's Development Research Group and its leading operational unit deploying case studies, the Global Delivery Initiative (GDI), and Princeton University's Innovations for Successful Societies (ISS) program, which develops policy-focused case studies of development.[3] Both programs worked for many years with people leading change in different contexts. From 2008 through 2021, the Princeton program helped a rising generation of leaders address the institution-building challenges facing governments in fragile states and neighborhoods, low-income countries, and crisis situations. Case studies were, and remain, the program's medium for enabling public servants to share experience with each other in an accessible manner. Similarly, the World Bank-based GDI, which launched in 2014, began as a collaboration among various development partners to help practitioners build a more systematic understanding of program implementation, promote policy dialogue, and improve operational effectiveness. The Global Delivery Library, one of the GDI resources, became an open repository of cases that tapped the tacit knowledge of field-level practitioners about how to navigate delivery challenges, enabling future operations to draw upon wisdom from past interventions.

---

[3] The Global Delivery Initiative's case studies are available via the Global Partnership for Effective Development Cooperation, accessed (by selecting "Case Studies" in the "Resource Type" category) at www.effectivecooperation.org/search/resources. Details on Princeton University's Innovations for Successful Societies program, along with all its published material, can be found at https://successful societies.princeton.edu.

13.2   From the Science of Delivery to Adaptive Management

Blair's observation – it's not the vision but the *how* that's the problem – had its roots in a prime minister's struggle to improve service delivery across different sectors, especially education, health, and policing. In the United Kingdom, as in every country, implementation is often the great bugaboo on which great ideas stumble. But offering reliable generalizations to help guide the work of front-line providers, managers, and ministers poses many challenges. The social world cannot be reduced to a set of laws or principles as easily as the natural world.

Efforts to frame a science of delivery exposed two different policy worlds: one in which it was possible to base generalizations on credible evidence, and another in which tracing the influence of actions on impact was more difficult, though still valuable. In medicine and education, for example, there were some strong points of agreement about measures that could have a big impact on broad outcomes, as Wagstaff (2013) has correctly noted. Take the example of vaccination against childhood diseases. There is mounting evidence about how best to scale vaccination campaigns. Though not completely reducible to a formula – at least not to one that works the same way to the same extent in every setting – it is possible to think systematically about how to achieve results, including estimates of the participation rates needed to create herd immunity and innovations to help maintain the cold-chain when lack of electricity threatens vaccine viability. Wagstaff (2013) points out that it is unsurprising, then, that champions of a science of delivery – the testable, relatively stable understanding of cause and effect within the implementation process – often started their careers in a field such as public health and that journals such as *Implementation Science* were specific to this policy area.

This science came together as the confluence of many strands of research and multiple methods of investigation. It is notable that the contributions in the pages of the Centers for Disease Control's *Morbidity and Mortality Weekly Report* have included not only analysis of epidemiological data, but also case studies based on field interviews.[4] The qualitative case studies help identify the nature of the many gaps between the release of a vaccine to a health worker and actual protection of an individual against the disease, and often to point to remedies. By tracing the breakdowns in the process,

---

[4] See www.cdc.gov/mmwr/index.html.

they spur adaptation that could help improve the match between the numbers of people a campaign aimed to protect and actual levels of vaccine administration. Through multiple cases, as well as larger tracking studies, practitioners are able to come closer to answering the key "How?" questions that Behn (2017: 94) rightly highlights as essential elements of a science of delivery: "How does this strategy produce results? What exactly are the causal connections between the strategies employed and the resulting outputs or outcomes?"[5]

Case studies have also aided understanding by enabling us to probe why outliers – exceptional successes or failures – differed from the patterns normally observed, thereby illuminating possible ways to improve performance across the board. This was the approach adopted by Brixi, Lust, and Woolcock (2015) to learn from local service success stories in parts of the Middle East and North Africa. Household survey data from several countries in the region indicated that student performance was often poor, despite the fact that school access and facilities had improved. If all schools in a country operated under the same set of regulations, these authors asked, why do some areas perform so much better than others, controlling for demographics? Did the differences stem from a condition outside the control of managers, or was it something that principals and teachers in one area just decided to do differently – a practice that, at least in principle, others could replicate? The household surveys did not contain the type of information that allowed them to answer these questions, so the team went to the successful schools and studied them. One hypothesis was that degree of parental engagement affected both teacher behavior and student performance. The questions the team posed therefore included several about interaction between school officials and the community. The case studies found that the successful schools were those where principals and teachers met with residents and there was more communication with families. The challenge was then to figure out how to generalize a practice that was at least partially sensitive to the orientations and aptitudes of school leaders. In this instance, qualitative case studies supported development of alternative explanations and illuminated a potential solution to the problem of low-performing schools.

Not all policy spheres look like either of these examples, however. In some, policy arenas, implementation involves multiple changes at once, which

---

[5] Behn (2017: 94) underscores this point, going on to argue that "For there to be any 'science' – anything close to 'science' – this experimentation has to result in an explanation about how, in a specific situation, specific management actions caused changes in human behaviors that produced better results."

means there are several possible causal explanations for outcomes. In Behn's (2017: 96) words: "Thus, the manager's ability to assign causal credit is difficult. And if the management team is just starting out – if this is the team's first effort to improve performance – which of the team's multiple actions deserves how much of the credit?" The answer to this question cannot be called "science," he says. "It could, however, be an intelligent guess."

An intelligent guess is a step in the right direction, a hypothesis rooted in facts, though it isn't the same as an evidence-based handbook, the kind of product Behn (2017) suggests a science would produce. Where it is hard to winnow out which conditions, circumstances, or actions carry the most weight in delivering a development outcome, and where we are therefore likely to have a high ratio of intelligent guesses in decision-making, implementation may adhere to a different model. Continual review, learning, and mid-course correction become essential. Though long practiced, this approach has more recently gone under names such as "adaptive management" or AdaptDev, which now has its own Google Group,[6] "Doing Development Differently" (DDD[7]), and "Problem-Driven Iterative Adaptation" (PDIA[8]). The common idea across these new platforms is that where a traditional after-action review, for example, is conducted at the end of an initiative, the push instead should be for feedback and learning to occur throughout an effort to implement a policy or institutional change. Booth et al. (2018: 8) point to a process in which implementers, in response to complex challenges, "deliberately set themselves up to learn by trial and error, testing initial approaches and adjusting rapidly as evidence on possible avenues of change is acquired." Matt Andrews (2018: 1), one of the key contributors to this approach, has written on the basis of his long experience: "We always ask of PDIA in practice: What did we do? What results emerged? What did we learn? What did we struggle with? What was next?"

Although both policy learning and learning-by-doing have a long history, the ambition of the Doing Development Differently and AdaptDev communities that have emerged in this space is to expand the practice of experimenting, learning, and adjusting in domains where broad evidence-based generalizations about implementation are out of reach. In these areas, the

---

[6] Accessed December 13, 2021 at https://groups.google.com/g/adaptdev?pli=1.

[7] Since 2014, a series of DDD workshops have been held around the world – Boston (2014), Manila (2015), London (2016), Jakarta (2017), Nairobi (2018), and Berlin (2019) – to consider practical ways in which donors, governments, and organizations can engage more constructively with implementation challenges that prevailing administrative systems and imperatives struggle to accommodate.

[8] On PDIA, see Andrews, Pritchett, and Woolcock (2017).

people responsible for translating ideas into practice will almost certainly encounter challenges and unexpected obstacles (Schon 1983; Pritchett, Samji, and Hammer 2013). If they do not step back, reflect, learn, and adapt, they risk persisting with interventions or strategies that are not well suited to the situation that they face. Therefore, these teams must be ready and willing to adapt mid-course, to experiment and scale up what works, and to iterate and integrate feedback into implementation. Together with careful planning and the elaboration of a clearly articulated theory of change, the incorporation of "rapid feedback loops" into an endeavor is crucial, as is using these processes for "learning in response to ongoing challenges" (Pritchett, Samji, and Hammer 2013: 1).

In this corner of the policy world, where causal relationships are less straightforward than they are in public health (and elsewhere), case studies help practitioners pool observations, recognize what has worked, identify where things aren't turning out as anticipated, flag surprises, and open up space for adaptation. They help make the tacit knowledge practitioners have accumulated as explicit possible. Although they may draw on focus groups, surveys, and quantitative evidence, they employ interviews to help trace the steps taken, departures from the roadmap, and intermediate results in order to help us better address both anticipated and unexpected circumstances and increase the probability of generating intended impacts.

In early experiments, embedding case development and data collection directly into projects not only strengthened the quality of evidence produced but also enabled managers to make mid-course corrections and secure stronger buy-in from other stakeholders. Innovative elements have sometimes included smartphone surveys to check whether a service reached intended beneficiaries or assess satisfaction, geotagged information displayed on maps to help spot service coverage issues, satellite photography to track crop conditions, and other information generated with relatively low-cost and flexible tools that have a broad variety of applications (e.g., see Danquah et al. 2019 on Sierra Leone). Workshops to document and review implementation steps taken to date help staff members spot omissions and bottlenecks and discuss creative ways to surmount unanticipated obstacles.

The World Bank's Global Scaling Up Rural Sanitation program aptly illustrates this kind of effort. With the goal of making a dent in the 2.5 billion people worldwide without access to improved sanitation, the project launched pilots in three countries, which served as learning laboratories for developing a theory of change. After this pilot phase concluded, the project then made the necessary adjustments and scaled up to a further 10 countries; to date, it has provided some 22 million people in 13 countries with improved sanitation.

The use of pilots in the initial "learning laboratory" countries provided crucial knowledge about what worked and what did not. This information was then disseminated through a global network, allowing team members to reflect on and analyze the results of their actions. Team leaders were able to learn from these initial lessons in real time, allowing for quick adaptation. An iterative and adaptive approach was also hardwired into the program, giving task team leaders both the freedom and the mandate to apply lessons learned in their countries or areas of responsibility, while also adapting and correcting course as they scaled up and collecting their own evidence locally to target effective behavior changes and interventions.

A second example from the GDI illustrates a slightly different approach, this time in the context of improving access of Nigerians to sustainable, clean, potable water. A case study indicated that governance reforms were difficult to implement, trust in the system was low, and monitoring was weak – with the result that progress had stalled. It was crucial to establish trust, build networks, and enhance relationships with a wide variety of stakeholders. To design a new phase of the project, the World Bank decided to share the case study and solicit ideas from each major stakeholder. It organized a series of meetings to invite observations and proposals. The first convened its Nigeria task team leaders. The subsequent meetings took place in Abuja and involved participation from representatives of more than sixty agencies, including the head of the Federal Program Implementation Unit, the high representative of the Federal Ministry of Finance, State Ministers of Water, State heads of the program implementation units, and the World Bank Country Director. Participants had a chance to discuss the case itself and introduce other information, then they charted out concrete recommendations.

13.3   Seven Qualities That Make a Case Useful for Practitioners

For purposes of learning and mid-course adjustment, not all case study formats are created equal. Moreover, the information and format needed are not always the same that academic colleagues seek. The GDI and Princeton's ISS program both ambitiously tried to tailor what they do to serve three distinct audiences: practitioners who want to improve implementation success, policy researchers or scholars who want to ground a (social) science of delivery, and aspiring leaders completing courses of study in universities and staff colleges or executive education programs. The jury is still out on whether it is possible to serve three masters equally well. Nonetheless, the experience to date has generated some wisdom – not yet formally tested! – about what helps a case to meet the needs of practitioners. This wisdom can be spelled out in seven principles:

1.   **A good case draws on a clear, shared lexicon.** A good part of what makes some cases more useful than others in development policy is the conceptual structure that underlies them, the lexicon. A good case is far more than a heap of facts the reader must somehow fit together. A good case focuses on subject matter that is central to a decision or series of decisions and helps reveal the development challenge and choice architecture, as well as the conditions or circumstances that affected the options available and the degree of success. The utility of a case depends on the ability to attach general names to the core challenges and in so doing facilitate comparison and consideration of alternatives.

A lexicon precedes a theory. It is a conceptual map, the key or index a practitioner, instructor, or researcher needs to identify other instances in which the same issue arose. For example, the difficulty people have in coming together to provide a public good, like a litter-free street, is a collective action problem. To be useful, qualitative cases that address this issue either have to use the term or employ the definition, minus the jargon, so that we can draw them into the pool of shared experience.

To employ an analogy, many of us have probably had the experience of moderating a discussion in which people with diverse experiences share their recent work. The moderator's job is to find the common ground, the shared problem on which the participants have something to say and could learn from each other. That job is much easier when the presenters share a lexicon and use that reference to define their focus and structure their remarks. Otherwise the moderator has to try to discern points of congruence based on fragmentary information – or ask the author, "this is a case of what?"

The ease with which we can learn from qualitative cases hinges partly on the degree to which the general names unlock the experience of others. It goes without saying that to be useful to development practitioners, this lexicon has to respond to how those practitioners think about their work and to what they seek to know. For example, to assist with implementation, both ISS and the GDI developed frameworks that featured a variety of delivery challenges (such as geographic fragmentation) and common impediments to success in achieving a broader development outcome (such as better health). But the aim was also to link users to broader theories and toolkits helpful for thinking outside the box and developing new approaches.

Located in an academic institution, ISS defined its lexicon by matching the problems governmental leaders said they encountered in trying to build more effective and accountable government with existing conceptual vocabularies in the social sciences. For example, some cases focus on coordination problems, and the program treats these in several different domains or policy spheres, including cabinet offices (centers of government), public financial management, disaster response, and business process improvement. In addition to coordination, collective action, and principal–agent/agency issues, the program focuses on problems that are especially difficult because they can lock a country into subpar performance: institutional traps, capacity traps, norm coordination traps, or thresholds, for example. (This approach led one reviewer to term the program's work "trapology.")

The GDI tried to secure a tighter fit between its lexicon and the mental maps of people in its diverse user base.[9] It reviewed more than 160 development publications to identify Original verb didn't seem to make sense. the delivery challenges most often encountered and conducted a text analysis on more than 4,000 Implementation Completion Reports from projects supervised by the World Bank and other development organizations. Focus groups reviewed the draft lists. The final result was a taxonomy with two levels. At the higher level, the program chose fifteen broad types of implementation problems across three dimensions: stakeholders, context, and project.[10] Below that were fifty-two additional keywords that presented a more granular view of specific delivery challenges. In the end, the effort yielded a taxonomy that included a mix of challenges, in several domains of application, mirroring the way many potential users searched for information and advice. This passage doesn't make sense. I can reword but it isn't really necessary.

2.   **A good case has a structure that communicates what a practitioner needs to know and facilitates cross-case comparison.** Whatever the realm of use, a good case is a story with a particular spin, in the sense that it helps the user

---

[9] Now housed within the Global Partnership for Effective Development Cooperation's open access resources, and the lexicon structures in the search menus for "challenge area" and "action area." Accessed December 13, 2021 at www.effectivecooperation.org/search/resources.

[10] Accessed December 13, 2021 at www.effectivecooperation.org/search/resources.

focus in on the information needed to draw conclusions. Structure is important for this reason, and the right structure depends on the intended purpose. If the focus is on implementation, then the case should track the stages of the implementation process, for example: problem recognition, likely delivery challenges, framing and strategy, steps taken to implement, adaptation processes, results obtained, and thoughts about what one might do differently. This ideal-type may not perfectly mimic the actual policy process in a given setting, but a decision-maker can easily follow the case narrative and relate to the subject matter if arrayed in this way, as well as compare and contrast with other cases.

The ISS program and the GDI both adopted templates to facilitate comprehension and comparison. With a few exceptions, the main actors – the "voice" of the story – are civil servants, civic leaders, task managers of projects, and occasionally managers based in international organizations. The text walks the reader through the context and the anticipated challenges (a set of hypotheses about potential sources of difficulty), and shows the options considered and the program design or strategy adopted to address these. Each case documents the new practices or policies a reform team created and the steps they took to win support, secure authorization, build awareness, reshape organizational cultures, and do the many other things often required to put a new system in place. In this respect, the approach resembles the classic Harvard Business School management case that puts the reader into the driver's seat alongside the person who has to solve a problem. The cases also document unanticipated obstacles and happy surprises, then conclude with results and participants' reflections on what they would do differently next time or in a different context.

3.   **A good case entertains multiple hypotheses.** Many different possible causes may account for an outcome. The case should make these visible to the reader and indicate where one or another appears to influence implementation, independently shape outcomes, or affect the scope conditions attached to solutions decision-makers employed. If the influence is negative, a work team can then think about how to solve the problem or mitigate the effects. If the influence is positive, the team might ask itself whether there are ways to amplify the impact. In this way, making hypotheses explicit facilitates adaptive management as well as instruction. This step also enhances the usefulness of a case for social scientists and policy-makers who aim to conduct cross-case comparison or internal process tracing to try to adjudicate among theories.

One sometimes hears that a good case must leverage a single underlying theory. But is that necessarily true? This approach is often too restrictive in practice, though it has its place. It would mean that, as in some kinds of social science research, the purpose of a case is to help us decide whether to accept or dismiss a particular account of results or impact. In areas where conditions may make a science of delivery achievable, as in aspects of public health, education, or economic policy, there is a rationale for constructing cases in this way. But for the purposes of adaptive management, in policy spheres where multiple causes are in play, it is preferable to entertain a range of theories and the hypotheses that flow from them.

There can be tension between the ultimate use of the case and making hypotheses explicit up front. The ISS program wrestled with this problem, sometimes with mixed success. Each series of its cases begins with a research design that highlights the many influences it wants to trace. Most of these become part of the challenges the decision-makers in the case confront, laid out in the second section. However, to ensure cases are engaging to read, ISS does not tag its hypotheses as such. Moreover, not all appear in the same section in every instance. Separate cross-cutting analysis carries the weight of this need. The decision to proceed in this way has consequences, however, and one is that many see the cases as purely inductive, scoping exercises. To conform more fully to a social science model, the program would have to produce a second, stylized version of each case that directly engaged hypotheses and shed other detail.

On the basis of its early experience, the GDI discerned five core categories of causal influence that development practitioners valued highly. Though not each was equally important in every instance, these dimensions provided an instructive set of entry points for assessing the dynamics of implementation and gradual accumulation of granular knowledge about these effects of contextual characteristics, political factors, and the actions of implementation teams on outcomes and impact.

The five dimensions (outlined below) were interconnected, complementing and enabling one another. Cases examined how particular challenges encountered along the way were managed with respect to:

a. *Citizen demands and citizen outcomes*: defining the goal as measurable gains in citizens' well-being; identifying the nature of the problem based on a thorough understanding of citizens' demands and local context; staying attentive to all factors that influence citizen outcomes, including, but not limited to, grassroots representation and bottom-up political pressure.

b. *Collaboration*: facilitating multistakeholder coalitions and multisectoral perspectives to identify and prioritize problems and coordinate (possible) solutions; convening varied development partners and building on their competitive advantages; tracing the impact of coordination structures on development outcomes.

c. *Evidence to achieve results*: using the best available evidence to identify problems and solutions; developing local evidence to refine solutions; collecting evidence of results throughout the project cycle; contributing to the global body of knowledge with the evidence collected for scaling up; whether outcomes were driven by evidence.

d. *Leadership for change*: understanding local political economies and drivers of change; identifying the incentives that motivate behaviors and integrating these into designing delivery solutions; evaluating whether incentive systems or political will accounted for outcomes.

e. *Adaptive implementation*: developing an adaptive implementation strategy that allows for iterative experimentation, feedback loops, and course correction; building a committed team with the right skills, experience, and institutional memory; maintaining the capacity to reflect on actions and their results; assessing whether institutional capacity for learning helped drive results.

GDI cases also included hypotheses drawn either from practitioner experience or research.

4. **A good case contains essential operational detail**. To serve development practitioners well, a case must speak to the issues that managers face with sufficient granularity that a counterpart in another country can follow the steps laid out. This quality often runs counter to what we seek in academe, where the aim is to test highly parsimonious theories that have broad applicability or scope, and where both the content and analysis of cases focuses on just a few key variables. The difficulty is to discern the difference between extraneous information and pertinent operational elements, which may include legal authority to act, the impact of political structures on jurisdiction, organizational routines, budget calendars, costs, information architecture, algorithms, and other elements, depending on the subject matter. From the perspective of someone trying to lead institutional change or implement a complex program, the devil is often in these details. An expert should see what she considers essential in a case and a novice should find the language easy enough to follow that the technical detail is clear.

When the person or team researching and writing the case (or facilitating case development) is unfamiliar with a subject area and the specific issues managers confront, reaching the right level of granularity may pose a problem. In some technical areas, both the ISS program and the GDI engaged experts to partner with them or to review initial briefings before case development began. Employing questions broad enough to allow practitioners to discuss their work in their own terms also helped the cases reach essential detail. It was always useful to ask, at the end of a conversation, "What would you like to know about how your counterparts in other countries have tried to reach the outcome you wanted to generate?"

5. **A good case pays attention to political will but need not make political will its focus**. Whether in the limited sense of having approval (authorization) from a department head or in the larger sense of having the backing of the head of state, implementation cases usually cut into a problem after there is at least a modicum of political will to proceed with a program and after an opportunity or ripe moment has already materialized. Sometimes sustaining political will is indeed one of the obstacles, but usually addressing this issue is antecedent to the steps taken to deliver a result. If there is no will, there is no policy intervention, and for those of us interested in improving implementation know-how, the "no will" cases are generally less interesting than others (though sometimes good ideas and initiatives bubble up without leadership).

A good practitioner case identifies the source of political will, as well as changes in intensity or motivation that may flow from political transitions, rotation in office, changes in popular opinion, unexpected events, etc. The case should identify how political backing was sustained or grew, or whether it was simply irrelevant and why. Were there self-reinforcing incentives built into the program design? Did program popularity make it difficult to change once the program started to deliver results? Were citizens groups able to lobby? Did leaders become part of a professional community favorable to a program's continued operation? It may be tempting in some instances to attribute a project's initiation or durability to outside pressure from a development partner, but rarely is that true. A good case explains why officials acceded, if in fact they did so.

6. **A good case discusses scope conditions**. One of the criticisms of randomized controlled trials is that they have limited external validity (Pritchett and Sandefur 2015). We often just do not have the information to know whether the same result would occur in other places, for other people, or during

different periods in history (Woolcock 2013). Learning from qualitative case studies can be prone to this same problem, but an implementation case usually provides some grist for thinking more systematically about whether the experience highlighted holds lessons for others. That grist comes in the form of a clear specification of context and analysis of how context shaped the steps taken and the results achieved. Such an analysis provides some basis for understanding how a change in implementation circumstances (context, scale, population) might alter the result.

Beyond encapsulating these broad principles, both ISS and the GDI made it a practice to offer the people who did the hard work of putting a program into practice a chance to think about how their experience generalizes, thereby capturing some of the tacit knowledge in the heads of these experts. For analytical purposes it is important to establish the parameters within which the findings of a given case apply, and experienced practitioners are often keenly aware of how slight differences in legal authorization, public opinion, or institutional capacity could make it hard for others to emulate their successes.

7. **A good case is fun to read**. Our two programs differ with respect to this seventh quality: the "engagement factor." People are busy. Senior officials, especially political leaders, are exceptionally so, and gaining their attention can be hard. If the purpose of a case is adaptive learning or diffusing experience, then a case ought to draw the reader in and get to the point fast. For this reason, the ISS program opted to follow a Harvard Business School management case model that puts a decision-maker in the driver's seat, uses names and quotes (cleared with the people interviewed), and keeps jargon to a minimum. Its cases put the reader right at the coal-face.

This approach had its pros and cons, however. In the program's view, while it boosted engagement with many practitioners and with students, it sometimes hurt credibility with a social science research audience, for whom this approach seemed to imply a "great man" theory of history. In the program's view these concerns were often misplaced. The style was similar to highly commended scholarly work on political development. The social science translation problem more often lay in the release of individual cases separately from cross-cutting analysis – and outside the realm of peer-reviewed journals.

For its part, the GDI, initially hosted within a multilateral organization, chose a different approach. Its cases usually treated an agency within a government or an institution as the lead actor, though it may mention the names of those involved. By virtue of being a consortium of more than forty partner organizations, of necessity the case writing style adopted had to balance ensuring adequate cross-program coherence with fitting the particular preferences and imperatives of its affiliate members. This approach also came at a cost, sometimes obscuring the internal negotiation dynamics within the agency in favor of a cleaner or more administratively procedural account. That said, adopting such an approach also allowed communities of practice to stand back and evaluate a situation more dispassionately.

13.4   Putting Cases to Work: Moderating a Case Discussion

A case is not usually a stand-alone document, though it can be so. If an important purpose of case studies is to promote learning and adaptation, then much rides on their capacity to stimulate group reflection, deliberation, and innovation. This in turn raises another question: How does one effectively moderate a case discussion?

Coming forward to the present, in our experience, the tone, sequence, and focus vary depending on whether the aim is to teach – to introduce key concepts and ways of thinking about a problem – or to help people who have participated in implementation reflect on their work. For the first purpose, the moderator may play a strong role in directing the discussion so that a group reaches key points, pausing to elaborate these. By contrast, for adaptive learning, where the point of a discussion is to help the people who carried out the work reflect and solve problems, the moderator may stand back a bit more to give participants a bigger opportunity to shape the agenda and to get into specific operational details in more depth than one might in a classroom setting. In both situations, however, there are some shared objectives, most importantly stimulating creative thinking about ways to: overcome obstacles that continue to impede success; mitigate the downsides of a generally successful response; reach difficult (isolated, marginalized) communities; take the intervention to scale; or adapt an approach for different circumstances.

To use a case for classroom purposes, we usually begin by reminding the group of the broader issues at stake. Every case has a *development challenge* at its core, the public value the people at the center of the action seek to create: the desired impact on citizens' lives. Every action also has an author, so naming names is important, or at least naming offices: "Minister Marina da Silva wanted to reduce the rate of deforestation in order to adhere to a new climate regime and preserve water quality and availability in her country"; "Sudarsono Osman wanted the land registries in Kuching to serve citizens faster, with fewer errors." The discussion leader may want to add some additional facts to situate the issue, identify what created the space for change, and add some more detail about the lead decision-makers.

Next comes the dramatic moment: "But ... something stood in the way." The discussion leader then poses a series of questions, beginning with "What was the main problem, the main *delivery challenge*?" At this stage, it is important to ensure that everyone can identify the general form of at least the major implementation problem in a case – process efficiency, aligning the interests of a principal and an agent, collective action, or coordination, for example: "Mr. X is responsible for making the program work, but he's stuck. At the start, what is his main problem? What is the general form of this problem?" Knowing the general form enables the case user to link to a general toolkit and consider whether solutions often considered in other settings might be useful in the circumstances at hand. The ability to abstract in this way enlarges problem-solving capacity. It is important to pause and sharpen familiarity with the general concept and the standard toolkit at this point.

Third, we help users connect with the context: "What do we know about the setting and the elements of context that might shape which tactics Mr. X can deploy?" Context is something that will come up throughout the discussion but especially at the end, when the focus is often on scale, scope conditions, and adaptations required to help a similar approach work in another setting. Context may include resource levels, diversity, socioeconomic conditions, government structure, legal authority, and many other conditions or circumstances, some of which may be malleable, while others remain fixed.

The real focus of the discussion comes after this point: "What options did they consider? Were there other possibilities and, if so, do we know why they weren't considered? What motivated the choices they made?" And then: "Let's work through the steps the team takes ... " The central objective is to develop a clear outline of the strategy and tactics employed. If the real issue the instructor wants to use as a focal point occurs later in the case, then it may be perfectly acceptable to expedite the discussion and simply throw the key elements of the initial response into a Powerpoint slide. "So here are the steps they initially took ... Have I got it right?" Usually, however, the aim is to pause to consider the purpose of each step, the appropriateness of the design, what proved difficult to do, any pleasant surprises, and how sensitive the actions taken were to the aptitudes of team leaders or context.

In the classroom, the instructor's job is to help participants identify concepts useful for analyzing problems that emerge at each step, as well as to bring external information to bear, where warranted. One of Princeton's Ebola response cases, for example, focuses on carrying out contact tracing in a very difficult context. If the group is unfamiliar with the key elements of contact tracing, it is helpful to call a short "time out" and explain these in some detail. Even if the elements are in the case text, pausing to reinforce the ideas is often helpful for nonspecialists.

Sometimes the focus of the discussion is not on the strategy or the main steps taken, but on an unanticipated obstacle a team confronts: "There is a big unanticipated obstacle in this case … They struggle to adapt. Put yourself in their shoes. How would you deal with this situation?" If the obstacle is minor and the response is successful, it is possible to fold this discussion into the previous stage of the conversation. If the obstacle is significant and incompletely resolved, the major part of the discussion could focus on this matter. The aim is then to help participants identify possible solutions by abstracting from the specific – giving the problem a general name that links to a toolbox – or by inviting each person to tap his or her own experiences and intuitions about how to solve the problem.

At this stage the moderator's role is to ensure everyone has a chance to contribute and to provide two or three alternative ways to structure the problem under discussion, in the event that everyone is stuck. For example, in one Smart City case, a public health unit used sophisticated math modeling to identify households at risk of lead poisoning, but the effort temporarily ground to a halt over the question of whether it could enter houses at risk and intervene, given concerns for privacy, personal autonomy/consent, and data security. Did it matter that those most at risk were too young to make informed choices on their own behalf? Would the answer to these questions be different if the issue was secondhand cigarette smoke or some other kind of risk – and if so, why? The moderator stimulated thinking by highlighting the ethical principles at issue and inducing participants to think about the implications by pointing to analogous issue areas where the same quandary was a matter of settled law or procedure.

The discussion moderator may want to summarize the results actually achieved and move on, but it is also possible to craft two important conversations around this segment of the case: one focused on causation and the other focused on metrics. Often the conversation will jump to the impact on the broad development challenge, the outcome highlighted in the beginning. In most instances many things affect this type of outcome, so it is important to identify the other things that contribute – the potential confounders – and then try to identify the specific lines of influence through which policy implementation shaped this "public value." To establish these lines of influence, we usually have to focus on intermediate outcomes or outputs: faster delivery times, lower rates of error, more inclusive coverage, etc.: "Were these the right metrics? Can you think of better metrics? If your office didn't have much money, is there a way to assess effectiveness inexpensively?" "What contributed most to these improvements?" "On one important dimension, there was little improvement . . . Why?"

Finally, if the purpose of the discussion is to assess the extent to which lessons from the case are applicable in other contexts, then it is possible to skim through some of the other stages and focus on this matter. Identifying the scope conditions, or the central factors and processes shaping the effectiveness of the solution case protagonists deploy, is central to this task. It is also possible to focus this part of the discussion on ways to improve further, to mitigate the downsides of the tactics selected, or to borrow from other fields to get around some of the limitations associated with the tactics actually used.

Some moderators subdivide the cases, asking participants first to read just the opening sections that outline the problem and the delivery challenges (possibly also the options considered and framing), so that the group has a chance to think about tactical toolkits available and how to proceed. The moderator then hands out further sections of the case, and the next phase of the conversation picks up with what the decision-makers actually did and the pros and cons of the approach, improvements, etc. A third handout might focus on an unanticipated obstacle or on results, prompting another turn in the conversation.

Over the years we have come to share the view of Harvard Business Case Publishing that providing moderators with teaching notes or discussion guides improves usage and enhances the quality of discussion. These notes provide some of the general concepts, toolkits, conceptual puzzles, options, and additional background information that moderators often need to move a conversation forward and inspire creative thinking. Generating them should become a part of the case development process, and they usually flow well from the initial research design and the cross-cutting analysis produced at the end, if there is such.

13.5   Using Case Studies as Part of Adaptive Management

Using cases for problem-solving or improvement within an organization entails a slightly different approach. In this setting, the case study becomes part of a participatory process designed to improve problem identification, foster development of solutions, and win agreement on accompanying changes in practice, including monitoring results. Since 2012, this form of adaptive management, long practiced in many major companies, has attracted a following in public sector development organizations. The United States Agency for International Development's adaptive management principles, treated as requirements in some of its assistance packages or awards, include elements such as regular monitoring of results; practices to support mid-course review of strategy and implementation and course correction; rewarding "candid knowledge sharing" and collaborative learning; and sharing results widely.[11]

The qualitative case study can play an important role in this approach. In some instances, the case writer's role is to conduct interviews before a mid-course review begins and to assemble observations of individual team members and beneficiaries in a form the moderator can use to structure discussion of what has worked, why some steps did not succeed to the degree anticipated, and what to do next. The project manager may then use the results of the conversation to revise the program so that there is a record for comparison after the next attempt to improve delivery. Alternatively, a designated writer may skip the first step and become the recorder for the group discussion, creating a case as a record or after-action report. Qualitative cases drawn from other settings may also enter the moderated discussion at various points in order to spur reflection and creative thinking about what decision-makers should do next.

Those developing the PDIA approach have given this issue a lot of thought. In their experience, one of the challenges associated with learning and adaptation is to induce team members to think hard about the sources of success and difficulty. For this purpose, they employ some of the tools of the trade that Toyota has developed – for example, the "Five Whys" exercise that asks participants to push themselves beyond an initial statement about the proximate cause of a problem to deeper reasons: If A was the cause, why did A happen? If B caused A to happen, what caused B?[12] They go through this exercise at multiple points, creating a "fish diagram" to help provide a record

---

[11] US Agency for International Development Learning Lab CLA Resources, available at https://usaidlearninglab.org/. For a clear, short list of adaptive management principles see also the opening of one of USAID's case studies on adaptive management: "Incentivizing Performance: USAID/Kosovo's Transparent, Effective and Accountable Municipalities (Team) Program," April 2018.

[12] See Toyota "Five Whys" discussion in Andrews, Pritchett, and Woolcock (2015); and Toyota Global on Toyota Traditions, available at www.toyota-global.com/company/toyota_traditions/quality/mar_apr_2006.html

of the discussion (see Figure 13.1). This discussion generates information and insight to incorporate in the next case draft, rendering the case study a collective, participatory product.

The next step is to encourage people to think outside the box in generating solutions for each problem the process identifies. The aim at this stage is to encourage people to draw on their own thinking. At this point it may be helpful to consider what others who have faced similar problems have done, drawing on cases from the libraries that the GDI and the ISS offer, or some other source. These stories take people out of their circumstances and surroundings, reduce defensiveness, and trigger new lines of thought. These conversations about other places usually quickly lead back to a more open discussion about the issues on the table. The moderator may summarize what another government or agency tried and then simply ask, "Would that work here, in your view?" "What would you do differently?" "What is the theory of change behind this idea?" "How will we know if this idea works?" Again, this part of the discussion can go into the case draft, if the case serves as the collective record.

But there is also a further step in adaptive learning. The PDIA authors ask participants to identify the space for change in connection with each problem identified in the previous step. That space includes three elements: Authority (who has the authority to act?), Acceptance (Do the people who will be affected recognize the need for change?), and Ability (Is there capacity – time, money, skill – to act?). This phase of the discussion may help set priorities – if the suggestion is to move where there is space or leverage – or it may lead to creative thinking about how to expand the space for change. This information may also become part of the case record.

Both the GDI and the Princeton ISS program have contributed to learn-and-adapt initiatives. In its first years, the GDI's Science of Delivery team helped more than sixty different projects use cases to broaden or deepen thinking during review of the initial concept note, decide how to address operational challenges, or present results. Participants sometimes convened their project staff to discuss and record their experiences as their work moved forward, resulting in the gradual development of a case, or they assembled at the conclusion of a project to develop an after-action report that documents the steps they took.

The GDI described its method, the Delivery Lab, as an opportunity to bring together thematic experts with specific operational knowledge from GDI's partner organizations and other invited guests who are working to

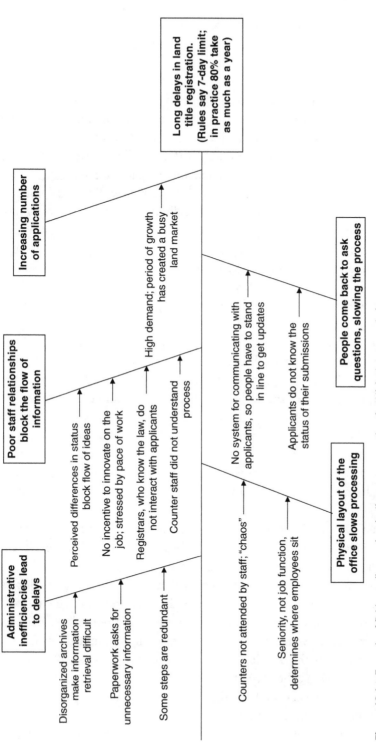

Figure 13.1 Example of fishbone diagram in adaptive management and participatory case study

Source: Andrews, Pritchett, and Woolcock (2015: 21)

overcome the obstacles and bottlenecks that can impede development efforts. Each lab began with a practitioner (the challenge holder) sharing an operational challenge that he or she currently faced in the context of an ongoing project. This brief presentation was followed by a facilitated group discussion and brainstorming session where experts shared relevant experiences. Ultimately, participants worked together to cocreate action-able solutions. The sessions allowed for peer exchange of experience-based knowledge, as practitioners explore problems and think through potential solutions.

13.6 Conclusion

Implementation-focused case studies play a vital role within the develop-ment community in the three key respects described here: (a) helping to develop better understanding of implementation dynamics (a science of delivery), (b) training, and (c) supporting adaptive management. But both the GDI and ISS program observe that practitioners have often employed qualitative cases for other purposes too.

Sometimes the aim is simply to help a manager or public servant structure a problem and think about the menu of options others have tried. A case study can provide a quick guide to key issues and enough operational knowledge to enable the decision-maker to figure out what s/he needs to know so as to pose the right questions in a more detailed person-to-person follow-up conversation. For instance, Princeton's ISS program has docu-mented the efforts of a number of governments to improve cabinet office coordination and support for policy decisions. These cases have helped chiefs of staff and deputy ministers learn from each other without having to take valuable time to travel abroad in search of ideas. But they have also facilitated face-to-face small group meetings that have matched those who have led impressive reforms with those who are just beginning to think about what to do.

To take another, similar example, the GDI used a case on accountability for mineral royalty funds to support Colombia's peace process. In Colombia, royalty funds from mining and natural resources held potential for financing local projects and building legitimacy. However, early experiences in man-aging natural resource funds were unsuccessful in part because local govern-ments lacked capacity to avoid misallocation, corruption, and poor planning, and the central government had no mechanism to remedy this problem.

As a result, instead of building peoples' confidence in their governments, the initial program undermined trust and the sense of government efficacy. The National Planning Department then created a new program that had flexibility to help local governments to build their capacity to implement projects, while also mobilizing community members to carry out "citizen visible audits." The case study on this program, which helped ensure that money was not stolen or misplaced and that projects met the real needs of the citizenry, helped foster agreement among parties to the peace process. In Colombia, an actual example of how to build local accountability and legitimacy and equitably use natural resources to develop the country moved policy conversations forward.

Apart from this kind of use, the programs have also found that people who have played important roles in the changes a case documents value the record of achievement. Those who labored hard to make something happen often immediately move on to the next project or crisis. The case provides welcome recognition and helps them explain their own contributions to others. They say the acknowledgment helps fuel another round of effort. Indeed, organizations often ask the programs whether they will commit to develop a case study on a specific program so that managers can say to team members, "If we do well, we will become a model . . . "

In other instances, people have written to say that they have used a case as a briefing to prepare for deployment to a new post. Operations documents and technical reports rarely contain names, but cases often do, thereby helping newcomers know to whom they can reach out for additional information while also offering historical context and an implicit heads up about sensitivities.

Finally, the case study is a vital tool for communicating to a wider audience what purpose a development initiative serves, the human story that unfolds around and within it, and the results achieved. It gives form and spirit to the numbers we often use to analyze policies. In an era when trust in governments and international organizations is low, the case study is a way to make the work practitioners do more accessible to fellow citizens and to rebuild shared understandings about the missions we pursue.

References

Andrews, M. (2018) "PDIA to inform budget reform in Mozambique." Harvard Center for Development. Available at https://bsc.cid.harvard.edu/files/bsc/files/pdia_in_practice_1_mozambique_pfm.pdf (accessed December 13, 2021).

Andrews, M., Pritchett, L., and Woolcock, M. (2015) "Doing problem driven work." Harvard University: Center for International Development Working Paper No. 307.

Andrews, M., Pritchett, L., and Woolcock, M. (2017) *Building state capability: Evidence, analysis, action* New York: Oxford University Press.

Barber, M. (2015). *How to run a government (so that citizens benefit and taxpayers don't go crazy)*. London: Penguin.

Behn, R. D. (2017) "How scientific is the science of delivery?" *Canadian Public Administration*, 60(1), 89–110.

Booth, D., Balfe, K., Gallagher, R., Kilcullen, G., O'Boyle, S., and Tiernan, A. (2018) *Learning to make a difference: Christian aid Ireland's adaptive programme management in governance, gender, peacebuilding, and human rights*. London: ODI Report.

Brixi, H., Lust, E., and Woolcock, M. (2015) *Trust, voice and incentives: Learning from local success stories in service delivery in the Middle East and North Africa*. Washington, DC: The World Bank.

Danquah, L. O., Hasham, N., MacFarlane, M., et al. (2019) "Use of a mobile application for Ebola contact tracing and monitoring in northern Sierra Leone: a proof-of-concept study," *BMC Infectious Diseases*, 19(1), 1–12.

Kim, J. Y. (2013) "Toward a global science of delivery," in *Voices on society: The art and science of delivery*. New York: McKinsey and Company, pp. 53–54.

Pritchett, L., Samji, S., and Hammer, J. (2013) It's all about MeE: Using structured experiential learning to crawl the design space. Washington, DC: Center for Global Development, Working Paper No. 322.

Pritchett, L. and Sandefur, J. (2015) "Learning from experiments when context matters," *American Economic Review*, 105(5), 471–475.

Schon, D. (1983) *The reflective practitioner*. New York: Basic Books.

Wagstaff, A. (2013) "So what exactly is 'the science of delivery'?" World Bank Let's Talk Development blog, April 8 [online]. Available at http://blogs.worldbank.org/development talk/so-what-exactly-is-the-science-of-delivery

Woolcock, M. (2013) "Using case studies to explore the external validity of complex development interventions," *Evaluation*, 19(3), 229–248.

World Bank (2013). *Knowledge-based country programs: An evaluation of the World Bank group experience*. Washington, DC: World Bank Independent Evaluation Group.

Index